Stories *of* Scottsboro

STORIES *of* SCOTTSBORO

James Goodman

PANTHEON BOOKS
NEW YORK

 Published in the United States by Pantheon Books, a division of Random House, Inc., New York, and simultaneously in Canada by Random House of Canada Limited, Toronto.

Library of Congress Cataloging-in-Publication Data

Goodman, James E.
Stories of Scottsboro / James Goodman.
p. cm.
Includes bibliographical references and index.
ISBN 0-679-40779-0
1. Scottsboro Trial, Scottsboro, Ala., 1931. 2. Trials (Rape)—Alabama—Scottsboro. I. Title.
KF224.S34G66 1994
345.761'02532—dc20
[347.61052532] 93-5589
CIP

Book design by Maura Fadden Rosenthal

Manufactured in the United States of America

First Edition

9 8 7 6 5 4 3 2 1

For Jackson, Samuel, and Jennifer

Contents

Preface

On March 25, 1931, a fight broke out between a group of white youths and a group of black youths on a freight train traveling through northern Alabama. Black and white alike had been stealing a ride. The black youths got the best of it, and the white youths complained to the nearest stationmaster. A posse stopped the train at the depot in Paint Rock, Alabama, and rounded up nine black teenage boys and two young white women. Someone said something about a rape. Sheriff's deputies arrested the blacks and took them to Scottsboro, the Jackson County seat. A crowd gathered outside the Scottsboro jail. The sheriff called the governor and the governor called out the National Guard. The crowd dispersed. Twelve days later the accused were put on trial for rape, and in four days four separate juries convicted eight of them and sentenced them to death. The Central Committee of the Communist Party of the United States assailed the verdicts, and the Party's legal affiliate, the International Labor Defense, announced that it would defend the boys. Countless people were outraged by the trials and death sentences. Countless others were outraged by the outrage. Appeals led to seven retrials and two landmark Supreme Court decisions. The defendants spent no less than six, and as many as nineteen, years in jail.

What happened? The defendants said they had been convicted of a crime they did not commit: the white boys had attacked them; they hadn't even seen any white women on the train. The women said they had been raped: the Negroes had attacked their companions, thrown them off the train, and then had their way. Communist Party officials said the charge was a frame-up and the trials were a circus, nothing but a legal lynching: the women were prostitutes who had to be coerced to cry rape. Thousands of northerners, white and black, agreed with the Communists and joined them in protesting the convictions. Nearly all black southerners assumed that the boys had been framed. A small group of white southerners concluded that the women had willingly had sex with the boys and cried rape only when they were caught. But most white southerners believed the women's story. They were proud that the citizens of northern Alabama had prevented a lynching and allowed the law to take its course. In all the protest, they saw nothing but the Communists' desire to foment race war and revolution. NAACP officials were as critical of the Communists as they were of the verdicts, and fought with the Party for control of the defense.

That was just the beginning—the first few months of a controversy that lasted a decade—and those were only a few of the ways that Americans living in the 1930s understood and explained it. What follows is a history of the court case and controversy, a narrative history in which I move, chapter by chapter, from one point of view to another, until I have recounted the events on that freight train, at the depot in Paint Rock, outside the Scottsboro jail, in and around the Scottsboro courthouse, and all over the country in subsequent years from the perspectives of a wide range of participants and observers. I answer the question "What happened?" with a story about the conflict between people with different ideas about what happened and different ideas about the causes and meaning of what happened—a story about the conflict between people with different stories of Scottsboro.

I retell people's stories, and I try to explain them, writing about what people saw and heard, where they got their news and information, and how their memories, ideas, and past experiences shaped their experience of Scottsboro. I show why some people were able to convince others that their stories of Scottsboro were "The Story of Scottsboro" and why others were not. I show how and why, in response to unfolding events and other people's stories, some people changed their minds about Scottsboro, how and why, in spite of events and other people's stories, others did not.

My sources include hundreds of letters written by the defendants; thousands of pages of trial transcripts and other court records; countless newspaper and magazine articles and editorials; the reports of private investigators; letters to newspaper editors and letters to Alabama officials; the manuscript collections of the organizations most interested in the case, including the Association of Southern Women for the Prevention of Lynching, the Commission on Interracial Cooperation, the American Civil Liberties Union, the National Association for the Advancement of Colored People, the Scottsboro Defense Committee, and the International Labor Defense. My sources include diaries, memoirs, oral histories, and autobiographies; previous histories of Scottsboro and numerous other works of history; Scottsboro songs, speeches, novels, pamphlets, posters, paintings, poems, cartoons, and plays.

I have struggled to be true to my sources. And I have kept myself, as a character, out of my stories, writing each of them from a third-person point of view. But readers should keep in mind that my stories are not transcripts of the stories told in the 1930s, any more than the stories told in the 1930s were transcripts of facts. I decided whose stories to tell and how to tell them. I chose central themes and some of the contexts in which I would like them to be understood. I decided who should have the first word, and who should have the last. I imposed order—at the very least beginnings, middles, and ends—where there was rarely order, created the illusion of stillness, or comprehensible movement, out of the always seamless, often chaotic, flow of consciousness and experience.

Stories of Scottsboro is my story of Scottsboro. In the telling, I weigh in on debates large and small, answer questions and ask questions, and in places address aspects of the controversy that few people talked or wrote about at the time. I have tried to convey my sense of the essential facts of the case—essential because nine lives were on the line and at least one of the poisonous ideas at the heart of the case, the idea that black men are rapists, still is. And, while leaving plenty of room for additional questions, explanations, and debate, I have tried to convey my sense of the conflict over those facts and their meaning. But I have tried hardest of all to convince readers that we cannot fully understand that conflict, or any other, without trying to understand it from many different points of view, without trying to understand—even as we evaluate and cast judgment upon competing points of view, and by those judgments live our lives—how and why other people make sense of their experience the ways that they do.

Once you get going, there is no end to understanding. I have not told all the stories of Scottsboro, and I have not told all the stories that follow with the same depth. I have left work for other historians. I hope some will think I have also left evidence of the value of experimentation in the writing of history, a search for historical forms that do justice to the richness and irresistible power of the past and the stories we tell about it.

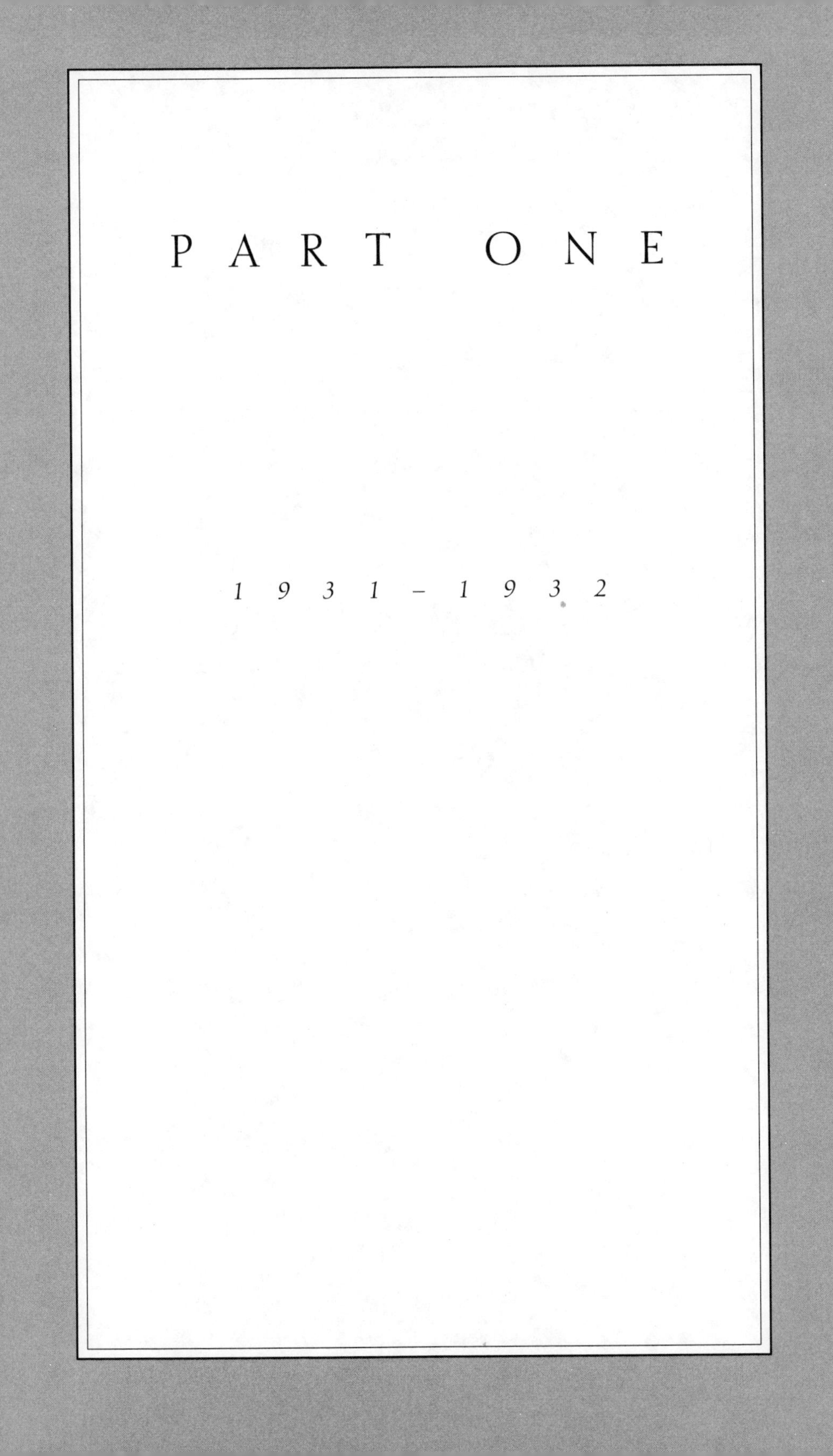

PART ONE

1931–1932

O N E

Something I Know I Did Not Do

A white foot stepped on a black hand. For four of the defendants, that's how Scottsboro began. The hand belonged to Haywood Patterson, an eighteen-year-old from Chattanooga, Tennessee. He was hanging on to the side of a Southern Railroad tank car. He and three friends had stolen a ride. The foot belonged to a white boy, who with four or five others had just walked across the top of the car; when they reached the end, they turned suddenly and walked back the other way. The second time the boy stepped on Patterson's hand, Patterson told him he had almost knocked him off the train and asked him not to do it again.

"The next time you want by, just tell me you want by and I let you by."

"Nigger, I don't ask you when I want by. What you doing on this train anyway?"

"Look," Patterson said, "I just tell you, the next time you want by you just tell me you want by and I let you by."

"Nigger bastard, this a white man's train. You better get off. All you black bastards better get off!"

A fireman or engineer or "railroad dick," Patterson said later, could have chased them off the train. They would have jumped, or at least tried to hide. But these were just white hoboes, with no more right to the freight train than he or his friends had. It was the first week of spring, 1931. Along with hundreds of thousands of other Americans, they had taken to the rails in search of a shorter breadline, a warmer place to sleep, and, if they got lucky, a few days' work.

"You white sonsofbitches," Patterson yelled, "we got as much right here as you."

The train was traveling west through northern Alabama en route from Chattanooga to Memphis. It had just emerged from the tunnel under Lookout Mountain when the argument began. After the tunnel, the train slowed down as it climbed a steep grade; the white boys hopped off and pelted the black boys with stones. Patterson and his friends took cover in another car, and then, when the train stopped at Stevenson, Alabama, to take on water and an additional car, they hopped off themselves. Before getting back on, they met up with six or seven other black youths; together they agreed to fight if the white boys bothered them again.

They did. As soon as the train left the station, they resumed their bombardment, not from the ground now but from another car. Patterson and about ten others confronted them and, after a short fight, chased or threw all but one of them, Orville Gilley, off the train. They would have chased Gilley off, but by the time they got to him, the train had picked up speed. He was hanging from the side of the gondola, and it looked as if he might get swept beneath it. Two of them grabbed him and pulled him back onto the car.

The train had stopped every hour or so all along the way, so the black youths thought nothing of it when it slowed down in Paint Rock, which was forty miles down the tracks. They had broken up into the small groups they had been in before the fight and spread out all along the length of the forty-two-car train. A few of them looked out to see where they were, and when they did they saw dozens of white men, armed with pistols, rifles, and shotguns, rushing toward them. The men grabbed Patterson, his three friends, and five others, questioned them briefly, and tied them to one another with a plow line. Then they herded them onto the back of a flatbed truck and drove them to the jail in Scottsboro, the Jackson County seat, twenty-one miles east of there.

At the depot in Paint Rock it was not clear to any of them what the trouble was about. Willie Roberson had been alone in an empty boxcar a few cars from the caboose. Olen Montgomery had been alone in a tank car on the same end of the train. Those who had taken part in or witnessed the fight may have guessed, especially if they had recognized, as Haywood Patterson and Clarence Norris did, some of the boys they had fought with among the crowd. Patterson asked the deputy who had hold of him what was going on, and the deputy said, "Assault and attempt to murder."

They were in jail for hours before they found out that there would be another charge. Not until the guards took them out of their cell and lined them up against a wall and the sheriff brought two white women by and asked them to point to the boys who had "had them" did they realize that they had been accused of rape. One of the women, Victoria Price, pointed to six of them. When the other didn't say a word, a guard said that "If those six had Miss Price, it stands to reason that the others had Miss Bates." The boys protested, insisting they hadn't touched the women, hadn't even seen them before Paint Rock, when they saw them being led away from the train. Clarence Norris called the women liars. One of the guards struck him with his bayonet, cutting to the bone the hand that Norris put up to shield his face. "Nigger," the guard hollered, "you know damn well how to talk about white women."

"I was scared before," Norris recalled years later, "but it wasn't nothing to how I felt now. I knew if a white woman accused a black man of rape, he was as good as dead. My hand was bleeding like I don't know what . . . but I didn't even think about it. All I could think was that I was going to die for something that I had not done."[1]

That was March 25, 1931. Two months later the youths were still in jail, and one of them, Olen Montgomery, wrote to one of their lawyers, George Chamlee, to ask about their case. Until the others learned to write as well as he could, Montgomery was the prison scribe. "Why SittinG down Worred Nilly Crazy," he wrote on May 25, "i Wont you all to Rite to Me and tell Me how is things Going on a Bout this Case of us 9 Boys Bee Cause i am in here For SomethinG i know i did not do. . . . i Was on My Way to Memphis on a oil tank By My Self a lone and i Was Not Worred With any one untell i Got to Paint Rock alabama and they Just Made a Frame up on uS Boys Just Cause they Cud." He wrote two and a half pages, and then, before a postscript of two more, included the names of the seven others who were sitting with him in Montgomery's Kilby Prison. They were on death row in Kilby, and their executions, scheduled for July 10, were less than six weeks away.[2]

Without some luck they would have been dead already. The

night they were arrested they were nearly lynched by several hundred "crackers" who had gathered around the old, dilapidated two-story jail as the news of the arrest spread through the hills of Scottsboro and neighboring towns. The men leading the mob threatened to break down the doors if the sheriff wouldn't let them in or let the "niggers" out. The boys could hear their voices through the window of their cell. Haywood Patterson laughed at Olen Montgomery when he twisted up his face and cried.[3]

They were saved by the Jackson County sheriff, M. L. Wann, who, unable to disperse the crowd, called the governor of Alabama, Benjamin Meeks Miller, who, in turn, called the National Guard. But the boys had no way of knowing that the National Guardsmen, white men with guns, distinguishable only by their uniforms from the men threatening to hang them, were not part of the lynching bee. Nor in the weeks that followed that sleepless night could they ever be certain that the guardsmen would protect them from the crowds that gathered every time they were moved from one prison to another or back and forth between prison and court. Men with uniforms had beaten or threatened them in every jail they had been in.[4]

The trials came fast—twelve days after their arrest—and passed even faster: four trials took a total of four days. When they were over, only the most frightening sights and sounds stuck in their minds: they remembered the people in the streets, more than they had ever seen in one place, and all the soldiers, their guns prominently displayed. They remembered the two women who had accused them in the Scottsboro jail; three days in a row they heard them tell their lies. They remembered the county solicitor, who badgered, threatened, and confused them; the jurors, who declared them guilty; the men in the audience who rose to their feet and cheered the first verdict; and the judge, who sentenced them to death. "The courtroom," Patterson said, "was one big smiling white face."[5]

Confusion did not end with the trials. Compared with what followed they had made a certain amount of sense. The boys had been framed: "Why I am sitting down, thinking of no one but you, mama," Andy Wright had Montgomery write a few days after the sentencing. "They didn't give me a fair trial. They are going to kill us for nothing. You know I would not do a thing like that. That got me all for nothing." But for nine poor, uneducated, southern black teenagers, only the degree and deadly consequence of this frame-up were new. They could all recall incidents in which they had been blamed for something they had not done. They could remember days of work for which they had not been paid. And, most of all, they could remember times when they had been threatened, bothered, badgered, and abused.[6]

What they could not remember was a time when white people had helped them, or even been kind. So they were completely bewildered when two white men in dark suits from an organization in New York they had never heard of came to visit them in prison and offered them aid. The men brought candy and soda and told them that to win their freedom they were going to raise money and hell all over the world. They had been receiving mail from white people, but until the two lawyers told them that the International Labor Defense (ILD) had been "causing around the country," telling people to send letters and cigarettes, they did not know why. "Mail from white people," Patterson wrote later, "was confusing to me. All my life I was untrusting of them. Now their kind words and presents was more light than we got through the bars of the windows." "I had never met white men like them before," Norris recalled. "These men brought the first kind words from the outside world since we had been arrested."[7]

Over the next three months a dizzying number of people visited. They said all sorts of different things, but one thing in common: disregard the advice of the people who were here the other day. First, Stephen Roddy, a lawyer they had seen in the courtroom in Scottsboro, came and told them to steer clear of the ILD. Roddy said the ILD people wanted to overthrow the government and were interested only in their own cause. They don't care about you, Roddy said. They say they want to help but couldn't even if they meant it, for southerners hate them nearly as much as they hate you. Associate with them, he said, and you are certain to die.[8]

The men from the ILD came back, bringing with them the parents of four of the boys. The ILD lawyers and parents agreed that Roddy had helped send them to the chair the first time and he would do it again. He was the tool of ministers and meddlers and "uplifters," who were themselves the servants of the southern bosses and lynch mobs.[9]

Next came four or five different men, white and black, from a group called the National Association for the Advancement of Colored People. They too tried to get the boys to ditch the Communists. They too wanted to handle the defense. This went on through

April and May, and then all summer. ILD people told them one thing. NAACP people told them another. Prison guards told them to disregard both: one was as bad as the other; if they didn't stop talking to Communists and Negroes and Jews from up north, the guards said, they would surely go to the chair. With each passing week their bewilderment grew. "I didn't know nothing about the ILD or the NAACP," Norris said. "I wanted all the help I could get from anybody. The ILD and the NAACP groups kept running in and out of the death house. Some of us signed with one group, then the other. But neither group wanted to handle the case unless all of us signed with them exclusive. I never did understand why they couldn't work together, since they all said they wanted to see us free."[10]

In the end the boys were swayed by the advice of their parents. As Andy Wright explained to the NAACP's executive secretary, Walter White, when White asked him if he thought that his mother, who consistently advised her sons to stick with the ILD, was wiser simply because she was older: "Mr. White, if you can't trust your mother, who can you trust?" Janie and Claude Patterson, Haywood's mother and father, Ada Wright, Andy and Roy's mother, and Mamie Williams Wilcox, Eugene Williams's mother, had backed the ILD in April and never wavered. "You will burn sure if you don't let them preachers alone and trust in the International Labor Defense to handle the case," Claude Patterson wrote to his son. Olen Montgomery's mother, Viola, joined them in the middle of May. The parents of the others went back and forth, as did nearly all of the boys, but by the end of the year all the parents were convinced that their boys were better off with the ILD.[11]

There were times when the defendants disagreed with their parents about who should defend them, and times when they disagreed with one another. That was not their first disagreement, and it would not be their last. There were nine of them. The two youngest, Roy Wright and Eugene Williams, were thirteen; the oldest, Charlie Weems, was nineteen. They were nine poor, barely literate and illiterate, hungry, scared, tormented teenagers, two of whom were seriously ill. From the beginning each of them experienced the mess they were in in his own way. Willie Roberson and Olen Montgomery had been nowhere near the foot that stepped on Haywood Patterson's hand. Ozie Powell had been in a gondola a few cars down the train. Neither Roberson, Montgomery, nor Powell had been in the fight on the train. Roy Wright's trial had ended in mistrial and he remained in the Birmingham jail. Nine young men, nine different lives. Andy and Roy Wright were brothers. Haywood Patterson, Eugene Williams, Andy, and Roy were friends. The four of them had never seen the other five; the other five had never seen one another before that day. After it, they spent a lot of time together, and like others their age they talked and dreamed and plotted and made up their minds and changed their minds and played; they broke up into cliques of four and three and two; they argued and fought and made up; they changed their minds and switched sides and argued and fought again. They sang and listened to music. They gambled and they prayed.

At the beginning of July, the boys received word from their parents that their executions had been postponed while their lawyers appealed their convictions to the Alabama Supreme Court. They had been on death row in Kilby Prison for over two months, two or three to a cell so small that five steps took them from one concrete wall to another. There were a dozen cells on the block; the electric chair was in a room at one end. They missed the sun and exercise they had been allowed at the Birmingham jail. They smoked cigarettes; they began to learn to read the letters addressed to them, which came every day in the mail; a few began to learn to write letters of their own. But for the most part there was "nothing much to do but stare at the walls and think about dying."[12]

They wanted to believe the news their parents had sent them, but the prison officials hadn't said a word. Just the opposite; the officials continued to taunt the boys, as they had done all along, telling them that their time was up. "You're going to die tonight," they would say. July 10 came. Clarence Norris recalled that guards brought eight boxes into the prison for their bodies. Haywood Patterson believed the letter from his people, and after it, a telegram from the ILD. "Yet," he said, "we were young, we didn't know the law, my folks could have been wrong, anything bad could happen."[13]

They didn't die that night, but Willie Stokes did. He was a black man, convicted of murder, the first man to go to the chair while they were on death row. There would be more. The guards took him out of his cell around midnight. "He went around and shook hands with all the prisoners," Clarence Norris said, "and wished them luck. He walked through the green door and they killed him. I couldn't see into the room where they had the electric chair, but I could hear every word and sound just like I was in there with them. . . . I was sick in mind and body after Will Stokes was killed. I didn't sleep or eat for days."[14]

"When they turned on the juice for Stokes," Patterson said, "we could hear the z-z-z-z-z-z of the electric current outside in the death row. The buzz went several times. After the juice was squeezed into him a guard came out and gave us a report." "Stokes died hard," the guards said. "They stuck a needle through his head to make sure." "If I live to be a hundred," Patterson remembered, "I will never forget that day. . . . Him going and us staying made us feel how life can hang by a hair."[15]

T W O

Beasts Unfit to Be Called Human

In the beginning, white Alabamans heard and told the story of a brutal rape. From the train station in Paint Rock and the jail in Scottsboro, news of the attack, the crowd outside the jail, and the averted lynching "spread like wildfire through Jackson County during the afternoon" and evening of March 25. No news spread faster in Alabama, or anywhere in the South, than rumor or report of rape; this was the rape of two white girls by nine black men. No one had ever heard of a more horrible crime.[1]

The story spread first by "mountain telegraph," as the men who had halted the train (every white man in Paint Rock with a gun) and the people who had gathered to watch the arrests returned to their homes in the nearby hills. It spread from town to town as salesmen who happened to be passing through Scottsboro or Paint Rock that afternoon continued on their way. It spread across the state by telephone and telegraph, across the country by the news wire of the Associated Press. It spread so quickly that even though the arrest had not been made until two in the afternoon, the story made the front pages of both of Scottsboro's newspapers, weeklies that went to press later the same day. The headlines of the *Jackson County Sentinel* read:

NINE NEGRO MEN RAPE TWO WHITE GIRLS

THREW WHITE BOYS FROM FREIGHT TRAIN AND HELD WHITE GIRLS PRISONERS UNTIL CAPTURED BY POSSE

ALL NEGROES POSITIVELY IDENTIFIED BY GIRLS AND ONE WHITE BOY WHO WAS HELD PRISONER WITH PISTOLS AND KNIVES WHILE NINE BLACK FRIENDS COMMITTED REVOLTING CRIME

It also made the headlines of the afternoon daily in Huntsville, the hometown of the victims, forty-one miles to the west.[2]

The victims, Victoria Price and Ruby Bates, talked to local newsmen the day after the assault and verified the story that had spread across the nation overnight. "Coming from the lips of the two girls," one reporter wrote, the details were "too revolting to be printed." Yet from the details that could be printed, white Alabamans learned everything they needed to know.[3]

Price and Bates told how they were returning to their homes from Chattanooga, where they had gone by freight to look for work in the mills. They had been riding on the side of a tank car, but the March "wind was howling" and it was "awfully cold," so when the train stopped in Stevenson they moved to a coal car, where they joined seven white boys. Suddenly twelve Negroes, some of them shooting pistols, others waving knives, leaped into the car and ordered the white youths off the fast-moving train. In no time they threw all but one of them off, and then they went after the girls. When they tried to flee, the Negroes grabbed their legs and pulled them back on the car; when they tried to resist, the men punched them, held knives to their throats, and tore off their clothes. "I guess you heard the rest," Price said.[4]

Alabamans learned that the twenty-one-year-old Price was the daughter of a poor Huntsville widow, the sole support of her mother since she was twelve. Her seventeen-year-old friend, Ruby Bates, was the daughter of another Huntsville widow. The two young women worked in Huntsville's cotton mills, and mill work was the only work they knew; they had been forced to leave home when their employers, who had been laying off workers and cutting hours and pay for over a year, finally just shut the mills down.[5]

The contrast between the girls and their assailants, who were reported to be "the worst negro characters in Chattanooga," could not have been starker. While J. Glenn Jordan, a reporter for the *Huntsville Times,* listened to the girls tell their story, he could hear the Negroes in their cells. They were, he said, telling jokes, "nasty jokes, unafraid, denying to outsiders that they were guilty, laughing, laughing, joking, joking, unafraid of consequences." They were "beasts unfit to be called human."[6]

Everything white Alabamans heard or read in the next few days confirmed the story that spread from Paint Rock and Scottsboro the day the posse stopped the train. The day after the arrest, newspapers reported that Price and Bates had identified the Negroes who had attacked them and that all of the Negroes had either confessed or been implicated by the others. Editors repeated these stories in every piece they ran about the case for a week; local reporters and editors, who lived in Scottsboro, Paint Rock, Huntsville, and Decatur and worked as stringers for the Associated Press, wrote the dispatches that the wire service carried all over the South, the first drafts of the newspaper articles most people read.[7]

On April 6, twelve days after the crime, Judge A. E. Hawkins called the Jackson County Court to order. Three days in a row Price and Bates told their story to four different juries, and to a standing-room-only audience, from which women of all ages and men under twenty-one were excluded. At recess and adjournments the audience passed the story on to the crowd outside; reporters rushed to the nearest phone or telegraph office, ensuring that highlights of the testimony made the front pages of papers published later the same day. The white audience listened to Price and Bates tell the white jurors how all nine of the defendants held knives at their throats, pinned down their legs, tore off their clothes, and raped them.[8]

"There were six to me," Price told the jury in the first trial, "and three to her, and three of hers got away. It took three of them to hold me. One was holding my legs and the other had a knife to my throat while the other one ravished me. It took three of those negroes to hold me. It took two to hold me while one had intercourse. The one sitting behind [the] defendants' counsel took my overalls off. My step-ins were torn off. . . . This negro boy tore them off. He held me while he took them off. Six of them had intercourse with me. The one sitting there was the first one. I don't know the name of the next one. . . . I know them when I see them. I can surely point out the next one. Yonder he sits, yonder. That boy had intercourse with me. The third one was the little bit of one; yonder he is. He held my legs while this one and that one ravished me and then he took my legs again." In what seemed like two or three hours, each of them was raped six times. They begged the Negroes to quit but the men ignored them, and even after they finished they stayed in the car with them, "telling us they were going to take us north and make us their women or kill us."[9]

Dr. R. R. Bridges, a graduate of Vanderbilt and a physician in town for seventeen years, testified that he had examined the two women about two hours after the assault and "found their vaginas were loaded with male sperm." Tom Rousseau, a clerk in Paint Rock who joined the posse, saw Victoria Price, eyes closed and unconscious, being carried from the train. Luther Morris, a local farmer who was up in the loft of his barn, roughly thirty yards from the tracks, when the train went by, testified that he "saw a bunch of negroes put off five white men and take charge of the two girls." He saw between eight and ten Negroes and two white women in the gondola, and "the two white girls were doing their best to jump and the negroes caught these two white girls and they were pulled back down in the car." When defense attorney Stephen Roddy asked Morris if he was sure about what he saw, Morris said, "I think I saw a plenty." The reporter for the *Chattanooga Daily Times* heard those words as "I saw 'em do a plenty."[10]

Other witnesses corroborated the testimony of Price and Bates, but in the minds of the jurors and spectators and all those who read reports of the trials in the papers the most damning evidence was the testimony of the defendants themselves. To the most sympathetic ears it was rambling and incoherent; to the least, it was riddled with inconsistencies, contradictions, and lies. In the first trial, Clarence Norris, called to the stand by his own attorney, testified that he had seen "every one of them have something to do with those girls after they put the white boys off the train": "I was sitting on top of the box car," he said. "I saw that negro just on the stand, Weems, rape one of those girls. I saw that myself. . . . I did not go down in the car and I did not have my hands on the girls at all, but I saw that one rape her. They all raped her, every one of them." The *Huntsville Times* reported that Norris "admitted that he had seen his companions outrage the girls and did the same." The *Chattanooga Daily Times* reported that Norris's testimony "was the highlight of the trial."[11]

Haywood Patterson, testifying in his own behalf at the second trial, at first said he had seen the girls in a gondola car at Stevenson but had had nothing to do with them. He said nothing about a rape. A minute later, under cross-examination, he said he had seen "all but three of those negroes"—all but his three friends—"ravish that girl." Yet before the solicitor was through with him he again testified that he hadn't touched the girls, or seen "any negroes on top of either one of those girls," or even seen "any white women" until he "got down to Paint Rock."[12]

Thirteen-year-old Roy Wright was called by the defense to bolster the least damning of Patterson's stories, which he did, up to a point. Wright said that neither Patterson nor any of the other Chattanooga boys—himself, his brother Andy, and Eugene Williams—had had anything to do with the girls. But he went on to say that he had seen the girls on the train and "nine negroes down there with them." "I saw all of them have intercourse with them," he said. "I saw all of them have intercourse; I saw that with my own eyes."[13]

Six of the accused, beginning with Charlie Weems, the first of the defendants to testify at the first trial, claimed they had not touched the girls and had not seen anyone else touch them, and they held fast to that story throughout the trials. But in the din that followed the testimony of Price and Bates, the accusations of Norris, Patterson, and Roy Wright, and the first of four guilty verdicts, no one in the courtroom took the testimony of those six seriously. By the fourth and last day of the Scottsboro trials, it appeared that all the Negroes had denied their guilt and accused all the others, as they had done in jail the day after their arrest. As one Scottsboro editor predicted five days before the first trial, the case against the boys turned out to be "so conclusive as to be almost perfect."[14]

Writers and editors all over the region agreed that it was the most atrocious crime ever recorded in that part of the country, perhaps in the whole United States, "a wholesale debauching of society . . . so horrible in its details that all the facts could never be printed," a "heinous and unspeakable crime" that "savored of the jungle, the way back dark ages of meanest African corruption." They were revolted by the story, but not surprised. Or if surprised, surprised only by the magnitude of the crime. They expected black men to rape white women. Blacks were savages, more savage, many argued (with scientific theories to support them), than they had been as slaves. Savages with an irrepressible sex drive and an appetite for white women. They were born rapists, rapists by instinct; given the chance, they struck. Two white women swore that they had been raped. Even if all nine of the boys had denied it and told the same story it is likely they would have been convicted; accusations much less serious and less substantiated had condemned black men. Bates and Price charged rape. Most of the boys denied it. There was no question in anyone's mind about whom to believe.[15]

That there had been a brutal rape most of the white Alabamans who paid even the slightest attention to the case agreed. But agreement over what happened on the train gave way to sharp disagreement over what should have happened after the women made the charge. Many would have liked to see the boys lynched—hanged, or burned, or both—right then and there. Others wanted to see more or less what they ultimately saw: the suspects shielded from the mob, taken to a secure jail, and then, at the earliest possible moment, indicted and tried.

Those who opposed lynching believed that it generated more violence and lawlessness than it deterred. Even in the rare instances when the crime was rape, the facts beyond doubt and the assailant of sound mind, the lynchers still undermined law and order, degraded every man and woman in the community, and hurt the reputation of the South. Opponents of lynching were battling an old tradition, but in Scottsboro, in late March of 1931, they had the Jackson County sheriff and the local newspapers, as well as the governor and the Alabama National Guard, on their side. While National Guardsmen kept the mob away from the boys, the editors called for patience. The state, they promised, would arraign the boys almost immediately, convene a special grand jury to indict them, schedule a trial shortly thereafter, and ask the judge to send them to the chair. "If ever there was an excuse for taking the law into their own hands," the editor of the *Scottsboro Progressive Age* wrote, "surely this was one." Nevertheless, he continued, the people of Jackson County "have saved the good name of the county and state by remaining cool and allowing the law to take its course."[16]

Those who would have liked to see the rapists lynched could point to the past and say they had always done it that way. Hundreds of black Alabamans, and thousands of black southerners, had been lynched in the fifty years since the end of Reconstruction, the heyday of a ritual that in one form or another dated back to Colonial America. Lynching, its late-nineteenth- and early-twentieth-century advocates argued, was the most efficient, humane, and effective means of punishing black men who violated the South's most fundamental taboo. Efficient, because it saved the community the time and cost of a trial, and eliminated the possibility that a jury would set a rapist free. Humane, because it spared the victims of the most horrible crime on earth from the wholly unnecessary trauma of facing their assailants in court. Effective, because the lynching of one black man sent the message to all that white men were superior and white women inviolable: rape a white woman, touch a white woman, insult a white woman, look the wrong way at a white woman, and you will die.[17]

Lynchings had been slowly, though not always steadily, declining since the bloody summer that followed the end of the First World War. There were ten recorded lynchings in 1929 and twenty-one in 1930 (out of thirty-seven and sixty-one attempts, respectively). In 1919 there had been eighty-three. By 1931, advocates and apologists had lost the support of most newspaper editors and many politicians. Since the decline of the Ku Klux Klan in the mid-1920s, they were not organized in any significant way. Yet those who still believed in lynching had more than history on their side. They also had numbers, in Alabama and all over the South. Two or three hundred of them threatened to break down the doors of the Scottsboro jail the evening of the arrest. Others talked of storming the jail the next day, keeping tensions high and thirty-odd National Guardsmen in town. If the mob had acted, the guardsmen, under Major Joseph Starnes, would have done their duty; yet when they surrounded the defendants with "glistening bayonets" every time they moved them, when they set machine guns at each of the courthouse doors, when they searched and checked the pistols of every spectator, they paid the mob their respect. At the same time, some of the newspaper editors who pleaded with their readers to remain calm displayed sympathy for those who might have been lynchers. "Officers had to point guns at friends . . . to keep them away from black men they themselves [w]ould have been glad to get to," wrote the editor of the *Huntsville Times*. The next day he noted, with a mixture of pride and regret, that the "nine brutes have been protected by the law since their apprehension." Now it was time for the courts to show that "the white man will not stand for such acts."[18]

Whether they were for lynching or against it, all the white southerners who spoke out in the two weeks before the trials and in the months after agreed that a black man who raped a white woman had to pay with his life. Privately some had doubts. "Of course the crime should be punished," one Alabama woman wrote to a friend, "but is death the right punishment? Are we not still intolerant because of racial prejudice?" A Statesville, North Carolina, man, arguing that the boys didn't know what they were doing, and had no sense of decency or honor, pleaded with the governor not to "let those miserable and half civilized young negroes die." The doubters, however, could not, or would not, speak louder than leading newspapermen, lawmen, and politicians. Editors who vigorously opposed lynching cheered when the solicitor announced that he would demand the death penalty. One of them, the editor of the *Fairhope* (Alabama) *Courier,* commended the sheriff and governor for thwarting the mob and then noted without lament that "if the facts in the case are as reported, the chair at Kilby will have a busy day." The first *Huntsville Times* editorial on the case, which praised the citizenry for its coolheadedness, ran under the headline "DEATH PENALTY PROPERLY DEMANDED IN FIENDISH CRIME OF NINE BURLY NEGROES."[19]

Those who picked up a newspaper the morning after the sentencing found that the Negroes had rioted shortly after National Guardsmen returned them to the Gadsden jail. They beat on their cell bars, demanded special food, tore up their bedding, cursed the court, prison officials, and white people in general, and fiercely attacked the guards sent to quell them. The sheriff had to call back the National Guardsmen, who subdued them and placed them in irons.[20]

THREE

Those Negroes Have Ruined Me and Ruby Forever

Victoria Price and Ruby Bates knew two versions of the events on that freight train, and they told one of them to the sheriff's deputies, local reporters, solicitor, judge, and jurors. In search of work, they had traveled to Chattanooga the only way they could afford. They had no luck in Chattanooga, and much worse luck on their way home, when they were brutally assaulted and repeatedly raped by nine black men. Had the posse not stopped the train in Paint Rock, the Negroes would have raped them again, or killed them, or taken them up north. "When I saw them nab those Negroes," Price told reporters, "I sure was happy. Mister, I never had a break in my life. Those Negroes have ruined me and Ruby forever. The only thing I ask is that they give them all the law allows."[1]

Price and Bates lived in Huntsville, a northern Alabama city set in a valley just west of the Cumberland Plateau, on the north bank of the Tennessee River. Huntsville had been an important cotton production and distribution center; counting the four mill villages right outside the town line, 32,000 people lived there. Only Birmingham, Montgomery, and Mobile were larger than that. When the mills were open and there was work, Price and Bates had worked in the Margaret Mill, the oldest, most dilapidated, and least prosperous of Huntsville's seven cotton mills. The Margaret was owned by local businessmen, and the only way they (and the owners of Huntsville's other small mills) could compete with the newer, larger, and more modern mills, financed by northern capital, was to keep wages low.[2]

Price first went to work in the mills when she was ten. Her mother had also worked in the mills; a bad fall forced her to retire. Since then Victoria's wages as a spinner were all that the two of them had, and in 1931 that wasn't much, $1.20 a day, half of what she had been making in 1929. To make matters worse, the mills had been running so slowly since "hard times" had come that she and Ruby could work only two, at the most three, days a week. And they were laid off every other week, which meant that they worked only five or six days a month.[3]

Bates had been in the mills for a couple of years. Her mother, Emma Bates, had come to the mill village from the cotton fields, following a path cleared and beaten down by thousands of other white southerners in the years after the Civil War. In the late 1920s, plummeting cotton prices, uncompromising landlords and furnishing merchants, inflexible crop liens, unmanageable debt, drought, and the boll weevil quickened the exodus of small landholders, tenant farmers, and sharecroppers from the land. Yet cotton was the least of Emma Bates's troubles. Her first husband died eight months into their marriage, and her second husband, Ruby's father, was no good. He drank, rarely worked alongside his wife and children in the fields, and never worked anywhere else, not counting his still. He made trouble with the family's landlords and beat Emma and their children. He hung around home only as long as Emma had money from the family's share of the crop at settlement time or from the laundry she took in. Once, on a binge, he sold their house, four rooms in the middle of eighty decent acres thirty miles south of Decatur, without telling her, then disappeared and didn't come back until he was sober and broke. Emma saved and bought another house, and he did it again.[4]

From then on, Emma rented, and when he was jailed for horse whipping one of Ruby's brothers, Emma packed up the children and their belongings and fled. He found them, she fled again, north this time, to a small town near Sheffield, Alabama, and east from there to Athens, where she found work in a mill. The mill went bankrupt, and it was the only one in town, so the family moved again. After a season of cotton picking outside Athens, they moved on to Huntsville, which was another twenty-three miles to the east. She found work in one of Huntsville's largest and most prosperous mills, but by the spring of 1931 she was permanently unemployed.[5]

Price and Bates worked in the worst mills. They came from families that had been battered by underemployment and poverty in the best of times. They had meager schooling if any at all. They lived with their mothers in unpainted wooden shacks in the worst sections of town. Bates's family was the only white family on their block, and their block was in the Negro section of town.

Their lives mocked the white South's most sacred ideal. More prosperous southerners liked to boast that the color line extended from the top to the bottom of southern society, and often it did. Yet no one who looked carefully could fail to notice that by the time it reached cities like Huntsville it was frayed beyond repair. Price and Bates lived among black people, played with them as children, roamed the streets with them as teenagers, bootlegged liquor and got drunk with them as young adults. They also went out with them, slept with them, fell in and out of love with them, apparently unaware of the widespread wishful thinking that made it possible for many white southerners to call all sex between white women and black men rape. No white woman, one Mississippi editor put it, no matter how degraded or depraved, would ever willingly "bestow her favors on a black man." Price and Bates had heard the words *white supremacy, segregation,* and *white womanhood,* but they did not live by them. In the eyes of "respectable" southern whites, Price and Bates had sunk as low as two women with white skin could sink. Perhaps lower. One frustrated Huntsville social worker complained that the whites in the mill villages were "as bad as the niggers."[6]

Until they were thought to have been raped. When sheriff's deputies found Price and Bates alongside the train at Paint Rock and realized they had been on it alone with the Negroes who had thrown the white boys off, their first thought was of rape. Later, no one could say for sure what came first, Price and Bates's accusation or the sheriff's interrogation. Some said that the girls had offered the charge without encouragement; others said that they had said nothing about an assault until a deputy asked if the Negroes had bothered them. Either way, Price and Bates were not deluded. They knew that the black youths had not raped them or bothered them in any way. But they also knew that if they had said nothing or no—"No, those Negroes didn't even speak to us"—the people who asked would have thought of them the way respectable white men and women had always thought of them: as the lowest of the low, vagabonds, adulterers, bootleggers, tramps. If, on the other hand, they complained or said yes, the same people would suddenly have thought of them as rape victims and treated them as white southern women, poor but virtuous, for the first time in their lives. It was a rare opportunity, and the choice was not a hard one for them to make.[7]

Dressed in new clothes furnished by the owners of the Margaret Mill, they talked with reporters in Scottsboro the very next day. Victoria Price did most of the talking. She was older and more self-assured, her face was colorless and grim, she looked tough and she was. She had a quick wit and a clever mind, and it was obvious from the beginning that she was leading her friend along. Every time she told the story of the rape, whether to newsmen that week or to four different juries the next, she demonstrated that even though poverty had pushed her across the color line, she knew what was going on in the minds of those who lived on the other side. She knew how to tell the story that most white southerners expected to hear, the story that would engage and enrage the men and women, farmers and artisans, shopkeepers and merchants, teachers and churchpeople who dominated the world that lay above the one in which she lived.

Words came slowly to Ruby Bates, and she resented the way smart and sassy Price upstaged her in the courtroom and pushed her around outside. Bates couldn't tell the story of the rape as confidently or colorfully, or make the audience laugh with her. When the defense attorney asked a question she didn't like, she was unable to put him in his place with a flip remark or an irreverent, irrelevant question of her own. Nonetheless, she too enjoyed the attention of newspapermen, who put her picture in the paper and seemed sincerely interested in her story—and the sympathy of the respectable men and women of Huntsville and Scottsboro, people who before had ignored her or shown her nothing but scorn. She too liked being a southern woman better than a piece of poor white trash.

Price told a story about ruthless, sex-crazy savages, and she told it in elaborate and chilling detail. She described not only what they did—how the Negroes beat them, tore off their clothes, pointed guns at them, pinned down their legs, held knives at their throats—but also the names they called them and the things they said to them, and to one another, while they were doing the deed: while Olen Montgomery raped her, Eugene Williams told her she had better keep her legs open. "He had a knife in his hand," she said; "he was standing up right over me." Another boy had told Montgomery to hurry, because they all "wanted their share." Willie Roberson pulled her legs apart, while the others told him to jerk them one way or the other. "Pour it to her, pour it to her," the other Negroes cried.[8]

On the witness stand there were all sorts of things about the trip to Chattanooga and the rape that Bates could not remember. She contradicted herself when asked whether she and Price had known the white boys on the train or traveled with them the day before. And unlike Price, she couldn't say positively which of the defendants had raped her, which ones had raped Price, or in what order. But considering what she had gone through, neither juries nor spectators held her bad memory against her; she got the most important part of the story right. She remembered clearly that two of the Negroes had guns and the rest had knives and that after chasing the white boys off the train they had thrown them down in the gondola, held knives at their throats, and raped each of them six times.[9]

Price and Bates alarmed spectators and jurors with their description of insatiable sex-mad savages. And even more with their description of self-conscious sex-mad savages, Negroes who knew exactly what they were doing, who were driven by a force much more frightening than instinct. The Negroes they described understood that they were violating the South's greatest taboo, and took great pleasure in it. The Negroes they described wanted more than sexual satisfaction. They wanted possession. As soon as they disposed of the white boys, they told Price and Bates that they were their women from then on. Andy Wright told Price that she was going to have his baby. When the Negroes were through, they told Price and Bates that if they didn't kill them they were going to take them up north. Price and Bates had been raped by Negroes who were thinking for themselves, acting on their own. That's not what white Alabamans, whether in the hills of northern Alabama or in the Black Belt below, expected. It was the last thing they wanted to see.[10]

FOUR

Legal Lynching

James Allen and Helen Marcy, editors of the Communist Party's *Southern Worker,* heard the news of the arrest over Chattanooga radio a few hours after the posse stopped the train. Allen, a twenty-five-year-old New Yorker who had taught philosophy before joining the Party in 1928, had come south in July 1930 to launch the paper, the CP's first in the South. His wife and comrade, Helen Marcy, joined him a few weeks later. Their small apartment was their office—a portable typewriter and a couple of boxes of files and books—and they moved often in order to keep one address ahead of the red squad.[1]

The paper's dateline was Birmingham, the logical place to publish, in light of that city's heavy industry. It was also the most dangerous. When the first Party organizers arrived in late 1929, police arrested them for vagrancy and private detectives raided their homes. Steel-company guards threatened to shoot them simply for setting foot on company grounds. Publishing a paper in Birmingham was out of the question. So Allen and Marcy set up in Chattanooga and found a printer in Rossville, Georgia, who agreed to print 3,000 copies a week for sixty dollars, cash on the spot. As it turned out, the printer's partner was a Klansman. He refused to speak to Allen when Allen came into the shop, but in 1930 he was as happy as his partner to have the business, and as anxious as Allen to keep the paper's origins a secret.[2]

The morning after the arrest, Allen and Marcy learned of the showdown between mob and militia outside the Scottsboro jail. They wired the New York office of the International Labor Defense—an officially non-Communist organization controlled by Party members and devoted to the legal defense of prisoners of class war—"alerting them to the danger of a mass lynching." Marcy and Lowell Wakefield, the ILD's southern representative, attended the pretrial hearings, and in the April 4 issue Marcy described the scene: the National Guardsmen with drawn bayonets who stood between the "surly and threatening" "lynch-hungry mob" and the "terrified youngsters." Wakefield and another Party organizer, Douglas McKenzie, traveled back to Scottsboro for the trials. Convinced that the boys were being railroaded, "legally lynched," Wakefield and McKenzie sent telegrams of protest to Alabama officials, demanding a stay of execution and protection for the boys against lynching, and informed the Party's Central Committee that they had another Sacco-Vanzetti on their hands. The Party issued a statement on the case on the last day of the trials, and within twenty-four hours of the death sentences, the ILD had voted to defend the boys.[3]

On the same day, April 10, under the headline "8 NEGRO WORKERS SENTENCED TO DIE BY LYNCH COURT," the official newspaper of the CPUSA, the *Daily Worker,* ran its first report on the case. Allen ran the *Southern Worker*'s first report the next day. Both were based on the dispatches of Wakefield and McKenzie, and told the story of a "frame-up from start to finish." The boys, unemployed workers from Chattanooga and Atlanta, were innocent of any crime except the crime of being poor and black. So innocent, that when the posse halted the train in Paint Rock they did not even try to flee. The four from Chattanooga were on their way to Memphis, where they had heard there was work on riverboats. Two of the five from Georgia, sick and penniless, were in search of medical care.[4]

The deputies discovered two white girls, dressed in men's overalls. Initially they said nothing about an assault. The first time the sheriff asked them if the boys had bothered them, they said no. Only under the pressure of the lynch mob outside the jail in Scottsboro and the prodding of the solicitor, "who kept saying, 'go ahead and say they did it, that boy attacked you, didn't he,' " did the girls finally agree to make the charge. Investigations after the trials revealed that the two girls were notorious prostitutes, who plied their trade in Huntsville and Chattanooga. One of them, Ruby Bates, had once been arrested for hugging a Negro in public.[5]

The boys were held without bail; local lawyers refused to defend them; local newspapers whipped up a mob spirit; and the judge scheduled the first trial for horse-swapping day, ensuring a tremendous crowd: ten thousand people, most of them armed with rifles and revolvers, poured into a town of fifteen hundred. Sheriffs beat the boys in an effort to extract confessions, but "in spite of the lies in the capitalist press," they did not confess, and they refused the advice of their "crooked lawyer to plead guilty and beg for life in jail." On the night of the first day of the trials, however, Clarence Norris was taken out of his cell, alone, threatened, and badly beaten. He turned state's evidence the next day. The verdict in the first case was greeted with applause and cheers from the spectators in the courtroom and a thunderous roar from the crowd outside. A brass band struck up a tune. The second jury had to be influenced by the reaction of the people of Jackson County to the verdict of the first.[6]

For Party theorists, the "reason for this murderous treatment of working class boys" was not hard to find. Southern landlords and industrialists used the charge of rape, the race prejudice of whites, and the stake and rope to divide white and black and keep both races enslaved. Yet in spite of the lynch mobs, workers were beginning to organize. And in response to unemployment, small business failures, and starvation wages in the mills and factories, in response to the mounting repression of sharecroppers and tenant farmers, whom planters kept in a state of virtual slavery sixty-five years after the Civil War, black and white workers had begun to work together, for the first time. Race prejudice was no longer doing the trick, and "the capitalists and landlords" feared that this movement would "destroy the basis of their super-exploitation of southern labor." They needed a new form of oppression to combat the union of workers across the color line. So they had turned to the courtroom, the "heartless and hypocritical pretense of a legal procedure," which in swiftness, brutality, and the denial of rights was "no different from the most cold-blooded 'illegal' lynching." Henceforth the façade of judge and jury would replace the rope as the primary instrument of capitalist oppression.[7]

Where the façade of capitalist justice looked especially thin,

Party leaders and organizers leapt at the opportunity to get Americans to look through it. By publicizing the plight of the boys and defending them in court, the Party saw the chance to educate, add to its ranks, and encourage the mass protest necessary not only to free the boys but also to bring about revolution. "The frame-up of the young Negro workers on a fake charge of rape," the *Daily Worker* predicted two days after the trials, "with two notorious white prostitutes brought by the bosses to testify against them, will be given a mighty answer in the May Day demonstrations in every part of the country and throughout the world." "Negro and white workers," the editors urged, "smash this murderous frame-up. Hold protest meetings. Wire protests to the governor of Alabama. Demonstrate May Day against lynching whether by a boss mob or by the bosses' state."[8]

In early 1931, mass protest was the key. Since the Sixth World Congress in 1928, the Party had been arguing that capitalism's end was near. More than a year before the stock market crash of 1929, the Party had predicted that worldwide economic depression would usher in the "third period" of postwar capitalism, ending five years of relative stability that had begun in 1923 with the defeat of the German revolution. Massive unemployment and agitation would prepare the way for the "radicalization of the masses," and militant workers, taking the offensive, in demonstrations, marches, and strikes, would seize capitalism by the throat and deliver the last blow.[9]

The "crime at Scottsboro" provided an ideal opportunity for mass education and mobilization. At the Sixth Party Congress, Party leaders had characterized Negroes in the deep South as an oppressed nation, deserving not only liberation—economic, political, and social equality—but also self-determination. Organizers didn't talk a whole lot about the idea of a separate black nation, and when they did, few seemed moved. James Allen found sharecroppers more concerned about "how they were going to get through the winter." Nonetheless, the call for self-determination signified an unprecedented emphasis on the "Negro question," and made southern blacks—whether struggling against planters or furnishing merchants, lynching or Jim Crow—the complete allies of northern workers. For black American Communists, long unhappy with their position in the Party and the Party's unwillingness to address the particular problems of black Americans, the practical consequences of this doctrinal shift were great: the shift allowed them to move the issues that most concerned them to the front pages of the Party's newspapers and the forefront of Party activities.[10]

Party leaders also saw an ideal opportunity to reveal the true character of the American "reformists," black and white, in the churches, press, and liberal organizations such as the National Association for the Advancement of Colored People and the American Civil Liberties Union. Liberals and socialists, Party theorists said, posed the greatest of all threats to the triumph of communism. Whether they believed in the capitalist system, as liberals did, or willingly compromised with it, as socialists ("social fascists") did, delayed the collapse of the system and, as they misled and co-opted workers who would otherwise have turned to revolution, sapped the Party of its strength.[11]

So in its effort to save the lives of the Scottsboro Boys in the spring of 1931, the Party had to contend with the "traitors" of the NAACP as well as the southern bosses and lynchers and Ku Klux Klan. In the beginning, Party officials said, the NAACP did nothing. The charge was rape, and if that was true, any association with the defendants would have sullied the organization's fine reputation. To protect it, Walter White and other "misleaders" were willing to sacrifice the boys. Only after the Party brought the truth about Alabama's legal lynching to the world's attention did the NAACP step in, and even then it could conceive of the case as nothing more than a rape case; the organization could set no goal greater than the "legalistic illusion" of a fair trial. It could not see that there was "no such thing as a 'fair trial' of a Negro boy accused of rape in an Alabama court," dominated as that court was by the southern ruling class. Nor could it see that "behind the ghastly crime of this frame-up" was "the whole question of the exploitation, persecution, disfranchisement, and constant murder of Negroes." The NAACP relied on alliances with southern attorneys, southern courts, and sympathetic southerners for justice and condemned publicity and mass mobilization. The result of that myopia was clear: the NAACP represented "an instrument of the white capitalist class for the perpetuation of the slavery of the negro people."[12]

The Communists organized meetings, rallies, marches, defense committees, petition drives, and postcard and letter-writing campaigns. They spoke, passed the hat, and recruited at churches, political clubs, booster clubs, fraternal organizations, and labor unions.

They published an illustrated *Story of Scottsboro* for children. They worked hardest in the black neighborhoods of northern cities, showering the black press with news releases, distributing pamphlets, stuffing mailboxes with leaflets. When black ministers, politicians, community leaders, or NAACP officials denied them a hearing, they broke up their meetings and took their story door-to-door. They took some of the defendants' mothers on a national, and then an international, publicity tour.[13]

Turnout increased dramatically in the spring of 1931, and the Party gained some new members. But not nearly as many as expected. Party organizers were dismayed by their inability to enlist a significant number of the people who attended meetings and rallies and signed petitions. They were also dismayed by their failure to maintain the loyalty of those they recruited; turnover was high. Even in Harlem, where the Party's role in Scottsboro, in consumer boycotts, in eviction protests, and in the organization of the unemployed put it at the center of the political scene, only a small number of people joined. Enrollment was a greater problem in Alabama, where time and submission to Party discipline were only a small part of the dues a prospective member might have to pay.[14]

Yet Party organizers had convinced Negroes all over the North that the CP was not simply the most militant force for racial justice in America, but also the most effective. And even in the South, despite the tremendous hostility of whites, stiff new criminal syndicalism laws, grave warnings against association with agitators, and the palpable danger for those who failed to take heed, Party organizers estimated that five to seven hundred people had joined in the Birmingham district, as many as five thousand in the Black Belt. Contrary to expectations, southern black churchpeople flooded the ILD with requests for Scottsboro speakers. Even the ministers who were not themselves aroused and outspoken, as James Allen found, were "subject to the pressure of their congregations."[15]

At the same time, a remarkable number of white liberals had come to see things the Party's way. A few weeks after the trials, Theodore Dreiser invited every literary person that he knew to his large Fifty-seventh Street studio, and more people showed up than could comfortably fit. Dreiser spoke about the misery and the breadlines and the starving and the unemployed. He spoke about Scottsboro and the epidemic of racial, industrial, and political persecution. "What are we, what is America, going to do about it?"

he asked. He suggested a committee to work with the ILD. They called it the National Committee for the Defense of Political Prisoners, and nearly fifty well-known writers and intellectuals joined. Dreiser, John Dos Passos, Lincoln Steffens, and Sherwood Anderson wrote widely circulated essays on Scottsboro. They also wrote dramatic one-page letters, mailed to thousands of people, alerting them to the "national emergency," asking them for contributions to the defense. Dreiser, Waldo Frank, Mary Heaton Vorse, and Edmund Wilson investigated labor conditions and conflict in the mines of Harlan County, Kentucky; others investigated violations of civil rights and civil liberties in the mill towns, mining towns, and prisons of the South.[16]

As the country sank deeper and deeper into the Depression, more and more minds came up for grabs. People whose friends and neighbors had lost their jobs, or who had lost their own. People who had grown tired of the sight of boarded-up shops, closed banks, and interminable food and relief lines, or who had grown tired of standing in those lines themselves. People who were struck by the gray, sunken faces that were everywhere, by all the people dismayed and disillusioned, distraught and dazed. People who had heard about bloody labor strikes in Kentucky, in Pennsylvania, and all along the West Coast; food riots and violence at the scene of evictions in Chicago and New York; tax and foreclosure sales in Iowa and Wisconsin; the army's rout of the Bonus Marchers, twenty thousand unarmed veterans of World War I, in Washington, D.C.

The dirty secrets of the 1920s—immigrants in the big cities, croppers, tenant farmers, and mill workers in the South, laborers in New England's old and invalid industrial towns, miners, railroad workers, and longshoremen—were, rather suddenly, out. Even for those with jobs, decent homes, and plenty of food on the table, the suffering of others was nearly impossible to ignore. People—not everyone, perhaps not even a large minority, but many more than, say, in early 1929—were asking questions, wondering what was going to happen, whether the system was going to survive, what could be done; they were pausing to listen to street-corner speeches or to take leaflets, and if not changing their minds, at least entertaining thoughts they might not have entertained before.

Listening to the Communists, people heard the most microscopic stories of Scottsboro, and the most macroscopic, the most abstract and the most concrete. To the Communists, of course, the extremes were inextricable: Capitalism was the theory. Unemployment, starvation wages, poverty, illiteracy, prejudice, peonage, disfranchisement, segregation, and legal lynching were the practice. Revolution would come when the American working class, black and white, saw the connection in the same light.

F I V E

The Negro and the Communists

NAACP secretary Walter White considered the Communists a band of lunatics. If he had had his way, he would have spoken exclusively about Scottsboro and the South: the near lynching, the mob outside the courtroom, the inadequate defense and disgraceful legal procedure, the all-white juries and the race prejudice that made the convictions and sentences all but a foregone conclusion. White would have liked to talk about the case quietly, not in the newspapers or streets but in the courts, and since most of the courts would be in the South, he would have liked to have southerners, interracial leaders and enlightened attorneys, do most of his talking for him. But he didn't get to say what he most wanted to say, in the way that he wanted to say it.

The Communist Party had broken the story, and for the first few weeks of the controversy, White, like everyone else skeptical of the first Associated Press dispatches, had to depend on Party papers for his news. (Even when he traveled to Alabama at the end of April to wrest control of the defense from the ILD, he couldn't forgo a briefing by the ILD's attorney, the former solicitor general of Hamilton County, Tennessee, George Chamlee.) Moreover, the Party had cast him and his Association as the Judases in its story, villains as dangerous as the lynchers themselves. They were attacked relentlessly in Party newspapers, pamphlets, and press releases, at every Party meeting and rally, and whenever Party members, planted in the audience, disrupted them at meetings and rallies of their own. How could the Association ignore the assault and not alienate northern middle-class blacks and northern white liberals, its most important constituents? How could it stay out of the fray and not squander the opportunity to associate itself with a cause drawing worldwide attention to the predicament of black southerners?[1]

It couldn't. The Association couldn't stay out, and thus it couldn't avoid a fight with the Communists, but this was a fight for which it was not prepared. The NAACP's forte was legal and political action; it was organized to lobby and litigate against lynching, segregation, disfranchisement, and the numerous other means by which black people were denied their constitutional rights. It did most of its fighting in state legislatures, Congress, and the courts. It drew its membership from the northern, urban black middle class—at the end of the 1920s it had only a handful of branches and not many more members in the deep South—and it had neither the means nor the inclination to fight with the Communists for mass support or membership. Dues and contributions sank with the stock market. By 1931 the Association was barely solvent and would have been more than happy simply to hold on to the members and branches it had.[2]

White couldn't compete with the Communists on their ground, but there were dangers for him even on his own. That's why he didn't enter the case the moment he read the first Associated Press reports of the arrests and near lynchings, or the moment black leaders in Chattanooga, writing a few days before the trials to report what they had done to assist the defendants, asked for help. He couldn't blindly associate the NAACP with what looked to him like nine pathetic teenagers, a motley crew of miscreants at best, at worst a gang of rapists, without risking the respectability it had taken two decades to gain. He might alienate powerful allies—politicians, philanthropists, journalists, lawyers—and at no time did he need those allies more, particularly the philanthropists. He certainly would have alienated the moderate southerners he desperately hoped to draw to his side. Yet once the Party beat him to Alabama, even the most cautious involvement in the case meant taking the chance that the Association would be confused with the

Communists, who were unpopular everywhere, and nowhere more than in the South, where they were treated with only slightly more courtesy than a gang of rapists.[3]

For Walter White, the fight was personal as well as political, and not simply because the Party's most vehement attacks were aimed directly at him. A man of immense energy and ambition, White had just been named secretary and he aspired not only to strengthen the Association but also to make it his own. He faced formidable obstacles: hard times, a white board of directors that had yet to yield the most important levers of power to the black administrative staff, and internal dissension that increased with each year of the Depression. Many young black activists—in 1931 White was an ancient thirty-seven—thought the Association's oligarchic structure and single-minded attention to constitutional rights would no longer do. The time had come, they argued, for a program broad enough to encompass the economic needs and rights of the black masses. The last thing White needed, or was prepared for, in the spring of 1931 was a controversial case and a battle with the Communists that not only threatened the Association's reputation but also put his own power, reputation, and respectability on the line.[4]

White was the blond-haired, blue-eyed son of an Atlanta postman and a former schoolteacher—both devout Christians who quietly believed in a friendly but omnipotent God and encouraged their seven children to do the same. (After White's father's death, his mother lifted the prohibition on bridge playing, but not on reading novels.) The family lived in the best-kept house on Houston Street and spent every Saturday preparing for Sunday with a fastidiousness that would have made Booker T. Washington, a quintessential Victorian, proud. The house sat squarely on the street's color line, and it was there, in the middle of the Atlanta Riot of 1906, that the fair-skinned twelve-year-old learned what it meant to be a Negro. On the first afternoon of the riot, while he and his father were delivering the mail, they watched a mob beat a black man to death. On the second night, they lay in wait, rifles in hand, as another mob, which had threatened to clear the Negroes from their block, approached the house "that was too nice for a nigger to live in." The next-door neighbor fired and the rioters fled.[5]

White attended Atlanta University and began work as a clerk at the Standard Life Insurance Company the morning after graduation. He got involved in local politics later the same year, when the Atlanta Board of Education proposed to cut costs by eliminating the seventh grade from the black grammar schools. It had cut the eighth grade two years earlier. Black Atlantans protested, and organized a local branch of the NAACP—White was elected secretary—to facilitate the fight, which they won. He was a superb orator, and he quickly gained the attention of James Weldon Johnson, the NAACP's field secretary, who in 1918 brought him into the New York office.

In the 1920s, knowing he could pass for white, White volunteered to go south to investigate lynchings. Except for the victims, no black man ever got as close as he did to the crime. Once, he was nearly lynched himself. He returned to New York with the most outrageous and incriminating details. White was equally successful as an administrator, a negotiator, a branch organizer, and, in the midst of the Harlem Renaissance, as a writer. He wrote two novels and a well-received study of lynching. Under the direction of Johnson and White (Johnson had become the NAACP's first black secretary in 1920) the Association flourished. When Johnson took a leave of absence in 1929, White was named acting secretary. When Johnson stepped down early in 1931, White was the obvious choice to replace him.[6]

From the beginning of the fight for control of the Scottsboro defense, White admitted privately what just about everyone close to the controversy already knew: the Party had rushed from its corner and stunned the NAACP with its first punch. Yet he never admitted it in public. Rather he argued that he and the Association had had everything under control—they had studied the case, secured attorneys, and quietly begun work on the appeals—when the Communists, with "a blare of trumpets," came charging onto the scene. The Party thereby transformed the Scottsboro case, which began "when two white women mill workers clambered aboard a freight train at Chattanooga," into "the most notable test of strength to date" between those seeking "justice for the Negro through American forms of government" and those seeking "to spread Communist propaganda among American Negroes." With the Depression devastating an already overburdened race, the Party had decided the time was ripe to capitalize on Negro unrest, to sow the seeds of revolution in America's most fertile field.[7]

With the Communist notion that there was no more fertile field,

White wholeheartedly agreed. Negroes were hungry. They were being thrown out of work in numbers well out of proportion to their share of the population, and the wages of those who kept their jobs were being reduced to levels that made starvation and homelessness inevitable. Since they were excluded from most labor unions, Negroes were always the last hired and first fired. Since four million black southerners—the great majority—depended on the cotton market, its collapse stung black farmers even worse than white, and added to miseries caused by gross disparities in state allotments for medicine and education, by the denial of voting rights, and by lynching. And as awful as these conditions were, White argued, they were only the most immediate causes of suffering and of the notion, growing in Negro thought since the World War, "that the problem he encounters in the United States is only a part of the whole structure of race prejudice" created by "the modern age of imperialism." To Negroes everywhere the "ruling classes among the white nations of the earth seem . . . to be as filled as ever with pride and greed and sublime contempt towards every race and color but their own."[8]

Hungry and homeless, oppressed and embittered, black Americans were more than willing to listen to talk of radical change. Had the Communists been honest, intelligent, and wise, White suggested, they might have made great gains. But, he contended, they were not. They turned Alabama officials against the defendants with their hostile telegrams and alienated the growing body of liberal white southerners. They not only eschewed cooperation with the NAACP, which in the preceding twenty-two years had built "a notable record of victories in State and Federal courts in protecting the Negro's constitutional rights," but attacked the organization, breaking up its meetings and insanely charging that the members were "in league with the lyncher-bosses of the South" and plotting to "murder the Scottsboro martyrs."[9]

The Communists' analysis was as unconvincing as their tactics were unwise. They charged that capitalist bosses were trying to lynch the boys and called for the workers to rise up and save them. Yet most Negroes saw, as W.E.B. Du Bois put it, that "the imported Marxist pattern did not fit." In Scottsboro, and all over the South, it was the capitalists, worried about the effect of racial violence on their profits, who saved Negroes from white proletarian mobs. In sum, the Communists gave many the impression that they were no more interested in the defendants than they were in the sharecroppers they led to slaughter in Alabama or the homeless killed in an eviction riot they incited in Chicago—the impression that the youths would be more valuable as martyrs. "If the Communists want these lads murdered," Du Bois wrote, "then their tactics of threatening judges and yelling for mass action on the part of white southern workers is calculated to insure this."[10]

The Communists failed this time, White said, but they might not the next. All over the country, people wondered if "Negroes were turning red." Walter White's answer was no, not yet, but chiefly owing to the Communists' stupidity. The Party might get wise, and if it did, who could blame American Negroes if, after three hundred years of loyalty, out of "sheer hopelessness" they turned on "their oppressors." The way to prevent that was simple: drastically alter "the almost chronic American indifference to the Negro's plight." Give the Negro a place to work and live, remove the barriers that keep him out of unions, protect his life and property, assure him justice in the courts, and give him the right to vote—then you won't have to worry about the Communists. "In brief," White wrote, "the only antidote to the spread among American Negroes of revolutionary doctrines is even handed justice."[11]

White talked about the case this way from the end of April 1931 until January 1932, and during that time he gained influential allies in the North. Although *The Nation,* the *Christian Century,* and *The New Republic* didn't always take his side completely (*The New Republic,* for example, thought both sides had "scored tactical victories and committed tactical errors") or uphold his refusal to join forces with the ILD, all agreed the case had nothing to do with class and the defendants would be better off if the defense were in conservative hands. White reinforced this view when he persuaded Clarence Darrow to undertake the defense with the aid of Arthur Garfield Hays. Anyone who cared about the best interests of the defendants, White said, would yield to the skill, reputation, and record of Darrow and Hays. The Communists couldn't do better than Darrow, but the NAACP couldn't defend the boys without their consent, and by the late fall of 1931 the boys all backed the ILD. In fact, it was the NAACP's failure to gain the support of all the boys that prompted Fort, Beddow and Ray (the reputable Birmingham criminal law firm White had first retained) to withdraw from the case, forcing White to turn, in desperation, to the retired Darrow. Attempts at compromise and a joint defense failed when ILD lawyers insisted that Darrow and Hays disassociate themselves from the NAACP and work under the ILD, and in January, a month after White's most powerful and confident telling of the story appeared in the pages of *Harper's,* the NAACP withdrew from the case.[12]

S I X

I Went Down There, All Innocence

"Can you go down to Scottsboro," Forrest Bailey asked Hollace Ransdall at the very end of April 1931, "and saturate yourself with the whole situation as regards those eight negro boys? It is quite clear that it is a frightful mess." Bailey was one of the directors of the American Civil Liberties Union; Ransdall was a young journalist, teacher, and activist who had worked for the ACLU before. She was born in Colorado and educated at the University of Chicago and Columbia's graduate school, where she took a master's degree in economics. She settled in New York, although when Bailey wrote her, Ransdall had just finished six weeks of teaching at the Southern Summer School for Women Workers in Louisville, Kentucky—a school for young women in the textile, garment, and tobacco industries, organized in the late 1920s by women trained in the social sciences and committed to social change.[1]

Ransdall traveled south, by herself, the first week in May, and spent ten days in Alabama, pretending, on Bailey's recommendation, "to know nothing at all" about the case. She scrambled all over the state—stopping in Birmingham, Tuscaloosa, Montgomery, Scottsboro, and Huntsville—and ended up in Chattanooga. It was just three weeks after the trials; every day's mail brought protest letters, and by all accounts the place was as flammable as a September forest after a summer without rain. Yet everywhere she dall asked the most provocative questions—about the ıl prejudice, Price and Bates—of everyone she met. She ıth the trial judge, the mayor of Scottsboro, the Jackson medical examiner, college professors, black clergymen, the leaders of the Birmingham chapter of the NAACP, and even strangers she met on the street. She spent her first evening in Alabama with Walter White, who had been hustling around the state in an effort to wrest control of the case from the ILD, and her last days with the defendants in Kilby Prison and the girls who accused them at their homes. She left on May 15, and two weeks later sent Bailey a thirty-one-page report.[2]

It all began when two mill girls from Huntsville donned overalls and hoboed their way to Chattanooga. Ransdall retold Victoria Price's story: the search for work, the train ride home, the fight between black and white gangs, the rape. She described the scene in Scottsboro on the first day of the trials: the crowd of eight to ten thousand that swarmed the narrow village streets; the 120 National Guardsmen who brought the boys to town, formed a picket line around the village square, and searched everyone who passed through the courthouse doors. Since the trials, local officials insisted, the crowd had been "curious not furious." But conversations with Scottsboro residents—one told Ransdall that she hoped they would leave the soldiers at home the next time so they could "finish off those black fiends and save the bother of a second trial"—and the presence of so many soldiers indicated just the opposite. If, as so many claimed, there was no lynching spirit in Scottsboro during the trials, why, Ransdall wondered, had the town looked like "an armed camp in war time"?[3]

Inside the courthouse Victoria Price testified with such gusto and treated defense attorneys with such irreverence that she brought down the house with laughter. She knew her audience was with her and played up to it. Ruby Bates was a much weaker witness. She could neither identify the boys who had raped her nor at crucial points corroborate the story Victoria had told. As for Orville Gilley—the white boy who had been pulled back onto the train and had allegedly witnessed the whole affair—the prosecution whisked him off the stand before he had a chance to say anything of substance. The testimony of the two doctors was as inconclusive as that of Bates and Gilley. Examinations revealed that both of the girls had had sexual intercourse around the time of the alleged assault, but there were no signs of rough handling. Nothing more serious than a scratch and a few small bruises, and when they were brought into the doctor's office "they were not hysterical."[4]

The boys' lawyer, Stephen Roddy of Chattanooga, was intimidated from the start. He told the judge that he was in court, informally, on behalf of friends of the boys' parents. He wasn't being paid, he hadn't the time to prepare, and he wasn't familiar with Alabama law or procedure. He simply wanted to help the court-appointed defense. But with Roddy before the court, the judge was reluctant to assign members of the bar to defend the boys. He told Roddy that if he appeared he wouldn't assign local counsel. If local counsel wanted to assist him, voluntarily, that would be another matter. Every time the judge seemed ready to leave it at that, Roddy backed down. He didn't want to do it alone. But members of the bar said they didn't see the need to be involved in the defense so long as Roddy was there. Roddy finally excused himself—"I think the boys would be better off if I stepped entirely out of the case." Except as an assistant. The judge said that with Roddy out, he would have to appoint someone, at which point Milo Moody, "an ancient Scottsboro lawyer of low type and rare practice," broke in and said, "I am willing to go ahead and help Mr. Roddy in anything I can do about it." The judge said once more that he would not require a lawyer to appear. The sixty-nine-year-old Moody said he was willing. The judge said, "All right." Roddy moved for a change of venue. The judge denied the motion, after which Roddy made "little more than half-hearted attempts" to defend the boys.[5]

Ransdall described the demonstration, inside and outside the courtroom, that followed the announcement of the first verdict, and then, more briefly, the substance of the second, third, and fourth trials. She pointed out that one of the boys, Olen Montgomery, was nearly blind and another, Willie Roberson, was suffering from so serious a case of venereal disease that it would have been painful if not impossible for him to have sexual intercourse. The case of Roy Wright was the most shameful of all. Wright was only thirteen, and the state, mindful of public opinion, asked only for life in prison. The jurors agreed with the state about what had happened but not what the punishment should be. When eleven held out for the death penalty, the judge declared a mistrial. "In three days' time," Ransdall concluded, "eight Negro boys all under 21, four of them under 18 and two of them sixteen or under, were hurried through trials which conformed only in outward appearance to the letter of the law." They had not had a chance to communicate with their parents. They had not seen a friendly face since they were arrested, yet, she wrote, "these eight boys, little more than children, surrounded entirely by white hatred and blind, venomous prejudice, were sentenced to be killed in the electric chair at the earliest possible moment permitted by law. It is no exaggeration certainly to call this a legal lynching."[6]

That was the history of the case, but to understand it, Ransdall wrote, readers would need "more than a mere knowledge of the events." She said that the Scottsboro trials, like the Dreyfus affair and the Sacco and Vanzetti case, "laid bare" the forces moving beneath the surface of the social structure. Most of the time these lay hidden. When they erupted, it was crucial for those who believed that humankind could exert control over social forces to examine them. So in the second part of her report Ransdall looked at the social and economic context of the case, paying special attention to the background of the girls and the prejudice of southern whites.[7]

Ransdall described the mills, the wages, and the appalling effect of the Depression on the workers. From local charity workers she had learned about living conditions and family life: the decrepit state of sanitation, health, and morality; the crime, drunkenness, insanity, and disease. Men often deserted their families when they lost their jobs, hoping that with them out of the way the charities would care for their wives and children. Husbands came and went. Women who took in male boarders were expected to share their beds with them. People gossiped, "but with jealousy for [their] good luck . . . rather than from disapproval of [their] conduct." "The distinction between wife and whore," Ransdall wrote, "is not strictly drawn. Promiscuity means little where economic oppression is great." "Why, just lots of these women are nothing but prostitutes," one social worker told her. "They just about have to be, I reckon, for nobody could live on the wages they make."[8]

Price and Bates came from the bottom of that world. With a social worker who knew them, Ransdall visited them at their homes. She found Bates a "large, fresh, good-looking girl," with "soft, melancholy eyes, as resigned and moving as those of a handsome truck horse." She was "shy, but a fluent enough talker when encouraged." Price, by contrast, was a lively, cocky young woman—"not bad to look at"—"who found it easier to talk than to breathe." Both of them spit snuff with wonderful aim.[9]

It was said that Bates's mother had a "boarder" living with her, "frequently got drunk," and "took men for money whenever she got the chance." But Ruby herself had been quiet and well-behaved—until she started running around with Price, who was in all kinds of trouble. The sheriff of Huntsville suspected that Price ran a speakeasy with a married man named Teller. He had caught Teller in her house but found no liquor, so all he could do was warn them. A neighbor of Price's claimed she was a "bad one," who more than once had been in scrapes with married men. She was the cause of the separation of one couple and might have been the cause of another, until the wife of the man threatened to kill her and Price moved out of the neighborhood. The same neighbor had seen Price shortly after the Scottsboro trials lying drunk in her backyard with a man asleep on her lap. Victoria's mother, the neighbor added, was "as notorious for her promiscuity in her day as Victoria is now."[10]

On her first evening in Alabama, Ransdall had heard from Walter White what White had heard from George Chamlee (the Chattanooga lawyer handling the defense of the boys for the ILD): that Price and Bates were notorious prostitutes. Price was known to solicit black and white men alike. A few days later a social worker told Ransdall that the chief deputy sheriff in Huntsville said that "he didn't bother Victoria, although he knew her trade, because she was a 'quiet prostitute, and didn't go rarin' around cuttin' up in public and walkin' the streets solicitin', but just took men quiet-like.' "[11]

The things that so outraged the respectable people of Scottsboro meant nothing to Price or Bates. Since the girls had been "in direct contact from the cradle with the institution of prostitution as a sideline necessary to make the meager wages of a mill worker pay the rent and buy the groceries," Ransdall reasoned, they had "no feeling of revulsion against promiscuous sexual intercourse such as women of easier lives might suffer." Nor did they have strong feelings about sexual relations between whites and blacks. George Chamlee had reported that it was not until after the girls were taken into custody that they cried rape. Only after they sensed the spirit of the armed men who had come to capture the boys did they agree to make the charge.[12]

Ransdall found Scottsboro a charming southern village of two thousand, situated in the midst of pleasant rolling hills. The people seemed mild-mannered, with kind, easy faces, friendly to one another and to her. Until she began asking about the trials. Then pleasant faces stiffened, laughing mouths grew narrow and sinister, soft eyes became cold and hard. Gentle and compassionate people were suddenly "transformed by blind, unreasoning antipathy so that their lips parted and their eyes glowed with lust for the blood of black children" who had done nothing to them, and may not have done anything to anyone. In those glowing eyes all Negroes were brutes, brutes who could be kept in their place, and away from white women, only by ruthless oppression. The people with whom she discussed the case, Ransdall said, made it "disconcertingly clear that they regarded the trial of the Negroes and the testimony given at it, not as an honest attempt to get the truth, but as a game where shrewd tricks were to be used to bring about a result already decided upon in the minds of every one of them. They all wanted the Negroes killed as quickly as possible in a way that would not bring disrepute upon the town."[13]

But why? Ransdall concluded it was because they lived on the enslavement of Negroes. They could no more afford to treat them with decency, honesty, fairness, or kindness than they could to grant them civil or political rights. They couldn't even afford to educate them, which was why, in a country that prided itself on its educational system, the defendants could neither read nor write. To maintain their social and economic position, southern whites had to keep the "nigger down." Repression, terror, and torture, Ransdall wrote, were the means to that end.[14]

Ransdall had hoped to publish her report, but each of the newspapers and magazines she queried told her they had already arranged to have someone else cover the case. Forrest Bailey and ACLU executive director Roger Baldwin thought the ACLU itself should publish it, but a number of their associates in the New York office, and a number of members of the governing board, blocked their proposal. Important people did not believe it, thought it too sensational, Ransdall recalled—"all these big, so called intellectual men who thought they knew it all." So Bailey and Baldwin mimeographed the report and sent it to individuals, organizations, magazines, and newspapers they thought would be interested. An ACLU press release reported Ransdall's conclusions and announced that her report was available upon request. The *New York Graphic* ran a story about it. So did the *Daily Worker,* its writer calling the report a "complete vindication" of the ILD's argument that the boys were the innocent "victims of a murderous frameup concocted by the Alabama bosses and their state and court machinery." He added that it wouldn't be popular with the NAACP, which had defended the state and its bosses. Yet it was: Walter White made extensive use of it whenever he wrote about the case.[15]

Ransdall did tell a sensational story, full of lurid anecdote and detail. She told it that way not because she wanted to shock her audience, but because she was shocked herself. She had never been to the deep South before. "I went down there, all innocence," she recalled, and got "more education" than "in all my eight years in college." She didn't even know enough to be scared, at least not until the judge, the mayor, and the doctor who examined the girls invited her into one of their offices, presumably to answer her questions. Instead they posted two policemen at the door and interrogated her, as if she were "St. Joan on the stage," asking who she was, why she was down there, who had sent her. Assuming that "no respectable organization would send a white woman down to ask about a lot of Niggers," they suspected she was a Communist, sent by Moscow. She didn't look like one, though; she looked more like a schoolteacher. Her parents had come from Kentucky. Puzzled, they concluded she was simply foolish, told her they wouldn't be responsible for her safety if she was not out of town in an hour, then offered to drive her to the train. She told them she could take care of herself, and resumed her investigation.[16]

Ransdall may not have been scared, but she was startled. The letters she wrote from Alabama reveal she could scarcely believe her own ears and eyes. She was astonished by the sordid backgrounds and unsavory characters of Price and Bates, "victims themselves but mercilessly cruel to other victims"; by the wretchedness of the boys, "diseased, destitute, and ignorant," "scared little mice, caught in a trap"; and, most of all, by the race prejudice of white southerners.[17]

Forrest Bailey had supplied her with the names of a half dozen Alabamans he thought would be sympathetic, but Bailey's contacts turned out to be as bad as the rest. Congressman George Huddleston, a "liberal friend of labor," hit the ceiling when she questioned the fairness of the trials. He didn't "care whether the boys were innocent or guilty. They were found riding on the same freight car with two white women, and that's enough for me." She tried to reason with him, reviewing some of the testimony she had just read, especially the doctor's, but she got nowhere. In desperation, she played what she thought would be a trump card and told him that "one of the women had been arrested previously for having taken a colored man as a customer in a house of prostitution." "It doesn't matter to me what the women had done previously," he said. "I'm in favor of the boys being executed just as quickly as possible! You can't understand how we Southern gentlemen feel about this question of relationships between negro men and white women." In Tuscaloosa, the "liberal lights of the university" "flared up" at the first mention of the case and all said the exact same thing.[18]

Ransdall wasn't sure if Alabamans believed what they said, if they really thought that the trials were fair. At times she felt that prejudice made them see the evidence differently from the way she saw it, or at least draw different conclusions from the same sight; thus the trial judge, A. E. Hawkins, "a dignified, fine looking, gray-haired Southern gentleman, who was absolutely convinced in his own mind that he had done everything to give the Negroes a fair trial, gave himself away so obviously at every other sentence he uttered, that any person with mind unclouded by the prejudice which infected him could have pointed it out." Other times she felt prejudice made them see one thing and say they saw another. Inside they knew the boys were innocent, or had strong doubts about their guilt and didn't care; racism led them to insist publicly that they were guilty and ought to be killed.[19]

How could anyone, she wondered, look at the crowd in Scottsboro during the trials, the demonstrations, the presence of troops, the slipshod evidence, the absence of friendly witnesses, the judge's refusal to allow questions about the reputation and conduct of the girls, and the all-white juries—and still maintain that the trials were fair? How could anyone look at the "eight terrified, bewildered young Negroes," lying miserably in their death cells, and then the two girls, enjoying excellent health and delighting in their fame—and still maintain that the boys deserved to die?[20]

S E V E N

A Stream of Vicious Literature

The first big wave of protest took Alabama officials by surprise. They had expected praise. They had snubbed Judge Lynch, called out the National Guard, held speedy trials, and thereby demonstrated that at least in Alabama the courts and not the mob would rule. And they got praise from all over Alabama and every corner of the South. But with the praise came condemnation, allegations about blood-hungry crowds, a Klan-dominated court, and a legal lynching: hundreds of telegrams, letters, and petitions addressed to the judge, local sheriffs, newspaper editors, and, especially, the governor. The judge and others dismissed the first few, which came during the trials, as pranks, but in the next few weeks there were too many to ignore. Although mainly from the North, they came from every state. Although mainly in English and from the United States, they came in every language from all over the world. Although mainly from ordinary men and women, they came from John Dos Passos, Theodore Dreiser, Fiorello La Guardia, Hamilton Fish, Thomas Mann, Albert Einstein, Maksim Gorky, and H. G. Wells.[1]

Letters arrived from unskilled laborers and business executives, schoolchildren and university administrators, barely literate but devout black Baptists and Episcopal bishops, tire manufacturers and temperance league activists, from people of every race, class, sex, region, and creed. Yet postcards, letters, and petitions from Communists, and mail from organizations that smelled radical or foreign or red, far outnumbered all the others. And most of the letters began something like this: "We the members of the Anti-Imperialist League"; "We the members of the Young Communist League"; "We the League of Struggle for Negro Rights"; "We the members of the Lithuanian Working Women's Alliance"; "We the Ukrainian Labor Temple"; "We the Frederick Douglass Interracial Forum"; "We the Karl Marx Pioneer Troops"; "We the Vegetarian Workers Club"; "We" the "Russian," "Finnish," "Scandinavian," "Croatian," "Hungarian," "Socialist," and "Jewish" toilers. Or worse: "We 900 white and colored workers assembled in a mass meeting in Kansas City"; "We white and black Birmingham workers"; "We four hundred white and black Communist workers gathered today in a social gathering." In April 1932 the attorney general of Alabama warned the telegraph companies they would be liable for prosecution if they continued to deliver telegrams regarded as "threatening" or "obscene."

It was a sea of mail, but it struck Alabama officials and editors as a powerful stream, a "stream of vicious literature" put out by "the Communists in an effort to capitalize on the negro case at Scottsboro." They quickly concluded that all the uproar about the convictions was the work of Communists or those misled by their propaganda, Communists whose aim was not to help the defendants—"these worthies probably care about as much for the fate of the convicted negro youths," wrote one editor, "as the average Tennessee farmer does about the banana crop in British Honduras"—but rather to use the case to incite race hatred and war. Who else would write such letters? Who else would call Judge Hawkins, who had cried as he read the verdicts, a "brutal slave driver"? Who else would look at the rebuff of mob rule and see "the threadbare lie of rape and a legal lynching"? Who else would write to the governor to demand the immediate and unconditional release of the defendants? Who else would call on Negroes and Communists to rise up and see to it that the guilty Negroes were turned scot-free?[2]

The rebuttal began with the facts: there was no lynching and the danger of a mob was never acute. Nor was there a legal lynching: the speed of the trials was for the boys' own good. There was a big crowd on hand, but the crowd and the music were merely coincidental; it was the first Monday of the month, a traditional trading day, when farmers from all over north-central Alabama came to town. At no time were the jurors intimidated by it. In a nine-part series on the case, *Birmingham News* reporter J. F. Rothermel, one of the few white Alabama journalists to suggest that there might be some validity to the charge that the speed of the trials hurt the defendants' chances for an adequate defense, otherwise dismissed the criticism of the trials, line by line. If the trials weren't perfect, they were as fair as humanly possible, as fair as they would have been anywhere, north or south. Grover Hall, editor of the *Montgomery Advertiser,* who had won a Pulitzer Prize in 1928 for his attacks on the Klan, expressed the sentiments of editors all over Alabama when he called readers' attention to the restraint of the people of Scottsboro, the prior records and confessions of the convicted men, and the testimony of the girls, before characterizing the trials as fair, orderly, and just. The only threat of disorder came from the activities of outsiders, which Hall called indecent and outrageous.[3]

Just one editor, F. T. Raiford, of the *Selma Times Journal,* was outspoken in his wholehearted dissent from those views. He wrote: "We are unable to take part in the outbursts of provincialism and purblind devotion to our institutions which are welling up in so many directions against the so-called 'pestiferous' groups and organizations that are leagued together in protest against the scheduled electrocution of eight Negro youths." Not until he was certain that the decrees of man-made courts were "ordained" by God and meant by Him to be obeyed as "emanations from the Source of all wisdom and truth" would Raiford consider all censuring comments seditious and treasonable. Raiford knew nothing of the guilt or innocence of the "black wretches." But he didn't need to in order to speak, in appalled tones, of the speed of the trials and sentencing, the armed militia, frowning machine guns, the courtroom surcharged with racial hatred, and the crowd. From a distance it looked like a mockery of justice, a "mob-dominated travesty" made to resemble "an impartial examination into the facts and the evidence." He hoped the Alabama Supreme Court would reverse the verdicts and order new trials.[4]

Raiford's was a lonely voice, and when Alabama's high court convened in late January 1932, Chief Justice John C. Anderson affirmed the more common view of the protest against the convictions. Anderson called the letters and telegrams "highly improper, inflammatory and revolutionary in their nature"; it was clear, he said, that they were intended to "bulldoze" the court. But the court would not be moved, and on March 24, the justices affirmed most Alabamans' view of the trials, upholding, by a vote of six to one, all but one of the eight convictions. (The court granted Eugene Williams a new trial, on the grounds that he may have been a juvenile at the time of the crime.) As most Alabama editors had been saying for a year, the majority, in a decision written by Justice Thomas E. Knight, Sr., held that the verdicts were amply supported by the evidence and the trials themselves were fair. Local press coverage, Knight said, was not inflammatory; neither a mob nor a mob spirit dominated the trials. "The presence of the militia, instead of having a coercive influence on the jury was a notice to everybody that the strong arm of the State was there to assure the accused a lawful trial." As for the speed of the trials, it was the majority's opinion that "if there was more speed, and less of delay in the administration of the criminal laws of the land, life and property would be infinitely safer, and greater respect would the criminally inclined have for the law."[5]

More scurrilous than Communist misrepresentation of what happened in Scottsboro was Communist interpretation of what it was all about, the charge that the verdicts were the result of class and race prejudice. The idea of class prejudice was preposterous. Alabama, and Jackson County in particular, was predominantly rural; most Negroes worked in the fields. Scottsboro had two small hosiery mills, a rug mill, a saw and planing mill, but the great majority of its people were farmers. Two-thirds of the 118 jurors were farmers; the rest were laborers, as the defendants were, or artisans and clerks. Only four could be said to be employers in any meaningful sense of the word.[6]

The charge of race prejudice was taken much more seriously, but it too was disputed vehemently, and in elaborate detail. P. W. Campbell, editor of the *Jackson County Sentinel,* led the way: there was, he claimed, not the slightest friction between the races, in Scottsboro or anywhere in Alabama, during the trials; nor had there ever "been racial trouble of any kind." Day-to-day relations were marked not by "hate" but by "friendliness and understanding." The races lived separately—Negroes had their own schools, churches, stores, and clubs—but in peace and harmony, for both races understood "the unwritten law and policy," the only law and policy that could ever "solve the race question in the South": segregation. It went both ways: "The white race let the negroes alone and the negroes let the whites alone." Intelligent Negroes had no more desire to cross the color line than intelligent whites. That was not to say there was never any trouble, but when there was, it was not racial trouble, but trouble caused by the "scum" of both races. Both races had that scum and recognized it as such. The proof was the reaction of the "best colored people" of Jackson County. They hadn't criticized the trials, they hadn't said a word, for they knew "it was a revolting crime and should be punished to the extreme."[7]

The great danger was that ignorant and trusting Negroes would be misled by the "wolves that came in sheep's clothing," infected by the prejudice and discord spread by alien influences intent on fomenting, and then exploiting, racial strife. And wherever even moderate Alabamans looked in the two years after the trials, they saw racial insubordination and insurrection.

In May 1931, 200 Communists, black and white, attempted to gather in Chattanooga, in violation of the city's segregation laws, to coordinate the protests against the trials. In July, having infiltrated the Black Belt, Party organizers rounded up some gullible sharecroppers around Camp Hill and duped them into joining a sharecroppers' union. The unionists, meeting to protest the Scottsboro verdicts, threatened the governor's life and then shot and severely wounded a sheriff who went to investigate. The shooting sparked a pitched gun battle between blacks and whites and then a general "uprising," which took a posse of hundreds to put down. In August, a Negro said to have been reading Communist literature kidnapped three Birmingham society girls, robbed them, railed at them for hours about the subjugation of his race, made improper advances, and finally shot all three of them, two mortally, when they tried to escape. In May 1932, 150 Negroes marched on Birmingham City Hall. In October, 300 turned up one week and 900 the next (along with 300 whites) in the hope of hearing William Z. Foster (the Communist Party's candidate for president) and Viola Montgomery (the mother of one of the defendants) address a rally. In December thousands attended a mass meeting of the unemployed. Every time police arrested a Negro for anything, anywhere in the state, he seemed to be carrying a Communist leaflet; every time they searched a house they found a membership list and piles of pamphlets advocating the violent overthrow of the government, an end to segregation, a minimum wage, race war, intermarriage, and social equality. "Demand what you want," the literature exhorted, "and if you don't get it take it."[8]

White southerners also wrote letters to Alabama's Governor

Miller, and most of them were as adamant as the state's newspaper editors and attorneys that the sentences should be carried out. They were often more candid about why. A Louisiana woman, writing for "the better class of people of the South," asked the governor to put all the Negroes, including the fourteen-year-old, to death at once. She had never heard of "so many crimes" and wondered whether it was because "we are too lenient with them," or because the Negroes think "the society in New York" will protect them. She was one of many worried about the effect of northern meddling on other Negroes; execution was necessary if for no other reason than to set a good example for the rest. "Our women," a Dothan, Alabama, man wrote, "have but little protection now and if these negroes are permitted to live they will have less." "The point which I do not understand," wrote a West Virginia man, after a meeting of Charleston businessmen at which a number of northern states were represented, "is why the great state of Alabama should be influenced by the complaints of the radical element throughout the world, when it is perfectly capable of administering its own affairs." "Not to enforce this law," he concluded, would "certainly lead to moral insurrection on the part of the negro race which can only result in race war." Everyone at the meeting agreed that the criminals should be put to death as promptly as possible.[9]

If Alabamans were to be criticized as severely for their trials as they once were for their lynchings, perhaps it made sense to go back to the old way. In April 1931, the editor of the *Jackson County Sentinel* had complained that the "ugly demands," "threats," and "filthy insinuations" had strained local notions of fair play, allowing "room for the growth of the thought that maybe . . . the 'shortest way out' in cases like these is the best." Six months later, the *Progressive Age* reprinted an editorial from a Georgia paper that predicted the result of interference by "reds and yellows" and long delays: "It would not be surprising that if another such crime should be committed in Scottsboro, or in that vicinity if the citizens should not take the matter in their own hands."[10]

E I G H T

The Real Facts Could Never Be Explained

Some white southerners had another view, and the men and women who led and belonged to the Commission on Interracial Cooperation (CIC) and the Association of Southern Women for the Prevention of Lynching (ASWPL) were the most prominent among them. The CIC was founded by Will Alexander, a Missouri-born former Methodist minister who had left the clergy in 1917, at the age of thirty-three, to work among blacks for the YMCA and the War Department. It was a moment of great optimism. Alexander hoped that wartime cooperation between blacks and whites would usher in a new age of race relations in the South. Such hope made the race riots that swept the country in the summer of 1919 all the more discouraging. There were more than twenty of them, and more ominous than their number was the unmistakable sign that blacks were fighting back, as they had in riots in East Saint Louis and Houston two summers before.[1]

The Commission grew out of the emergency interracial committees organized in Atlanta that summer. Its members were schoolteachers, social workers, clergymen, churchpeople, missionaries, journalists, college professors, and a doctor, lawyer, and businessman here and there. Like Alexander, many of them came from the evangelical Protestant churches and church organizations infused with the spirit of Social Christianity. Some traced their liberalism back further, to antebellum unionists and Whigs. Some came from liberal colleges and universities, where, in the early decades of the twentieth century, the new sociology and anthropology gave the lie to scientific racism. Some, coming of age amid the politics and reform movements of the Progressive Era, had by the 1920s and 1930s been able to free themselves of the vicious racism of that era. Some came to racial liberalism almost accidentally, in the conflict with the "masses" and their powerful agrarian political leaders (the enemy of my enemy is my friend). Some came to it concerned about morality, social order, reason, justice, the restraint of passion, the rule of law, and cautious, incremental social and cultural change. Some, believing that racial turmoil scared away northern investors, came concerned about economic development. Many, motivated by desires as disparate as profit and pride, progress and honor, came to racial liberalism concerned about the South's image in northern minds.[2]

The CIC's idea was to bring together the best of both races, the most responsible men (and, separately, women), to provide a forum in which blacks and whites could meet, share experiences, and air grievances about parks and recreation, public transportation, sanitation, health care, education, and police brutality. The hope was that the understanding generated would trickle down. With the resurgence of the Klan in the 1920s, and the dramatic increase in lynchings, the CIC turned most of its attention to racial violence, and as it did, two additional organizations took form. The first was the Southern Commission for the Study of Lynching, chaired by George Fort Milton, historian and editor of the *Chattanooga News*; the other was the Association of Southern Women for the Prevention of Lynching. The latter was founded in late 1930 by Jessie Daniel Ames, former director of women's work at the CIC, who had come to interracial work and then Atlanta from the women's suffrage movement and other progressive politics in Texas. Along with many of her colleagues, Ames had grown dissatisfied with the lynching commission's faith in research and with the separate and unequal place of women in the CIC. They knew enough about lynching, a number of women thought; it was time to try to stop it.[3]

In neither the thought nor the politics of the 1920s or early 1930s South did these organizations play a dominant role. If an antilynching woman, standing between a lynch mob and a black suspect at some rickety jailhouse door, held a mob at bay, editors put the story on the front page. More often, southern liberals did their work without attracting much attention. The CIC was an arbitrator, regularly brushed by the blows of the parties that it set out to reconcile: blacks saw a reincarnation of the kind master; whites saw carpetbaggers or abolitionists with a southern drawl. Nonetheless, the people who directed, joined, and sympathized with these organizations saw things differently from most white southerners, and they were confident that for every southerner outspoken in his or her support there were scores of others who quietly occupied the same uncertain ground.

When they spoke about Scottsboro, liberal southerners hoped middle-class southern blacks and northern whites were listening. Yet they were white southerners speaking primarily to white southerners, and most white southerners were convinced that the defendants were guilty, the proceedings just, and all those who thought otherwise Communists. So the first thing CIC executives thought to say was something only the most reactionary southerners could disagree with: the trials were a step in the right direction. They began their description of case and controversy with the "heartiest commendation" for the State of Alabama, its governor, and local officials, whose "prompt and vigorous action . . . undoubtedly prevented what otherwise would have been one of the most appalling holocausts of mob violence in our history." Alabama officials not only prevented a lynching but "endeavored" to give the accused "as fair a trial as possible under the circumstances." It was the circumstances, Will Alexander said—the swiftness of the trials, the inadequacy of the defense, the tension in town, the contradictory evidence—that made fair trials "exceedingly difficult" and raised serious doubts about the guilt of the defendants. Alexander argued that Alabama "could not afford to execute" the boys "until the case had been thoroughly reviewed by the higher courts."[4]

In the spring and summer of 1931, James Burton, the CIC's field secretary for Alabama, investigated the case. Stephen Roddy, the Chattanooga attorney who had helped Scottsboro attorney Milo Moody defend the boys, told Burton there had been more than twenty Negroes on the train and though some of them may have had "immoral relations" with the girls, without resistance, it was unlikely that they were the same ones who were on death row. Roddy also reported that both Price and Bates were immoral. George Chamlee, the attorney retained by the ILD, also provided some "very damaging" information about the state's witnesses, and Leo Thiel, the white principal of a Seventh-Day Adventist School in Huntsville, told Burton that he had met with J. A. Hackworth, a local private detective, who was "not at all backward about saying these girls were prostitutes." Hackworth, who was looking for work, offered, for a fee of $100, to obtain affidavits proving that the girls were prostitutes. The CIC couldn't afford his price, but at a hearing in Scottsboro in June—on a motion for new trials—Burton watched Chamlee present the affidavits to Judge Hawkins, who wouldn't allow Chamlee to read them aloud.[5]

"I did not read Mr. Chamlee's affidavits personally," James Burton wrote Will Alexander, "but I learned through legal sources that the statements said that these two girls resided in Chattanooga in 1929 and part of 1930, that they were of bad reputation, lived in a house of prostitution conducted by Negroes, and that colored men were their patrons." Price denied it. Burton found her bent over a washtub on the back porch of her home, a small house "in an alley or narrow street." She came down off the porch, emptied her mouth of snuff, and said that the boys were guilty of rape and she hoped to see every one of them "burned." Besides her three ex-husbands, she had never known any men. She had been a virtuous woman until that day.[6]

Reviewing the trial transcripts, Burton realized why none of the information about Price and Bates had had any influence at the trials: the prosecution had objected to every question about their characters and Judge Hawkins sustained every objection. Burton found the testimony, particularly that of the doctor, revolting, plainly incomplete, and full of approximations and contradictions. The defense had been unprepared and so haphazard that Burton couldn't even figure out who was in charge. One of the prosecuting attorneys Burton spoke with offered one explanation: Roddy came to court on the first day of the trials so "stewed" he couldn't walk a straight line.[7]

Long before he had completed his investigation, Burton and the CIC and ASWPL officials with whom he shared his findings were certain that the defendants deserved new trials. Yet when it came to determining what they should do about it, how they ought to use all the facts they had uncovered, whom they should tell what they knew, they were full of doubt.

They were full of doubt first because the ASWPL's stated purpose and the CIC's primary concern were to prevent lynching, reduce tensions in places where capital crimes had been committed, and facilitate speedy trials. In Scottsboro, all these objectives had been achieved without them. How could they protest the results of the trials when they themselves argued that one of the causes of lynching was frustration over legal delays. The trials convinced many antilynching activists that lynching might not be the only problem with southern justice, that when it came to the courtroom, speedy might not be synonymous with just. Nevertheless, most concluded that to protest convictions in a case in which the mob had been thwarted would raise serious questions about their motives and compromise their six-month-old cause.[8]

Antilynching women were unnerved also by reports of Price's and Bates's promiscuity. Most of them had never considered the possibility that behind many lynchings were interracial affairs, or white women who had solicited sex from black men. Was it possible, they now wondered, that to avoid humiliation (or worse) when they were caught, white women cried rape? If so, an ASWPL activist wrote, "the law should differentiate between the respectable women and the immoral women in defining . . . assault and fixing a proportionate penalty." Yet antilynching women could not imagine what they or CIC officials could say or do about Price and Bates without being "terribly misunderstood." "The real facts," wrote one Alabama woman, who described herself as "amazed beyond expression," "could never be explained."[9]

The interference of the Communists turned uncertainty and confusion into partial paralysis. CIC officials believed, just as fervently as the NAACP's Walter White (with whom they regularly corresponded, shared confidential reports, met, and schemed), that the case had nothing to do with class struggle and that the Party did not care at all about the lives of the boys. On the contrary, many suspected the Party hoped to provoke Alabama to kill the defendants. Why else, George Fort Milton asked in January of 1932, would the Party bombard the Alabama Supreme Court with "outrageous and insulting" letters, if not to "irritate and outrage" the justices and "prejudice them against the Negroes"? Milton assumed the Communists wanted the boys killed so that they could parade around the country making the "damnable charge that they were electrocuted because of their color."[10]

CIC officials produced their share of reports on "Radical Activities in Alabama." Yet it made no sense for them to tell the story of Scottsboro as if it were a story about the dangers of communism and nothing more. That was precisely what reactionary white southerners were doing. If liberals also conflated the two issues, how could they possibly put their distinct message across? The CIC had to try to separate communism and Scottsboro in the minds of other Alabamans—liberal, moderate, and conservative alike. They had to convince others (and at times themselves) that they *could* be separated, that one could have nothing to do with the Communists or radicalism of any kind and still believe that the defendants had not had fair trails and should not be executed.

The CIC had continually to maintain its anticommunist credentials. But unlike Walter White and other anticommunist northern liberals, who could at once bash the Communists and capitalize on their alleged threat, southern liberals couldn't play it both ways. They couldn't put the case and the fight over the defense in the context of a great struggle between those who wanted reform—the eradication of racism by democratic, capitalistic means—and those who wanted revolution. Too few southerners would have recognized the difference. Not even all liberals did: writing to Bruce Bliven at *The New Republic,* George Fort Milton said he hoped that the CIC would "divest further legal details from the odium which will accrue to it through Communist or radical negro auspices." When Milton wrote "radical negro auspices," he meant the NAACP.[11]

CIC and ASWPL officials did their Scottsboro work behind the scenes: they tried to secure editorials that expressed their hope that the defendants would be given the "full benefit of the courts"; they spoke to white church and civic leaders, encouraging them to call for calm reconsideration of the verdicts; they talked among themselves (and with the NAACP) about approaching the governor with the revelations about Price and Bates and asking him to commute the sentences. When people wrote to Will Alexander to ask what they could do to help, he discouraged petitions and letters to the governor. If you must send something, he said, send money for a competent defense. Protests only "complicated the case" and made it more difficult to obtain the support of many liberals and moderates "who otherwise would have been willing to push it to the limit."[12]

As early as June 1931, Will Alexander expressed confidence that "an increasing number of people in the South," aware of the facts of the case and the passion and prejudice that reigned, were "willing to help in every possible way" to see that the defendants were "given a chance." By early 1932, there were signs on the pages of a few big-city Alabama newspapers that some hard lines were softening; there was hope that there would be new trials and great disappointment in April when the Alabama Supreme Court upheld the guilty verdicts.[13]

New information about the case changed some minds. So did travel outside the region. Many southerners were stung by the criticism they were subjected to while traveling in the North. And also in Europe. Earl Sims, an Atlanta lawyer who described himself as the son of a Confederate soldier, the husband of an Alabama woman, and "neither a nigger lover nor a communist," was prompted by talk of the trials he had heard overseas in the winter of 1932 to write to Alabama's Governor Miller; there had been Scottsboro demonstrations in Switzerland, France, Germany, and Spain. Sims asked the governor whether "a barbarous penalty" was to be applied to "children." He wasn't criticizing the trials, and he understood the governor's exasperation with the radicals, Negroes, and South-haters who were. It was "merely the age-old issue of civilization versus savagery," and, Sims concluded, the governor had the opportunity "to demonstrate that, in his state, at least, civilization" was "in the ascendancy."[14]

N I N E

The Blackest Member of Our Commonwealth

There were black schoolteachers in the South and black ministers. There were some prosperous black farmers who, in spite of the invasion of the boll weevil and the collapse of the cotton market, had acquired or held on to tools, livestock, and land. There were black artisans who had not been forced out of their trades. There were black newspapermen, insurance executives, and undertakers; there were a few black doctors and lawyers. They were the heart and soul of the southern black middle class, and they said what they had to say about Scottsboro in their schools, churches, civic organizations, chambers of commerce, lodges, social clubs, letters to leading editors and elected officials, and in the few newspapers that withstood the first two years of the Depression. They were a very small group of ambitious, assiduous, accommodating, assertively moderate, at times conservative women and men. There was danger all around them, yet under the most unbearable pressure they displayed the most amazing grace.[1]

Below was the mass of poor, rural southern blacks, who had neither their caution, optimism, or patience—nor much more than their lives to lose for their lack of it. To many middle-class black southerners, the unwashed and unlettered were a disturbing reminder of where they had come from, and also, if in the early 1930s any reminder was needed, of how swiftly the fruits of years of striving could be swept away. All around them were southern whites, most of whom thought they were moving too far, too fast. Middle-class and upper-class whites hovered above while poor southern whites swarmed around them like bees. If blacks steered clear of whites when they could and knew their place when they couldn't, they might not get stung. But the penalties for the slightest infraction were grave. A black farmer or merchant who insisted on a price, goaded a white man to keep his word, or pushed too hard to collect a debt, risked more than his livelihood. Self-esteem, ambition, success—any one of these was provocative. Black people who wanted a higher education or aspired to practice medicine or law; those who rode through town in too fine a horse and buggy or too well polished a car; and those who simply displayed an air of equality or superiority found their lives threatened, their property destroyed, themselves and their families run out of town.

These were the spiritual heirs of Booker T. Washington, the former slave who, in the first decades of the age of segregation, at the very moment when white southerners transformed discriminatory social, economic, and political attitudes and practices, old and new, into law, founded Alabama's Tuskegee Institute and built not only a great school but a center for a paradoxical form of black power. He pleased white people by pleading with black people to trade political aspiration for economic opportunity, asking them to forget all they learned during Reconstruction, to pick up a trade, and use it to climb up from slavery. In the process, he became one of the most powerful politicians, black or white, in the South. He pleased whites by denying the importance of social equality, labor unions, and the ballot box. And in the process, he secretly channeled money (so freely in part because of his denials) into court cases challenging segregation and disfranchisement. It might not be unkind to say that in the New South, Washington perfected and took to its logical conclusion the cunning that had once assured the survival and sanity of slaves.[2]

Washington died in 1915. The fiftieth anniversary of Tuskegee's founding was celebrated the week after the Scottsboro trials. Editorials and essays honoring Washington, pointing to the strides that his race had taken in the half-century since the end of Reconstruction, thanks in no small way to his life and work, appeared in newspapers all over the country. As much as the accolades, Washington would have appreciated the way that those who followed in his footsteps tiptoed into the Scottsboro affair. The carefully worded letter his successor at Tuskegee, Robert M. Moton, wrote to the governor a couple of days after the trials read as if the founder's ghost had guided his hand. Moton thanked Miller for preventing a tragedy. A lynching, he said, would have "shocked the moral sense of the whole country, and placed a stigma on our great state," a "wholly undeserved" stigma in light of Alabama's record for law and order. "The prompt and orderly process of punishing crime meets with the hearty approval of all worthy citizens of both races." But, he concluded, "the end of law" was "justice": "I am confident that in this case you will see that such protection as the courts can give will be meted out to the humblest, the poorest, and the blackest member of our commonwealth."[3]

Black newspaper editors in the deep South handled the controversy with the same delicacy and tact. Oscar Adams, the editor of the *Birmingham Reporter,* had grown up in Mobile, graduated from the Agricultural and Mechanical College at Normal, and moved to Birmingham and purchased the paper in 1906. Adams was skeptical of the proceedings from the first and grew more skeptical over time. He wanted to see new trials held in a new place and he wished the Communists would disappear. In his own comments on the case, Adams was bolder than the CIC and more diplomatic, quieter, less forceful than the NAACP. Yet those who listened to what Adams said without watching what he did could not have understood what he was up to.[4]

When the story broke, Adams didn't even cover it. He must have concluded, as Washington would have, that it was best to say nothing, at least nothing critical of the courts, until the storm passed and its damage could be assessed. It was not until the beginning of May that Adams first mentioned the case, and even then his coverage was discreet: columns about the status of the appeals, based exclusively on news releases of the NAACP. His first editorial did not appear until the middle of June, and it too was restrained in substance and tone. For whites and blacks alike, he argued, the truth was paramount: "If these young fellows, poorly trained, primitive," were "guilty of the vile attack charged to them, then the punishment prescribed by law . . . should be administered." In their opposition to such violence against womanhood, all decent citizens, regardless of color, region, or station, agreed. The question, Adams said, was whether the evidence was conclusive, and whether the fear and race prejudice that rode with the mob made a judicious deliberation impossible. Every effort to find the truth, to secure justice, "should be taken by those who believe in fair play and honest dealings with all human-kind. . . . The case should not be decided upon race prejudice, or because certain sexes are involved. The dominating forces of Alabama should seek only justice in this matter, as justice is all to which any of us are entitled."[5]

That was the substance of Adams's editorials for the next few years. He did not call Price and Bates prostitutes or even report the allegations of those who did. Nor did he suggest that the "lie" of rape was behind most lynchings, or that the death penalty did not in any way fit the crime. He called for new trials, equal justice under the law, criticized the Communists, and warned his readers to stay away from them.

Yet he said more than that, he just didn't say it in his own words. In the weeks after the sentencing, Adams used ostensibly unrelated news stories and other people's words, drawn from the wire services and set on his front page, rather than explicit articles or his own editorials, to let his readers know what was on his mind. His layout was ingenious. In the edition that carried the *Reporter*'s first story on the case, which ran under a two-inch headline in fat block letters, "NEW TRIAL SOUGHT FOR BOYS," Adams ran a small story—also on the front page, and near the top—about two Norfolk, Virginia, women whom a grand jury had just indicted for perjury; earlier, on their false testimony, a court had convicted a black man of rape and sentenced him to death. The next week, Adams printed a story from California, picked up off the Associated Negro Press news wire, about a California judge who, prior to giving up his seat, pardoned (with no strings attached) 116 convicted felons who had been on probation. Among them were sixteen "white men convicted of criminal assaults on young girls and women." The article was wholly out of place—front, top, and center—in a small Alabama paper, except for the significance of the headline it allowed Adams to run: "JUDGE RELEASES 16 WHITE RAPISTS." Two weeks later, under the banner headline "NEGRO BOY FOUND NOT GUILTY," Adams printed a story about a twenty-year-old South Carolinian who was acquitted on charges of attempted rape. (Although the alleged victim described the crime in a dramatic manner, the defendant convinced the jury that he was out of the state on the day of the alleged crime.) Juxtaposition was another of Adams's tricks: at the beginning of August he printed two stories of the same length, with the same size headline, both high and perfectly centered on page one, separated by a single column. One read: "NEGRO BOY SAVES WHITE FRIEND FROM DROWNING"; the other: "NEGRO BOY LYNCHED IN ALABAMA."[6]

Adams had run similar stories before Scottsboro. They were at once sensational and immediately relevant to the concerns of the race. After the trials, he ran them more often, displayed them more prominently, and included more news from distant cities and states. One story after another about perjury, sexual assault charges thrown out of court, heavy fines levied on counties to compensate the families of wrongly lynched men, black people accused, nearly lynched, lynched, or sentenced to die for crimes to which whites later confessed.[7]

When in early 1932 a few white southern newspaper editors began to express skepticism about the Scottsboro trials, Adams reprinted their editorials and opinion pieces on his editorial page. The practice of printing other papers' editorials was a common one, but Adams and other black editors did it more often than white editors, for obvious reasons. When a white southern newspaper ran an editorial (about lynching, discrimination, voting rights, education, or anything else) with which Adams agreed, he would reprint it. Sometimes he placed a white editor's editorial right beneath an editorial of his own that expressed an identical point of view. Other times he ran their editorials alone, allowing a prestigious southern editor to speak for him, to say things he too was thinking but did not feel free to say.[8]

Sol Johnson was a black newspaperman in Georgia, the editor of the *Savannah Tribune,* and his first editorial on Scottsboro sounded a lot like Adams's. He commended the state for preventing "summary punishment." He too was sure that if the charges were true, there would be little sympathy. But, he added, there appeared to be some doubt. There had been long deliberations, one mistrial, and hundreds of people outside the courtroom bent on summary punishment; it was natural for the jurors to echo the sentiment of the crowd. Had officials really wanted fair trials, they would have moved them. And like Adams, Johnson allowed wire-service news stories and editorials from white southern newspapers to stand in for his most subversive opinions.[9]

Johnson had a lot to say about the trials in his own words as well, and he said it sooner than Adams did (the week after the trials), more explicitly, and more often, and he never shied away from what he saw as the larger context of the controversy: the court system and the charge of rape. The four hundred miles between Birmingham and Savannah may have reduced his inhibitions. Johnson firmly supported the NAACP; he was on the executive committee of the Savannah branch. He often rebuked the Communists or printed condemnations of the Party by others. Yet after the NAACP withdrew from the case, Johnson took his news from the Communist news services (including, for the first time in his pages, allegations about the reputations and the police records of Price and Bates). He did not stop criticizing the Communists, but he criticized less. He printed stories and pictures about Communist-sponsored Scottsboro meetings, and about the appearance of the defendants' parents at demonstrations. After James Ford, a black man born in Alabama (the grandson of a Georgia man lynched for "being fresh to a white woman") was chosen to run with William Z. Foster on the Communist Party ticket for the presidency, Johnson devoted much space to their campaigns. (That was June 1932; one month later, the Party nominated another black man for the governorship of Alabama.) Every few weeks, Johnson would print a picture of a well-known figure—Countee Cullen, Langston Hughes, Theodore Dreiser—who had endorsed the Party ticket, or an account of a Party rally."[10]

Johnson himself wasn't a Communist or fellow traveler. He distanced himself from much of what the Party said and did about Scottsboro and the larger struggle for equality. When fighting between sharecroppers and sheriffs broke out at Reeltown in December 1932, he reprinted an editorial from the *Atlanta World* characterizing militant resistance as absurd. His own editorial criticized the critics of the officials at Tuskegee Institute hospital who had turned two wounded croppers over to the law. "We often protect the accused," he admitted, "because we fear summary punishment. At times our sympathy goes out to the hunted culprits. In the face of law we must not allow our sympathy to control." Yet he printed the Party's version of the story, usually on his first page; the following week he ran the Communist account of the funeral for the dead croppers, describing how "thousands filed past two martyred leaders who gave their lives to protect their homes."[11]

Johnson's coverage, though bolder than Oscar Adams's, was equally eclectic. That's because, like Adams's, his budget was low and his methods of gathering news relatively primitive. He couldn't afford to be choosy about where he got his stories, and he rarely had time to rewrite news-service reports to express his particular perspective. And that's because, again like Adams, Johnson was a man in the middle, pushed and pulled between races, classes, and world views.

T E N

A Poor White Man at My Door

In the North, black newspapermen, clergymen, teachers, intellectuals, and artists were as quick as Walter White to recognize that Scottsboro made the Communist Party and its appeal to black America impossible to ignore. Scottsboro raised big and important questions about the Communists. Much to White's surprise, not all northern blacks, not even all of the black intelligentsia, in the past the Association's mainstay, saw things his way.

The NAACP's most vocal support came from clergymen, for whom a distaste for radical politics and Communist irreligion was often heightened by a powerful personal loyalty to Walter White. Nowhere was that truer than in Harlem, home to White and other NAACP executives and one of the great battlegrounds in the fight between the two organizations for popular support. Black clergymen denounced the Communists from their pulpits while also aiding the Association in more practical ways, refusing, for example, to allow ILD organizers to use their churches for Scottsboro meetings.[1]

Almost all of the ministers who got involved in the fray stuck with the Association until it admitted defeat in January 1932. Yet the black clergymen were not of one mind, and those who supported the NAACP were not always able to keep their congregations in line. In the middle of May 1931, after a long debate, the members of the Cooperative Business League, an auxiliary of Chicago's Pilgrim Baptist Church, voted to split the money it had raised for the Scottsboro defense between the NAACP and the ILD. At first a majority wanted all the money to go to the ILD. Then the minority raised the problem of the Communists' attitude toward the church, and the balance swung the other way. Compromise came on the third day.[2]

A few well-known northern blacks took sides as quickly and unhesitatingly as the clergymen. Robert Vann, editor of the *Pittsburgh Courier,* rushed to White's side and never wavered. And when it came to Scottsboro, W.E.B. Du Bois, editor of the NAACP's journal, *Crisis,* held fast to the Association's line. On the other side, the *Chicago Defender*'s editor, Robert Abbott, endorsed the ILD in the beginning of May. Boston journalist Eugene Gordon laid into the NAACP in *New Masses* in July, suggesting it change its name to the "Nicest Association for the Advancement of Certain People." Langston Hughes, though a personal friend of Walter White, was furious that the Association was so slow to act and so tentative in its actions. Hughes published his Scottsboro poems and play not in *Crisis* but in *Opportunity* and especially in *New Masses.* He published a few more poems in *Contempo,* a journal of radical politics and modernist literature courageously published for a few years at the University of North Carolina at Chapel Hill. One of them, in the December 1931 issue, was "Christ in Alabama":

Christ is a Nigger,
Beaten and black—
O, bare your back.

Mary is His Mother—
Mammy of the South,
Silence your mouth.

God's His Father—
White Master above
Grant us your love.

Most holy bastard
Of the bleeding mouth:
Nigger Christ
On the cross of the South.

Alongside that poem was Hughes's equally incendiary essay about the case, "Southern Gentlemen, White Prostitutes, Mill-Owners, and Negroes."[3]

But Vann, Du Bois, Abbott, and Hughes were the exceptions. At first most northern black writers and editors, like their counterparts in the South, simply wanted to figure out what the controversy was all about. Most were annoyed to learn that the NAACP had moved slowly in the aftermath of the trials, but few thought the Association's hesitation was cause to reject it completely. And few thought that war between the two organizations was inevitable, a point made painfully clear to the NAACP toward the end of April when its own field secretary, William Pickens, sent a letter of support along with a contribution to the ILD. (The national office had a fit, and Pickens was reprimanded severely; in the months that followed, he was responsible for the Association's harshest attacks on the ILD.)[4]

Even the editors who had endorsed the ILD before the NAACP was fully involved in the case ended up giving equal time to both sides and calling for cooperation. As the battle heated up in the spring of 1931 and raged through the summer and fall, the articles in many of the black papers read like informal dissertations: they described the alleged crime and the trials, introduced the competing organizations, outlined their histories, explained what they stood for, what they had done, and what they proposed to do now. In the midst of a vitriolic debate, those articles were models of balance and fairness to both sides, and that balance was as much the consequence of uncertainty as dispassionate journalism. The newspaper editors and reporters struggled not just to clarify a confusing controversy for their readers but to make sense of it themselves. They tried to explain why the two organizations couldn't work together, but their editorials reveal that they, like the defendants, did not know for sure.[5]

When it became clear that a joint defense was impossible, most black newspaper editors and intellectuals, including many who had expressed reservations about the Communists, ignored Walter White's criticisms and warnings about the Communists and blamed the NAACP. "What does it matter whether God, the devil, or Communists save those helpless black boys?" asked Roscoe Dunjee, editor of the *Oklahoma City Black Dispatch*. Carl Murphy, the editor of the *Baltimore Afro-American,* argued that communism was "no menace to Negroes"; on the contrary, the reds were "ready," "courageous," and in Scottsboro, "ahead." The *Defender*'s Robert Abbott added that the Party was "distinguished for its love of justice, although unpopular among the wealth and power of the land." Both editors insisted it was not necessary to accept all the Party's ideas and aims to recognize they were as radical as any white group since the abolitionists—"the first white group since Emancipation to advocate race, social equality, and intermarriage for those who wish it." They were as radical as the NAACP had been twenty years earlier, and, as the *New York News and Harlem Home Journal* put it, they deserved "full credit . . . for arousing the nation over the impending doom of the eight boys."[6]

Editors could forgive the NAACP's slow start, and even its apparent self-centeredness, but they tired fast of its unrelenting attacks on the ILD. All agreed that the Association had every reason to boast of its record. "As the leading organization for fighting our enemies," the *Washington World* wrote, it had "done a great deal of good." The problem was that lately it seemed as if the NAACP had decided that the greatest service it could render was to fight communism. That suspicion was confirmed in July 1931, shortly after sheriffs in Camp Hill, Alabama, broke up a meeting of black farmers who had gathered to air sharecropping grievances and draft a letter to the governor protesting the Scottsboro verdicts. Sheriffs killed one and wounded five, burned down the church where the meeting was held, arrested dozens, and terrorized the countryside for days; when the dust settled, five black people were missing, and when inquiries were made, officials reported they had been sent out to cut stove wood and had lots to cut.[7]

The NAACP immediately distanced itself from the croppers, blamed the affair on the Communists, and said we told you so, we told you "trouble would result from the campaign of bombastic and empty threats." The *Afro-American,* which happened to have a reporter, posing as a minister, on the scene, denied that the Communists had anything to do with the affair. The only reds involved, its headline screamed, were rednecks. The trouble started when colored farmers refused to pick cotton in Alabama for fifty cents a day when they found they could get at least a dollar more by crossing over the border to Georgia. Communists or no Communists, the editor of the *Washington World* was stunned that the Association used the incident to attack the ILD. He couldn't believe that the Association had not a "word of condemnation for an illegal shooting match staged by officers supposed to represent law and order." The

NAACP had "outlived its usefulness," he wrote, if it felt that "fighting the spread of communism" was "more important than fighting white Southerners who will lynch, massacre and slaughter and expect to get away with it." Only a "traitorous clique" would use "a tragic massacre of colored workers to malign an organization that is fighting in its way for the release of the Scottsboro boys."[8]

In April 1932, the editor of *Crisis,* W.E.B. Du Bois, asked the editors of seventeen Negro newspapers to contribute to a symposium on communism. Many expressed reservations and doubts. P. B. Young, of the *Norfolk Journal and Guide,* thought that the Communists had failed to consider the "rank-and-file" American's "traditional aversion" to " 'the blood and thunder' appeals of 'revolution' and 'mass action.' " Young thought that most black Americans were too patriotic to turn to communism. So did E. Washington Rhodes, editor of the *Philadephia Tribune,* who talked of the Negro's "peculiar love" for "America and American institutions," a love he believed transcended human understanding. The *Louisville Leader*'s editor, I. Willis Cole, was certain that Negroes would never turn to a party that scoffed at civil liberties and democratic government, or one that demanded that all members subscribe to every one of its principles and tenets. In courting Negroes, Cole argued, Party organizers kept certain of their principles in the background; once Negroes found out about those principles, the Communists would find it much more difficult to recruit them. Cole was just one of the editors to ask if black people could possibly make themselves at home among men who "hated god and all forms of religion."[9]

Cole and other black editors, including Du Bois, worried that the Communists had not fully explored the relevance of their theories to America, where race prejudice complicated class prejudice and sometimes seemed to turn Communist descriptions of the world upside down. How much faith should black people put in a dictatorship of the proletariat, the great majority of which, in the words of William Kelley, editor of Harlem's *Amsterdam News,* would come from the "same ignorant white class in the North and South which now fails to respond to just and intelligent appeals for racial and religious tolerance—the same ignorant white working class which forms the backbone of every lynching mob"? How hard should blacks fight to destroy capitalism, Cole asked, quoting Du Bois: after all, it was the "American courts from the Supreme Court down," dominated by "wealth and Big Business," that had given the Negro his "only protection against complete disfranchisement, segregation and the abolition of his schools"; and it was "Standard Oil, the Power Trust, the Steel Trust together with the aristocratic Christian Church" that had given him higher education and 40,000 black leaders to fight white folks on their own level and in their own language."

Yet even the most skeptical were amazed—not that some Negroes had joined the Party, but that many more had not. Every editor understood why Negroes would join, and every editor implicitly or explicitly asked, "Who could blame them?" P. B. Young provided a list of the Communist Party's good deeds: it proposed and practiced racial equality, aided evicted tenants, boycotted segregated establishments, and fought against white-only labor unions. J. E. Mitchell of the *St. Louis Argus* summed up that list in one sentence: "The communists say that they are for the equal protection of the law for all citizens alike, and many of their followers have gone to jail and suffered to demonstrate their belief." W. P. Dabney of the *Ohio Union* replied to oft-heard criticism of Party motives by asking whether drowning men demand reasons for helping hands. Fred Moore of the *New York Age* felt the same: "When Communists attack labor unions for keeping the Negro from earning his bread and butter I find no reason to disagree. When in speech and on large banners Communists advocate fair play for the Negro and launch a movement to secure the freedom of eight lads illegally convicted of rape, I do not accuse them of being wholly prompted by selfish motives. I find all political parties more or less selfish as are most organizations." In the end, however, Moore thought the Negro's problems were "going to be solved in the U.S., not in Russia, and not by Russia."

If one editor captured the mixed feelings of many black northerners, it was the *Black Dispatch*'s Roscoe Dunjee. For years Dunjee had hoped that poor whites would eventually come to see that their problems and interests were inseparable from the problems and interests of blacks, realize that the ruling class had kept them all down by keeping them apart. "The mental picture I have carried of the day when the two races would sit down side by side, on a basis of equality and brotherhood, has always been my rainbow." Now, Dunjee wrote, suddenly "I have at my door a poor white man," preaching brotherhood and equality. The white man wanted to "fight about it." "He calls meetings and stages parades. Boldly he carries banners through the streets of Dixie, with inscriptions which fairly scream and say all my previous demoted citizenship must vanish. Jim Crow, segregation and anti-marriage laws, yes, everything which has hitherto separated the white and the black" in America. The white man brought along "his woman," and she joined him in "the demand for racial equality."

That poor white man had faults as well as virtues. He wanted to destroy democracy along with capitalism. He was against individualism, and not long ago he had been part of the mob. But, Dunjee asked, at a time when we are "standing on the brink of revolutionary changes in our social and racial attitudes," a time when white wrath, generated during Reconstruction, had perhaps spent its force, were those good enough reasons for blacks to turn their backs on communism? "Yonder stands the poor white with a bomb under his arm—yet love in his heart for me. What shall I do about it? Does that unsanitary looking human being hold within his grasp my rainbow of promise, and the power which I so sorely need?"

E L E V E N

What Has Been Will Be Again

A few days after Alabama sheriffs shot up the sharecroppers' union in July 1931, Hosea Hudson, a thirty-three-year-old black Birmingham iron molder, heard that fifteen "leading negroes, preachers and some businessmen" had condemned the union and put up a $1,500 reward for the capture and conviction of the men who were down in Camp Hill "agitating and misleading our poor, ignorant niggers." Hudson couldn't understand it. He tried to figure it out, asking people what they thought about it, and he found that "a whole lot of them was sympathetic to the sharecroppers. They wanted to see something done, too, to break up the persecution against the Negro people."[1]

Hudson was born in Wilkes County, Georgia, in 1898, the son of sharecroppers; he had been a sharecropper himself until he was twenty-five. Then, plagued by family troubles and the failing cotton market, he quit farming and moved to Atlanta with his wife, Sophie, and their son. He found a job cleaning the pit in a railroad roundhouse, but the job was dangerous and he was unable to persuade his boss to make it safe. He was also unable to persuade him to promote him to machinist's helper, and so he decided to move to Birmingham, having heard from friends that he could make five dollars a day there. He found work immediately, at Stockham Pipe and Fittings, an iron foundry, where he was trained to be a molder, though not for five dollars a day. That was 1924.[2]

As long as he could remember, Hudson had resented the way Negroes were whipped and mobbed and chased with hounds. If only the older people could get together, he thought, "we could stop that kind of stuff." As long as he worked for wages he wondered why blacks were paid less than whites for the same work. Yet except for occasional talk about a presidential election or the tariff, he hadn't had "any mind" about politics or racial issues. His loves were baseball, singing, and girls. He sang bass in the L&N Quartet (named after the railroad the group's leader worked on); they were the first black singers to perform on Birmingham radio. Even when the Communists first came to Birmingham, blanketing the city with leaflets and organizing meetings in the park, he paid them little mind. He was busy figuring out where he would sing that night.[3]

It was talk all over town about the trials in the hills and the bold headlines in the *Birmingham News* that finally turned his head. He began buying the *News* and bringing it home for his wife to read. He and his friends were angry and wanted to know all they could about the case; Communist leaflets were an important source of their news. Working only a few days a week, as they had been since 1925, they had time to kill, to walk the streets and hang out at Tommy Clark's grocery, where they ate sandwiches and talked about the case. They wondered why it was that the better class of whites, the ones from whom they always expected assurances after a frame-up, had been unable to straighten this one out. The talk went on, and grew louder after the trouble at Camp Hill, "when the jails were full of negroes and people were wiring from all over demanding that they not be hung."[4]

Not long after, Hudson attended his first Party meeting, against the advice of many friends who warned him not to "fool with that mess" or he'd lose his job. He had run into Al Murphy, a guy he used to work with, and asked him why he was no longer in the shop. Murphy said he'd been fired for participating in the organization defending the Scottsboro Boys. He had just returned from New York. Hudson wanted to know all about it. He was "looking for somebody to say something, looking to see what [was] going to be said out of all these telegrams." He asked so many questions that Murphy became suspicious. Hudson wanted to know when and where the next meeting was, but it was not until a few weeks had passed and they had had a few more conversations that Murphy concluded that he was okay.[5]

There were a dozen people in a small room and Murphy did most of the talking, on and on about the case, the Depression, self-determination, and the imperialist war. Hudson didn't understand most of it. But he knew about Scottsboro, lynching, and Jim Crow, and what Murphy said about speedups, machines replacing people, the stagger plan, and unemployment made sense. He signed up that night and was immediately elected to be a shop organizer, which is what he did until January 1932, when a snitch reported that it was Hudson who had distributed a leaflet full of criticism of how his plant was run. He was fired. Hudson's wife, Sophie, had been working in a white woman's home, and when the woman heard why Hudson had lost his job, Sophie was fired too. "It was cold in the heart of the winter," Hudson remembered, "and everyone was unemployed."[6]

Hudson stuck with the Party. He and his comrades continued to distribute leaflets and CP newspapers; to avoid attack or arrest, they went house to house at night and drove small bundles of literature out to the country, leaving them for croppers in old barns and the hollows of trees. They sparred with the "better negroes," cajoled ministers to speak out about the Scottsboro case, organized marches on city hall, met among themselves to study the *Liberator* and the *Daily Worker,* and attended district and regional conferences. Most of all, they worked among the unemployed, organizing neighborhood councils. "The main thing that attracted people," Hudson said, "was unemployment relief": "Unemployment relief didn't just mean food. It meant getting some coal, it meant also paying the rent, cause a lot of people couldn't pay the rent, and the landlords would be threatening to put them outdoors. We'd get us a postcard, get the landlord's name, go to writing down, demanding not to put the people out the room."[7]

Eighty-five miles southeast of Birmingham, in Reeltown, Tallapoosa County, a tenant farmer named Ned Cobb was forty-six years into a lifelong struggle to maintain the freedom his parents and grandparents had won in the Civil War. His foes were landlords, furnishing merchants, white neighbors, bad weather, boll weevils, and the ups and downs of the cotton market. For a tenant farmer with a family of eleven, he fared well. Even through the twenties and the first years of the Depression, he kept up payments on his land, maintained possession of his house, stock, and tools. Cobb, like Hudson, first heard of the Party, which he called "the union," in the wake of Scottsboro and Camp Hill. Camp Hill was twenty miles northeast of his Reeltown home. He immediately liked what he heard, for he hadn't been "over ten or twelve years old" when he "came into the knowledge of more different things wrong than" he could "really tell." "It was just like slavery," he said. "In place of ever changin and gettin better, it was gettin worser and worser. . . ." He figured the union meant "a turnabout on the southern man, white and colored." He was further encouraged when a big old skunk of a white man warned him not to join.[8]

The "teachers" were traveling through the country, holding meetings, and attracted the attention of Cobb and several friends by their talk "bout the future comin." "He told, and we greed, the future days follows the present. And if we didn't do somethin for ourselves today, tomorrow wouldn't be no different." The first thing the organization wanted, Cobb recalled, was the right to organize. That was "one of the best things they ever could fight for and get on foot," Cobb said: "From my boy days comin along, ever since I been in God's world, I've never had no rights, no voice in nothin that the white man didn't want me to have—even been cut out of education, book learnin, been deprived of that. How could I favor such rulins as have been the past?" The teachers "sent out literatures," and though Cobb "couldn't definitely say what them literatures said—I aint a readin man"—he knew they said things big white men didn't like.[9]

The unionists' first demands were simple enough. They wanted food advances (which landlords and merchants had cut off after planting in the spring of 1931) to continue until settlement time. At settlement they wanted their share in cash, rather then credit or supplies, so they could buy what they needed from the merchant who gave them the best price. Croppers wanted the right to work for whomever they chose, wherever they chose; tenant farmers wanted the right to sell their crops to whomever they chose, whenever they chose, freeing them from the monopoly—on credit, supplies, tools, stock, settlement prices—of particular landlords and merchants. They also wanted the right to a garden for home use and a three-hour rest at midday. Not too much to ask for, yet enough to strike a blow at the heart of the man-made causes of their misery:

the crop lien system, the laws and practices that gave the men who furnished the drastically scarce credit control over every aspect of their working lives.[10]

Neither Cobb nor Hudson had a hard time finding friends and neighbors who thought, as they did, that the Communists proposed to do precisely what needed to be done. "It's a whole lot of Hudsons around," Hudson said, "you just haven't never met them." Yet not all the Hudsons were willing to join the fight. "Don't think everybody was with us," Hudson said, "cause it was a lot of them among our own ranks, right in that lower class, was against us, just as much as them in the other class was. We had to do a lot of straightening up."[11]

Some suspected the Communists were insane. After hearing an insensitive organizer lampoon religion or question the existence of God, many a potential convert concluded he was an "infidel" and refused to listen to another word. Others didn't trust the Communists simply because so many Party organizers were white. But most black people, Hudson and Cobb believed, were simply scared. They approved of what the organizers, black and white, were saying and doing, but they were afraid of losing their jobs, homes, credit, horses, families, or lives, so they put up with a world they didn't like as best they could, or found less dangerous forms of subversion.

Not a few of those who were hostile or afraid turned informer, and there were times when the "stooges," "stool pigeons," and "uncle toms" seemed to pose a bigger threat to black Communists than the surveillance of whites. But the informers, no matter how well placed, were often as susceptible to black peer pressure as they were to white intimidation, and Hudson and Cobb were convinced that the great majority of their peers were quietly on their side. Some would argue with Hudson for hours and then give him a contribution, on one condition: "Just keep what I say and do to yourself, and don't ever call my name to anyone." "All of em was willin to it in their minds," Cobb said, "but they was shy in their acts."[12]

Cobb himself was not shy. In December 1932 he stood up to one of the high sheriff's deputies who had come to Reeltown to attach Cliff James's stock. James was one of the last black landowners in Tallapoosa County and one of Cobb's neighbors and friends. The merchant who held the mortgage on James's farm had heard from the high sheriff that he was the head of the local Sharecroppers Union and in retaliation signed a writ of attachment against two mules and cows. Hearing that the deputy was coming "to take everything" that James had, and knowing that he was next, Cobb and a number of others gathered at James's farm. Cobb pleaded with the deputy not to take the animals. Without his stock, Cobb told the deputy, James would not be able to feed his wife and children. The deputy said he had orders and he would be damned if he "ain't goin to take it," but when he and the two black boys he had brought with him to do the dirty work made a move toward the lot, Cobb stood in their way. The deputy left, threatening to go and get the sheriff, who would "come down there and kill the last damn one of you."[13]

A few hours later he returned with a car full of white men. Most of Cobb's friends took cover in the house or behind it, but Cobb went out front to meet them. They surrounded the house and two of them, a deputy sheriff and a man named Platt, approached him, pointing shotguns. Deputy Ward walked toward the front door, while Platt walked up to Cobb, who stared him down for a moment and then turned toward the house. Ward grabbed him, but Cobb threw him off and started through the door. Platt opened fire, hitting Cobb three times in the back. Cobb turned and emptied his .32 Smith and Wesson in Platt's direction, and by the time he stopped to reload, the deputies had finished shooting and "hitched up their ass-wagon and took off." Cobb was covered with blood. A friend who had been in the house was dead.

The next week reminded blacks and whites alike of the week of terror that had followed the riot at Camp Hill a year and a half earlier. Small armies of heavily armed whites, perhaps five hundred in all, scoured the countryside in search of union members (they had found a list in James's house), disarming and interrogating, when not beating or shooting, every black person they could find. There were some subtle differences: more were killed, at least four, including Cliff James and Cobb's brother-in-law, both of whom died of gunshot wounds; dozens were wounded, and many more would have been had not nearly every black man, woman, and child in Tallapoosa County taken to the woods. And this time, according to the *Birmingham Post,* "a good many white farmers expressed sympathy with the negroes' desperate plight, although thoroughly disapproving of their resistance to the law."[14]

Back in Birmingham, Hudson spent the night preparing new leaflets. ILD people spent it looking for an undertaker willing to prepare the bodies for a public viewing and arrange a mass funeral.

The first few they approached wanted nothing to do with it, but according to Hudson, Hickman Jordan agreed to do it, and forever after his business flourished. It was no easier to find a preacher. Two horses pulled Jordan's hearse, and behind it was a long line of trucks, wagons, and buggies, and every policeman in Birmingham. That was the first time, Hudson said, that white people in Birmingham "recognized" a "Negro funeral."[15]

Cobb's trial for attempted murder began in late April 1933. It would have begun weeks earlier, but so many black people came to town on the appointed day that the trial was postponed. "Cotton Tom" Heflin prosecuted the case, asking loads of questions, mostly about who was with him, but none of the important ones, like where he was shot. The ILD defended him, and after his conviction, appealed, unsuccessfully, on procedural grounds. Cobb felt they were with him from beginning to end, asking all the right questions (which the judge ignored) and doing everything they could possibly do. Suspected of being a union leader, Cobb received a stiffer sentence than the four others with whom he was tried—twelve to fifteen years.[16]

"That was my education right there," Cobb said. "The nigger was disrecognized; the white man in this country had everything fixed and mapped out. Didn't allow no niggers to stand arm and arm together. The rule worked just like it had always worked: they was against me definitely just like they was against those Scottsboro boys. . . . The Negro stood a light show; he wasn't allowed the full extent of his oath. . . . They already had the dope they wanted on me and they didn't ask me for my story."[17]

The "better class of Negroes" warned Hudson and Cobb and other "hotheads" away from the agitators, but they offered nothing in their stead. The "big preachers" weren't speaking out; the three tiny NAACP chapters in Alabama were made up almost exclusively of "the better class of folks." An "ordinary Negro," Hudson said, "didn't feel that was his place." The Communist Party was the first and only group, white or black, to speak to them about Scottsboro and Camp Hill. The Party was the first and only labor and protest organization to invite them and other rural and working-class southern blacks to join.[18]

Cobb's and Hudson's "deeds," their willingness to act, set them apart from most of those around them. Yet they were connected by the experiences that informed those deeds—connected by the memories, ideas, and experiences of family, work, community, religion, economics, politics, and history—elements of African and American heritages that in America alone were three hundred years old. Hudson said that he had been prepared for the Party's coming by a militant grandmother and other "old slave people" who liked to talk about the war and Reconstruction and the "Yankees whupping the South. They used to sit around and talk about the Yankees. It used to be some Jewish peddlers to come through with bags of things to sell on their shoulders, and they would talk about the North. I heard that talk so much until I always looked for the Yankees to come back one day and finish the job of freeing the Negroes like how the old people talk about."[19]

Cobb had been prepared by his Grandmother Cealy, who knew her Bible and liked to say, "What has been will be again." She was "right smart," Cobb said. "Colored people once knowed what it was to live under freedom before they got over in this country, and they would know it again." Cobb thought of the "teachers" who helped him and his friends organize the Sharecroppers Union as the descendants of the white men who had come down during and after the Civil War, the whites who had come "to bring emancipation, and left before it was over." "Now," Cobb said, "they've come to finish the job."[20]

T W E L V E

I Am with Them to the End

The lives of the parents of the defendants were, in broad strokes, a lot like the lives of Hudson and Cobb. Claude Patterson worked in Chattanooga's steel mills, on the stagger plan; for three days of work per week he made seven dollars, with which he had to help feed a family of eight. His wife, Janie Patterson, like Ida Norris, Viola Montgomery, and Josephine Powell, worked in white people's homes, washing and ironing, cooking and cleaning; at one time they had all worked on farms. Ida Norris was the mother of ten, two of whom had died in infancy. Montgomery, who married at fifteen and was separated by 1931, was the mother of three children, none of whom was healthy. Josephine Powell was the mother of four.[1]

They believed their sons and wanted to do what they could to help. Like Hudson and Cobb and most other ordinary black southerners, they hadn't heard of either the NAACP or the ILD before the trials. Unlike Cobb and Hudson and most others who wanted to help, after the trials the defendants' parents had a choice between the two protest organizations. The parents had signed with the ILD before they learned of the NAACP and its interest in the case, but once the NAACP got into the fray, the parents had every opportunity and plenty of time to change their minds. Between April 1931 and January 1932 they were under enormous pressure from nearly everyone—black and white clergy, leading white Alabama attorneys, local and national NAACP officials, the warden and jailers at Kilby Prison, at times even their own sons—to abandon the ILD. They refused.[2]

ILD organizers got to them first and approached them, as they had approached their sons, as partners and friends. "A few days after the trial," Ada Wright wrote, "people from the ILD came to see me in Chattanooga. Of course I didn't know anything about the ILD at that time. . . . They told me they were out to defend the workers black and white and asked my consent to defend our boys." When the Interdenominational Ministers Alliance of Chattanooga approached Janie Patterson a month after the trials and tried to talk her into switching to the NAACP, she refused. The ILD, she explained, had "been very honest from the beginning, being the only organization or individual that ever came to the parents and discussed the case with them, and asked their support." "I can't be treated any better," she wrote two weeks later, "than the Reds has treated me."[3]

The Communists asked not only for their endorsement, but also for their help. They asked them to join an international campaign to free their sons. If, in a hierarchical organization that had not cleansed itself of the "white chauvinism" it was fighting against, the defendants' parents were not always treated as equals, they were treated as equally as they had ever been treated before. And ILD officials were not merely flattering them when they asked them to join the fight. Foreseeing that the mothers of the "Scottsboro Boys" would draw crowds, Party organizers sent them right into the field. In the fall and early winter of 1931, Ada Wright, Mamie Williams, Viola Montgomery, Ida Norris, and Janie Patterson traveled all over the country to raise money and spread the word. In 1932, Ada Wright accompanied the ILD's national secretary, J. Louis Engdahl, on a six-month, thirteen-country tour of Europe sponsored by International Red Aid.[4]

The contrast with the NAACP could not have been starker. When Association executives approached them, they did so as stewards, asking them only to sign on the dotted line. When some of the parents refused, saying that they were with the ILD, and others hesitated, saying they would need time to think about it, Walter White and other NAACP executives explained their behavior in ways that made it unlikely they would ever win them over. ILD officials, White said, got the parents' attention with checks, money for food, clothes, rent, and sometimes bus or train fare to Kilby Prison. Then they took advantage of their meager educations, their inability to see through Communist propaganda. In private, Walter White called them "frightfully ignorant." William Pickens went further, calling them "the densest and dumbest animals" he had ever seen. In public, White and Pickens were only slightly more discreet. They were "humble folk," White explained, "and [had] few opportunities for knowledge."[5]

The parents had no intellectual pretensions. But, said Mamie Williams, one of the first to get behind the ILD, "we are not too ignorant to know a bunch of liars and fakers when we meet up with them, and not too ignorant to know that if we let the NAACP look after our boys, that they will die." Mrs. Patterson told a crowd in New Haven that people tried to tell her "the ILD was low-down whites and Reds." "I haven't got any schooling," she said, "but I have five senses and I know that Negroes can't win by themselves." After the first execution day had passed, Ada Wright told of neighbors trying to warn her away from the ILD. They said, "Ada you better keep away from the reds." But she said, "It looks like the reds are the only ones that want to help us, and today I know this is true, because if it had not been for the reds, and the mass protests of the workers, our boys would have died July 10."[6]

That was the bottom line, the lives of their sons. In the spring of 1931, ILD attorneys had won a stay of execution, pending appeals to the Alabama Supreme Court. A year later, they won a second stay of execution, pending appeals to the U.S. Supreme Court. In May 1932, they won a hearing before the Supreme Court. In October, they made the arguments for new trials on which the justices were expected to rule any day. They continually protested mistreatment by sheriffs and prison guards.

"Our boys were being whipped and beaten until they came in," Mamie Williams had told a protest meeting in Charlotte, North Carolina, in May 1931. "I never heard of them before they came and looked up us parents. They've done everything they could. . . . If it hadn't been for the ILD we mothers wouldn't have been able to see our boys, I guess, until judgment day." A year and a half later, all the parents felt the same way. "I don't care whether they are Reds, Greens or Blues," Janie Patterson liked to say, "they are the only ones who put up a fight to save these boys and I am with them to the end."[7]

T H I R T E E N

The History of Liberty

On November 7, 1932, by a vote of seven to two, the U.S. Supreme Court overturned the Scottsboro convictions. Justice George Sutherland, reading the majority opinion in *Powell* v. *Alabama* from the bench, stated that the question before the Court was whether the defendants had been denied counsel, and if so, whether that denial violated the due process clause of the Fourteenth Amendment.[1]

Sutherland discussed the facts of the case and circumstances of the prosecution that shed direct light on the question of counsel. He noted that the defendants were arraigned immediately after the return of indictments and that at their arraignment the judge did not ask them if they had counsel, or if they were able to employ counsel, or if they wished to have counsel appointed, or if they had friends or relatives who might assist in obtaining counsel or making a decision about it. Nor, apparently, did he ask their consent before assigning all seven members of the Scottsboro bar to handle their defense. That assignment, Sutherland said, imposed a specific obligation on no one and was tantamount to assigning no one, a conclusion Sutherland supported by noting that even before the case was called, one of the attorneys assigned to the defense had accepted an offer to work with the prosecution.

Six days later, Sutherland continued, the judge called the first case and asked whether the parties were prepared for trial. When no one answered for the defendants, Stephen Roddy, a Chattanooga attorney, stepped forward. Although he had not been employed by the defendants, he said he was a friend of people interested in the case. He hoped to appear alongside the attorneys the court appointed—assuming, as the judge seemed to assume, that at least some of the attorneys he appointed to represent the defendants at the arraignment would undertake their defense.

Sutherland quoted at length from the record of the tense, halting, and circular conversation that followed between the judge, Roddy, and some members of the Scottsboro bar about who was going to defend the boys. The conversation ended in confusion, and the trials began. "The defendants," Sutherland said, "young, ignorant, illiterate, surrounded by hostile sentiment, hauled back and forth under guard of soldiers, charged with an atrocious crime, regarded with especial horror in the community where they were to be tried, were thus put in peril of their lives within a few moments after counsel for the first time charged with any degree of reponsibility began to represent them."

"The failure of the trial court to give the defendants reasonable time and opportunity to secure counsel," Sutherland argued, was "a clear denial of due process." Nothing made clearer the difference that time would have made—with the "defendants' friends and families in other states and communication with them necessarily difficult"—than the appearance of able counsel immediately after their conviction. But, Sutherland concluded, the denial of due process in this case was not simply a matter of time. Even if the trial court had been right to assume that time would not have helped the defendants get themselves better counsel, "the failure of the trial court to make an effective appointment of counsel was likewise a denial of due process within the meaning of the Fourteenth Amendment."

Justice Pierce Butler wrote and read the dissent, in which Justice James McReynolds concurred. Butler noted curtly that the Court had put aside two of the appellants' contentions—one about fair and impartial trials and the other about the exclusion of Negroes from juries—"as utterly without merit." Butler and McReynolds agreed with the majority that the denial of counsel was a denial of due process. But, quoting extensively from the opinion of the Alabama Supreme Court, they argued that the accused had been ably represented, that the state's evidence was adequate to warrant convictions, and that three of the defendants, while asserting their own innocence, had testified that they had seen other defendants commit the crime. Butler concluded by arguing that the majority had no good reason to consider and proffer an opinion on any matter other than the opportunity and time the defendants had been given to secure counsel. But, he said, the majority did not stop there, and its subsequent declaration that the trial court's failure to appoint an effective counsel was itself a denial of due process was an "extension of the Federal authority into a field hitherto occupied exclusively by the several states."

At the foot of the steps of the Court that morning, a hundred people, carrying signs that read "EQUAL RIGHTS FOR NEGROES," "JOIN THE ILD," and "SCOTTSBORO BOYS SHALL NOT DIE," had gathered for a demonstration. Police ordered them to disperse, and when they refused, lobbed tear gas and charged with clubs. The demonstration was aborted, but Party officials knew that the picketers, and all the picketers before them, had carried the day. The hand of the Court, the Party said, was again forced by "the powerful mass protest, embracing millions of workers throughout the world at the initiative of the Communist Party and the International Labor Defense."[2]

If the cause of the decision was clear to Party officials, the value and significance were not. The decision was full of contradictions, grounds for indignation as well as celebration. On the one hand, it was a victory of revolutionary struggle over "reformist betrayal," a victory that demonstrated just how correct the Party's strategy of mass agitation and provocation had been. On the other, it was an elaborate trap, "calculated to revive the faith of the masses in bourgeois-democratic institutions," to deceive the workers into thinking that the system was just. The justices ignored all the important political questions raised by the defense—the frame-up, the savage lynch atmosphere, the barring of blacks from the juries—and, in a long-winded document filled with "befogging terminology," based their decision on the narrowest grounds. So narrow, Party analysts charged, that the decision could be read as a set of instructions from one capitalist court to another, a manual on "How to Lynch in the Courtroom Without Violating the Constitution."[3]

Evidence for that argument was everywhere. When the *New York Times* editors wrote that the decision would "abate the rancor of extreme radicals, while confirming the faith of the American people in the soundness of their institutions and especially in the integrity of their courts," Party officials read their words as evidence that the capitalist press was being (uncharacteristically) honest about the justices' intentions. When Felix Frankfurter—a professor of law at Harvard and one of the founders of the ACLU—pointed out that the decision left the fate of the defendants untouched ("Upon the question of guilt or innocence it bears not even remotely; the Supreme Court has declared only that the determination must be made with due observance of the decencies of civilized procedure"), Party officials found a mainstream legal scholar frankly admitting that the Court's decision was nothing more than instructions for legal lynchings.[4]

Few non-Communists agreed with the Party's explanation of the Court's decision. Walter White claimed the decision vindicated not Communist agitation but the strategy of strictly "legal redress," the NAACP's method for twenty-two years. A Michigan editor argued that the decision illustrated the "utter uselessness" of the Communist demonstrations. The *New York Times* thought the decision was proof that the Communists were wrong to charge that "a spirit of wicked class prejudice pervades the United States, and that here no justice can be had for the poor and ignorant." The *New York Daily News* put it more forcefully: by granting new trials, "the highest court in the world's greatest capitalist country has silenced most of the radicals' Scottsboro thunder."[5]

Even many of the liberals and radicals who credited the Communists with getting the case to the high court and thereby saving the defendants' lives considered absurd the Party's characterization of the decision as a trick or a trap. Some were as dismayed as the Party by the narrow grounds on which the Court based the decision Morris Ernst, a socialist, called the decision "an empty and meaningless victory" because the majority disregarded the two contentions that carried the deepest social significance: the absence of fair, impartial, and deliberate trials and the exclusion of blacks from the juries. But many more people, black and white, celebrated victory. Even the editors of *The Nation*, who had printed Ernst's "Dissenting Opinion," and who accepted many of his contentions, refused to accept his conclusion. "The right to counsel was no mere technicality," they insisted, "but as fundamental as the other two."[6]

Felix Frankfurter wrote a long essay on the decision for the *New York Times*. The importance of the case, Frankfurter wrote, transcended and extended beyond the fate of the "pitiful" and "illiterate" defendants. That's because the Supreme Court had applied the due process clause of the Fourteenth Amendment to review a state court's conduct in a criminal trial. In the past, the justices had used the conveniently vague words of that amendment to protect property rights and ward off the regulation of economic enterprise. Now, Frankfurter wrote, in the hands of the same justices, the same words "return to their more immediate purpose of protecting black men from oppressive and unequal treatment by whites."[7]

Frankfurter argued that in limiting its decision to the question of an adequate defense, the Supreme Court did not, as some critics of the decision complained, turn its back on *Moore* v. *Dempsey* (1923), the decision in which the Court had overturned the conviction of a half-dozen black Arkansas sharecroppers on the grounds that the court that had sentenced them to death had capitulated to a threatening mob. (A court dominated by a mob, the Court said, was not a court but a mob.) Rather, the Supreme Court extended it, enunciating another "fundamental requisite of the judicial process," another aspect of state criminal procedure to which the high court would pay close attention. In *Moore* v. *Dempsey,* the Court said that a fair trial requires a court free from coercion. In *Powell* v. *Alabama,* it said that it also requires that the accused be furnished with means of presenting his defense, especially counsel and time. "The history of liberty," Frankfurter concluded (citing Justice Brandeis), "cannot be dissociated from the history of procedural observances." Frankfurter didn't think that the *Powell* Court was declaring its desire or intent to become a general tribunal for the correction of criminal errors. Nonetheless, in his mind the deepest significance of the case was the signal the justices sent that, though the Court would continue to act with hesitation, it would "not suffer, in its own scathing phrase, 'judicial murder.' "[8]

F O U R T E E N

Stuck in the Same Old Cell

The defendants had stories of their own. They told them to one another and to other prisoners. They told them to their many visitors, though the defendants often found that when their visitors told stories about their visit, the stories the visitors told were not the defendants' but their own. The defendants told them in hundreds of letters, scribbled on dime-store letter paper, or dictated to fellow prisoners who knew how to write.

They wrote asking for help, as Haywood Patterson did hours after his trial: "Do all you can to save me from being put to death for nothing. Mother do what you can to save your son. We did not get a fair trial, and you try to have it moved somewhere else if we get a new trial. Do you all try to come down here and try to get me a new trial, or I will be put to death on July 10." They wrote to express their thoughts about the fight between the ILD and the NAACP, as Charlie Weems did in a letter to George Maurer of the ILD: "Stop Walter White from butting in my case." They wrote to apologize when they changed their minds: "Mr. White," Clarence Norris wrote, "the other boys and I was talking about you today. I think all of them have made it up in their minds that you were write and Mr. White I am sorry that the boys acted like they did when Mr. Beddow [the Birmingham attorney White had hoped would agree to defend the boys] was down here. Please don't think hard of him [Haywood Patterson] because I really don't think he knows any better. I am too glad for somebody to help me out of this trouble. . . ."[1]

They wrote to ask for things they needed. "While in my cell lonely and thinking of you," Roy Wright wrote to his mother, "I am trying by some means to write you a few words. I would like for you to come down here Thursday. . . . I feel like I can eat some of your cooking Mom." Wright asked for chicken, paper, stamps, peanuts, and cake: "If nothing else the chicken." They sent Christmas wish lists. Ozie Powell asked for "1 coconut, 2 nice cakes, chocolate and coconut, 1 pound mixed nuts, 1 doz. apples, 1 doz. oranges, 1 doz. bananas and candy, 3 blocks of grape chewing gum, 2 pairs of socks and some cheese and some fried rabbit and sausage and some fried potato pies. and some sauce meat. and some rex-all tooth paste and some stamps envelopes and tablet."[2]

They wrote to say thanks: "Since the Supreme Court have granted we Boys a new trial," Olen Montgomery wrote to ILD chief William Patterson, "I thank it is my rite to express my thanks an appreciation to the Whole party for thair care of me and the wonderful and faithful struggle for my rites." Haywood Patterson wrote ten days later: "Now I only wish I was more educated so that I could express my sincere appreciation to the people in New York for all that they have did for we boys while here in prison."[3]

Sometimes they wrote simply to say what was on their minds. "Just stuck in my same old cell at 4:30 a.m.," Roy Wright wrote to George Maurer. "I haven't slept much since three nights and I just had to drop you a line or two about myself and my troubles to kinder ease my pain a little and to get a little consolation if there is any more in life for me. While I am trying to write this letter probably I'll get some. You know Mr. Maurer that at times it is really hard for me to get myself together in this place. . . . Oh, to think what I am charged with. If there is a god as they say he knows I am not guilty of such hideous crime. . . . You know I pray every night of my life. Maybe he knows that I know nothing of that crime. . . . You know I am idle in here and I think the whole thing over and over. To think there is people so unjust that they put things on people they don't know anything about. Well, nevertheless the good lord don't like ugly things so I'll trust in him for those that try to punish me for a deed I didn't commit. I forgot to tell you that I got a letter from Mama. She's Ok. Well I guess I'll close for this time. I hope I get out of here this month so I'll close."[4]

Roy Wright was thirteen in March 1931. His brother Andy was nineteen. Their mother, Ada Wright, and three sisters lived in Chattanooga, where the two boys were born and raised. Roy had three or four years of school before he quit to work in a grocery store and run around with Andy and Andy's friends. Andy began school at eight or nine and made it through the sixth grade. He had liked it and done well, but he had to quit to help his mother with Roy and his younger sister after his father died. Andy drove a truck for a produce distributor for seven years, working his way up to twenty-one dollars a week; then his boss's insurance company found out how young he was and forced his boss to let him go. After that he worked for a while as an extra hand in a furniture store. Having heard about government jobs hauling logs on boats, he and Roy and two friends, Haywood Patterson and Eugene Williams, hopped a freight bound for Memphis. Andy and Roy didn't tell their mother they were going, though it was Roy's first time away from home.[5]

Both Wrights could read and write a bit, but eighteen-year-old Haywood Patterson couldn't write at all. Born in Elberton, Georgia, in 1912, Patterson was the fourth of nine living children; four of his mother's babies had died before he was born. His father, Claude Patterson, had been a sharecropper until he got fed up with the white man in charge of his land. He had bought a secondhand car, and when the boss tried to tell him when he could work on it and when he couldn't, he decided he had had enough. But he couldn't just walk up to the man and tell him that he had decided to leave. He owed money for food, stock, rent, and seed. So he slipped off, and Haywood's mother pretended that he had disappeared. She went to the landlord in distress, said that he had left her and all the children alone. The man believed her, and when she said that her only choice was to go live with her father, he let her go.[6]

Patterson started school at six or seven and made it as far as the third grade. He never went regularly—his parents thought he did, but he often pretended to go and played instead—and he stopped for good when he was about fourteen. He did odd jobs while he was in school and worked as a delivery boy after he quit. At fourteen he began riding the rails, looking for work, eating away from home as much as possible. His parents had younger mouths to feed. "Many freight rides I had by the time I was sixteen," he said. "I knew all the nearby states, southeast to Georgia and down to Pensacola, Florida, north to Ohio, west to Arkansas. I knew the train schedules, when the freights left and where they arrived. I could light a butt in the wind on top of a moving boxcar."[7]

But he couldn't write, and he regretted not having paid more attention to school the moment he found himself in jail. "In the death cell," he recalled, "I held a pencil in my hand, but I couldn't tap the power that was in it." He could read a bit and he taught himself to write with the help of his two best friends, a dictionary and the Bible. He copied passages from the Bible and looked up words he didn't know; he bet guards and visitors they couldn't name a state he didn't know the capital of. By December he was able to write the note he sent along with his mother's Christmas gift, and he began writing his own letters, from the "Condemned Dept." at Kilby to the ILD: "We are well and hoping to be free soon and also hoping you will remain in fighting for us boys. Have you all got Mr. Darrow. I heard that Mr. Clarence Darrow was going to fighting for us boys, and I would like to know if possible because I am innocent, as innocent as the tiny mite of life just beginning to stir beneath my heart. Honest, Mr. Engdahl, I haven't done anything to be imprisonment like this."[8]

He had no choice but to learn to write, he said, because in Kilby you had to "find a world in yourself." The prison, only eight years old, was the pride of the Alabama prison system, complete with dairy farm, cotton mill, slaughterhouse, and hospital. A special wing of the prison had been designated death row, and the condemned were kept apart from the regular prison population at all times. The cells, Patterson said, were "no bigger than a small bathroom in a city house. Just big enough for an upper and lower cot. There was a face bowl there and a toilet stool. A dark screen was over the cell door. One small window was in the back of the cell. You could look out the window but only see the cell block wall of another building. This was the 'blind side' of death row." There was "no air, no sight of the sky, no exercise." Death row inmates left their cells only once or twice a week, when they were handcuffed and walked to the shower, a few yards down the row.[9]

Clarence Norris was born in 1912, the second of eleven children, two of whom, a sister and a brother, had died in infancy. His parents were sharecroppers. He remembered fresh air, fresh milk, fresh butter, fresh collards, mustards, turnips, tomatoes, corn, beans, okra, cabbages, potatoes, and yams. The family hunted, fished, spent all day Sunday in church; Clarence liked the singing. They participated in revivals that lasted for weeks, which for Clarence meant picnics behind the Mount Olive Baptist Church, tables and tables of free food spread beneath the trees.[10]

Bad memories were mixed with the good. Norris's father was a hard worker and a good provider, but he was a better man to have working for you than to work for. He was hard to please, and he had a temper that only violence could ease. Being his son was an impossible job. He told his children he had been a slave and tried to keep them straight with stories of slavery days: the finger he had lost to his master's ax when he was late getting up one morning; the sister he'd lost to an overseer when she forcefully resisted the man's advances—he killed her with a hoe. Once Clarence "got some size," his father talked about little but the work to be done. Clarence and his siblings worked in the fields from the age of seven. By ten he was pulling cotton, plowing, and planting: "Everything a grown man could do I did or my daddy would whup me good." He started school at seven, but his father wouldn't let him go more than a day or two a week, and he didn't get beyond the second grade. "You didn't bite my daddy's bread and go to school after a certain age."[11]

The family moved from Warm Springs to Neal after their landlord killed the horse that pulled his father's brand-new buggy and then threatened to kill his father.

Hating farming and his father's beatings, he left home for the first time when he was about fifteen, for a job down the road that paid wages. A year later, after his father died of a heart attack, he returned to Warm Springs, where he found work as a caddy at a country club. His first trip far from home was by freight to Birmingham, but he got seriously ill along the way. He was taken in and nursed by a black family that lived along the tracks. Word of construction jobs drew him to West Point, Georgia, where he took a room in a boardinghouse and quickly fell in love with his landlady's niece. They moved to Gadsden, where Clarence got a good job in the brand-new Goodyear plant, working eleven to sixteen hours a day. They rented a house and furnished it on credit; he was as happy as he had ever been. A year later, his girlfriend fell for another man and left him. He imagined killing her, and the night he realized he might actually do it, he fled, leaving house and furniture behind and heading back to the railroad tracks.[12]

The hoboing was harder than ever. Everyone was hungry, looking for work, begging for food. Food cost nothing, but there was no work and thus no money to be had. Breadlines were segregated. With plenty of company, he scrounged around town all day and returned to the hobo jungles at night, jungles crowded with men talking of their troubles, telling their stories, passing along rumors about jobs. He went days without eating, but starvation was not the greatest worry of the homeless and unemployed in the deep South. Sheriffs had their eyes out for hoboes, whom they often arrested for vagrancy, curfew violations, and other trumped-up charges and then sold to chain gangs. Found guilty of nothing more than vagrancy, a man might find himself sentenced to seven to thirty days in a quarry busting rocks, in a field picking cotton, or out in the middle of nowhere digging ditches for pipe or putting down a road. It was work without wages, and that man would be awfully lucky to be free of it in thirty days.[13]

When Norris found work, employers often paid him less than they had promised to pay him. Sometimes they refused to pay him at all. Norris remembered the last job he had before he was arrested. Word had spread that many men were needed to dig out the foundation of a new building; fifty showed up in the hope of making twenty cents an hour. "The boss went down the line and picked the biggest, healthiest-looking men," Norris said. "The men not hired stood around waiting. They knew somebody would quit or be fired, 'cause they was working us like mules. We were using shovels. The foreman come around to me and said, 'Every time the man next to you brings up a shovelful, you bring up a shovelful.' After an hour of this my pace slowed some, here come the boss: 'Keep up now, I got a bunch of fellas to take your place.' I threw down the tools and told them they could have my place. And they wouldn't give me my twenty cents!"[14]

Tough as times were, Norris dreamed of saving enough money to hire a teacher and learn to read and write. He was eighteen. In Kilby Prison he dreamed mostly of killing the guards who tormented him. Once a few of the men he had met on death row were executed, he began to dream of dying in the chair.[15]

Executions were carried out after midnight, in the room behind the steel door at the end of their cell block, in a chair built by a former prisoner, an expert cabinetmaker. That chair had replaced the gallows in 1923. Willie Stokes, convicted of murder, was the first to go, on the day in July 1931 when the defendants had originally been scheduled to die. Then Charlie Williams, for rape. Then Richard Ashe, Willie Johnson, and Charlie Jones. Then Isaac

Mimms and Percy Irvin. Mimms, Irvin, and a third man named Strickland had been charged with the robbery and murder of a white man. According to Mimms, Irvin had turned state's evidence, testifying that he had been an innocent bystander. But the only person who profited from his testimony was the solicitor. All three men were convicted and sentenced to death. Strickland's family had some money, and at the last moment his lawyer persuaded the governor to commute his sentence to life. A few hours before Mimms and Irvin were scheduled to die, Mimms split Irvin's head open with an iron pipe. Doctors slowed the bleeding with bandages, and led him to the chair. Mimms told fellow prisoners that he knew he was scheduled to go first; he wanted to be sure that the man who had cost him his life would be losing his. Norris never forgot the screams of Mimms's mother. She had to be carried out of the prison, not just out of the death cell, but all the way out to the gates.[16]

Blake Ruff tried to stab himself to death a few hours before he was set to die. Afraid to enter his cell while he was conscious and had a knife, guards knocked him out with gas. Orderlies bandaged him up, bathed him, put clean clothes on him, and a few hours later took him to the chair. Ruff, who was executed the last week of March 1933, was the tenth man executed in the two years the defendants had been on death row. All ten were black.[17]

The following evening, L. J. Burrs was on duty on death row, and as he made his rounds he told Patterson, Norris, Weems, Andy Wright, Roberson, Montgomery, and Powell to get ready to go. Late that afternoon the warden had received orders to transfer them, after dark and under heavy guard, to the Jefferson County Jail in Birmingham, en route to Decatur for their new trials. They began to pack up their belongings. Burrs stopped them. "Hell," he said, "leave all that here, you'll be back." They left their things. But, Patterson recalled, "that wasn't all we left for Burrs. We had our opinions of the death house and we left them in the beds and covered them with sheets. We gave them a nasty job. They had put it on us and we put it on them. In hell, if the guests get the chance, they don't treat the devil any better than he treats them."[18]

In Birmingham, those seven were reunited with Eugene Williams, who had been there since April 1932, when the Alabama Supreme Court overturned his conviction, and Roy Wright, who had been there all along. Wright's first trial had ended in a mistrial when seven jurors held out for the death penalty despite the prosecution's plea for life. On March 9, 1933, two weeks before Patterson and the others arrived, *New York Times* reporter Raymond Daniell was allowed a rare jailhouse interview with Wright.

Wright, who was now fifteen years old, and four inches taller than he had been in March 1931, told Daniell that he, his brother, and their two Chattanooga friends had neither fought with the white boys nor seen Price or Bates. They hadn't known there was trouble until they saw the posse. His memory of the hours and days that followed was not clear. He knew he had had a trial because the Supreme Court declared that it was not fair. He remembered taking the stand but couldn't say which of the men asking him questions were lawyers for the prosecution and which for the defense. He remembered one of them urging him to plead guilty "and get a life sentence instead of a chair." And he remembered what happened just before he was called to testify in Haywood Patterson's trial:

> I was sitting in a chair in front of the judge and one of those girls was testifying. One of the deputy sheriffs leaned over to me and asked me if I was going to turn State's evidence, and I said no, because I didn't know anything about this case. Then the trial stopped awhile and the deputy sheriff beckoned to me to come out into another room—the room back of the place where the judge was sitting—and I went. They whipped me and it seemed like they was going to kill me. All the time they kept saying, "Now will you tell?" and finally it seemed like I couldn't stand no more and I said yes. Then I went back into the courtroom and they put me up on the chair in front of the judge and began asking a lot of questions, and I said I had seen Charlie Weems and Clarence Norris with the white girls.[19]

Roy Wright's mistreatment began in Scottsboro, when one of the militiamen jabbed him with a bayonet, leaving a scar on his cheek. It continued in the Gadsden jail, where the boys were moved for safekeeping the day after their arrest. Back in Gadsden after their trials, Haywood Patterson got fed up and seized a gun from a deputy sheriff and warned him not to come one step nearer. "Haywood ain't afraid of nothing or anybody," Wright said. "He just took the gun away from that deputy sheriff and said: 'We've been sentenced to death already for nothing and we ain't going to take any more beatings. Go ahead, now, and shoot if you want to, but I'll shoot too.' "[20]

"It wouldn't have been no good, though," Wright said, "because the gun Haywood got was only a .32 and they had all those machine guns and things. I don't believe it would have gone off, even." Only once before March 1931 had Wright been in trouble with the law. He and some friends had been to a late movie; it ran to eleven-thirty, and on the way home they were picked up "for keeping late" hours. They spent the night in jail.

Wright said he was anxiously awaiting his new trial, but he wasn't pleased that it was going to be in Decatur. "I don't like that much better than Scottsboro. It's right next to where those girls live."[21]

PART TWO

1933

F I F T E E N

Brave and Chivalrous Generations of the Past

In January 1933 the ILD retained Samuel Leibowitz to lead the defense in the second trials, thereby depriving the Party's foes of a dear and damaging bludgeon: the accusation that the Party did not truly want to "free the Scottsboro Boys," but rather hoped to goad Alabama into executing them. In a fifteen-year career, Leibowitz had defended seventy-eight individuals charged with first-degree murder, and not one of them was executed. Seventy-seven of them were acquitted, and the trial of the other ended in a hung jury. Lawyers and laity disagreed about who was the best criminal lawyer in the country, the next Clarence Darrow. But everyone agreed that the thirty-seven-year-old New Yorker was the man to call if you were accused of a crime for which the jury might send you to the chair.[1]

Leibowitz was the son of Isaac and Bina Lebeau, Romanian immigrants who, frustrated by anti-Semitism, had come to America in 1897, when Samuel was four. Isaac changed Lebeau to Leibowitz after a neighbor convinced him he would do better in New York with "an American name," and the family prospered, climbing from the Lower East Side to Harlem's Little Italy to East New York–Cypress Hills, Brooklyn. Along the way, Isaac traded in his pushcart for a series of dry goods stores. Samuel worked his way through college and law school at Cornell, and then, though his teachers advised him against it ("Anything but that," the dean said), he decided to go into criminal law. He was ambitious and had concluded that a Jew without money or connections could make a name for himself only in a branch of the profession that the best and brightest shunned. He began by taking the cases of indigents, untalented pickpockets, and petty thieves, but because he won even those that prosecutors and court-watchers had considered airtight, his name got around. Before long he had some of the most infamous accused rapists, murderers, gangsters, corrupt cops, and their kin knocking at his office door.[2]

Leibowitz had a big oval head, a fleshy face, a gracefully receding hairline, and an expanding waistline, not all of which was lost in his six-foot frame. On his way to court, dressed in well-cut and neatly pressed business suits, he looked like a banker, or a banker's lawyer. In court, he was a showman, fiery and flamboyant, a triple-threat man, one writer noted, a master of cackles, thrills, and tears. At Cornell he had excelled at drama and debating, and his vibrant voice and extraordinary sense of timing were as useful to him as his prodigious preparation, attention to detail, and mastery of the law. He loved to popularize science—the reports of doctors, coroners, and ballistics experts—for the edification of his juries, but he knew juries liked entertainment at least as much as instruction. So he entertained them. He was especially adept at playing to a public familiar and fed up with stories of police corruption, to jurors who came to the courtroom with a sense that "the law" broke the law as much as it upheld it—and who could easily be convinced that the police had manufactured evidence, bought a witness, or tortured a suspect to extract a confession.[3]

Characteristic was his defense of the "Baby Killer," Vincent Coll. The twenty-two-year-old Coll had been a rising star in the underworld until he was accused of firing one of the two submachine guns aimed at Anthony Trobino, as Trobino walked along East 107th Street in Manhattan one afternoon in late July 1931. Trobino ducked and escaped injury, but five children on that same sidewalk were less fortunate. One of them, four-year-old Michael Vengalli, who had been sitting in his "baby buggy," died. The murder "evoked howls of outrage throughout the entire country." Police and local newspapers posted a thirty-thousand-dollar reward, and Coll was arrested two months later.

The chief witness against him was George Brecht, an ex-convict and professional surprise witness, who just happened to be walking along East 107th Street on the afternoon of the shooting. Leibowitz had a nose for professional witnesses as well as for ex-cons, so sharp a nose, legend had it, that he could tell not only how long an ex-con had been in prison but what prison he had been in. Brecht had lots of experience himself, and under a long cross-examination he remained calm and composed. It wasn't until he testified, in a Bob Burns (Arkansan) drawl, that he made his living on the streets of New York selling Eskimo Pies that Leibowitz smelled a rat.

At lunch Leibowitz sent out for a handful of the ice cream bars, and when court reconvened he distributed them to prosecutor, judge, and jurors, before continuing his cross-examination with questions to which every customer, let alone every peddler, would have known the answers: Describe the wrapper. What does the ice cream look like? How do you keep them cold in July? Brecht had never heard of dry ice and insisted that the pies kept themselves cold in the summer sun. The little lie told Leibowitz there were big lies, and a probation officer who had known Brecht in St. Louis—Brecht had testified that he had never been in jail or even on a witness stand before—told him everything else that he needed to know. It took Leibowitz only a few minutes the next morning to get Brecht to confess that he was an ex-con, that for the last three months he had been a special guest of the police department, and that since the age of nineteen he had made a career out of taking the witness stand and saying, "That's the man." After an embarrassed district attorney ordered the prosecutor to move for a directed verdict of acquittal, Coll went free. He was murdered, gangland-style, soon after.[4]

Nothing about Leibowitz but his record could have appealed to the ILD. He was not a radical, a fellow traveler, or a crusader of any kind; he was not even opposed to capital punishment. He had no experience putting social classes or economic systems on trial. He took the case of anyone who said he or she was innocent. When critics called him gullible, or worse, he said it was the judge's and jury's job to determine who did what. His was to ensure that every defendant was presumed innocent until proved otherwise in the face of the most spirited defense. He was a mainstream, organization Democrat, as full as any American of the democratic and legalistic illusions the Communists were so eager to shatter.

The ILD's new national secretary, a black Communist attorney named William Patterson, told Leibowitz that the ILD couldn't pay him, or even reimburse him for his expenses. It offered him nothing but "an opportunity to give [his] best in a case which for its humanitarian appeal has never been equalled in the annals of American jurisprudence." He would be representing not only "nine innocent boys" but also a "nation of twelve million oppressed people struggling against dehumanizing inequality." Patterson promised Leibowitz that he would not be asked to give up any of his political, economic, or social views.[5]

Leibowitz asked Patterson for the court records, studied them, found Victoria Price's testimony rebutted by the science of one of the state's own witnesses, Dr. Bridges, and concluded that the defendants were innocent. He saw an opportunity to right a wrong and at the same time to "increase the realm of his renown," by associating himself at last with a cause that others would see as noble. He wrote to Patterson: "Your organization and I are not in agreement in our political and economic views." But, yes, he was interested, because the case touched no "controversial theory of economy or government" but only "the basic rights of man."[6]

His wife, Belle, and many friends had warned him not to take the case. They feared that the defendants had been prejudged, "doomed" because their skins were black. Leibowitz told Patterson he could not "partake of that opinion." "North and South, East and West, we Americans have a common tradition of justice. And if it is justice that these black men be adjudged innocent—if it is justice, I repeat—I cannot believe that the people of Alabama will be false to their great heritage of honor, and to those brave and chivalrous generations of the past, in whose blood the history of their state is written." He acknowledged that "customs" differed, that "social usages and points of view" were "dictated by tradition." "But," he added, "persons of substance in the Southern States have recognized for many generations a moral obligation toward the simple and generous folk, whom slavery brought them first as chattels."[7]

Patterson hoped that Leibowitz would keep his ideas about the case to himself. They would only provide fodder for the cannons of the hard-line Party leaders who thought that by his choice of Leibowitz Patterson had sold out the masses. They would characterize Leibowitz's talk of common traditions of justice and the basic rights of man as bourgeois naïveté. They would dismiss as absurd his view of the South. Yet by late 1932, Patterson and other ILD officials had concluded that the case would continue to be of revolutionary value only if in the upcoming trials the Party could persuade the workers, particularly southern white workers, that the defendants had been framed. "I am satisfied that there are thousands of sincere and conscientious people who are firm in their belief of the guilt of the defendants," Patterson wrote to George Chamlee. "Every effort must be made by us to win them over and to show them the nature of the conspiracy." To those ends Patterson was prepared to sacrifice ideological purity. Leibowitz's reponse to his invitation had simply made it clear how great that sacrifice would be.[8]

Patterson wrote back to say again that he wasn't asking, and he did not expect, Leibowitz to adopt the ILD's views. His appeal grew out of the ILD's "intense desire to secure for these boys" what it regarded as "the best possible legal counsel." Patterson insisted that mass protest was inseparable from the legal defense, and then, after offering a brief lesson on class and race relations in the South, gently suggesting that "as an attorney" Leibowitz had probably not "delved into these sociological trends," he accepted Leibowitz's services. When in conference with Patterson and the ILD's chief attorney, Joseph Brodsky, Leibowitz spoke confidently of his ability to scratch the superficial layer of prejudice off the rock of decency in every human being, even in Alabama, Brodsky said: "You will be a sadder but wiser man when you are finished. We have been down there and we know what we are talking about."[9]

Leibowitz had not been down south, but his ideas about southern justice and race relations were rooted in widespread ideas about southern history. It was a history full of romance, courage, and honor, of a section defeated but not destroyed, of a forever struggling people (white) who by the second decade of the twentieth century had largely triumphed over the triple burdens of slavery, the Civil War, and Reconstruction. It was a tragic history, but a strange form of tragedy in which everything had worked out in the end.

The view from the North had not always been so rosy. Abolitionists had persuaded many northerners that slavery was pure evil, white southerners were brutal and depraved, and southern society was backward and degenerate. The antipathies and traumas of the Civil War made that dark view darker, and during Reconstruction, radical Republicans did their best to make it darker still. But by the first decades of the twentieth century the white South had won smashing victories in one of the civil wars that followed the Civil War, the war over the memory and history of the sectional crisis and the nineteenth-century South.

Southern historians, led by Ulrich B. Phillips, who taught at the University of Wisconsin and the University of Michigan before settling at Yale, persuaded northern historians, who in turn helped to persuade the public, that slavery—"the peculiar institution"—had been an unhappy inheritance, a bond the region unconsciously despised but could not break. Earlier generations, north as well as south, had handed it down and profited from it, but by the nineteenth century it remained exclusively in southern hands. Southerners made of it what they could. Slavery had cost a lot and returned little. The balance sheet looked nothing like what the abolitionists had made it out to be. Whites were the big losers; the price they paid was corruption, degeneracy, stagnation, and, most of all, lost time: the nineteenth century left them behind. If anyone gained it was the uncivilized slaves, "the simple and generous folk" Leibowitz had referred to, for they were the beneficiaries of the white man's benevolence, the kindness and paternalism of their masters.[10]

Early-twentieth-century historians argued vigorously about what caused the sectional crisis, secession, and the Civil War. Some thought it was a clash of irreconcilable cultures. Some thought it was a clash of irreconcilable economic systems, a predatory, industrial North versus an agrarian South. Others thought it was a conflict between two different ideas of government, one giving the most power to the federal government, the other leaving it in the hands of the states. A few persisted in seeing the Civil War as many northerners had seen it in the generation after the war—as a fight between slave states and free, with slavery as the fundamental cause. But in the years between the two World Wars, many more thought it was about nothing at all, or next to nothing: blundering politicians and wild, intemperate agitators, abolitionists and fire-eaters, north and south. Yet historians of both sections and almost every persuasion agreed on one thing about the war: once it began, both sides fought long, hard, and valiantly for values and ideals in which they truly believed—and for which more than half a million men gave their lives.[11]

Then a few radicals nearly spoiled it all with Reconstruction, perverting Lincoln's grand vision of rapid reconciliation, "with malice toward none and charity for all." In the thesauruses of white historians, north and south, *Reconstruction* became a synonym for venality, vengeance, brutality, and humiliation; it was characterized by military occupation, Republican state governments that could not have been more corrupt, and worst of all, black rule: the empowerment of black men who moments before had been slaves and who were not even prepared for freedom. Black historians dissented vigorously, but white historians and white Americans were as close as any large group ever gets to being of one mind in thinking that "all thoughtful men" saw black suffrage as the "greatest political crime ever perpetrated by any people" and Reconstruction a "savage tyranny" that "accomplished not one useful result," and which southerners had justly and heroically risen up to overthrow.[12]

In the early twentieth century, the capital of Reconstruction history was Columbia University, where Tennessee-born political scientist John Burgess and New Jersey–born historian William Dunning reigned. Dunning's and Burgess's interpretations of Reconstruction were not entirely new. Aging Confederates and younger southern partisans, amateur and professional, including Woodrow Wilson, had laid the foundation. And a northern amateur historian, James Ford Rhodes, had had similar things to say about Reconstruction at the same time. But Dunning was blessed with many students, loyal as they were prolific, and on the foundation he laid in his books and in his famous seminars, they built a monumental southern history of Reconstruction, state by state. Dunning's students had students of their own, so that the history that had its origins in his seminars dominated the way historians looked at Reconstruction for more than fifty years.[13]

The scholars had help from novelists, moviemakers, and popular historians, the three most important of whom were Thomas Dixon, D. W. Griffith, and Claude Bowers. Dixon's Reconstruction novel, *The Clansman,* was a best-seller in 1905 and later a popular play. (*Civil War and Reconstruction in Alabama,* by Walter L. Fleming, a student of Dunning's, appeared the same year.) Yet Dixon's subsequent collaboration with D. W. Griffith, which produced *Birth of a Nation,* dwarfed his earlier success. Millions of Americans viewed the movie, and, just as Dixon and Griffith hoped, millions of Americans came to understand Reconstruction as the time when Klansmen on horseback rose from the ashes of defeat to rescue white women and the white South from radical Reconstruction, from black rapists and black rule. President Woodrow Wilson invited Dixon, a friend from his college days, to show the film at the White

House. It was "like writing history with lightning," Wilson is reported to have said, "and my only regret is that it is all so terribly true."[14]

Fourteen years after Griffith turned the reigning interpretation of Reconstruction into a classic film, Claude Bowers, a fiercely loyal and terminally unreconstructed southern Democrat, intent upon healing the divisions that Al Smith's 1928 presidential candidacy had revealed in the Solid South, turned it into a vivid and immensely readable racist melodrama, in which Andrew Johnson and the Democrats are full of unrealized good intentions, Thaddeus Stevens and the Republicans full of all too well realized malevolence, and the former slaves full of unredeemable stupidity and lust. Bowers' earlier histories had done well, and his publisher, Houghton Mifflin, had great expectations for *The Tragic Era*. They printed a hundred thousand copies, and spent generously to promote it. Their efforts paid off. The book was a Literary Guild selection, a best-seller in 1929 and a moneymaker for years after—a critical as well as a popular success.[15]

Arthur Schlesinger, Sr., was one of the few white historians who had serious reservations. Schlesinger called Bowers' research meager, his interpretation unoriginal, and his method excessively melodramatic. Because he portrayed only great heroes and even greater scoundrels at moments of high drama, Bowers failed to notice that Reconstruction was "exceptionally mild as such things go in history. The Radicals stopped short of the crowning blunders: they confiscated practically no enemy land and put no one to death for a political offense. They established public schools in the South. And in spite of their lamentable misdeeds, economic progress went on." It wasn't his kind of history, yet Schlesinger had to admit that by applying "the art of the motion picture" to "historiography," Bowers had written a flowing narrative that swept "the reader breathlessly along from one thrilling climax to another." If by the end of the book he grew weary, "surfeited with scandal, corruption and fraud," it was "not the author's fault"; it was "history's."[16]

The Reconstruction of Rhodes, Dixon, Dunning, Burgess, Griffith, and Bowers was pure evil; its termination could be nothing but good. The federal government withdrew the troops. The carpetbagger and scalawag governments were run out of town. White southerners returned to power. Responsibility for the freedpeople was back where it ought to have been all along, in the hands of southern whites who knew them better than northerners did and were best prepared to civilize them. With the noose removed from the southern neck, blood once again began to flow. Southern capital began building cotton mills. Northern capital began building railroads and producing iron. White southerners built a New South on the unstable, shifting ashes of the old. In the 1890s, propelled by the desire to purify a political system still polluted by the tailings of Reconstruction, whites began turning the wheels of disfranchisement, and by the first years of the new century the Fourteenth and Fifteenth amendments had effectively been annulled. Almost suddenly, the Civil War looked not only inevitable but glorious and good: the South had been freed of slavery, and one great nation had been forged in the flames that destroyed it. In the next war, thirty-three years after Appomattox, northerners joined southerners in a fight that had much to do with white supremacy.[17]

It was this history of the South, which was both a cause and a consequence of sectional reconciliation, that allowed most white northerners in the worst and bloodiest years of segregation to agree that the fate of the freedpeople was best left in southern hands. It was this history that allowed white northerners to take white southerners at their word when they said that the region's fiercest racial tensions had been relieved. Not that there weren't problems. There were, and they were attributed to the long half-life of the damage done during Reconstruction, to the poor whites and the demagogues who egged them on, and, most of all, to the ignorance, laziness, and stupidity, the unreasoning recalcitrance and regression, of black women and men. As black and immigrant ghettos took shape in the North, as freedpeople north and south failed to live up to abolitionist expectations, and as scientific racism captured the popular imagination, northerners were inclined to look at the problems of southern whites with sympathetic eyes. Perhaps, many began to think, southerners had been right about Negroes all along.[18]

That was by no means the only northern view of the South. By the 1930s there was also the image of the benighted South, the savage South, the retarded and demented South of the fundamentalists, prohibitionists, and the dying but never dead Ku Klux Klan. H. L. Mencken didn't invent those images, but he contributed to them with such ardor and elegance that he helped make their creation an intellectual vogue. Journalists and scholars in the South as well as the North made a living trying to live up to the standard he set. But during the twenties the "benighted South" remained largely the South of intellectuals. The Klan was healthier in the industrial states of the North than it was in the South; fundamentalist religion, the defense of which killed William Jennings Bryan in 1925 and made Dayton, Tennessee, the butt of so many jokes, was hardly unknown above the Mason-Dixon line.

Samuel Leibowitz hadn't given much thought to the South or southern history before he was asked to lead the Scottsboro defense. He was a busy criminal lawyer, in a city as provincial as a big city can be. Yet Leibowitz had ideas about the South and southern history. Or ideas had him. They surfaced the instant he was called to speak about the South. He had ideas about the South, and on the eve of his first trip south, he had expectations.

S I X T E E N

The Buzzards Swarm Again

The attorney general of Alabama, Thomas E. Knight, Jr., led the prosecution. Knight was born in Greensboro in 1898 and attended the public schools there and then the prep school at Greensboro's Southern University. He enrolled in the University of Alabama but in 1917 left for the war, fighting with Alabama's 1st Cavalry and then the 117th Field Artillery. Home again after the armistice, he took up the law, which in his family and state was also to take up Democratic Party politics. After three years as Hale County's solicitor and five years as Alabama's assistant attorney general, in 1930 he was elected attorney general. Knight described himself as a Democrat, a Methodist, an Elk, a Knight of Pythias, and a member of the American Legion.[1]

Knight was short, wiry, good-humored, and, at thirty-four, still quick to blush. He was ambitious and made no secret of it; he had risen fast and hoped to rise higher. Yet he never got too busy or too big for his old friends, and perhaps because he neither flaunted his family and its political connections nor tried to pretend that his good fortune was all of his own making, few seemed to begrudge him his success. He knew as well as anyone his genealogical debt. His grandfather, William Knight, had fought in the Civil War, rising to the rank of captain in the 36th Alabama. During Reconstruction he served as sheriff and county commissioner, and in 1886 was elected to represent Hale County in the state legislature. Five years later he was a delegate to Alabama's Constitutional Convention, the main purpose of which was to write white supremacy—or, more exactly, black disfranchisement—into law without too grossly violating the Fourteenth and Fifteenth amendments.[2]

His son, Thomas Edmund, Sr., took his start in politics right where the elder Knight left off, winning a seat in the legislature two years after his father stepped down. He served two terms, then retired and passed the next thirty years practicing law. In 1926 he was elected circuit court judge. In 1931 Governor Miller appointed him to fill an unexpired seat on the Alabama Supreme Court; in 1932 he was elected to the same seat. In between appointment and election, he wrote the majority opinion in *Powell* v. *State,* the decision in which the Alabama Supreme Court upheld the Scottsboro convictions. Point by point he picked apart the appellants' argument that newspaper accounts of the rape had inflamed public opinion and contributed to the ill will toward them that made fair trials in Jackson County impossible. Despite the appellants' repeated references to *Moore* v. *Dempsey,* the case of the Arkansas sharecroppers whose murder convictions were overturned when the Supreme Court held that the court that tried them had been dominated by a mob, Knight ruled that "by no stretch of the imagination" was there the slightest resemblance between the two cases. Having taken half of his thirty-four-page opinion to uphold the trial judge's decision not to grant a change of venue, Knight went on to rebut or dismiss the appellants' arguments about the speed of the proceedings, the demonstration that followed the first guilty verdict, the reputations of Victoria Price and Ruby Bates, and the prejudice of the jurors.[3]

In January 1932, Attorney General Knight had argued the state's case before his father and the six other justices of the Alabama Supreme Court. In October, he argued before the U.S. Supreme Court. Neither father nor son could have been pleased in November when the high court, in a decision written by a conservative, Justice Sutherland, reversed the Alabama Supreme Court, stating frankly, by analogy, that execution of the defendants without a retrial would be "judicial murder." In only one aspect of the ruling could they take solace: both of them had shrugged off the appellants' argument about all-white juries. In his opinion affirming the original convictions, Justice Knight ruled that the argument was both out of place—the defense had raised no objection to the juries at the trials—and groundless: "The State of Alabama has the right, within constitutional limitations, to fix qualification for jurors." Much to the Alabamans' relief, the Supreme Court majority had refused to comment on the jury question in *Powell* v. *Alabama,* limiting its ruling to the question of counsel. And the minority had insisted, with the Knights, that the argument was utterly without merit. When, in early 1933, defense attorneys made clear that in the upcoming trials they would lay the ground for appeal by demonstrating that Negroes were excluded from Alabama's juries, Attorney General Knight decided to defend the jury system and lead the prosecution himself.[4]

Knight believed that the attack on the jury system was an attack on the sovereignty of Alabama. Countless white southerners agreed. Historian Frank Owsley called the Scottsboro defense the "third crusade, the sequel to Abolition and Reconstruction," and when he presented a paper with that title at the annual meeting of the American Historical Association in Urbana, Illinois, in 1933, the southerners in the audience "shed tears of joy" and even the westerners were impressed. (Easterners, Owsley complained, didn't come to western meetings.)[5]

In each of the first two crusades, Owsley argued, northern crusaders—not authentic crusaders but "sentimental dupes," "hired tools cloaking motives of material gain in robes of morality"—had attempted to ride the Trojan horse of Negro rights into the South in order to gain power for themselves at the expense of white and black people alike. In each instance, northeastern industrialists and their intellectual allies had used the Negro as a pawn to further their own political and economic ends. In each instance, the northerners' great mistake—interfering with the relationship between blacks and whites in the South—developed into war upon the South. In each instance, the North's pillaging of the South in the guise of a moral campaign resulted in the worsening of relations between whites and blacks. After abolitionism began, southerners were forced to defend and tighten an institution they had previously considered abolishing. After redemption, whites retaliated against black men and women for their conduct during Reconstruction.[6]

Now, sixty years later, "the buzzards were swarming again." Grover Hall, editor of the *Montgomery Advertiser,* used that popular metaphor to describe northern meddlers in July 1931 when a black man guarding a meeting of sharecroppers called to protest the Scottsboro convictions opened fire on two sheriffs. Just like some of those sharecroppers, Hall saw the Communists who had come south to help organize the union as the direct descendants of the northerners who had come south during Reconstruction. The "white buzzards that swarmed into the afflicted South in the wake of the heroic Union Army, after Appomattox, lit on the shoulders of the Negro freedmen and whispered tales of wealth and power into their trusting, gullible ears. While the Negroes listened the buzzards fingered their pockets, put dangerous notions into their heads, made countless new enemies for them to contend against and in the end caused many of them to be slain and many more to be flogged, and deprived of the full advantages which accrue to those who have the full confidence of their neighbors." That was an old story. Anyone who knew anything knew it.[7]

"The negro should have learned then," Owsley wrote, "that in the end the relationship good or bad between himself and the white race of the South must be settled between them and that no outside power could dictate permanently the terms of this relationship." But the Negro didn't learn, and the crusaders didn't give up, and now—discrediting the South in the eyes of the North by ridiculing the section as backward, ignorant, and unprogressive, by "creating as much friction between the races as possible," by screaming about unfair trials, all-white juries, and the nullification of the Fourteenth Amendment—they were at it again.[8]

If Scottsboro was the third crusade, the Communists were the third crusaders, and what white southerners thought and feared most about them was what they had in common with the first two. Although every southern discussion of communism included a few unfocused phrases about the confiscation of private property, the abolition of religion, and the inevitability of class war, at the heart of the white southern idea of communism were matters of race. When white southerners thought of communism they thought of two classes, but these were not the bourgeoisie and the proletariat, not the propertied and propertyless. White southerners thought of the black and the white. They imagined intermingling and intermarriage, integration and every form of equality.

Except for a handful of Communist Party theoreticians, no one took more seriously than white southerners the Party's proposal for a black republic in the Black Belt. As Frank Owsley explained after reading a pamphlet called *The Communist Position on the Negro Question,* the proposal had three parts: first, the Party proposed to confiscate and return to the Negroes the "land of the southern white," on which Negroes and their ancestors had slaved for centuries, for there was no other way to "insure economic and social equality." Second, the Party proposed to "break up present artificial state boundaries and to establish the state unity of the territory known as the Black Belt." Finally, the Party proposed to grant Negroes the "complete right of self-determination; the right to set up their own government in this territory and the right to separate, if they wish, from the United States." The Negro, Owsley summed up, "incited to attack the white man, is promised his property, is promised an independent state where he will either rule or destroy the white—is promised in effect the same things which the industrialists offered him as the price of his support during reconstruction."[9]

History provided justification for opposition to outside interference and communism. But history was not some long-dead and distant relative whom white southerners revived to repel northern invaders. History was alive, and lived nearby: "If one could just shut his eyes for a bit," wrote *Jackson County Sentinel* editor P. W. Campbell, "and have someone read to him the proceedings in the case and motions at Decatur or could walk into the court room blindfolded and listen, or could read some of the dispatches being published in the northern newspapers, he would think the years had dropped away and the Civil War had just ended and the dark days of reconstruction were in full bloom." Scottsboro, Campbell said, was nothing but "an old song—with new singers": "Seventy years ago the scalawags and carpetbaggers marched into the South with negro troops and said to the white people: 'The Negro is your equal and you will accept him as such.' Today, in 1933, the 'Reds of New York' march into the South with a lawbook written purposely to humiliate a white people because of sectional hatred, and again say, 'The Negro is your equal and you will accept him as such.' "[10]

Yet the memory of Reconstruction, and the hostility to outside interference, was not simply the memory and fear of blacks sitting on juries, or of blacks voting, or even of integration and social equality, a tipping of the scales of race relations so that blacks and whites were level. It was a fear of black mastery—of the world turned upside down, as white southerners thought it had been during Reconstruction. Among the images that Claude Bowers used to evoke that world was the image of armed, uniformed black men, in charge in 1865. "Nothing short of stupendous ignorance, or brutal malignity," he wrote, could explain "the arming and uniforming of former slaves and setting them as guardians over the white men and their families." Even northerners, "not prone to sympathize with the prostrate foe, were shocked and humiliated by the scenes they saw":

> In streets and highways they took no pride in the spectacle of thousands of blacks with muskets and shimmering bayonets swaggering in jeering fashion before their former masters and mistresses. These colored soldiers were not so culpable as the whites who used them to torture a fallen enemy. These were children, acting as children would under the circumstances. Marching four abreast in the streets, they jostled the whites from the pavements. In rough and sullen tones the sentries challenged old crippled and emaciated men in tattered gray. So insolent did their conduct become in some communities that women no longer dared venture from their doors, and citizens in the country no longer felt it safe to go to town.[11]

"The Negro is a great, big manchild," wrote a prominent Birmingham man in a letter about Scottsboro to the *Birmingham News*. "His conception of law is a policeman's club, and his idea of liberty is license; basically he is a human negation. His idea of civilization is limited by something he can get into his mouth. Sex is the dominating quality of his makeup and he can no more help it than can a monkey or an African Gorilla." The memory of Reconstruction was the memory of a time when those Negroes, suddenly cut loose from the bits and harnesses that for generations had restrained them, and "drunk with a sense of their power and importance," were viciously turned against their former masters and friends by the northern whites, who put the idea of ballots, land, and equality in their heads and encouraged them, in the words of Frank Owsley, to "pillage, murder and rape." It was the memory of a time when those Negroes were on top. A memory of a time when those Negroes could be put back in their place and kept there only by unrelenting, terrifying violence.[12]

The memory of Reconstruction was a reminder to most of the white southerners who filed into the yellow brick Decatur courthouse at the end of March 1933, a reminder to most of the white southerners who followed the case from afar, a reminder to Attorney General Knight, and to Alabama Supreme Court Justice Knight, just as it had been a reminder to Justice Knight's father at the Constitutional Convention thirty-two years before, a reminder that if they weren't careful, the past—that past—would be present again.

SEVENTEEN

The Good People of the Great South

In the middle of March, Samuel Leibowitz traveled by car to Chattanooga to meet with Joseph Brodsky, the ILD's chief counsel, and the Chattanoogan working with him, George Chamlee. Two weeks earlier, Chamlee had won a change of venue, not to Birmingham—the only place in Alabama, he had argued, where the defendants might get fair trials—but to Decatur, a town of eighteen thousand, fifty miles west of Scottsboro. It was the Morgan County seat, and Judge James E. Horton, Jr., would preside.[1]

Leibowitz knew that most white Alabamans would suspect he was a Communist. And he knew suspicion would turn to certainty the moment he confirmed reports, which had been circulating for weeks, that he would challenge the jury system. So the first thing he did when he arrived in Chattanooga was hand reporters copies of his first exchange of letters with ILD chief William Patterson. The first thing he said was that he was not "a red." He wanted everyone to know that he was not "in sympathy with the political activities of the communists or any other radical organization." He made it clear that he was not taking a cent from the Communists, not for legal fees, not for expenses.[2]

He wanted the people of the South to know that he was not there "to try to tell them how to administer their laws or run their affairs." He was interested solely in saving "innocent boys from the electric chair," and he would do his best to see that their lives were not "endangered by propaganda or agitation from any quarter." He was not putting Alabama justice on trial; he was defending his clients, laying the foundation for possible appeal. "I am a Democrat," he said, "a staunch supporter of Franklin Delano Roosevelt" who served "my country" to "the best of my ability in the World War." He came "simply as a lawyer to try a law case, fully mindful of the sincere desire of the good people of the great south to give every living thing on god's green earth a square deal." If guilty, he said, the men should die. But if the girls were making a false accusation, he was sure that there was not "a red-blooded upstanding American citizen below the Mason-Dixon line" who would not "pray with heart and soul for their acquittal." "I cannot subscribe to what in some quarters is the prevailing notion, that the Southerner will not give these Negro youths an absolutely fair chance for their lives."[3]

It was only a matter of days before his faith in red-blooded American citizens began to fade. The warden of Montgomery's Kilby Prison, citing a prison rule, refused to allow him to confer with his clients without a guard looking over his shoulder. Attorney General Knight said he would not waive the rule unless a court ordered him to, but when Leibowitz threatened to go to court with a writ of *habeas corpus,* Knight agreed to let him meet alone with the defendants in the Decatur jail, and had them moved there. Leibowitz found them all in one cell, the only cell in the crumbling building with a decent lock. The jail smelled of urine and dead animals and, besides the boys, was occupied only by roaches and rats; it had been condemned two years earlier and had not been used for white prisoners since.[4]

He expected prejudice. Friends had warned him. The record of the first trials and the appeals made clear to him not just the shoddiness of the original defense and the contradictions in the testimony, but the procedures and passions arrayed against the defendants. The sounds of racism and signs of segregation were everywhere on his car ride down. But neither friends nor record nor car ride down prepared him for the prejudice he found. He had expected to see it on the street, perhaps at gas stations and grocery stores, on the green outside the courthouse, and in coffee shops—wherever men and women spoke off the record, among themselves. He knew that two years earlier prejudice had found its way into the courtroom. He assumed it must have sneaked in. It never occurred to him it could have knocked, introduced itself, and then walked right in the front door.[5]

The defense opened the pretrial hearing on the afternoon of March 27 with the motion it had promised: Leibowitz asked Judge Horton to quash the indictments on the ground that Negroes had been excluded from the rolls from which the Jackson County grand jury, the body that handed down the indictments, had been drawn. That exclusion, he argued, was a clear violation of the Fourteenth Amendment. In support of the motion, Leibowitz called James Stockton Benson, editor of the *Scottsboro Progressive Age*. With a smile on his face, and without hesitation, the fifty-one-year-old Benson, a former schoolteacher, postmaster, state legislator, and president of the Alabama Press Association, said that for as long as he had been around he had never seen or heard of a Negro juror. As far as he knew, not one had ever served or been called.[6]

When Leibowitz asked Benson to explain the absence of Negroes on juries, Benson said that it was a matter of selection, not exclusion. There were some Negroes with "good reputations," but none had been trained for jury duty and none had sound judgment. Benson said he would say the same thing about women. When Leibowitz pushed him, asking if the judgment of Negro preachers, teachers, and deacons was any less sound than that of the illiterate whites on the jury rolls, Benson admitted that "some of them has got education enough . . . but, as a matter of a fact, I think they wouldn't have the character." Leibowitz asked him if by character he meant honesty. Benson said, "Yes Sir, they will nearly all steal."[7]

No one who knew Benson, and certainly no one who had read his editorials on the case, could possibly have mistaken him for a friend of the defense. Northern editors and pamphleteers regularly cited his editorials in order to demonstrate race prejudice in Alabama and the desperate plight of the defendants. Yet on the witness stand he was so quick to admit that he could not name a single instance in which a Negro had been put on a jury roll that Attorney General Knight suspected that he had been tampered with, and on cross-examination, treated him as a hostile witness.[8]

Leibowitz's second witness, J. E. Moody, the head of the jury commission, also denied that the absence of Negroes was a matter of exclusion. Leibowitz read him the names of prominent Negroes. Moody said they weren't qualified. Leibowitz asked him to give the court a general sense of the requirements for jury service, as set forth in the state's statute. Moody said he could recall only the requirement of character. Leibowitz took the opportunity to demonstrate that the president of the jury board was completely ignorant of the law he was supposed to administer. But when pushed, Moody, like Benson before him, protested that specific qualifications were largely immaterial, and that the defense counsel's suspicion that there was some kind of plot to exclude Negroes was mistaken. No one ever talked about either the qualifications or the race of prospective jurors. Negroes were not excluded for a particular reason. They were simply "never discussed."[9]

What most surprised Leibowitz about Benson and Moody—and the jury commissioner and commission clerk who followed them to the stand—was their candor. They were some of northern Alabama's leading citizens. Yet they revealed their worst sides to him without the slightest sense of embarrassment and without the slightest understanding of how they sounded to him or to others who might be unfamiliar with white southern ways. When Leibowitz accused them of prejudice, they denied it. When he accused them of excluding black men from juries, they at first seemed not to comprehend what he was accusing them of. It was as if, to these middle-aged men in the middle age of segregation, the exclusion of Negroes from juries, like the prejudice that generated it, was unconscious. Leibowitz had imagined the process as a highly self-conscious conspiracy. But these men took it for granted, did it without thinking. Where Leibowitz saw racism, they saw nothing at all.

After the last of his white witnesses stepped down, Leibowitz called John Sanford, a plasterer from Scottsboro. Sanford was followed by C. S. Finley, a former trustee of a Negro school; Finley by Mark Taylor, the operator of a cleaning and pressing business; Taylor by Travis Moseley, a Pullman porter. He called nine black men in all, and asked each of them how old they were, where they were born, where they lived, how long they had lived there, how much education they had, what they did for a living, whether they were U.S. citizens, owned property, were family men, belonged to a church, could read, whether they read newspapers and followed the affairs of state and nation. And he asked them if they had ever been called to serve on a Jackson County jury. He read them the names of other Jackson County Negroes, and asked them to identify the people they knew and discuss their qualifications: Were they generally reputed to be honest and intelligent men? Were they esteemed in the community for their integrity, good character, and sound judgment? Were they habitual drunkards? Or afflicted with any physical weakness? Could they read English? Had they ever been convicted of any offense involving moral turpitude? One after another, they boldly took the stand. Sanford began late Monday afternoon and continued first thing Tuesday morning. The other eight were on the stand through the early afternoon. Hour after hour, question after question, name after name: Yes, they were qualified. No, they had never been called, nor had anyone they knew.[10]

Knight examined each of Leibowitz's black witnesses at length, and from the first revealed that not even he, the attorney general, was immune to the prejudice that infected the state. Except perhaps for the way he pronounced the word *nigger,* northerners who encountered him only outside the courtroom never would have guessed. He invited reporters to his rooms in the Cornelian Arms (where prosecution, defense, and most of the white reporters stayed) to sit back and discuss the case over a glass of the finest Alabama moonshine. He dropped in on others, including the Leibowitzes. Everyone found him charming.[11]

Inside the courtroom, Knight was another man: high-strung, short-tempered, and belligerent. Alternately patronizing and abusive, he drilled and badgered, pointed and shouted at, at times even seemed to be threatening, the highly respected black witnesses Leibowitz had called to prove that there were black men qualified for jury service in Alabama. Beginning with John Sanford. Leibowitz leaped out of his chair and objected: "You are not going to bully this witness or any other witness." He asked Horton to ask Knight to stand back, lower his voice, and "stop sticking his finger" in Sanford's eyes. Knight's face turned two shades of red, one in surprise, one in fury. Knight's bearing toward Sanford came as naturally to him and his audience as breathing. Yet Leibowitz, who had seen his share of badgering, and was himself rather good at it, had not seen anything like it before. Certainly not in a courtroom, and certainly not by a state attorney general. After Knight composed himself, and asked the question again—"And you don't know what the word esteemed means John?"—Leibowitz told him to call the witness Mr. Sanford. Knight replied as calmly as he could that he was "not in the habit of doing that."[12]

Knight asked black witnesses to recite the statute that defined jury selection, even though the head of the Jackson County jury commission himself had been unable even to paraphrase it. He then asked them to define words and phrases that appeared in the statute—*esteemed, integrity,* and *moral turpitude*—words that they had used, in response to Leibowitz's questions, to characterize black men whom they knew. He asked a few if they were Communists; others about difficulties their children had had with white men or the law. He asked one witness if he had recently had some trouble with his wife. ("If everyone who has had trouble with his wife in any community was barred from jury service," Leibowitz objected, "there wouldn't be any juries.") Leibowitz continued to object, and the clashes between him and Knight—all that disturbed the constant chatter and even the slumber of spectators through hour after hour of the same answers to the same questions in the overheated courtroom—became more frequent and less civil. So frequent at times that the two lawyers began to address each other directly and Judge Horton had to remind them to address their objections to the bench.[13]

After a day and a half of testimony, Horton overruled the motion to quash the indictments. The defense had expected that he would, and asked for a day's recess, time to gather witnesses in support of an identical move against the Morgan County venire, from which the jury would be drawn as soon as pretrial motions were exhausted. Arguments on the second motion lasted another day and a half. Knight called Arthur J. Tidewell, one of the three Morgan County jury commissioners, and asked him to peruse the long list of Negroes the defense had compiled. Some, Tidewell said, had been considered for jury service, and none had been excluded because of his "race or color." Leibowitz surprised Tidewell and Knight by demanding the county's jury lists, and Horton surprised them even more by ordering the sheriff to bring the immense, red-leather-bound book into court. Leibowitz read names, asking Tidewell whether they were the names of whites or Negroes. He said he didn't know or he wasn't sure. He also said that he had never met a Negro fit for jury duty.[14]

All day Thursday and half of Friday another dozen black men, Morgan County's most prominent—doctors, educators, businessmen, civic leaders—most of whom had college degrees, some more than one, took the stand and introduced themselves to the judge, jury, spectators, press, and nation. They presented lists of names of people they knew and thought to be qualified for duty—and then paged through the jury rolls to see if any of the names were there. Leibowitz threatened to call hundreds of Negroes if that was what it would take to prove what the prosecution and jury commissioners refused to concede: that every person on the list was white. "I want to go back 20 or 30 years and show this court that there has been systematic exclusion of Negroes from the juries in Morgan County, and I am going to if it takes the rest of my life."[15]

Judge Horton had heard enough. He called a halt to the testimony, and denied the motion. But he ruled that the defense had made a *prima facie* case that Negroes had been excluded from the juries, providing defense attorneys with solid grounds for an appeal. Jury selection for the first trial, Haywood Patterson's, took another acrimonious afternoon. Leibowitz tried to cleanse the venire of "crackers." Knight went after the "liberals," young Decatur residents he feared might be sympathetic to the defense. Horton recessed for the weekend, asking jurors not to talk about the case. First thing Monday morning, April 3, 1933, after opening arguments, the prosecution called Victoria Price to the stand.[16]

E I G H T E E N

A Foul, Contemptible, Outrageous Lie

Knight's direct examination of Price was sixteen minutes long. She told an unadorned version of the story she had told four times in the Scottsboro courtroom, about the futile job-hunting trip to Chattanooga, the fight on the train ride home, and the gang rape. Haywood Patterson, she said, was one of the Negroes who had attacked her. What was different in Decatur was that when she was finished she had to face a cross-examination by a defense attorney who did not believe a word she had said.[1]

There was nothing particularly original about Leibowitz's cross-examination. He asked Price whether she had been raped before, whether she had been scared, whether she had screamed, scratched, bit, kicked, or clawed. He asked whether she had tried to lock her legs and whether she knew that her thighs were the strongest part of her body. He drew her out about the details of her story—the blood, semen, and bruises—that he expected the two doctors who had examined her shortly after the train ride to contradict. He moved from the alleged rape to her past, and from her past to her activities in the hours and days before the alleged crime. Certain that her character, as revealed in her criminal record, would cast doubt on her veracity that no amount of prejudice could overcome, Leibowitz tried to introduce police and court records to show that the twice-married woman was a convicted vagrant, bootlegger, adulterer, and fornicator.[2]

Attorney General Knight objected, angrily and often. He said he didn't care whether Price had been convicted of "forty offenses." The charge was rape, and she had never been convicted of "living in adultery with a negro." Leibowitz insisted that Price's criminal record had a direct bearing on her credibility. What's more, he said, his questions about Price's movements and activities in the days preceding the alleged rape were not intended to show "general acts of lewdness" as much as to show how she had ended up in the condition she was in when Dr. Bridges examined her. Horton would not allow Leibowitz to read into the record evidence that Price had recently been convicted of fornication and adultery. For those crimes, the Alabama Supreme Court had ruled, only state court convictions could be brought to bear on a witness's credibility. Price had been convicted in Huntsville's municipal court. But Horton said he would allow Leibowitz to "show commerce with any man within twenty-four hours of the crime."[3]

Leibowitz did more than challenge Price's story. He made it clear that he knew another one, and thus the motive for her lies. He suggested that two nights before the alleged assault she and Bates had spent the evening in a Huntsville hobo jungle with two men, Lester Carter and Jack Tiller, the latter a married man. Price denied it, insisting that she had never met Carter and that she and Bates had traveled alone. He suggested she had traveled to Chattanooga often. Price insisted she had never been there before. He suggested that she and Bates had spent the night immediately before the alleged assault with Carter and another man in another hobo jungle, this one in Chattanooga. She insisted that she had spent the night at the home of Mrs. Callie Brochie. Leibowitz suggested that there was no Callie Brochie in Chattanooga and that Price had, in fact, taken the name from a character in a short story in the *Saturday Evening Post*. Price insisted that she had been repeatedly raped on the train ride home. Leibowitz suggested that when the train was stopped and she saw the posse and the Negroes and thought that she would be arrested for vagrancy or for being a hobo on a train in the company of Negroes, to save herself she decided to say that they had raped her. Leibowitz handed Judge Horton a photograph of Ruby Bates with a Negro man, asked that it be entered into the record, and took his seat.[4]

Leibowitz wanted to convince the jury, as he himself was convinced, that Victoria Price was a tramp and a liar. But in that four-hour cross-examination, which took the entire afternoon, he discovered that Victoria Price was no ordinary tramp or liar. He had a dozen years' experience in New York City's criminal courts, much of it defending gangsters. Price was not the first hardened witness he had faced, and certainly not the most depraved. Nor was she the first witness who tried to stare him down and, failing that, who seemed as if she were about to leap out of her seat and strike him. She wasn't the first witness to be evasive, sarcastic, and crude. She was, however, the first witness to use her bad memory, truculence, total lack of refinement, and, at times, even ignorance, to great advantage.[5]

In order to point out inconsistencies between Price's story and virtually everyone else's, Leibowitz had asked the Lionel Corporation to build a model train exactly like the one on which Price said she had been raped. It was thirty-four feet long. When he tried to use it, she refused to admit that it looked anything like the one she had been on. "That's much smaller," she said at one point; at another: "That's just a toy." When he asked her how old she was, and then, skeptical of her answer, when she was born, she said, "I ain't got that educated that I can figure it out." When he asked her about a conviction for adultery, she said she didn't know what the word meant. She repeatedly accused Leibowitz of talking too fast and using words she didn't understand.[6]

Nor had he seen anyone turn his preparation, memory for detail, timing, and tone against him. Her testimony was full of holes, unlikelihoods, inconsistencies, and improbabilities, yet she herself was hard to shake. She repeatedly avoided the biggest traps he set for her by simply saying "No" or "I won't say," and more than once turned her failure of memory to her own advantage by saying that although she couldn't remember what he wanted her to remember—it had been two years, she reminded him, since the crime—she did remember one thing: "Those Negroes and this Haywood Patterson raped me." "You are a pretty good actress, aren't you?" Leibowitz asked, to which she replied: "You're a pretty good actor yourself."[7]

When he was through with Price, Leibowitz asked and received permission to question the conductor of the train. The witness testified that he had seen Price and Bates standing next to the fourth gondola, a car which had gondolas in front of it and in back of it, and that he had found Price's snuffbox in the same car, casting doubt on Price's repeated assertion that the Negroes had jumped from an adjacent boxcar. After the conductor stepped down, the state called Dr. Bridges, and he gave the same testimony he had given in Scottsboro. But on cross-examination, Bridges acknowledged that Price and Bates had been composed and calm; that he and his assistant had been able to find barely enough sperm to make a smear; that the semen they had found was nonmotile, though sperm usually lived from twelve hours to two days; and that neither Price nor Bates was bleeding. "In other words," Leibowitz asked, "the best you can say about the whole case is that both of these women showed they had sexual intercourse?" "Yes, Sir," Bridges said."[8]

Bridges was not the last of the state's witnesses Leibowitz turned to his advantage. On Tuesday, the second day of the trial, W. H. Hill, the ticket agent at Paint Rock, testified that he had seen the defendants and the girls on the same car; on cross-examination Leibowitz forced him to admit that he hadn't actually seen the girls until after they got off the train. Tom Rousseau testified he had seen all of the defendants on one car; on cross-examination he admitted that the black youths he had seen had been scattered across the front part of the train. Lee Adams said he had seen a fight on the train; on cross-examination he admitted that he had been a quarter-mile from the track and hadn't seen any girls. Ory Dobbins followed Adams, and Dobbins repeated the dramatic testimony that he had given at Scottsboro: he said he had seen Price and Bates about to jump from the train when the defendants grabbed them and pulled them back on. Leibowitz introduced photographs to demonstrate that from where Dobbins said he was standing he could not have seen the broad scene he described but only a narrow slice of the train, which at that point was passing at a good clip. Was he sure it was a woman he saw? Leibowitz asked. "I reckon so," Dobbins replied. "She was wearing women's clothes."[9]

"Women's clothes?" Judge Horton interrupted. Horton knew as well as Leibowitz, as well as anyone who knew the slightest bit about the case, that Price and Bates weren't wearing women's clothes. The fact that they had put overalls over their own clothes was something that nearly everyone who spoke and wrote about the case thought worthy of note. "Are you sure it wasn't overalls or a coat?" Horton asked. "No sir," Dobbins insisted, "a dress."[10]

The state rested its case Tuesday afternoon and Leibowitz called Dallas Ramsey, a Chattanoogan whose home bordered the hobo jungle that Price denied ever having been in. Ramsey testified that he had seen Price and Bates near his home the morning of the day of the alleged rape. He had also seen them get on a train with a white man.[11]

On Wednesday, the third day of the trial, Leibowitz called six of the accused. Willie Roberson testified that at the time of the alleged crime he was suffering from syphilis and had sores all over his genitals. He was in such severe pain that he could not walk without a cane, let alone jump from one car to another, take part in a fight, or rape Victoria Price. He had been in a car toward the back of the train. Olen Montgomery said he had been alone on a tank car the entire ride. He had neither been in nor known of the fight. Ozie Powell also denied having been in the fight. But he had seen it: he had been riding between a gondola and a boxcar. After several youths passed above him, he looked into the gondola and saw the fight. A few minutes later, he saw several white boys jump off the train. Roberson, Montgomery, and Powell all insisted that they had not known one another or the other defendants before they met in jail. Andy Wright, Eugene Williams, and Haywood Patterson had known one another. They admitted that they had fought with the white boys after the whites had tried to throw them off the train. But they denied even having seen Price and Bates before Paint Rock.[12]

When it came to cross-examining them, Knight had only one trick: he read from the transcripts of the trials at Scottsboro, and over Leibowitz's repeated objections, he asked petty, stupid questions about words they were alleged to have said on days they couldn't remember at trials the Supreme Court had declared unfair. Powell had a miserable time. Roberson, Williams, Montgomery, and Wright did better. They stuck to their stories. But each of them wished he could have been as sharp as Haywood Patterson, who, emboldened by the thought that he knew something that the attorney general of Alabama did not, frequently put Knight in his place.[13]

Knight asked Patterson if he had joked to fellow prisoners in Kilby about how the girls cried while he raped them (as a convict hoping to talk himself out of the chair had just testified). His answer was as full of unbelieving sarcasm as it was of disgust: "No sir, I haven't mocked no girl crying, how could I mock them—how could a man rape a girl with a man [Gilley] hanging on the side when we taken him and put him back and saved his life."[14]

Knight persisted, about the mocking, about the rape. Patterson said it again: "No sir, I didn't do such a thing as that; I pulled this white boy back up on the train and saved his life." When Knight finally got the point—namely, why would he, or the craziest black man alive, have pulled Gilley back up on the train if he were about to rape Victoria Price—he said: "Stop talking except when you are being talked to." Then he moved on to Patterson's testimony at Scottsboro:

"I will ask you if when you were in Scottsboro you were tried at Scottsboro."

"Yes sir, I was framed at Scottsboro."

"Framed at Scottsboro."

"Yes sir."

"Who told you to say you were framed?"

"I told myself to say it."[15]

Early Wednesday afternoon, Judge Horton suddenly stopped Patterson's trial and ordered the jury out of the courtroom. He had received word from a reliable source that a large crowd had gathered the night before and had discussed storming the jail, lynching the defendants, and then either lynching the defense attorneys or running them out of town. Horton announced that he had ordered sheriffs and National Guardsmen to defend the prisoners with their lives. Every man who defied them, he said, had better be prepared to take a lawman's life or forfeit his own. The contrast between the "vigorous tones" with which he spoke, almost shouted, those words and the quiet with which he had presided and ruled over even the fiercest clashes between Leibowitz and Knight made it impossible for anyone to mistake his resolve. Spectators understood—and the press reported—that Horton had ordered the guardsmen to "shoot to kill."[16]

Horton asked the court clerk to bring the jury back in and Leibowitz called the train's fireman, Percy Ricks, who testified that moments after the posse stopped the train in Paint Rock he had seen Price and Bates slinking along the side of the train, as if they were trying to run away. Leibowitz then called Dr. Edward Reisman, a Chattanooga gynecologist, who gave an elaborate presentation on female anatomy, complete with a diagram of a woman's body large enough for all the spectators to see. Whenever Leibowitz thought Reisman was speaking in terms only specialists could understand, he asked the doctor to put his explanations—of the functions of various parts of the body, of the size of the vagina, of the amount of sperm in the average ejaculation, of where exactly he would expect to find that sperm—in laymen's language. In response to Leibowitz's questions, Reisman said that it was hard for him to believe that six men raped a woman and left so slight a trace; that all the sperm would have died; that the woman's respiration, pulse, and pupil dilation would be normal—as Dr. Bridges had found them—so soon after a savage rape.[17]

Leibowitz saved his two most spectacular witnesses for last. Thursday morning, the fourth day of the trial, he called Lester Carter, the white youth whose name had come up repeatedly in Leibowitz's cross-examination of Price but whom Price had insisted she hadn't known before the day of the alleged crime. Carter raced through the story that Leibowitz had tortuously tried to extract from Price. He had met Price and Jack Tiller in the Huntsville jail. They were there for adultery, he for vagrancy. When they got out, Price introduced Carter to her friend, Ruby Bates. They hit it off, and the three of them decided they would travel together to Chattanooga to look for work; Tiller planned to join them later. The four of them spent the night before the trip making plans and making love in a Huntsville hobo jungle. In Chattanooga, Price, Carter, and Bates met up with a man named Orville Gilley. After a day of fruitless job hunting, the four of them spent the night by the railroad tracks in Chattanooga, and the next day they decided to return to Huntsville. There was a group of white boys in the next train car, and when Carter and Gilley heard that they were fighting with some Negroes, they climbed over. When they saw that they were greatly outnumbered, they decided to get off the train. Carter got off easily. Gilley fell between two cars and would have been hurt if two of the defendants hadn't pulled him back up onto the train.[18]

Knight cross-examined Carter, and Leibowitz rested his case, with reservations. In fact, he only pretended to rest his case, then approached the bench and, in a whisper, asked Judge Horton for a short recess, which Horton granted. Spectators stirred but stayed in their seats. Ten minutes later, National Guardsmen suddenly opened the back doors of the courtroom. In walked a Birmingham social worker, and a few steps behind her, Ruby Bates. Spectators gasped. Bates had been missing from her home for weeks, and rumors about her whereabouts abounded, along with charges and countercharges of foul play. More than once, when Bates's name came up in Leibowitz's questioning of witnesses, Knight had angrily asked Leibowitz where she was. Now she was in the courtroom, as a witness for the defense, and no one was more surprised or dismayed than Knight. Horton called the courtroom to order, and under Leibowitz's direct examination for fifteen minutes, Bates corroborated Carter's testimony completely, and went on to tell the court what happened after Carter left the train: the defendants did not rape, touch, or even speak to her and Victoria. She had claimed they had raped them, because she was excited. Victoria had told her to say it, told her they "might have to stay in jail" if they didn't "frame up a story for crossing the state line with men." Late Thursday afternoon, the defense rested for good.[19]

The day before, it seemed as if Horton had prevented a disaster. By Thursday evening it seemed as if the hostility against defense attorneys and witnesses spreading through Morgan County was out of his control. Inadvertently, the judge may even have contributed to it, for Communist Party officials took Wednesday's warning as a confirmation of their worst fear. Leibowitz had asked Party officials to soft-pedal mass action, and they had agreed—there had been no demonstrations, no leaflets, and no telegrams—as long as the lives of the defendants and ILD attorneys were not in danger. But now they clearly were, and the Party began sounding the alarm, most noticeably in a fusillade of telegrams to prosecuting attorneys, the governor, local editors and officials, and the judge.[20]

Reports of mobs got the Communists going. The testimony of Carter and Bates further encouraged those who might have joined a mob. After dark on the day they testified, there were reports of burning crosses. A mob was said to be gathering in Huntsville, Price's and Bates' hometown. One unit of National Guardsmen hid Bates while another, with riot guns, stood outside the Cornelian Arms. In the courtroom, Mary Heaton Vorse, covering the trial for *The New Republic,* had heard more than one person whisper, "It'll be a wonder if Leibowitz gets out alive." "They ain't advertising or makin' speeches," a man sitting next to her said, "but they'll know what to do when the time comes." Captain Joe Burleson, the commander of the National Guard, had heard similar talk and assigned five uniformed guards to Leibowitz's side. Moments after he learned of the cross-burnings and the mob in Huntsville, Burleson told reporters that he had 150 men ready to move.[21]

The following day the Morgan County solicitor, Wade Wright, whose courtroom style was that of a fire-and-brimstone preacher, took some of that fury, which up to that point had been expressed only in whispers, meetings in the hills, and unsigned letters to Leibowitz, and turned it into a rambling and raving closing argument. Referring to Ruby Bates's evasion under Knight's cross-examination, Wright said that she "couldn't understand all the things that happened in New York because part of it was in the Jew language." He mocked the way Lester Carter had waved his hands about as he testified; that was the Brodsky in him, Wright said. He said Carter now ought to be called "Mr. Carterinsky" and described him as "the prettiest Jew" he ever saw.

> That man Carter is a new kind of a man to me. Did you watch his hands? If he had been with Brodsky another two weeks he would have been down here with a pack on his back a-trying to sell you goods. Are you going to countenance that sort of thing? Don't you know these defense witnesses are bought and paid for? May the Lord have mercy on the soul of Ruby Bates. Now the question in this case is this: Is justice in the case going to be bought and sold in Alabama with Jew money from New York?[22]

Leibowitz pounded the defense table with his hand, leapt to his feet, and moved for a mistrial. Horton called the comments improper but denied the motion. Wright's speech prompted cross-burnings in Huntsville and Scottsboro and brought new death threats against Leibowitz and Brodsky. John Spivak, who covered the trial for the Associated Negro Press, surveyed Decatur's hardware stores and found them all sold out of guns and ammunition.[23]

Leibowitz began his closing argument by calling Wright's summation an appeal to prejudice, sectionalism, and bigotry. What was he saying but "Come on, boys, we can lick this Jew from New York. Stick it to him! We're among home folks." It was "the speech of a man taking unfair advantage, a hangman's speech." New York was full of decent people, just as Alabama was, Leibowitz said. He was proud of his state, would die for it just as he would die for his nation. The state's attorneys talked of Communists; they meant to "befuddle": "I'm a Roosevelt Democrat and I served my country when the Stars and Stripes were in jeopardy and when there was no talk of Jew or Gentile, white or black." They talked of "Jew money," but he wasn't getting a cent for his services, nor for his and his wife's expenses. "I'm interested solely in seeing that that poor, moronic colored boy over there and his co-defendants in the other cases get a square shake of the dice, because I believe, before

God, they are the victims of a dastardly frame-up. Mobs mean nothing to me. Let them take me out and hang me. My mission will have been served if I get these unfortunates the same justice that I would seek to achieve for any of you gentlemen if you came to New York and were unjustly accused."[24]

He pleaded for tolerance and reason, and most of his summation, which went from the end of Friday afternoon to the middle of Saturday morning, was a careful review of the testimony of the previous four days. The state's case depended on Victoria Price, he said, for the state's other witnesses cast as much doubt on her veracity as the witnesses called by the defense. But Price was an "abandoned," "brazen" woman, her story a "foul, contemptible, outrageous lie." He closed with a recitation of the Lord's Prayer and a plea for all or nothing, acquittal or the chair.[25]

Late Saturday morning, after Attorney General Knight's summation (which was fairer than Wright's, except when he referred to Haywood Patterson as "that thing" and told the jurors that if they acquitted him, New Yorkers would "dress him up in a high hat and morning coat, gray striped trousers and spats"), Horton charged the jury. He had the difficult task of persuading the jurors to put not just Wright's words but all the irrelevant issues out of their minds.

Horton told the jurors that throughout the trial he had acted as he believed to be right—no matter what the personal cost. He asked them to do the same. He mentioned that his forebears, like many of their own, had been among the earliest settlers, and that his father and grandfather had fought for the Confederacy. But, he said, "You are not trying lawyers, you are not trying state lines." He referred to the telegrams that messengers had been delivering in handfuls throughout the closing arguments as "baubles" and instructed the jury to ignore them. Instead, he said, you should "take the evidence, sift it out and find the truths and untruths and render your verdict. It will not be easy to keep your minds solely on the evidence. Much prejudice has crept into it. It has come not only from far away, but from right here at home as well."[26]

The only question before them, Horton told the jurors, was that of rape. He told them not to be swayed by the "natural sympathy" for a woman who says she has been attacked. He told them that they could consider that Price and Bates were "women of the underworld," "of easy virtue." In considering Bates, they could consider not only her lack of virtue, which she admitted, but also her recantation. Price was also "a woman of easy virtue," and there was evidence to show that she had given "false testimony about her movements and activities in Chattanooga." He told them that if in their minds a guilty verdict depended on the testimony of Price and they were convinced she had not sworn truly about any material point, they could not convict the defendant. And he told them that they were deciding whether Haywood Patterson forcibly ravished a woman, not whether he was black or white: "We are a white race and a Negro race here together—we are here to live together—our interests are together. The world . . . is showing intolerance and hate. It seems sometimes that love has almost deserted the human bosom. It seems sometimes that hate has taken its place." But, he concluded, only for a time. "The great things in life, God's great principles, matters of eternal right, alone live. Wrong dies and truth forever lasts and we should have faith in that."[27]

Horton gave the case to the jury just before one o'clock on Saturday, April 8. Ten and a half hours later, the foreman announced that the jurors were still deliberating. Horton ordered them locked up for the night.

NINETEEN

What Better Evidence Was Ever Put Up to a Jury?

Hundreds of locals watched Leibowitz grill jury commissioners about their juries, watched him question the veracity and integrity of the most respected men in their communities, some of them their neighbors and friends. They watched him fight with Knight, telling him where he ought to stand, how he ought to speak, what he should and shouldn't do with his hands. They watched him treat Negro witnesses with more respect than white witnesses, heard him address them as "Mr." and insist that the attorney general do the same. They watched him probe prospective jurors for prejudice. And if their own names had been plucked from the jury rolls, they themselves sat there in front of the courtroom and answered his questions. Jury commissioner Arthur Tidewell asked Leibowitz if he was calling him a liar. Prospective juror Fred Morgan complained to Horton, "Us jurors in Morgan County are not accustomed to taking the charge from the defendant's lawyer and we don't like it. I never heard the like of the way this man is questioning us."[1]

After a week of that, Knight called his first witness, Victoria Price, to the stand. Jurors sat dead still as she thrust her finger at Patterson and said that he was one of the ones who had raped her. Knight introduced as evidence a torn pair of panties. Price claimed she had been wearing them the day of the rape. After Knight had asked his last question, Leibowitz rose, walked toward the witness chair, which was up on a platform directly in front of the bench, and asked, "Shall I call you Miss Price or Mrs. Price?" Four hours later Price stepped down, and everyone who was there, and many who were not, agreed with Tom Davenport, who covered the trial for the *Decatur Daily* and the Associated Press, when he described that cross-examination as "merciless." James Benson, editor of the *Scottsboro Progressive Age*, called it "an attempt to rip to shreds the reputation and character of Mrs. Price by showing she consorted with Negroes." The editor of the *Huntsville Times,* who based his story on Davenport's (as did editors all over the South), wrote that Price did a "remarkable" job maintaining her composure in spite of the defense's efforts "to break down her testimony." The editor of the *Athens Courier* wrote that the "New York lawyer" representing the "brutes known as the Scottsboro nine" did everything "possible to shake her testimony but failed." The headline of the *Montgomery Advertiser* article read: "FOUR HOUR QUIZ FAILS TO SHAKE ATTACK VICTIM'S STORY"[2]

Few of the people inside the courtroom and not many more outside had any grand illusions about Victoria Price and her mysteriously absent friend Ruby Bates. Two years earlier, local newspapers had portrayed them as pure, young, and white, the flower of southern womanhood. The worst that was said about them at the time was that they were poor—poor, but virtuous and white. Soon after the trial, the virtue, like the flower before it, withered away. They became simply white women, with emphasis on the word *white*, or as the *Jackson County Sentinel* put it, "poor country girls and mill workers" who were likely to have been "knocked about some."[3]

It made little difference to the people of Morgan County that Price was not what she was first thought to be, not all she ought to be. They weren't either. The Louisville & Nashville Railroad had brought great prosperity to Decatur when it opened up fifty-five acres of repair shops in the late 1880s. Forty-one new industries followed the railroad; people talked of a Chicago of the South; the county seat was moved from Somerville. Cutbacks began in the 1920s; they accelerated sharply in 1931, and in 1933 the company closed the shops completely, bankrupting numerous local merchants who had become dependent on the railroad trade. A textile mill and a hosiery factory also went under in early 1933. In two years, two of the town's three largest businesses, along with seven of its eight banks, had gone bust.[4]

The unemployment rate was 13 percent and rising, and those with work were not necessarily much better off than those without it. The Decatur jurors—three farmers, two mill workers, two bookkeepers, a barber, a salesman, a bank cashier, a storekeeper, and a draftsman—knew many people who, like Price, had been knocked around a bit; people down on their luck or on the verge of falling. They were their brothers and sisters, their daughters and nieces, and the daughters of their friends. They didn't always treat them well, didn't necessarily have charitable thoughts or kind words for them when they passed on the street. But they deserved sympathy even when they didn't deserve respect.[5]

The jurors watched Price do her best, which at times was damn good, against the slick, smug, patronizing Jewish lawyer from New York. She stuck to her story, beating back his every effort to break her down. She complained repeatedly that Leibowitz talked too fast or that he used too many words she didn't understand. More than once she said she couldn't figure out an answer because she hadn't had as much education as he, knowing that only a handful of people in the courtroom had. She protested that he was trying to "blacken her character," knowing spectators and jurors would feel the same way. Her animosity toward him, as well as theirs, spread by spoken and printed word well beyond the courtroom. The editor of the *Sylacauga* (Alabama) *News* said he didn't think anyone "possessed of that old Southern chivalry" could read about the first day of the trial and publish an opinion without breaking the law. The "brutal manner in which the attorney employed by the International Labor Defense" cross-questioned Price made him feel like "reaching for his gun."[6]

The conductor of the freight train, R. S. Turner, followed Price to the stand. Turner called off the location of the various types of cars while Leibowitz put together his colorful toy train. Turner then testified that he had seen Price and Bates alongside the fourth gondola from the engine, and found Price's snuffbox in the same car. Price had said repeatedly the rapists had jumped them from an adjacent boxcar. The prosecution countered by recalling Price, introducing as evidence the knife she said was held at her throat during the attack, and asking her to tell the court what the defendants had said during the attack. She said that one of them "pulled out his private parts" and said, "When I put this in you and pull it out you will have a negro baby." Another made fun of her for hollering and said, "You haven't hollered none yet until I put this black thing in you and pull it out." Leibowitz interrupted, angrily asking if she wasn't embarrassed uttering those words, but Knight objected before she had a chance to reply.[7]

Dr. Bridges was next. According to the *Decatur Daily*'s Tom Davenport, who was sitting in the front of the courtroom, at the press table right behind the prosecution table on the right side, the Scottsboro doctor's testimony "contained so many medical terms the court reporter and press correspondents worked frantically to follow it." Davenport wrote three articles about the first day of the trial, six newspaper columns in all. But partly because he found Bridges' testimony difficult, partly because he knew most editors wouldn't print testimony about semen and vaginas, Davenport devoted only one short paragraph to it: "Dr. Bridges," he wrote, "testified as to the physical condition of the women and found evidence of intimacies." He also testified that "Mrs. Price had bruises on her back and that neither was hysterical at the time, but the following day appeared nervous."[8]

After Bridges, W. H. Hill, the Paint Rock depot agent, testified that he had seen the defendants scrambling out of a coal car, the same car that Price and Bates had been in. The girls were excited and crying. Tom Rousseau, a member of the posse, testified that "all of the negroes were climbing out of the car and running up to the engine." "Yes sir," he said when Leibowitz asked him if Haywood Patterson was among them. Lee Adams, a farmer, saw scuffling on the train and later saw two white boys wiping blood off their faces. Ory Dobbins, another farmer, testified that as the train passed he saw a woman trying to escape; the next thing he saw was a Negro grab her and throw her back down on the train. Arthur Woodall, a Stevenson merchant and deputy sheriff who helped search the defendants after they had been brought to Scottsboro, testified that he found a penknife on one of the defendants, the same penknife that on the previous day of the trial Price had said belonged to her.[9]

Three of them—Hill, Rousseau, and Adams—had a tough time with Leibowitz, and the fourth, Dobbins, who told the court the girls were wearing dresses, had a miserable time. But the stories they told on direct examination made a more vivid impression than the revisions they made in the course of Leibowitz's long and methodical cross-examinations. And the fifth of those prosecution witnesses, Arthur Woodall, got the better of Leibowitz, providing clearer corroboration of Price's story in response to one of his questions than he had in response to all of Knight's. Woodall said he had taken a knife from one of the defendants but couldn't remember which one. Leibowitz asked Woodall if he had asked the one he had taken it from whether it was his knife. Woodall said yes, he had: the boy had said "he took it off the white girl Victoria Price." Leibowitz choked on Woodall's words and the look on his face made Knight laugh and clap his hands and then dash out of the courtroom in an effort to conceal his glee. After Leibowitz moved for a mistrial, Knight apologized to judge and jury. Horton denied the motion, instructing jurors to ignore Knight's reaction.[10]

The state rested, and after a short recess the defense called Dallas Ramsey, a Negro who lived next to Chattanooga's railroad yards and hobo jungle. Jurors heard him say that he had seen Price and Bates get on the train with a white man. Then they heard George Chamlee, a defense attorney, testify that there was no one by the name of Callie Brochie in Chattanooga. First thing the next morning Leibowitz called Willie Roberson to the stand, and, after him, five of the others. Each of them denied that he had raped anyone. One of them, Ozie Powell, withered under Knight's cross-exam. Knight drilled him about the discrepancies between his testimony at Scottsboro in 1931 and his testimony a few minutes before, in response to Leibowitz's direct examination. Powell's answers were so contradictory that when Knight was through with him, Leibowitz felt that all he could do to minimize the damage was to call him back to the stand and ask the seventeen-year-old about his education. "Ozie, tell us about how much schooling you have had in your life?" "I ain't had ever about three months," Powell said. The other five fared much better, but three of them, including Haywood Patterson, admitted they had been in a fight with the whites and in that fight one of the whites had been pistol-whipped by a Negro who left the train before Paint Rock.[11]

Lester Carter testified Thursday morning, the fourth day of the trial. He told a long, detailed, sordid story, the essence of which was clear to all: Price made up the story about the rape. On cross-examination, Thomas Knight went to great lengths to convince the jurors that Carter's story was too fantastic to be true. There were too many accidents, unlikelihoods, absurdities, and missing pieces. Hoboing across the country, Carter had camped in a hobo jungle near Wynne, Arkansas. Also in that jungle was a minister, who heard Carter talking about the rape trials and told him that there were people in New York and in Alabama who would be interested in hearing what he knew about the case. Carter opted for New York, hoboed there, and naturally went right to the top. He found himself in Governor Roosevelt's office. The governor, of course—now President Roosevelt—wouldn't see him. So he left, bummed around a bit more, and ended up in the lap of defense attorney Joseph Brodsky. How he got there, he could not recall.[12]

Carter stuck doggedly to his story, but the attorney general undermined it by establishing Carter's indisputable ties to the defense and by suggesting—or, rather, arguing—what he himself believed: namely, that Carter had been bought by the ILD. Carter admitted that he had lived in New York in a room Brodsky paid for; that Brodsky had furnished his meals and bought the suit he was wearing; and that he didn't know who provided or drove the car that had carried him back to Alabama.[13]

When Bates appeared in court later the same day and recanted her original testimony, Knight minimized the impact of her recantation, perhaps even turned her surprise appearance to his advantage, in the same way. Knight knew the jurors would think, as he did, that Bates's story was as unlikely as Carter's. They knew she had disappeared a few weeks before the trials were scheduled to begin and that the prosecution had searched for her up and down Alabama and in parts of Tennessee. Where had she been? It turned out that she, too, had traveled to New York. She hadn't gone to the governor, but instead found her way to one of the city's most famous ministers, the Reverend Harry Emerson Fosdick, who, after hearing her story, bought her clothes, gave her money, and told her to go back down to Alabama and tell the truth. Which she had done. She had traveled by car, and though she didn't know whose car it was, who drove it, or with whom she stayed along the way, she just happened to show up a few minutes after the defense rested its case, with reservations. Knight also knew that jurors would agree with him in thinking that she was a woman of no virtue. What he wanted to prove to them was that worse than selling her body, or giving it away, Bates had sold her soul—and the South—to northerners and Communists, "lock, stock and barrel."[14]

At times cheered on by spectators, Knight jumped abruptly and erratically from the trials two years earlier to that very day. He asked her which gondola she had been on and then where she had gotten the coat she was wearing on the stand. He asked her who had given her the money to buy the coat, where she had gotten her hat, where she had gotten her shoes, how long she had had the pocketbook she held in her lap. He asked her whether she had seen Haywood Patterson on the train and whether she had seen the fight on the train. He asked her who was with her when she had bought the hat, when she had gone to New York. He asked her how she got to New York, where she got the money to travel from Huntsville to Montgomery, Montgomery to Chattanooga, Chattanooga to New York, and then from New York back down to Alabama.[15]

He asked her whom she had traveled with, if she knew Danny Dundee, if she had been drunk when she wrote the letter to her boyfriend in which she said she hadn't been raped. He asked her who had given her the money to stay in New York, whom she had worked for in New York, whether she had been in Montgomery the day there was a Communist meeting there. He asked her if she had seen Lester Carter in New York. He asked her how she had found out about Reverend Fosdick, whether she had met with Joseph Brodsky in New York, and whether she had met with Brodsky in Birmingham.[16]

He asked her whether or not she had syphilis. Leibowitz objected, and Horton sustained the objection. When Knight insisted that he was going to prove the connection between Roberson's disease and Bates's, Leibowitz moved for a mistrial. Horton overruled the motion, but at Leibowitz's urging told the jury to disregard the question and Knight's remarks. But Leibowitz could not make the words go away. At another point in his cross-examination, Knight asked Bates whether she had told a doctor who treated her for syphilis shortly after the first trials that she had gotten the disease from one of the rapists. She admitted that she had, and in the minds of most of those in the courtroom that admission turned Leibowitz's contention that Willie Roberson was syphilitic—so severely syphilitic in 1931 that he could not possibly have raped anyone—into evidence for the state.[17]

Whether Knight's questions concerned events two years or two days before, Bates hesitated and vacillated just the same. With her eyes to the floor, she contradicted herself repeatedly, evading questions as often as Price but much less adroitly. Sometimes she paused so long before answering that it seemed she was making up her answers on the spot. The attorney general was intimidating. But the biggest traps Bates stepped into she had set for herself, by testifying to one thing in Scottsboro and the opposite in Decatur, by writing a note to her boyfriend one day in January 1932 and signing an affidavit repudiating it the next, by telling Knight one story in a meeting with her in Birmingham in December 1932 (a meeting at which Price and two prosecuting attorneys were also present) and another story on the witness stand that very day.

It is not clear what could have been more damaging to Bates's credibility than the exchange that came with Knight's questions about the Birmingham meeting. "I will ask you," he said, "if I didn't tell you then and there I did not want to burn any person that wasn't guilty?" Horton overruled Leibowitz's objection. "Yes," Bates said. She thought that he had said that. "Did I not tell you the only thing I wanted was the truth?" Knight asked. Again Leibowitz objected. Again Horton overruled. Again Bates said, "Yes."

"At that time I also told you I would punish anybody who made you swear falsely, did I not?"

"Yes, sir."

"Didn't you then and there tell me substantially what you swore to at Scottsboro as to what happened on that train?"

"I didn't tell you. Victoria Price told you and I was sitting there."

"You say Victoria told me?"

"Yes, sir, Victoria told the whole story."

"Didn't I ask you questions about it?"

"If you did, I don't remember it."

"If I did you don't remember it, but it was told in your presence?"

"Yes, sir."[18]

Solicitor Bailey's summation came first. He spoke of "sinister influences" in New York and then about clothes. Unlike Bates, he said, Price didn't come to court in "New York clothes." "She didn't come here in a hat bought in New York. She didn't come here in a New York coat, but she told you she went to Chattanooga to look for work. We don't say that she is what she should have been. She has erred, but our laws say no man shall lay a hand on a woman against her will." Price could have "rouged her lips and cheeks and stood on the streets of Huntsville," Bailey said. But she didn't. She went out "to seek honest toil."[19]

Bailey was followed by Wade Wright, the Morgan County solicitor. Wright mocked Carter's manner and his dress, his voice and his wild gesticulations. He accused Bates of perjury, and asked the jurors if they were going to allow Alabama justice to be "bought and sold with Jew money from New York." Leibowitz followed

Wright. He told the jurors that unlike Wright he would appeal to them as "logical, intelligent human beings," determined to give even a "poor scrap of colored humanity a fair, square deal." To that end he reviewed the evidence, exhaustively, from Victoria Price—"on whose testimony alone," he said, "the state's case rested"—to Ruby Bates: "If Ruby Bates had been subjected to the sort of treatment described by the state she would be howling for this Negro's blood—not pleading [for] his life." Leibowitz closed with a prayer.[20]

The attorney general had the last say, and he began by trying to distance himself from Solicitor Wright, by whom he appeared to be genuinely embarrassed. "I do not want a verdict based on racial prejudice or a religious creed," he shouted. "I want a verdict based on the merits of this case. On that evidence, gentlemen, there can be but one verdict, and that verdict is death—death in the electric chair for raping Victoria Price." Bates, Knight said, had "sold out for a gray coat and a gray hat." He reminded the jurors that he had told Ruby Bates a few months earlier that he didn't want to "burn" an innocent Negro, "this negro, or any other." "I'm no murderer," he said in closing. "The very fact that the state did not prepare this case to the minutest detail," he said, was "proof that the State of Alabama has not framed that negro. . . . I don't have to have people come down here and tell me the right thing to do. I'd *nolle prosse* the indictments if I thought these negroes were innocent. This is no framed prosecution. It is a framed defense."[21]

Dozens of witnesses had testified. In reaching their verdict, the jurors appear to have decided, as Leibowitz suggested they might, that the state's case depended entirely on the testimony of just one, Victoria Price. The question was whom to believe: Price, or Carter and Bates. Leibowitz had saved Carter and Bates for the last day of his defense not simply because they were his most sensational witnesses but also because they were his whitest. All of the other witnesses who obviously and flatly contradicted Price were black: Percy Ricks, the train's fireman; Dallas Ramsey, the man from the hobo jungle; and the defendants themselves. But in a maze of complicated, conflicting testimony—about how far from the Paint Rock depot the defendants would have been able to see the posse; about who was with whom on what night or day in what hobo jungle; about who was in what type of car and where on a long freight train; about what Ory Dobbins could have seen from a field of vision of sixty feet during a two-second look at a freight train moving at twenty-five miles per hour; about motile and nonmotile spermatozoa; about how long after ejaculation sperm lives in a woman's vagina and how much sperm ought to have been found—one thing was perfectly clear: Ruby Bates was a liar. Either she had lied in Scottsboro or she was lying now.

As she testified, spectators laughed. Afterwards many southerners advised Knight to charge her with perjury. Knight didn't see why he should bother. "At the present time," he wrote, "she is making me such a damn good witness I prefer to leave her on the ground." Bates was a liar, and Carter was suspect too, tainted by his apparent eagerness to testify, his high-pitched voice, the speed at which he spoke, the strange way he threw around his arms and hands as he talked, and the northern way he said the word *Negro*. Bates too, to the ears of many northern Alabamans, talked like a New Yorker. And both of them came to court dressed like New Yorkers. Bailey, Wright, and Knight each referred to Carter's fancy suit and Bates's gray coat and matching hat and contrasted them with Price's inexpensive, plain black attire. They need not have bothered. The contrast was at least as obvious to the Morgan County jurors as it was to them.[22]

Moments after they retired, the jurors took their first ballot and voted unanimously to convict. Eleven hours later, eleven of them finally persuaded the foreman, a draftsman named Eugene Bailey, who was holding out for life imprisonment, to send Haywood Patterson to the chair. *New York Times* reporter Raymond Daniell interviewed the jurors after Horton excused them. One of them told him they had not even discussed Bates's testimony.[23]

It was as if the defense had rested Wednesday afternoon, after Knight cross-examined the last of the accused. After court adjourned that day, James Benson returned to his office at the *Scottsboro Progressive Age* to write an editorial for the next day's paper and put the paper to bed. He weeded his mail of telegrams and angry letters, some of them attacking him personally for the testimony he had given about the jury system the week before. Then, still puzzling over the criticism, he sat down at his desk.

No one in Jackson County, he wrote, had done more "in a humble way to promote harmony between the races." Whenever Negroes asked for it, he gave them space in his paper. He visited their schools and churches and helped them raise money for various causes.

So, Benson continued, "we cannot for our lives understand the attitude of many supposedly good people of our great nation who so vilely abuse Scottsboro and Jackson County for our efforts to protect our womanhood." No one who had heard or read in the newspapers the testimony of the state's witnesses could condemn them. "The attacked girl states positively that these negroes assaulted her and her companion. Farmers along the road said they saw a fight between negroes and whites as the train passed along. The doctors positively say there were evidences of assault. The white boys were thrown from the train and their lives jeopardized. What better evidence was ever put up to a jury?"[24]

T W E N T Y

That Godforsaken Place and the People Who Live There

Leibowitz was stunned. On the testimony of Dr. Bridges alone, a prosecution witness, he thought he should have won the case. With Carter's testimony and Bates's recantation on top of it, he didn't see how he could have lost. He knew he had been hurt by the testimony of the Stevenson storekeeper who claimed that he had taken Price's knife from one of the boys. He knew Knight had succeeded in making Ozie Powell look bad, and Ruby Bates look worse. He knew the prosecution's appeals to race, section, and religion had been effective. Nevertheless, most of his witnesses, and many of the state's, had helped him reduce Price's story to dust. But the jurors saw rock and found Patterson guilty. Leibowitz approached the bench and said to Horton, "I am taking back to New York with me a picture of one of the finest jurists I have ever met. But I am sorry I cannot say as much for a jury which has decided this case against the weight of the evidence."[1]

A few hours later, he told reporters he couldn't understand "how any twelve sane men could convict even a dog upon the uncorroborated word of a woman many times convicted herself" when "every decent piece of testimony proved conclusively she had framed" the defendants. The verdict was nothing but "the act of bigots spitting on the tomb of Abraham Lincoln." Back in New York a *New York Herald Tribune* reporter asked him to explain the outcome of the trial. "If you ever saw those creatures," he replied, "those bigots whose mouths are slits in their faces, whose eyes popped out at you like frogs, whose chins dripped tobacco juice, bewhiskered and filthy, you would not ask how they could do it."[2]

Two weeks earlier, in remarks to reporters in Chattanooga that revealed his rosy view of the South as well as his tact, Leibowitz had described the same men as red-blooded Americans. He had changed his mind about the Communists too. Before the trial, he had charged that they were getting in his way. After the trial, he told reporters that if it had not been for the ILD, "those nine Negro boys would be in their coffins now, buried back of the county jail." And the case itself, which before he had thought was just a simple frame-up, was now something more: "The issue is no longer confined to this case. It has become a question of the bigoted whites of the south against the 14,000,000 Negroes of the nation." "The last trial we fought on technical grounds, legal grounds," he said. That's how he had wanted it. He had told ILD people he wouldn't work for them if they insisted on taking the trial to the streets. He now planned to drag "every sociological, religious and political issue" right out into the open: "We'll hold those bigots right up to the mirror of public opinion."[3]

Many white northerners were as shocked and dismayed as he. Unlike the first trials, which few paid attention to until after they were over, this one had been followed as it happened. Unlike reports critical of the original verdicts, broadcast most often and most vociferously in African-American and Communist Party newspapers, the reliability of which was not taken for granted by most people, the reports of the Decatur trial were written by widely respected journalists—Tom Cassidy of the *Daily News,* Raymond Daniell of the *New York Times,* and staff writers for the United Press and the Associated Press—all of whom had been right in the courtroom. And when northerners read articles based on Alabaman Tom Davenport's AP reports, they read not what Davenport wrote but what northern editors, who usually rewrote his reports or, at the very least, put headlines on them, made of what he wrote; there was no mistaking one for the other. In two weeks, all the northerners who had heard about the case but had a hard time believing that things were as bad as they looked to the Communists and other radicals, got the headlines—"CREDIBILITY OF STATE'S MAIN WITNESS AGAINST NEGROES ATTACKED BY DEFENSE"; "THREATS ARE REPORTED"; "JUDGE TELLS GUARDSMEN TO SHOOT TO KILL"; "LEIBOWITZ PRO-

TECTED"; "MEDICAL WITNESS IS SKEPTICAL OF TESTIMONY GIVEN BY ALLEGED VICTIM"; "RUBY BATES MAKES DRAMATIC REAPPEARANCE AT ALABAMA TRIAL TO DENY ASSAULT"; "NEW YORK ATTACKED"; "JURY OUT"; "JUDGE WARNS OF BIGOTRY"; "PLEA MADE TO ROOSEVELT"; "ACLU FEARS MOB VIOLENCE"; "NEGRO FOUND GUILTY"—and the stories beneath them from editors and reporters they trusted.[4]

The verdict, wrote the editors of the *Herald Tribune,* would be received "with a profound sense of shock by justice-loving Americans." "The result," wrote the editors of the *New York Times,* "comes as a surprise and shock to those who had followed the evidence given in court." "National opinion everywhere," the *Tribune* predicted, "will accept this outcome as proof of the impossibility of securing a really just verdict in Alabama." And to the extent that by "national" the *Tribune*'s editors mostly meant northern, they were right: the hue and cry was deafening. People who had cried out about the trial before cried louder. Many people got involved for the first time. In churches, schools, colleges, on street corners, in parks and other open spaces in cities all over the North there were rallies, meetings, marches, and demonstrations. Out of those gatherings scores of new protest organizations were born. Newspapers all over the country covered the melee that ensued when part of the throng that met Leibowitz's train in New York tried to march back to Harlem without a permit for a parade.[5]

Some editors, confusing the word *Negro* with the word *red,* called the melee a "red riot," but it was not only blacks and Communists who protested the verdict. Leibowitz's role in the Decatur trial apparently made protest safe for regular old Democrats: John O'Brien, the mayor of New York, and John McCooey, the Kings County Democratic leader, joined Leibowitz in addressing a huge protest meeting in Brooklyn. The Presbytery of New York, in a compromise that followed a heated debate about whether the group should make a public statement, and if so, what the statement should be, praised Judge Horton and condemned the verdict. The Association of New York Congregational Churches and the Federal Council of Churches also condemned the verdict and urged other church groups and congregations to express their views. Within twenty-four hours, twenty-five thousand people had sent telegrams to the governor of Alabama. Northerners argued vehemently about the reasons for the verdict, the fairness of the trial judge, the tactics of the defense. Many thought that the defense—by injecting, however inadvertently, so many extraneous issues into the trial, and thereby inflaming prejudices against Communists, northerners, blacks, and Jews—shared some of the blame. But even those who expressed the harshest criticism of the defense and the greatest sensitivity to the right of southerners to govern their own affairs thought, as Leibowitz did, that the verdict was outrageous.[6]

The trial was a front-page story in Alabama, in black newspapers nationwide, and in Communist Party newspapers. It was a prominent national news story in mainstream metropolitan papers. After reading the United Press and Associated Press reports about Ruby Bates's reversal, dozens of editors moved the story to their front pages. Still, it was just one story in late March and early April 1933, the end of the worst winter of the Depression. American industry, agriculture, and finance were in general crisis. FDR had been inaugurated on March 4 and had closed the banks on March 6, three weeks before the trial began. Reports about the economy and Roosevelt's first days dominated domestic news. Dominating international news were dispatches from Europe, especially Germany, about the rise of Hitler and the first wave of repression against German Jews.

Throughout March there had been reports from Germany of legal and extralegal "outrages": the destruction of property, the disruption of Jewish businesses, raids on Jewish organizations, the intimidation of Jewish teachers, mass arrests, beatings, and murders. There was talk of mass emigration, and a growing outcry from Jews in the United States and all over the world. There were mass meetings of Jews and Jewish sympathizers in the United States and Western Europe, and calls for boycotts of German goods and other forms of economic reprisals. Germany denied the reports and harshly criticized outside interference in its sovereign affairs. In retaliation for the boycotts and anti-German propaganda, the Nazis ordered an official boycott (there was already an unofficial one) for April 1 of Jewish businesses, professions, and schools until all foreign protest ceased. Jewish merchants were forbidden to close or lay off employees. Storm troopers blocked entrances to shops. Police photographed people going in. Violence against Jews, though officially frowned upon, increased.[7]

That boycott was the culmination of a month of atrocities. News stories about it and the violence that attended it came on the same pages as reports of nine abused black teenagers, mobs, cross-burnings, and near lynchings. Stories of southern racism and anti-Semitism appeared alongside reports of Nazi racism and anti-

Semitism, and for many northerners one story became an aid to understanding the other. People who knew more about Germany, as many recent immigrants and first-generation northerners did, used what they knew to make sense of the news from Alabama. For those who knew more about Alabama, the stream of understanding ran the other way. Newspaper editors, columnists, and readers debated the relation between the two, and though some denied that anything fruitful could be made of the connection, most found in it a powerful mixture of metaphors, in which Scottsboro was Hitlerism come to America, and Hitlerism was racism and anti-Semitism in Germany.

The week of Haywood Patterson's trial, the *New York Evening Post* ran a special series on Germany. The writer argued that Americans could best imagine the effect of Hitlerism by imagining a Klan takeover of the United States; it meant "vast changes in the habits and outlook of the German people." A Hamburg professor on tour in the United States made precisely the same point. At rallies called to protest the atrocities in Germany, speakers repeatedly juxtaposed the two events, optimistically predicting that the world would crush Nazism just as Americans had crushed the Klan.[8]

When, just one week after its special series on Hitler, the editors of the *New York Evening Post* suggested that Leibowitz, in his comments about the jurors, was just as bad if not worse than the white Alabamans he criticized, a reader asked if they would say that "the Jews were worse than Hitler if they protested and in protesting used some pardonably hard words." The world needed more "intolerance of intolerance," he wrote. "This is not the time to pamper bigots," whether they were in "Germany, Alabama, or anywhere else." Numerous others argued that whether or not Alabama "faithfully represented" America, the verdict made it hard for Americans to be self-righteous in their criticism of Germany. "How can we hope through our influence to help those unfortunates in Germany who are being hounded and destroyed," wrote the editors of the *New York Mirror,* "when right here in America such a prejudiced miscarriage of justice is permitted as in this Scottsboro case?"[9]

Black Americans made the connection often and angrily. Samuel Leibowitz himself made the connection, characterizing all but a few "fair-minded" Alabamans as the "baying pack," the "wolves of bigotry who raised the Hitler cry of 'Jew money from New York' because we dared demand a square deal for men whose skin was black." He was responding not just to his first experience of racism, the way white southerners treated black southerners, but also to fear, to the way white southerners had treated him.[10]

Leibowitz was one of those northerners for whom Alabama was a foreign land. The clothes people wore, the language they spoke, the food they ate, and the way they carried themselves were all unfamiliar. And it wasn't just language, habits (spitting snuff), and manners. The people themselves looked strange. Unprovoked, unfamiliarity breeds apprehension, and apprehension often makes the unfamiliar appear menacing. Leibowitz's apprehension was provoked. First by threatening letters. Then angry muttering in the courtroom that spilled out to the streets. His wife, Belle, afraid someone would try to poison him, began cooking all his meals. Leibowitz was no longer simply a defender of the victims of prejudice. He was the object of prejudice. "The hatred of New York and other metropolitan centers of commerce and modern enlightenment," he said, was even more vicious than the "hatred manifested by this outrageous verdict against the Negro." Halfway through the trial it seemed as if it were not just Haywood Patterson but also Leibowitz and Brodsky whose lives were on the line.[11]

Prejudice against him, coupled with fear, bred prejudice in him. The South was transformed from God's green earth to a godforsaken place. White southerners were transformed en masse from chivalrous citizens into creatures: "lantern-jawed morons"; "bigots whose mouths are slits in their faces, whose eyes pop out at you like frogs"; cowards who, while burning crosses at night, wore masks so that "decent people" could not see the "sordidness and venom in their hideous countenances." Prejudice against him also bred new sympathies. Leibowitz returned to New York with a new understanding of what it was like to be a black man, at least a black man in a southern court. And a new respect for the Communists, who understood what the Scottsboro defendants were up against, and who were willing to fight for their freedom until "hell froze over."[12]

Three thousand people gathered at Pennsylvania Station the day after the verdict and carried Leibowitz out to the street on their shoulders. Three nights later, nearly four thousand people gathered at Harlem's Salem Methodist Episcopal Church to hear him say that he would sell his home and fight with every drop of blood in his body if that's what it would take to free the Scottsboro Boys. Friday he spoke at two large rallies: twenty-five hundred people gathered at the Methodist Episcopal Church of St. Marks, and ten thousand in Union Square, where Haywood Patterson's mother, Janie, was among those who addressed the crowd. This was not the first time in his career that Leibowitz had been at the center of controversy, but it was the first time that he was on the popular side. He was hailed by most liberals, and a great many moderates and radicals as well. On Sunday, seven days after the verdict, a wildly enthusiastic crowd of seven thousand greeted Leibowitz at Brooklyn's Arcadia Hall.[13]

The next day, April 17, Judge Horton convened his court to sentence Patterson to death and begin Charlie Weems's trial. He sentenced Patterson, setting his execution day for June 16, and immediately suspended the sentence on a motion for a retrial made by Joseph Brodsky. Then, instead of calling the new venire, Horton postponed the rest of the trials indefinitely—until he had determined that a fair and impartial trial was possible. The comments about the jurors attributed to Leibowitz had inflamed public opinion and prejudiced the case against his own clients, Horton said. Whether Leibowitz actually said what he was purported to have said did not matter; the effect would be the same and Leibowitz would be a "millstone" about his clients' necks.[14]

Leibowitz didn't disavow the statements; he simply tried to clarify them and put them in context: he wasn't sure if he had been quoted word for word; he had been speaking of the spectators more than the jurors. Nonetheless, he and his associates had heard laughter coming from the jury room toward the end of the deliberations. When the jurors filed into the courtroom to deliver their verdict, they had smiles on their faces. Good omens, Leibowitz had thought. The foreman announced the verdict and, Leibowitz said, "the sight of twelve human beings sending an innocent creature to his death in such a spirit of joviality was more than anyone with a spark of human decency in his makeup could bear without emitting a spontaneous outcry of chagrin and revolt."[15]

What's more, Leibowitz argued in a long letter to Horton, his comments could not have created "one-thousandth of the prejudice" against Patterson that had existed before the trial began and that had been "intensified immeasurably" by the challenge to the jury system, the attorney general's treatment of witnesses, and the Morgan County solicitor's anti-Semitic diatribe. Leibowitz reminded Horton that the defense had moved for a continuance immediately after the verdict, on the grounds that passions were too high for a fair trial. It was only after his own comments, Leibowitz said, that

Horton decided that for the time being it would be impossible for a jury to reach a "just and impartial verdict."[16]

Throughout the spring and summer of 1933, Leibowitz continued to speak out at meetings and rallies. He shared platforms with Socialists, Communists, regular old Democrats, mothers of the defendants, Ruby Bates, Lester Carter, and executives of the ILD, ACLU, and NAACP—with anyone who wanted to see the defendants free. He spoke passionately for the freedom of the defendants and against the anti-Semitism and racism he had experienced in Alabama. "We have fought the good fight," he said. "We have kept the faith and will carry on. The nine innocent Scottsboro Boys will not die so long as decent men and women survive and there exists in Washington the Supreme Court of our land." Leibowitz said he would carry the case up to the highest court and then back down to Alabama "ad infinitum." "It'll be a merry-go-round, and if some Ku Kluxer doesn't put a bullet through my head I'll go right along until they let the passengers off."[17]

T W E N T Y – O N E

Sometimes We Laughed about It

After Haywood Patterson's trial, he and the other defendants were taken to the Jefferson County Prison, in Birmingham. The seven who had spent the past two years in Kilby Prison—Patterson, Weems, Norris, Roberson, Montgomery, Powell, and Andy Wright—hoped that they would remain in Birmingham for as long as they remained in jail. The few days they had spent there on their way from Kilby to Decatur for Patterson's trial, and the many evenings they had spent there during the trial, when guardsmen ordered them returned for safekeeping, were as bearable as any of the days they had spent in jail. They had been allowed out into the prison yard for air and exercise. Each morning they had been moved from the small cells they slept in to a spacious day room. Their visitors had been allowed to walk right up to their bars.

By the time Horton postponed the remaining trials, it seemed like another place. Guards took every opportunity to rub the guilty verdict in their faces. The warden, unhappy about all the visitors, decided to move them to a special day cell at the back of the prison, instead of their regular day cell at the front, every Thursday, which was Negro visiting day. The defendants now suspected that during the trial, with all the lawyers and reporters coming and going, the warden had ordered guards to put on a good show.

The defendants decided not to take the restrictions. One Thursday at the end of April, they fashioned weapons out of plumbing and lighting fixtures and refused to go back to their regular cells at the end of the day, daring the guards to come get them. The guards ordered several trusties to disarm them, but fearing for their lives, the trusties refused. The next day the defendants surrendered their weapons and returned to their cells, but only after negotiating a compromise: they would pay for damages; they would not be punished; and they would get exercise, visitors, and their "rights."[1]

They awoke each morning knowing that violence was as likely to be a part of the day as walls and bars. They fought with guards. They fought with other inmates. They fought with one another. In April, guards had to separate Patterson and Powell. In May, they broke up a fight between Patterson and the Wrights. Patterson suffered a small stab wound. Guards reported that Roy and Andy said they attacked Haywood because he was overbearing and arrogant. The Wrights told Atlanta attorney Benjamin Davis, Jr., a regular visitor, that the fight grew out of mutual kidding, a friendly rivalry, dating back to Chattanooga days. The kidding became extremely personal and ended in the knife fight. They had been bored and irritable. Afterwards, they all regretted they had let their tempers get the best of them.[2]

Southern newspapers reported when they "rioted" or fought among themselves. Northern newspapers reported when violence against them was exceptional. Most of the violence was routine. The lash—which meant fourteen to twenty-one blows to the back with a three-inch-wide leather strap while three guards held them pinned facedown on the floor and a prison doctor and the warden looked on—was sanctioned by Alabama law and defended by the governor as well as wardens and guards. Much more frequent were the beatings by guards that doctors and wardens did not see and which were not recorded in the prison log.[3]

Yet even hell had its regions, better and worse, and once the defendants learned their way around the jail and demonstrated, by fighting back, that they would not be stepped on, they quickly found that their first impressions were right: any sane prisoner would prefer Birmingham to Kilby. The joint was run by guards and trusties whose goodwill was often for sale. Prisoners could get what they wanted in Birmingham: clothes (they didn't have to wear prison uniforms), liquor, food, even guns and knives. Cooperative guards shopped for the prisoners, as did the trusties who had jobs outside the jail. Clarence Norris paid the kitchen trusty three dollars a week to bring him his favorite food: "ham and eggs, steaks, chicken, fish, desserts." All cooked, Norris said, "just the way I liked it."[4]

The jail housed women as well as men, black men and women in one part of the jail, white men and women in another. The Scottsboro defendants had girlfriends, and the guards carried letters and gifts from cell to cell. Clarence Norris paid one guard to buy him an iron so his girlfriend, Ernestine, could press his clothes. He paid another three dollars a night to make arrangements with the guard on Ernestine's block to allow her to spend the night in his cell. When things went smoothly, Birmingham was as bearable for prisoners with money as an Alabama prison could be.[5]

"The feeling was very high about our case between my second and third trials," Patterson remembered. "Hundreds of dollars came in to us. I ate the same food as the warden and the jailers, just the same. The chef, he would cook our food specially. We paid for it, never had to eat the prison food. Sometimes we laughed about it, the ups and downs. Outside we were hoboes; inside the prison we had some respect. By our being in jail we were getting the food there that our families never was able to buy us. It was a twist of the case we were in. We took advantage because we didn't know when we'd go back to the death row."[6]

"Life is funny," Clarence Norris said, "we would laugh about it. We had the death sentence hanging over our heads, but we were eating and dressing better than a lot of men on the outside, including our guards. Good people all over the world were making our lives a lot easier. The letters and money was still coming in from everywhere. The money made it possible for us to eat and dress better than we ever had in our lives. But I would much rather have been on the outside looking in."[7]

T W E N T Y - T W O

The Tragic Error

In 1913, John Roy Lynch, a former slave, speaker of the Mississippi House of Representatives, and Reconstruction congressman, published *The Facts of Reconstruction*. Four years later, in the second and third volumes of the *Journal of Negro History,* Lynch published two piercing critiques of the errors and biases in James Ford Rhodes's *History of the United States from the Compromise of 1850 to the Final Restoration of Home Rule at the South*. In defense of the reconstructed state governments, the bane of every white historian of Reconstruction, Lynch wrote:

> I do not hesitate to assert that the Southern Reconstructed Governments were the best governments those States ever had before or have ever had since, statements and allegations made by Mr. Rhodes and some other historical writers to the contrary notwithstanding. It is not claimed that they were perfect, but they were superior in every way to those which are representative of what Mr. Rhodes is pleased to term the restoration of home rule. They were the first and only governments in that section that were based upon the consent of the governed.[1]

George Myers, a black barber and politician in Cleveland, Ohio, cut Rhodes's hair when Rhodes was a Cleveland businessman, and the two corresponded for thirty years after Rhodes moved to Boston in 1891 to devote the rest of his life to writing history. Despite Myers's relative conservatism and his close friendship with Rhodes, he took Lynch's side in his heated debate with Rhodes about Reconstruction.

"There are always two sides," Myers wrote to Rhodes, "and no two people ever see each side alike." Myers thought Rhodes made the mistake of "not seeing and talking with the prominent Negro participants," whom he could have put him "in touch with." Because he didn't, his history of "the restoration of home rule" was written purely from the perspectives of the winners, who, "flushed with victory," "painted the other fellow and his methods a little blacker than either was." Myers admitted that if he himself had written a critique of Rhodes's work, he would have been "less verbose and less virile and not confounded the happenings of today with those of yesterday."[2]

Or perhaps he would not have: "Of course in this day of intense color prejudice, race discrimination and persecution, particularly in the South, it is hard for any colored man to discuss a public question without interjecting this question. You cannot fully appreciate this because you have never been discriminated against. I do not perhaps feel it so much as some by reason of a wide and beneficial acquaintance, but it has been brought home to me on many occasions."[3]

A decade and a half later, in 1931, the seventy-three-year-old Lynch reviewed Claude Bowers' history of Reconstruction, *The Tragic Era*. He found "a composition of errors, misstatements, misrepresentations, and false assertions," and thought the title of the book should have been "The Tragic Error." Carter G. Woodson, editor of the *Journal of Negro History,* also reviewed the book: "Of this book the thinking element will take little notice, because it is downright propaganda in the interest of the defeated opponents of Congressional Reconstruction." Woodson overestimated the discrimination of the thinking element, but he was prescient about the overall influence of the book: "With the efficient advertising machinery now behind this book, it will probably have a large circulation among the gullible of our population. The teaching of history, too, will be rendered more difficult by the sinister influence of such a work written for notoriety and published to exploit the uninformed. Only a few citizens have given sufficient attention to history to distinguish between truth and error." Woodson called

Bowers insincere and ignorant, and granted him only "knowledge of human weakness," enough of it "to know that in the present state of race hate any book exposing merely the faults of a statesman who favored the elevation of a Negro to a higher status will now prove immensely popular."[4]

W.E.B. Du Bois had put his own ideas about Reconstruction into two iconoclastic essays, "Of the Dawn of Freedom" (1903) and "Reconstruction and Its Benefits" (1910). In 1935 he would publish his monumental history, *Black Reconstruction in America.* In that book's last chapter, a devastating critique of the historical literature, he wrote: "Three-fourths of the testimony against the Negro in Reconstruction is on the unsupported evidence of men who hated and despised Negroes and regarded it as loyalty to blood, patriotism to country, and filial tribute to the fathers to lie, steal or kill in order to discredit these black folks." "One fact and one alone," he wrote, "explains the attitude of most recent writers towards Reconstruction: they cannot conceive Negroes as men; in their minds the word 'Negro' connotes 'inferiority' and 'stupidity' lightened only by unreasoning gayety and humor."[5]

Black and white historians agreed on one point: Reconstruction was a great tragedy. In the minds of Du Bois and others, however, the tragedy was not that their parents and grandparents were empowered, but that they did not gain enough power to ensure that when northerners lost their will no one would be able to take it away. The tragedy was not that the vengeful, victorious North went too far, but that it didn't go far enough in aiding them in their struggle for political and economic democracy and equality.

That was Reconstruction in the minds of countless black Americans, from the highly educated black men and women Du Bois called the "talented tenth" to black men and women without a day of formal education, like Alabama sharecropper Ned Cobb, like Cobb's Grandmother Cealy, like Alabama steelworker Hosea Hudson, like the eighty-eight-year-old former slave who, speaking to a WPA interviewer in the 1930s, summed up one of Lynch's and Du Bois's central themes in a line: "I know folks think the books tell the truth, but they shore don't."[6]

And that was Reconstruction in the minds of some of the seventeen thousand Harlem residents who, in the first four hours after the news of the Decatur verdict reached New York, signed the petition calling for a march on Washington that William H. Davis, publisher of the *Amsterdam News,* had pinned to the bulletin board on the wall outside his office. Five thousand more were reported to be waiting in line to sign. It was Palm Sunday and people were out in the streets. Theodore Bassett, a Communist Party organizer, said afterwards that he had never seen such "anger or indignation before or since." "Some people were ready to march to Alabama that night. If there were ever a revolutionary situation, I imagine that's what it would be like." Communists, Socialists, Garveyites, Democrats, Republicans, and preachers spoke from the same platforms. Within twenty-four hours, forty thousand had signed Davis's petition.[7]

Black Americans were angry and indignant, but they were not surprised. They had expected the verdict, and they believed they understood it. It was an old story, and they retold it to convince white Americans of what they already knew. The trial would show "the whole world that despite the Fourteenth Amendment the black man has no rights in the South," wrote the editor of the *Philadelphia Ledger.* It would expose the "brutal, savage, calloused depravity of southern conscience," wrote the *Black Dispatch*'s Roscoe Dunjee. "It proves that the mob rules the courts in Dixie, and that in such courts of injustice the color of a human being's skin determines his guilt or innocence."[8]

Some black northerners, including the national officers of the NAACP, agreed with the many white northerners who thought that the Communists were partly to blame for Haywood Patterson's fate. But when Walter White expressed that belief a few days after the trial, the backlash in the black press and on the streets was so great—"On every corner up here now we are catching hell," NAACP ally I. F. Coles wrote from Harlem—that White reversed himself almost immediately. By week's end White had offered to contribute to and raise money for the defense.[9]

The period of relative peace between the NAACP and the ILD that followed the ILD's acceptance of that offer was short-lived. The first fight was about the march on Washington: moderates wanted a delegation of representative citizens; the Communists and their closest allies insisted upon a mass march. Yet White had once again been reminded that many black people—some humble, others very well placed—thought that the Party deserved not scorn but praise. Debates about communism raged anew on the editorial pages of black newspapers, in schools, churches, lodges, and on the streets. There were numerous points of view, and no one knew how many believed one thing or another. But one thing was clear to Party people and NAACP people alike: in the wake of the Decatur trial, the ILD's black sympathizers were more confident of their stance than ever, and their critics were on the run.[10]

"WE SAY NO," cried the editor of the *Baltimore Afro-American* when the editors of big-city dailies called for the withdrawal or removal of the ILD. The *Amsterdam News*'s William Davis thought the NAACP should "deem it a privilege" to cooperate with the defense no matter who sponsored it. The editor of the *New York Age* told Walter White to "snap out of it": the ILD was "conducting a fight for the lives of these innocent lads in a most praiseworthy manner" and it was "up to every Negro and pro-Negro organization" to support them. A Birmingham man wrote to the NAACP: "I am under serious consideration and knowledge if International Labor Defense dont fight to save the lives of the Scottsboro Boys they would have been dead." The writer said he often saw "the name of I.L.D. in the newspapers about fighting for the Negroes. I never see the name of N.A.A.C.P. in the paper since that time I consider I.L.D. lead the world in fighting saving the lives of the Scottsboro Boys."[11]

T W E N T Y - T H R E E

The Pathology of Women

The editor of the *Huntsville Times* said the Decatur verdict was just as expected, meaning not only that it was predictable but also that it was right. Most white southerners agreed. But most white southerners were not *all* white southerners. A significant number of white southerners believed that the jury had made a tremendous mistake. Virginius Dabney, editor of the *Richmond Times-Dispatch,* found it "inconceivable that the jury could have brought in a verdict of guilty." Jonathan Daniels, editor of the *Raleigh News and Observer,* called the verdict "shocking" and "outrageous." The editor of the *Richmond News Leader,* saying that it was a question not merely of "reasonable doubt" but of "unreasonable conviction," concluded that Haywood Patterson had been sentenced to death "primarily" because he was "black."[1]

Not all of the white southerners who concluded that the verdict was unjust had turned to the trial with the same sense of the case or the same expectations. Some, like the editor of the *Richmond News Leader,* had been "suspicious" of the first verdicts and found their suspicions confirmed. Some, like Virginius Dabney, had hoped the second trials would clear up the confusion—about what happened on the freight train—generated by the first. And some had expected the second trial to confirm their sense that the defendants were guilty as charged. Judge Horton, for example, had studied the transcripts from the first trials, and saw much that cried out for correction. But he still went to Patterson's second trial thinking that the defendants had done it and thus that the Scottsboro juries, even if for the wrong reasons, had got the verdicts right.[2]

The white southerners who criticized the Decatur verdict, like the interracial leaders and antilynching activists who two years earlier had expressed doubts about the Scottsboro trials, were mostly middle-class and upper-middle-class men and women from cities and towns. Few of them were wealthy, but none of them were mill workers or miners, sharecroppers or tenant farmers, clerks or unskilled laborers, uneducated or poor. Their position in southern society was important to them, and to their understanding of Scottsboro. What bothered them most about northern opinion and criticism was not that it came from northerners, which was what bothered most white southerners. It was that the critics, ignorant of the class structure of the South, did not distinguish among southerners, but assumed that southerners were monolithic in their attitudes and behavior toward blacks.

"If there were only two classes in the South—white and black," wrote Ben Cothran, a Tennessee-born journalist whose United Press reports of the Decatur trials appeared in the *Birmingham Post*, "perhaps things wouldn't be so difficult." But there were three: "black, white, and poor white." And, wrote Alabama journalist and journalism professor Clarence Cason, "no one could pretend to understand the South unless he assumes the existence of enormous differences between the heritage and temper of the 'poor whites' and the 'quality.' " "Feeling toward the Negro," Cason explained to the readers of the *North American Review*, "is remarkable for its diversity. In fact nothing more immediately establishes the outlook and background of a southern white man than his attitude toward the Negro."[3]

"The Southerner of plantation descent," Cason said, "carried with him a definite sympathy for the Negro." That sympathy was part of his "mental heritage" and it left relations between the better people and the Negroes "warm and personal." The better people might not help the "Negro attain his more radical social aims," but they would protect him from "actual cruelty and flagrant injustice." It was the poor whites—the sharecroppers and mill workers, "descendants of the independent farmers who had been driven to the hills and poor lands by slavery"—who mistreated the Negro. "They are used just as the Negro is," Cothran said, "but still they are told they are superior to him and must assert this superiority, when the only way they know how to do it is to knock the black man down."[4]

They were poor and used but full of pride, and, since the 1890s, under the regalia of the Populists, the Anti-Saloon Leaguers, and the Klan, and under the leadership of the "fiercely belligerent" Bilbos, Bleases, Heflins, Vardamans, and Longs—all of whom manipulated "emotional prejudices against Negroes with telling effects at the polls"—the once underprivileged majority had "tasted political power from Texas to the Carolinas." "In the final analysis," Cason concluded, " 'white supremacy' really means 'poor-white supremacy,' for this term accurately represents the people most concerned in that valorous movement, and the end which they have sought to achieve."[5]

To support their claims, Cason and Cothran and like-minded southerners pointed to the work of contemporary social scientists, including Arthur Raper, a sociologist who worked for the Commission of Interracial Cooperation. In 1930, working with Morehouse College professor Walter Chivers, Raper investigated twenty-one lynchings. In 1931 he published an influential pamphlet, *Lynchings and What They Mean*; in 1933, a five-hundred-page book, *The Tragedy of Lynching*. Raper's analysis was always trenchant. Yet the parts of the pamphlet and book that moved most effortlessly from writer to readers—and from readers to press releases, newspaper articles, editorials, book reviews, and lectures—were a few simple conclusions, easy to cite and explain: fewer than one in six victims of lynching was accused of rape; blacks were safest from the mob in the old Black Belt counties; blacks were in the most danger in the poorest, remotest, most sparsely populated areas, where tenancy was high and literacy low.[6]

In the minds of a great many of the southerners who came to see the Scottsboro and Decatur verdicts as unjust, the injustice in the courtroom, like the injustice of lynching, was the consequence first and foremost of the poor white southerner's problem with the Negro. When in 1931 Will Alexander was asked about the Communist Party's charge that the verdicts were caused by class prejudice, he responded by saying that "the Scottsboro case had nothing of class struggle in it. It originally grew out of contacts between low-class whites and low-class Negroes, who happened to be bumming their way on a freight train." Ben Cothran reminded his readers that the "Scottsboro juries were typical of the poorer, rural sections—right out of the class most in conflict with the Negro, knowing least about him but hating him hardest." "Remember," Cothran wrote,

> these jurors would have been in a mob; they have been in an economic battle with the Negro for generations. Their living is wrested from a savage Nature, so they in turn are savage to competitors in living. Their minds are flabby from disuse and lack of proper mental food; they have never been taught to grasp or understand anything outside their immediate daily routine; so why expect them to understand involved medical testimony? Eliminate that, and you have only the word of the Negro against the white.[7]

Alexander spoke of the young black and white hoboes on the freight train. Cothran spoke of the white men who sat in the jury box in Scottsboro and Decatur. But to get from the fight between lower-class whites and blacks on the train to the juries of lower-class whites sentencing the blacks to death, there had to be a charge of rape. The way the white southerners who were critical of the verdicts understood the events on the freight train and the events in the courtroom had much to do with the way they thought about lower-class whites. But it was of no small consequence that two of those lower-class whites were women, for many people's attitudes toward poor white southerners were reinforced by their attitudes toward women. At the very bottom of the social hierarchy, and at the very top rung of the ladder of causation, were two poor white women who had cried rape.

Not everyone thought it necessary to distinguish Price and Bates's sex from their class. When the black Presbyterian minister and civil rights advocate Francis Grimké wrote that the Decatur verdict showed that southern whites hated blacks, James E. Clarke, chairman of the CIC in Tennessee, responded by saying that not all whites hated blacks. "Of course there is such an attitude on the part of some. It was appealed to by the women who sought to escape some punishment or disgrace themselves by putting the blame upon Negroes—a very common method for a low grade of white people, male or female." In many more minds, the sex of the two lower-class people who charged rape had everything in the world to do with the case. If the white southerners who were skeptical of the verdicts tended to blame poor whites for racial injustice, they tended to blame women when that injustice began with an accusation of rape. The charge of rape, Ben Cothran wrote, "nearly always comes from a white woman, and it isn't uncommon for the charge to be a false one. There is no explanation for this, without exploring obscure psychological factors. It just sometimes happens."[8]

Cothran didn't go into the psychological factors, but many others, laypeople and self-proclaimed experts, did. It was four years before social psychologist John Dollard applied Helene Deutsch's ideas about the rape fantasies of white women to his classic study of caste and class in Indianola, Mississippi. It was eight years before Wilbur Cash, at the beginning of what was otherwise a very shrewd discussion of the "southern rape complex," took aim at the "neurotic old maids and wives, and hysterical girls." And it was a decade before Deutsch's ideas themselves became well known.[9]

Nonetheless, the air that carried the Scottsboro debate was thick with popular psychology, popular speculation about the origins of the false cry of rape. "It is difficult to understand," wrote the *Raleigh* (North Carolina) *Times,* "how two women—even such as Ruby Bates and Mrs. Price—could have gone the length of attempting to perjure away the lives of a number of innocent men. But the phenomenon is a common experience in the pathology of women—sometimes good as well as bad." The case, the editors concluded, should serve "to give solemn warning to the South, all too apt to execute judicially, as well as by lynch law, when some psychopathic woman has a day dream and sticks to it on the witness stand."[10]

J. F. Hayden, of High Point, North Carolina, who identified himself as "an intensive student of sex," a "reader of several hundred of the late scientific books on the subject," and the author of *The Art of Marriage*, told Alabama's Governor Miller that studies agreed on two things. First, he said, "nine out of ten charges of rape are false and are due to a peculiar psychological condition of the woman." Second, it is "practically impossible for a man to rape a woman if she uses all her resources of resistance; the only exception being where she is beaten into an unconscious condition." Innumerable critics of the verdicts said the same thing: women fantasized about being raped. Hysterical women made up stories about being raped to fulfill masochistic yearnings. Women asked to be raped, or otherwise egged their rapists on. All of which was another way of saying what the author of *The Art of Marriage* implied when he said that a woman who resists cannot be raped: defined as an act of intercourse against a woman's will, rape did not exist at all.[11]

In the confusion of Scottsboro, some southern men and a few southern women, struggling to make sense of the case and figure out how to persuade others to see it the way they did, anticipated Helene Deutsch's most famous ideas about female psychology and rape. Those ideas were not new, neither in the way white southerners used them in popular debate nor in the way Deutsch used them in professional psychology. What was new was that some white southerners were pushed to apply them to the problem of interracial sex. Few if any southerners were pushed so far as to suggest, as Deutsch concluded, that white southern women had a special attraction to black men, that white men knew it, and, thus, that white men were reacting to their sense of that attraction when they overreacted to charges of rape. But a significant number of white southerners, women and men, acknowledged something they would not have acknowledged before: not all sex between white women and black men was rape.

The most careful southern observers of southern society—the Georgia writer Lillian Smith was one—would have been as wary of Deutsch's interpretation of southern sexual psychology as Arthur Raper and other careful observers of lynching were wary of the class interpretation of race relations. They knew that charges of rape came from a wide variety of places. They came from white women trying to hide interracial transgressions. They came from white men trying to hide their own crimes. They came from white men playing deadly trump cards in personal, business, or political conflicts with black men. Sometimes they came from white women who had been raped. And then there were times when the charge of rape was generated by fantasies and fabrications. What Lillian Smith and others knew, and what Deutsch failed to notice, was that the charge was at least as likely to be born in the fantasies and fabrications of white men as in the fantasies of white women.[12]

Likewise, Raper knew that the lessons that many southerners (and not a few northerners) drew from a superficial reading or review of his book were misleading. Lynchings may have been more prevalent in poorer areas, but in those areas the people who participated in and condoned lynchings came from the top as well as the bottom of the social scale. Without the help or tacit approval of the best people—lawyers, judges, journalists, sheriffs, teachers, and preachers—lynchers could not have succeeded at the rate they did. Lynchers usually had the help or tacit approval of the best. After Clarence Cason observed a series of brutal lynchings in his hometown in the summer of 1933, even he was forced to admit it.[13]

Like many Alabamans, Cason blamed the Tuscaloosa lynchings on the infuriating presence of the ILD. He was still convinced that the "best people" supported justice. But he was also convinced that lynching would be around until the best people were "unrelenting in their demands for a civilized attitude" and "willing to take personal and commercial risks in making these demands known." The tendency to blame the mistreatment of the Negro on "hill billies, red necks, and white trash," he now argued, was snobbery in its most perfidious form. The idea that a special bond existed between Bourbons and Negroes was largely sentimental.[14]

Cason quoted court officials as saying that the lynchers, who were not even indicted, would have been apprehended in a day if public opinion had been "unflinchingly and aggressively on the side of the law." But it wasn't, because for a people deeply divided by social class, lynchings were a powerful expression of racial solidarity. The same was true for legal lynchings. Many racial liberals and even some moderates came to see that Scottsboro could not be explained simply as a consequence of the poverty and prejudices of poor white men any more than it could be explained simply as a consequence of the dispositions of two poor white women asking to be raped or imagining that they were. But in the minds of most of them, those two attitudes combined to make a powerful, and almost irresistible, explanation, an explanation that was at once a cause and a product of the way that many white southern critics of the trials made sense of the case. Preexisting prejudices against lower-class whites and women made it likely that when the South's "best people" searched for Scottsboro villains, they would look beneath themselves before they looked anywhere else. At the same time, their perceptions of the crowds outside the courthouses, the spectators, Leibowitz's defense, Price and Bates, the juries, and the verdicts themselves reinforced those prejudices and the ideas in which they were expressed.[15]

The southerners whose minds were changed by the Decatur verdict did not talk exclusively about Price and Bates. They talked about sectional bitterness, race prejudice, and the psychology of southern juries. They talked about the smoke screen of rape hysteria, sectional prejudice, and anti-Semitism thrown up by the prosecution. They talked about the inevitability of an appeal. They talked about the reputation of the South. They talked about what they could do to help the defendants while the defense was in the hands of Communists, and many concluded, as the CIC's Will Alexander did, that there was nothing they could do without associating themselves with the Communists and their "very reprehensible methods." They talked about what they could do to force the Communists out of the case. Or, in the tactful words of Jonathan Daniels, one of the few white editors below the Mason-Dixon line to credit the ILD and Leibowitz with saving the lives of the boys and awakening the nation and the South to the "danger of injustice in Alabama," they talked about what they could do to bring about the "withdrawal" of northern counsel and their replacement by the "most eminent southern attorneys willing to fight for the acquittal of the Negroes with the same vigor."[16]

What so frustrated southern liberals about the interference of the Communists was that it "played into the hands" of the demagogues, the hands of the Heflins and Longs. It did that, first, by erasing the distinction between past and present, rendering irrelevant a slight but crucial difference between the historical memories of the minority of liberal white southerners and the historical memories of the white majority.[17]

For the liberals, the past was past. Reconstruction had been dreadful. George Fort Milton called it the "age of hate." Virginius Dabney called it a "nightmare" in which the "leading whites" were "deprived of the ballot in many states and the ignorant and illiterate Negroes" were "in control." But it was over, long over. Scottsboro was complicated by Communist interference, but it wasn't, as Frank Owsley would have it, "the third abolitionist crusade." And though for most white southerners Reconstruction was a reminder of the dangers of all change, for liberals it was a reminder of the dangers of only certain kinds of change: sudden change, violent change, change forced upon the region from outside. "History is one thing and 1933 another," wrote *Birmingham Age-Herald* columnist John Temple Graves II in an essay asking southerners to reconsider their "inherited" objection to Negro jurors. "The 'tragic era' is dead these 60 years now," Graves wrote, "and all of us who are honest with ourselves know that there are many Negroes today perfectly qualified in education and outlook for jury service."[18]

Outside interference blurred the lines between past and present, history and current events. With those lines went distinctions between change generated from within and change forced from without, between northern critics of the South and southern critics, between moderates, liberals, and radicals. Heightened racial and sectional conflict fostered among southern whites the mentality of a people under siege. It became a simple thing for the demagogues to convince people that there was only one kind of change: change for the worse; and two kinds of people: the South's friends and the South's enemies, upholders and violators of southern honor. As Birmingham's Episcopal Bishop William McDowell argued, by deliberately "prolonging the trials" and "inciting race prejudice and class hatred," the Communists were "undoing all of the interracial work of the last thirty years." They were also destroying any hope for the future, for when all criticism was effortlessly characterized as subversive, southern critics of the South lost their jobs.[19]

The southerners whose minds were changed by the Decatur verdict did not talk exclusively about Price and Bates. It was only in the upper South that they thought it prudent or productive to talk about them publicly at all. Persuaded that an injustice had been done and confident that they knew why, many moved on to other aspects of the controversy. But when it came to explaining what had gone wrong at Scottsboro and Decatur—when newspaper editors in the upper South tried to convince their readers that the verdicts were unjust, when Alabama interracial leaders tried behind the scenes to convince allies and powerful politicians of the same—they often raised one concern, one part of a large body of evidence, over a host of others, plucked one cause of the injustice from a messy knot of causes, and severed Price and Bates from the circumstances in which they made the charge and the context in which so many people believed them.

What went wrong in northern Alabama in 1931? Two wretched white women cried rape and nearly lied nine Negroes into the electric chair. Sure, they couldn't have done it if the jurors had not believed them. But once those poor white southerners heard two white women charge that black men had ravished them, they went out of their minds, lost what little self-control they had to begin with. Many liberal southerners knew what Helene Deutsch would soon conclude: "rape fantasies" often had "such irresistible verisimilitude that even the most experienced judges" were "misled in trials of innocent men accused of rape by hysterical women." If judges were misled, how could jurors be expected to separate right from wrong, justice from injustice, truth from lies?[20]

What went wrong in Scottsboro and Decatur? The state's case, wrote the editor of the *Greensboro Daily News* a few days after the

Decatur trial, "depended on two alleged victims, neither with any character, of lax morals, attired in men's clothing, bumming freight trains with a group of male hoboes when the attack occurred, if it occurred at all. Bates repudiated her original testimony. Horton said both had perjured themselves. So we ask: what constitutes reasonable doubt in the eyes of an Alabama jury?" The *Charlotte Observer* noted Bates's recantation and then went on to point out that neither of the women was representative of "southern womanhood." The "characters which they bore," the editor said, invited "forcible approach by their Negro companions on the train." Jonathan Daniels, editor of the *Raleigh News and Observer,* was one of many southern liberals to argue that in light of Judge Horton's charge alone the verdict was "shocking."[21]

But even before the verdict, even before Horton's charge, Daniels had known where to place the blame. In an editorial the day after Bates recanted, he wrote about Bates and Price: "A woman sat on the witness chair in an Alabama courtroom on Thursday and declared that she had testified to a whole narrative of falsehood which resulted in the sentencing of seven Negroes to the electric chair." Daniels thought "a terrible crime" had been committed in Alabama, but "unless the pattern of lying in the Scottsboro case" was even more complex than it appeared, Bates's recantation made it clear that the crime was "done not by the Negroes but by those who posed as their victims." "With the confession of Ruby Bates," he concluded, "the honor of the white South is far more on trial in Alabama than it was when it was being defended against seven Negro hoboes. Today the honor of the South must be defended from the attacks of whites who would, with cold-blooded ruthlessness, have lied seven Negroes to death."[22]

TWENTY-FOUR

History, Sacred and Profane

On June 22, 1933, two months after he had sentenced Haywood Patterson to death and postponed the remaining trials, Judge James E. Horton convened court in his hometown of Athens, Alabama, to hear the defense's motions for a new trial. The defense had so little hope for success that Leibowitz remained in New York; it was simply the next step toward the Supreme Court. George Chamlee and Osmond Fraenkel, a mild-mannered New York attorney with years of experience in civil liberties litigation, prepared oral arguments, but they didn't get the chance to deliver them. Instead of listening, Horton spoke, reading a single-spaced, seventeen-page decision.[1]

The fifty-five-year-old judge was descended from southern pioneers, planters, soldiers, and politicians, and he took his ancestry seriously. He thought of his social responsibility in vertical rather than horizontal lines; it ran "up and down the genealogical tree rather than around the contemporary lot." His grandfather was a native of Virginia and one of the earliest settlers of Alabama's Madison County. He had built a large plantation and served in the state legislature. Horton's father, also a planter and small slaveholder, served in the Civil War under General Daniel S. Donelson. After the war he married the general's daughter Emily. Emily's mother was the daughter of John Branch, a governor of North Carolina and Secretary of the Navy under Andrew Jackson.[2]

Horton studied medicine at Vanderbilt for a year before transferring to Cumberland University, where he received his B.A. in 1897, and a Bachelor of Law in 1899. His father was a probate judge, and Horton clerked in his court for a few years before entering private practice. He ran for the state legislature in 1906 and lost, ran again four years later and won. He served one term, then in 1914 ran successfully for a seat in the State Senate, giving up that seat the following year when he was appointed to fill an unexpired term in the chancery court. In 1917, Alabama's chancery courts were consolidated into its circuit courts and Horton returned to his law office and his land. In 1922, he was elected judge of the Eighth Circuit Court. In 1933, Judge Horton was in the fifth year of his second six-year term.[3]

Horton was over six feet tall and lank as Abraham Lincoln, whom he resembled, except that Lincoln wore a beard and Horton occasionally wore horn-rimmed glasses. When it was announced that he would preside in Decatur, a local paper praised him as a man of "unusually equable nature, great legal ability and fairness." The editor of that paper, the *Limestone Democrat,* expressed confidence that the "foreign defense" would have no good reason to be dissatisfied with the trial. Months after the Decatur trial, Thomas Knight complained to a friend that his troubles with the judge began the moment the defense "told him that he looked like Abraham Lincoln." But before the trial, Knight had thought Horton would "make an excellent Judge."[4]

Knight had had every reason to be hopeful. Horton was a large landholder living in a small town in a rural corner of the state. His land lay along the Elk River, and he lived in Athens, a quiet town in which oak- and elm-lined streets led to the courthouse square. He was a planter, and though he insisted he was not politically ambitious—he always had to be begged or petitioned to run—he was a politician as well as a judge. In office, his concerns were Prohibition (he was a local-option man); election reform (he introduced a bill that would have authorized county courts to divide each county into districts and allowed local candidates to run for office by district as opposed to at-large, but it never made it out of committee); and roads. He was not, as one observer put it, "very notably social-minded," and he was "liberal only in the sense of putting the rules of the game above the desire to win."[5]

Yet from the first day of the trial, Horton had revealed in deeds and words that he shared the attitudes and concerns of moderate and liberal southerners, if not their backgrounds, temperament, or style. When two black journalists, Bernard Young of the *Norfolk Journal and Guide* and William Jones of the *Baltimore Afro-American,* approached the bench to thank him for the letters he had sent to help them get into the courtroom, he greeted them warmly and, "after a slight hesitation, offered his hand." Before jury selection he warned prospective jurors and spectators against prejudice and extralegal violence: "Under our law when it comes to the courts we know neither native nor alien, we know neither Jew nor Gentile, we know neither black nor white . . . but to each it is our duty to mete out even handed justice." It was also the duty of all citizens, Horton said, to abide by the decisions of the courts: "I trust that no one . . . will . . . show anything different from calmness, courtesy, and the proper regard for the law and the restraint of their passion." On the third day of the trial, the soft-spoken judge called those talking of lynching the defendants "cowardly murderers," and promised that he himself would stand with the sheriffs and soldiers responsible for protecting the prisoners' lives. "I am speaking with feeling," he said, "and I know it, because I am feeling it. I absolutely have no patience with mob spirit, and that spirit that would charge the guilt or innocence of any being without knowing of their guilt or innocence. Your very civilization depends upon the carrying out of your laws in an orderly manner."[6]

Horton went to the trial thinking that the defendants were probably guilty. Years later he implied that though Price's evasiveness on the stand the first day of the trial had shaken his faith in the first verdicts it was the words of the two Scottsboro doctors, Dr. Bridges and his assistant, Dr. Lynch, that upset it. Bridges testified for the state on the afternoon of the first day and the morning of the second. Lynch had been scheduled to follow him, but as he was about to take the stand the prosecution asked Horton to excuse him, arguing that his testimony would only be a repetition of Bridges'. Horton excused him, but Lynch then approached Horton and asked if they could talk privately, which they did, in the men's room, with the bailiff guarding the door. Lynch told Horton that he had never believed that the girls had been raped. In Scottsboro he had accused them of lying, and they had laughed at him.[7]

Horton urged him to testify. Lynch said that he wanted to, but that he couldn't. If he testified for the defense he would not be able to return to Scottsboro. He was four years out of medical school, and he had just begun to build a practice. Horton didn't end the trial. He did not want to expose and ruin a young man at the beginning of a promising career, especially one he thought honest and courageous for doing what he had just done. Nor did he want to make a judicial decision based on one man's opinion. But Bridges' testimony and Lynch's confession were probably enough to convince him that Price had not been raped.[8]

Reading from the bench on June 22, Horton said he would base his decision solely on questions of law, carefully abstaining from "the assumption of those not within its proper sphere." The defense had moved for a retrial on numerous grounds. It contended that mob sentiment had precluded a fair trial; that Solicitor Wright had injected religious prejudice into the trial with his charge of "Jew money"; that Attorney General Knight had injected race prejudice by treating the defendants and other black witnesses with utter disrespect; and that Negroes had been excluded from the jury rolls in violation of the Fourteenth Amendment.[9]

Horton said he would neither consider them all nor make a judgment about whether the arguments he would not consider were justified. The vital ground of the defense motion, and the basis of his decision, would be whether the verdict of the jury was contrary to the evidence. He cited a series of precedents for setting aside a verdict on that ground; in one case, the Alabama Supreme Court ruled that a jury, without conscious violation of duty, had been moved by bias, passion, and prejudice. He cited rulings in other cases in which the evidence had been insufficient, or in conflict with experience and common knowledge. He then went on to discuss the law "as especially applicable to the crime of rape." Finally, he turned to the "facts of the case": Was the evidence of the chief complainant reliable? Was it corroborated or contradicted by other evidence in the case?

Horton outlined the circumstances of the alleged crime and the facts as set forth by Price. He asked if, in the "rich field" from which corroboration might be gleaned—from the seven white boys on the train at the beginning of the fight (and also an eighth boy, Orville Gilley, who supposedly witnessed the whole thing) to "the cloud of witnesses at Paint Rock" to "the mute but telling physical condition of the women or their clothes"—there was "some one fact in corroboration" of Victoria Price's story. In all, Horton listed nine areas of potential corroboration, and explored each of them in exhaustive detail, going on for four pages, most of which had to do with the contradictions between Price's testimony and that of Dr. Bridges. Of Bridges, Horton said: "His intelligence, his fair testimony, his honesty, and his professional attainments impressed the Court and certainly all that heard him. He was frank and unevasive in his answers." It was Horton's opinion that he "should be given full faith and credit." Horton devoted an entire page to Bridges and Lynch's examination of Price's thighs and vagina. He concluded that "the State's evidence" corroborated Price "slightly, if at all."

Horton then asked whether Price's story was reasonable or probable. He argued that although rape was a crime usually committed in secrecy or in a secluded place, Price claimed she was raped around noon, on a sunny day, high up on a gondola car in plain view of anyone observing the train as it passed. Was it likely, he asked, that on top of that car, with the train speeding up and slowing down as it traveled the forty miles through the heart of Jackson County, nine Negroes had undressed Price, thrown her down, and (while one or another held a knife at her throat) successively had intercourse with her? Was it likely that the white boy Gilley (under no compulsion or threat from the Negroes, who had pulled him back on the train when, while trying to jump off, he got caught between two cars) sat off in a corner of the car and watched the whole thing, without attempting to jump off again and run for help or else run up the train and find the conductor or engineer? Was it likely or just a coincidence that just before the train pulled into Paint Rock the rapists happened to cease and the women happened to draw up and fasten their overalls, so that when the posse spotted them they appeared to be fully clothed?

The "natural inclination of the mind," Horton said, was to doubt that it happened that way. Price's "manner of testifying and demeanor on the stand" only increased that doubt. "The gravity of the offense and the importance of her testimony demanded candor and sincerity." Yet "her testimony was contradictory, often evasive, and time and again she refused to answer pertinent questions." In addition, "the proof tends strongly to show that she knowingly testified falsely in many material aspects of the case."

Only toward the end of his decision, when he considered Price's credibility, did Horton review some of the evidence offered by the defense. Before doing so, he made it clear that he would "exclude the evidence of witnesses for the defendant who themselves appear unworthy of credit." He didn't have to say that he meant Ruby Bates. Lester Carter was a somewhat different story. Whether he was "entitled to entire credit," Horton said, was "certainly a question of great doubt." But in the areas "where the facts and circumstances corroborated him," and where the state made no effort to contradict him, Horton saw "no reason to capriciously reject all he said."

Horton used Lester Carter's testimony to point out the places in Price's testimony where he thought she had knowingly testified falsely: her assertion that she hadn't known Lester Carter until she met him at Scottsboro; that she and her boyfriend Tiller spent the night before their trip to Chattanooga in her home, not in a hobo jungle; that she and Bates spent the night before the alleged rape at the home of Mrs. Callie Brochie; that the defendants had seven knives and two pistols. He used the testimony of the train's conductor to point out that although Price claimed the rapists had jumped them from a boxcar, the gondola in which she and Bates were riding was in the middle of two others.

In the last paragraph before his conclusion, Horton mentioned for the first time the testimony of Patterson and the five other boys who took the stand in his behalf, noting the contradictions between their stories and Price's. All of them denied that they had raped her, denied that they knew anything about it, denied that they had seen any white women on the train. Four testified that they had been in a fight with the white boys on the train. Two testified that they had known nothing about the fight or the girls; they said they had been on an entirely different part of the train, and that because of physical infirmities, near blindness in one, venereal disease in the other, they couldn't possibly have committed the crime with which they were charged.

Compared with the other white southerners who thought Price's sexual history had some bearing on her credibility as a witness, Horton was balanced and restrained. In examining the law applicable to rape, he cited a former chief justice of the Alabama Supreme Court:

> Her known want of chastity may create a presumption that her testimony is false or feigned. Whether it creates such presumption, the jury must determine from all the evidence. She may be of ill fame for chastity, but she is still under the protection of the law, and not subject to a forced violation of her person, for the grat-

> ification of the propensities of the man who has strength to overpower her. No principle of law forbids a conviction of her uncorroborated testimony though she is wanting in chastity, if the jury are satisfied of its truth.

Horton then gave the other side of the law its due, citing three precedents in which judges warned against rape convictions based on uncorroborated testimony or generated by the natural indignation of the jury against the alleged perpetrator. Each quoted or plagiarized Lord Matthew Hale, who in the seventeenth century wrote that the charge of rape was "an accusation easily to be made and hard to be proved, and harder to be defended by the party accused, though never so innocent."

Horton discussed Price's reputation and character only in relation to the specifics of her testimony and that of others. He noted that the defense contended that Price had charged the defendants with rape to avoid being charged with vagrancy or some other charge, but he resisted the temptation to say what the other charge was. In only one place in his decision did he refer to Price's life prior to two days before the alleged crime, and he did that only to show that she had lied when she testified that she had not met Lester Carter before she arrived at Scottsboro. Horton noted that Carter claimed that he and Price had met in jail, but he refrained from mentioning what Price had been in jail for. He reviewed Price's activities in the days before the train ride, but he did so only in the specific context of claims she made, facts in dispute, findings of the doctors. In short, he did so only when they had a direct bearing on her accusation.

Price said she had been thrown and abused upon the jagged sharp rock that filled the gondola. Horton noted that Dr. Bridges had found only small scratches on her wrist and blue marks in the small of her back and shoulders, adding that Price had traveled round-trip from Huntsville to Chattanooga by freight, that she had spent the night in a hobo dive, and that she had had intercourse with a man shortly before the time when the doctor examined her. "The few blue spots and this scratch," he concluded, "would be the natural consequence of such living."

Price charged that she had been raped six times, that "she was wet on her private parts," and that "each negro wetted her more and more." Horton noted that Dr. Bridges had found only a small amount of semen, semen in which the sperm were dead, and then said: "When we consider, as the facts hereafter detailed will show, that this woman had slept side by side with a man the night before in Chattanooga, and had intercourse at Huntsville with Tiller on the night before she went to Chattanooga . . . the conclusion becomes clearer that this woman was not forced into intercourse with all of these negroes upon that train, but that her condition was clearly due to the intercourse that she had had on the nights previous to that time."

Price said she had fainted. Horton noted that Bridges had said that when the women were brought to his office neither was "hysterical, or nervous about it at all." There was "nothing unusual about their respiration and their pulse was normal." That was not the physical and mental condition one would expect of the victims of so horrible an experience, one of whom claimed she had fainted, Horton said. "The fact that the women were unchaste might tend to mitigate the marked effect upon the sensibilities," but, he added, "such hardness would also lessen the probability of either of them fainting."

Price claimed she hadn't met Carter before Scottsboro. Horton noted that Carter claimed he had known her at Huntsville and had seen her "commit adultery on several occasions with one Tiller." Price claimed she had spent the night before she left for Chattanooga in her home, with Tiller, who was her boyfriend. Horton noted that Carter claimed that the four of them—Carter, Bates, Tiller, and Price—had been out and engaged in "adulterous intercourse," and that Tiller, though present in the courtroom, was not put on the stand to deny what Carter had said. Price claimed she and Bates had traveled to Chattanooga alone, and spent the night, alone, at Mrs. Callie Brochie's. Carter said that he, Bates, and Price had traveled to Chattanooga together, and "all went to what is known as the 'Hoboes Jungle,' a place where tramps of all descriptions spent the night in the open."

It was not until the first paragraph of his brief conclusion that Horton leapt from a discussion of the evidence—skillfully woven into a logical, seemingly irrefutable argument—to a speculative explanation of the origins of the case:

> History, sacred and profane, and the common experience of mankind teach us that women of the character shown in this case are prone for selfish reasons to make false accusations both of rape

> and insult upon the slightest provocation, or even without provocation for ulterior purposes.

No one paying close attention two months earlier, when in his charge Horton reminded jurors that Price and Bates were women of easy virtue, would have been completely surprised by those words. When "women of the underworld" come before the court, he had said, "the law says it is the duty of the jury to consider that fact. Not that the law would trample them down." Nor anyone paying close attention to the way Horton used words and phrases like *tramps, hobo dives,* and *unchaste women* in the body of his decision. Yet the first paragraph of his conclusion, more than anything Horton had said or written before it, most clearly revealed the similarities between his interpretation of the case and the interpretations of so many of the other white southerners who thought the Decatur jurors got the verdict wrong.[10]

In that conclusion Horton not only put Price and Bates at the center of what happened (and what did not happen) on the train and at the depot at Paint Rock. He also put them at the center of the events, controversy, and injustice that followed from that fateful day. What derailed the train of justice at Scottsboro and Decatur? The characters of two women. For selfish reasons, to spare themselves, two white women lied. History and common experience teach us that women of Price's and Bates's character were prone, with or without provocation, to do what they did. Price and Bates didn't just top Horton's list of culprits. They were the only names on the list.

The last few lines of Horton's conclusion were perfectly consistent with the close, careful, legalistic reading and arguing of the body of his decision:

> The law declares that a defendant should not be convicted without corroboration where the testimony of the prosecutrix bears on its face indications of unreliability or improbability and particularly when it is contradicted by other evidence. The testimony of the prosecutrix in this case is not only uncorroborated, but it also bears on its face indications of improbability and is contradicted by other evidence, and in addition thereto the evidence greatly

> preponderates in favor of the defendant. It therefore becomes the duty of the Court under the law to grant the motion made in this case.

Judge Horton set aside the verdict and death sentence and ordered a new trial.

T W E N T Y - F I V E

Some Very Damaging Information

"History, sacred and profane, and the common experience of mankind teach us that women of the character shown in this case are prone for selfish reasons to make false accusations both of rape and insult upon the slightest provocation, or even without provocation for ulterior purposes." Horton's words spread north like wildfire from the packed Athens courthouse. Here was a white southerner, an Alabama politician and judge, the son of a slave owner and a planter himself, who, in setting aside an Alabama jury's guilty verdict, had condemned a white woman who had charged a black man with rape.

Horton and other like-minded southerners were not the only or even the first people to apply that particular idea of history and common experience to the case. Back in April 1931, Communist Party editors had printed allegations about Price and Bates, based on the investigation of ILD organizer Douglas McKenzie, in the *Daily Worker*'s very first articles about the Scottsboro trials. After the trials, George Chamlee, the quixotic Chattanooga attorney retained by the ILD, took over the investigation. Five years earlier, Chamlee had strongly suggested that lynching—when considered in the light of southern fears of social equality, especially of intermarriage—was a reasonable response to attacks by Negroes on white women and sometimes even attacks by Negroes on white men. Yet the same man had "helped to quell four mobs"; had liberated without trial, with a lynching otherwise imminent, a Negro whom he knew to be innocent of the charge of rape; and was best known for his defense of people—striking streetcar workers, blacks, and Communists—whom no other Chattanooga lawyer would touch. Chamlee's grandfather was a decorated Confederate soldier, and when, during the trial of some Communists, the prosecutor charged that the accused had called for the overthrow of the government and forsworn loyalty to the flag, Chamlee reminded him that their own grandfathers had repudiated the government and pledged their allegiance to another flag.[1]

In the weeks after the first trials, Chamlee passed the word about Price and Bates to the CIC's James Burton, the NAACP's Walter White, and the ACLU's Hollace Ransdall. After a meeting with Chamlee at the beginning of May 1931, White wrote back to his office to say that although the reputation of the boys was "exceedingly bad," the reputation of the two white girls was "infinitely worse: They are notorious prostitutes and one of them, according to reputable individuals in Chattanooga, was arrested in a disorderly house in *flagrante delicto* with a colored man." A few days later, White met with Hollace Ransdall. He told her the "full story" and then suggested she visit Huntsville, where, Ransdall wrote in a memo to New York, "the two prostitutes" lived and plied "their trade."[2]

Chamlee also tried to tell it to Judge A. E. Hawkins. On June 4, 1931, he presented affidavits from ten Chattanooga Negroes as part of the defense's first motion for new trials. Oliver Love swore that during 1929 and 1930 Price and Bates had rented rooms in his boardinghouse and entertained "negro men in their rooms all night" and that "it made no difference whether she slept with a white man or a negro to her and they would both get drunk and they danced with and embraced colored men, and would hug them and kiss them." Love said that once in early 1930 Bates had asked him to help her make some money. She said it was payday at the Casey & Hedges Shops and she wanted to "meet and have intercourse with three men that afternoon." Love let her have the front room, and after they had gone home and changed clothes and washed up, "three men came and visited with her in that room that day." Love said that Price also "frequently met and entertained negro men in her room and ate her lunches there and she had a great many negro men meeting her there." Love permitted it because he needed the money.[3]

McKinley Pitts lived at 2330 Forest Street, near one of the houses in which Price and Bates roomed in early 1930. Pitts saw them "dance with negro boys and men in negro houses," saw them "drinking intoxicating liquor with negro boys and men," saw them "embracing negro men in dances in negro houses," and heard them asking "negro men" the size of their "privates." Pitts said that "she was greatly in love with Shug Moore," a "young Negro man," and "she wanted to make dates with him." And he said that "she was a hot proposition, a common street prostitute of the lowest type" who "did not seem to care for decency or anything."[4]

Issac Hinch, a twenty-two-year-old who said that he was personally acquainted with Bates, said she had "the reputation of being immoral and associated with more colored people than any woman" he had ever known. J. P. Hobby, who lived in the factory district of Chattanooga and had once "retailed a little liquid refreshments" at his home, said that Price had come by often to "get liquor and get drunk." Hobby had "a piano at his home and she would dance and put herself on the lowest terms that she could." She was "grossly immoral," Hobby said, "and danced in a vulgar fashion and she would dance with colored men and was guilty of the highest order of immorality and her conduct was disgraceful and scandalous and this fact [was] known to a great many colored people in that section and in that neighborhood."[5]

Annie Linson was also personally acquainted with Price and Bates. She had seen them in her neighborhood on numerous occasions when "they would visit the homes of negroes and would dance with colored men and put their arm around colored men, and smoke cigarettes with them and hug them and carry on with them just like colored girls would do with their own husbands." Their reputations, Linson said, were "bad for lewdness, drunkenness, for going dressed half naked, and dance with negro men and boys and associate with negro men and boys and smoke cigarettes and be out at all hours of the night and curse and swear, and were a general nuisance to the negro population near where they stayed." Once she even had to throw them out of her home.[6]

Tom Landers once saw Price drunk and "dressed in a lewd and almost nude fashion"; another time she was "drunk and in a fight with another woman and she had her clothes up around her body and she had on only two garments, and exposed her private parts and it was a drunken, disgraceful spectacle in the presence of a number of colored people." Like all the others, Landers swore that Price and Bates were "not entitled to full faith and credit of belief on oath in a court of justice."[7]

One week prior to the hearing before Judge Hawkins, the *Jackson County Sentinel* had reported that "Reds and their lawyers" had gathered affidavits of "unspeakable vileness and absolutely false" from "negro wenches and bootleggers, who denied knowing what was in the affidavits." The day after the hearing, the *Chattanooga Daily Times* reported that two of Chamlee's affiants, when visited by the assistant solicitor and a Chattanooga detective, had retracted their sworn statements and said that Chamlee had paid them fifty cents to sign. Chamlee insisted that the fifty cents was for carfare to his office.[8]

Knowing what was coming, Jackson County solicitor H. G. Bailey came to court with affidavits of his own. One was a sworn statement from the editor of the *Scottsboro Progressive Age,* who along with Bailey and two Huntsville detectives had also tracked down a few of Chamlee's affiants. One of them, Ashberry Clay, told them that there were statements in his affidavit that he did not make and which he did not know were in there. Clay also said that he had told Chamlee that he wasn't sure that the women he was talking about were Price and Bates. Chamlee had bought him dinner and paid him seventy-five cents. Tom Landers told them that at the time the girls were alleged to have been living in Chattanooga he was a convict in the state penitentiary.[9]

Bailey also presented an affidavit signed by the superintendent, the secretary, and the paymaster of the Margaret Mill, where Price and Bates had worked. They knew Price personally and said "she was a good worker and her character around the mill was good, except that she possibly had a fight or two." She was "absolutely above having anything wrong to do with negro men." Bates was "quiet and reserved and bore a splendid character," as far as they knew. They had never heard "one thing against her."[10]

Judge Hawkins didn't allow Chamlee to read his affidavits in court, and Alabama newspaper editors were of no more help to Chamlee in his effort to spread the allegations about Price and Bates around the state. Will Alexander (of the Commission on Interracial Cooperation) and Jessie Daniel Ames (of the Association of Southern Women for the Prevention of Lynching) shared what they learned about Price and Bates only with the small group of associates they thought would take it the right way. That meant that most of the allegations about Price and Bates that circulated in the South in the first two years of the controversy came in the leaflets, newspapers, letters, and affidavits scattered by "reds" and "radical Negroes." Some white southerners read them, and showed that they took them seriously by immediately and vigorously repudiating them. But when a black man or a Communist charged that a white rape victim was a prostitute, there was no mistaking his word for fact.

Outside the South, the allegations moved with much less resistance. They moved north in Communist Party papers and pamphlets, where Price and Bates were occasionally described as honorable toilers forced into degradation by capitalism, and most of the time described as "notorious professional prostitutes." They spread in the fund-raising letters of organizations of fellow travelers, such as the National Committee for the Defense of Political Prisoners. They spread in the news releases and pamphlets of the NAACP and in the articles and editorials of African-American newspapers. They spread in the report Hollace Ransdall prepared for the ACLU, and even more in newspaper reports of that report. And the allegations spread in articles about the appeals process in the northern commercial press. The *New York World Telegram* published its report of Chamlee's affidavits and motion for new trials under the headline "DENOUNCE GIRLS IN NEGRO APPEAL." "The reputation of these women is bad," Chamlee told a UPI reporter. The proof was in the affidavits and in the fact that the women "admitted going to Chattanooga as hoboes and leaving as hoboes, on a train with a crowd of men in the night time." "As a man who has practiced law in the criminal courts for many years," Chamlee said, "I can assert that the most dangerous and one of the most undependable witnesses in the world is a woman testifying in an assault case against a Negro."[11]

Only a few of the people who dug up and spread stories about Price's and Bates's sex lives made an effort to say anything about other aspects of their lives. Hollace Ransdall was one of them. Her own observations were as straightforward as her reporting of the observations of others, but she went to great lengths to ground her sensational revelations in the day-to-day life of Huntsville's mill villages: the chronic unemployment, low wages, broken families, hunger, and disease; the "dreary," "hopeless" struggle to "make some sort of a living even in the best of times." Ransdall came to see that words and concepts like *respectability, promiscuity,* and *sexual morality* meant something different to Price and Bates (and the people they lived, worked, and ran around with) than they did to most of the men and women who spread the gossip, rumor, and hearsay about them. And with wide, nearly innocent eyes, she described the family arrangements in the mill villages, and Price's and Bates's lusts and loves, from a perspective markedly different from that of most other middle-class observers.[12]

Ransdall found that the word *whore* had many meanings, one of which was a woman who shared her bed with a man she wasn't married to; and she understood, at least in the moment she wrote those words, that if the term was laden with value, it was not necessarily laden with derogation. She also found that many of her informants used the words *promiscuous* and *prostitute* synonymously. A woman who had sex before marriage, at least without a commitment to marry, was often called a prostitute. A woman who slept around, for whatever reason, was always called one. Bates wasn't married, and if any of the boys she went out with had made any commitments to her, she never mentioned them. Price was married, though not to Jack Tiller, the man she was hanging around with, sleeping with, and making plans to travel with in March 1931.[13]

Two years after Ransdall filed her report, labor journalist Mary Heaton Vorse traveled to Decatur to cover the second trials for *The New Republic*. She was one of two or three women in the courtroom. In her essay "How Scottsboro Happened," Vorse used the testimony of Carter and Bates to try to imagine the circumstances in which the behavior that sickened most observers, the behavior that she herself called a "story of degradation and horror that rivals anything written by Faulkner"—riding freights, drinking hard, making love in the company of other couples, making love in boxcars and fields, sleeping in hobo jungles, finding love, money, food, fun, and companionship wherever it came—was understandable, even sane. Their amusements, Vorse wrote, were their promiscuous love affairs; their playgrounds were hobo swamps and the unfailing freight cars:

> Why not? What was to stop them? What did Huntsville or Alabama or the United States offer a girl for virtue and probity and industry? A mean shack, many children for whom there would not be enough food or clothing or the smaller decencies of life,

> for whom at best there would be long hours in the mill—and, as now, not even the certainty of work. With hunger, dirt, sordidness, the reward of virtue, why not try the open road, the excitement of new places?[14]

If, among all the people sympathetic to the Scottsboro defense, it was only two northern women who tried to put the allegations about Price and Bates in the context of their lives, it was only a few southern women who argued that those allegations were irrelevant. It was left to those southern women, for no one else sympathetic to the defense even suggested that a woman's character and reputation had no bearing whatsoever on the question of rape. No one else left evidence of a dissent from the idea, implied or expressed most often by northern liberals and radicals, that rape was not quite as bad as white southerners made it out to be.[15]

The women who dissented from the dominant view had been taught, as so many white southern women had been taught, to think of themselves as the powerless prey of black rapists. But unlike most white southern women, they had become outspoken opponents of lynching. They believed that the lynch mob demeaned women, brought contempt upon the South, the nation, and Christianity itself, and undermined the law and all social order. Yet many of the women who had summoned the courage to oppose lynching found it impossible to discard their fear of rape like an old-fashioned dress the moment Jessie Daniel Ames (let alone Arthur Raper or Walter White) garnered statistics to demonstrate that it was based on misinformation and myth.[16]

"Whether their own minds perceive danger where none exists, or whether the fears have been put in their minds by men's fears, it is difficult to determine," wrote Jessie Daniel Ames. "But some women appear to live in a state of constant terror of being criminally assaulted." Antilynching activists were not immune from that fear, and some of them, like the southern women who favored lynching (and many of those who voiced no opinion), associated rape exclusively with black men. When in discussions of Scottsboro those women discovered that the alleged victims were "immoral," they did not immediately say, "Well, then I guess it is wrong to call it rape," or, "In that case it was their own fault." Those women cringed when Theodore Dreiser called the penalty for rape in Alabama "a horrible travesty on natural conduct"; or when John Spivak wrote that in the "depths" where Price was "born and lived . . . all feeling was killed. Being raped does not trouble her. She rapes easily and apparently likes it"; or when Langston Hughes ended an angry attack on "Southern Gentlemen, White Prostitutes, and Mill-Owners" by asking, "And who ever heard of raping a prostitute?"[17]

The voices of those southern women were faint, and it was not always possible to distinguish them from the mass of southern defenders of the verdicts, just as it was not always possible to distinguish Ransdall from critics of the verdicts with less information about Price and Bates and far less understanding of them. In the spring and summer of 1931, it was the most sensational and least nuanced stories about Price and Bates, told by ILD organizers, defense attorneys, school principals, social workers, sheriffs, private detectives, black Chattanoogans, NAACP officials, and northern investigators and journalists that circulated among critics of the trials, north and south, black and white. Those stories continued to circulate in late 1931 and throughout 1932, albeit more slowly, for outside Alabama, Chattanooga, and New York the case and controversy were only periodically in the news.

Then came Haywood Patterson's second trial, in March 1933. The heart of Samuel Leibowitz's defense was his attack on Victoria Price. He began that attack in his cross-examination of her on the first day of the trial, followed it up with most of the witnesses he called, and finished it in his summation. His aim was to convince the jury that Price's story about being repeatedly and forcibly raped at gun- and knifepoint was a complete fabrication. "The whole damnable thing," he argued, was "a frame-up of two irresponsible women."[18]

Yet Leibowitz was too good a lawyer to let his case and Patterson's fate rest on the slim chance that jurors would come to see things exactly as he did. The evidence and insinuation of fornication, adultery, and relationships with Negroes, the testimony of Lester Carter and Ruby Bates about their activities in the days before the fateful train ride, might well convince jurors that Price had made the whole thing up and bullied Bates into going along with the lie. But even if jurors were not convinced, even if some continued to imagine that something had happened on that train, Leibowitz had hoped and expected that the evidence and testimony would at least convince jurors that, whatever had happened, they should not call it rape.

TWENTY-SIX

Of My Own Free Will and Accord

Victoria Price made an accusation that could have resulted in the lynching or execution of nine black boys she had never seen before. She was in a tough spot. Fresh out of jail for adultery, with a long history of trouble with the law, she had to be alarmed when the train slowed down in Paint Rock and she looked up out of the gondola and saw that it was no ordinary water stop. Lester Carter and the other white boys had jumped or been thrown off during the fight, and as far as she knew, the black boys had jumped off too. That left just her, Ruby, and Orville Gilley. Wherever she looked she saw heavily armed men, nearly as frightening a sight for her and Bates as it was for the nine black youths scattered along the length of the train.

She didn't know why the posse was there, and even if she had guessed she would have been worried. She knew that she and Bates were violating vagrancy laws. She thought they were violating the laws against crossing state lines with a minor for immoral purposes—Bates was only seventeen. She also thought she was in danger of once again being arrested for adultery: a married woman traveling with two men, Orville Gilley and Lester Carter, neither of whom was her husband, with plans to meet her boyfriend, Jack Tiller, a few days hence.

Price and Bates climbed down, ducked their heads, and ran

along the tracks toward the engine. When they saw that there were men ahead of them, coming in their direction, they turned and ran the other way. There were men at the back of the train too. Unable to escape, Price leaned on Bates's shoulder and pretended to faint. Sometime after she came to, someone said something about a rape. It wasn't entirely clear which one of them made the charge. Bates said it was Price; after Bates reversed her testimony, the prosecution said it was Bates. Nor was it clear whether one of them volunteered the charge or was responding to a question (a question "suggestive of an answer," as Judge Horton put it) posed by the station agent or another member of the posse: Did they bother you?[1]

It was common for white people to accuse black people of crimes to conceal or divert attention from their own transgressions. It was acceptable and reasonable, and it was done by women as well as by men. Rape was the most serious accusation a white person could level against a black person, and as women, Price and Bates were the victims of the ideas that gave the accusation its power: ideas about the bestial nature of black men and the corresponding danger of integration and equality; ideas about the powerlessness and vulnerability of white women and the corresponding precondition of personal safety, complete deference and submission to white men. But power rarely rests squarely or completely in one place or another, once and for all; in this instance Price and Bates took hold of a weapon that was usually used against them and turned it on nine black boys.[2]

Victoria Price had a choice between her own well-being and the well-being of a bunch of black teenagers whom she had never seen before but who had the misfortune of being on that freight train when the posse stopped it in Paint Rock. She made the choice that most southern whites would have made, thinking that blacks were inferior and knowing that they were vulnerable: she chose her own well-being. She charged rape and forever after stuck to her story with the tenacity of a person who believed what she said. Perhaps she believed it from the moment she said it. More likely, confusing her treatment at the hands of the defense and other champions of the defendants with her treatment at the hands of the youths they defended, she came to believe it over time. Mary Heaton Vorse described Leibowitz's cross-examination as the shredding of her life with a patient scalpel. John Spivak described her as "nervous and boiling with fury as Leibowitz quietly and persistently bore into her past life and activities." Spivak's editors ran his story under the headline "LEIBOWITZ IMPALES PRICE GIRL AS PROSTITUTE."[3]

Price's sense of morality began with her own well-being and spread out from there to that of her lovers and friends. She was streetwise, wild, and tough, and moved among people whose lives were full of grit and danger and fun. She couldn't depend on anyone to look out for her, at least not for long, and not as carefully as she could look out for herself. Her boyfriend, Tiller, had decided that rather than risk arrest for violation of the Mann Act or another arrest for adultery he would stay in Chattanooga and meet up with her later. Price had lived among black people. She "treated" with them, trading sex for liquor, favors, money, food, companionship, and love. She appears to have loved black men as easily as she loved white men, but that did not mean she thought of her black lovers as equals. White hoboes thought nothing of telling black hoboes to get off a freight train or at least to keep it segregated by staying off their car. The white men around Price thought nothing of trying to get the best of black men when trouble arose. Why shouldn't she do the same? She might have been in big trouble with the law in Paint Rock. No reason in the world not to trade the fortunes of a bunch of Negroes—strangers—for her own.[4]

Ruby Bates's life was a lot like Price's, and the brown-haired, blue-eyed seventeen-year-old was like her older friend in all sorts of ways. It was not until Bates's recantation, at the Decatur trial, that most observers came to see that she and Price were not two women cast out of one mold. Yet from the moment one or both of them made the charge at the depot in Paint Rock, Bates was a thorn in the side of the Jackson County officials who were convinced that the two women had been raped.

Bates had trouble identifying the accused in jail, and on the stand in Scottsboro she was a miserable witness for the prosecution. Annoyed sheriffs and solicitors immediately called her slow, stupid, and dumb. She was not as quick or as articulate as Price. But she was not stupid or dumb. She was shy, insecure, and fearful in the face of authority. Some people are better at lying than others; afterwards some people regret it less. Whether Bates didn't like lying because she did it badly, or did it badly because she didn't like it, she didn't do it well and she had regrets. She had them as soon as she and Price were taken to the Scottsboro jail, feeling perhaps, as she said Orville Gilley had felt at the time, that they would all "go to torment" if they told anything but the truth. She ended up sticking by Price's side, but she did so nervously, if not reluctantly, and once the thrill of her few days of fame wore off, and the money she was paid as a witness was gone, the burden of what she had done became more than she wanted to bear.[5]

A job was no easier to come by after the trial than it had been before. In August 1931, Ruby and her mother decided to move; they hopped a train heading west. Huddled in the corner of a boxcar, she thought back to her last train ride, and to the boys in jail. She and her mother were doing just what she and Victoria had been doing. She and Price had lied to get themselves out of trouble, but, she wondered, "what good had telling those lies done for me." They spent the night in Sheffield, with her mother's sister, and then went on to Russellville, where they found work in a mill. Ruby got sick and three weeks later they returned to Huntsville. Her mother took in washing and ironing to feed them until Ruby recovered.[6]

Ruby met a man named Earl Streetman and they started going out. Then they had a falling-out over another girl, Mary Sanders. Sanders had bad-mouthed her, something having to do with Scottsboro. She may have told Streetman he ought to go with her instead of Ruby, for the simple reason that Bates had been ruined by Negroes. Or that she had heard that the rapists had given Bates a venereal disease. One night in early January 1932, Bates wrote a note to Streetman and gave it to a friend, Marion Pearlman, to deliver. Pearlman, an ex-prizefighter who had fought under the name Danny Dundee, was under surveillance by Huntsville police, who suspected he was involved in the Scottsboro case and perhaps also in bootlegging. Later the same night an informer told police that Pearlman had read Bates's letter aloud to several Negroes at a local restaurant. They put a tail on him, and when, at a local dance, he got in a fight with another man, they arrested him for assault. They searched him, and they found the letter:

Jan 5 1932
Huntsville Ala
215 Connelly Ally

dearest Earl

i want to make a statement too you Mary Sanders is a goddam lie about those Negroes jassing me those police man made me tell a lie that is my statement because i Want too clear my self that is

> all to it if you Want too Believe ok. if not that is ok. You Will be sorry some day if you had to stay in Jail With eights Negroes you would tell a lie two those Negroes did not touch me or those white Boys i hope you will believe me the law dont. i love you better than Mary does are any Body else in the World that is why i am telling you of this thing I was drunk at the time and did not know what i was doing i know it was wrong too let those Negroes die on account of me i hope you Will Believe my statement Because it is the gods truth i hope you Will Believe me i was jazed But those white Boys jazed me i Wish those Negroes are not Burnt on account of me it is these white Boys fault that is my statement and that is all I know i hope you tell the law hope you will answer
>
> P.S. this is one time that i might tell a lie But it is the truth so god help me.
>
> Ruby Bates[7]

Afraid that he was going to go to jail for public drunkenness or assault, Pearlman told the Huntsville police that George Chamlee had paid him to ply Bates with whiskey and get her to write the letter. The police visited Bates the next day, interrogated her, took her down to the station and threatened her with a hundred days on the chain gang if she didn't sign the paper the sheriff put in front of her. She signed, and the next day she read in the papers that she ("of my own free will and accord and without any threats, promises, or inducements of any kind made against or to me by any person whatever") had sworn that her "evidence against the negroes at Scottsboro was absolutely the truth." If she had written a letter to Earl Streetman the day before, or any other day, contradicting that testimony, she did so when she was "so drunk" that she "didn't know what she was doing."[8]

Chamlee admitted he knew Pearlman, but he insisted that Pearlman's story was "absolutely false," an effort to use the letter the police found on him to get himself out of trouble. Huntsville police and everyone else hostile to the defense had good reason to want to believe that Bates hadn't written the letter on her own, that someone had put her up to it and perhaps even drugged her. But an investigation into Pearlman's claim by the Huntsville police went bust, and another by the local bar association found no evidence of wrongdoing.[9]

Chamlee hadn't approached Pearlman. Pearlman, who lived in the same boardinghouse as Bates, had approached him at a newsstand, having overheard Chamlee ask a newsboy who was a friend of his which papers had articles about the case. Pearlman introduced himself and told Chamlee that he knew Ruby Bates. Not long after, George Proctor, a writer for *New Masses,* came to Chamlee looking for leads. He said he was especially interested in the reputation of the two girls. Chamlee introduced Proctor to Pearlman, and Proctor offered Pearlman train fare between Huntsville and Chattanooga plus ten dollars in exchange for information on Bates. Proctor denied telling Pearlman to get Bates drunk, let alone getting her to write or sign a letter while she was drunk. He thought that Huntsville detectives had "terrified" Pearlman into telling a story "for the express purpose of injuring Mr. Chamlee's reputation" and discrediting "the whole Scottsboro defense."[10]

The prosecution hoped that the publicity generated by the incident would keep defense attorneys away from its witnesses. It was not to be. At the end of 1932, Bates, along with a boyfriend and another girl, left Huntsville for Montgomery. Unable to find work there, she and her girlfriend decided to go to Chattanooga, and then New York. As with most of Bates's comings and goings, there was more than one version of her decision to go north. Some thought the ILD had approached her in Chattanooga and brought her to New York. Walter White and others thought that she had "voluntarily gone over to Chattanooga and offered to tell the truth" to defense attorneys and anyone else who cared to hear it. She herself didn't say anything about meeting with ILD or defense attorneys in Chattanooga or a free ride. She said she had thirty-five dollars, twenty of which her boyfriend had given her, and her friend had more. They pooled their money and bought two bus tickets to New York.[11]

Bates found a job in a tourist camp outside the city. It was the middle of March 1933 and Scottsboro was in the news. She wanted to talk to someone about the case but couldn't figure out whom she should talk to. She saw an article in the newspaper about a Reverend Harry Emerson Fosdick. And a photograph. She studied his face and decided that she ought to try to see him. He was the pastor of the Riverside Church, and she called at his office and identified herself. He said he would see her right away. She persuaded him that she had testified falsely in Scottsboro, and he encouraged her to return to Alabama to testify in the defendants' behalf.[12]

Under Leibowitz's direct examination on the witness stand, Bates said she had not been raped. Victoria had told her to say that they had been raped, told her that if she didn't, they would be in trouble for vagrancy and crossing state lines with men. Under Knight's cross-examination, she had as much trouble trying to tell the truth as she had had two years earlier trying to lie. "He shouted the questions at me," she said afterwards, "and hardly gave me time to answer before he asked another one." She had on a new dress. It wasn't "really new," she said, "but was new to them. I didn't have on the faded print dress that I had on when I worked in the mills." The first thing Knight asked her was where she got the dress. He asked numerous questions about her sex life, about what she did with her boyfriends. He asked her whether they paid her, and whether she had had intercourse with the salesmen with whom she said she had traveled from Huntsville to Montgomery before she went to New York. He kept coming back to the dress and her hat and slippers. He pointed at her and once stuck his finger right in her face and hollered.[13]

Bates answered his big questions truthfully but hemmed and hawed in answering many of the small ones. By the time she stepped down she had told a lot of obvious lies, both in a futile attempt to put a few small patches over the gaping holes between the stories she had told Knight in the past and the story she was telling on the stand that day, and in an equally futile attempt to keep the prosecution from finding out what she had decided they shouldn't know about the aid she had received from the defense ever since she had decided to switch sides.

As soon as word spread about Bates's reappearance and reversal, she replaced Leibowitz as the object of greatest loathing among locals. Feelings ran so high, and talk of violence was so openly expressed, that just before midnight a detail of heavily armed deputies whisked her out of the Cornelian Arms and took her into hiding. Spared the mob, Bates was vilified by the press and by people who recognized her on the street, and her life was threatened on numerous occasions. She decided to go north, where many people, delighted by her honesty and courage, considered her a hero. Some of those people were Communists, and as the parents of the defendants had found two years earlier, the Communists treated her better, and with more respect, than anyone had ever treated her before. Considering what she had been through, it was no more difficult for her than it had been for the defendants' parents (or, more recently, Samuel Leibowitz) to come to see things their way.

Bates began appearing at rallies and meetings, talking about her life and the case in language that was an awkward mixture of the Party's and her own. She admitted that she didn't understand Communist slogans and much of what Party people said. But, she said, she used to think a lot about the mills and "all the people having to work so hard and getting practically nothing for it." "I'd wonder what could be done and didn't know there was anything." Now she understood that "if the people would all work together instead of against each other it would help everybody." "Well," she added, "I guess it wouldn't help the bosses, but it would help all the workers."[14]

The first week in May 1933, she and Lester Carter addressed a crowd of five thousand at the Union Baptist Church in Baltimore. "Friends," she said with a southern accent exaggerated by her nervousness,

> I want to tell you that the Scottsboro boys were framed by the bosses of the south and two girls. I was one of the girls and I want you to know that I am sorry I said what I did at the first trial, but I was forced to say it. Those boys did not attack me and I want to tell you all right here now that I am sorry that I caused them all this trouble for two years, and now I am willing to join hands with black and white to get them free.[15]

Baltimore was one stop on the Scottsboro March on Washington. Three thousand people continued on to the White House, where the president's secretary, Louis Howe, ushered Bates and a few others into his office and then turned them away. The president, Howe said, was meeting with a German envoy. So they marched, in the rain, to Capitol Hill, where they met with Speaker of the House Henry Rainey and Vice President John Garner. They asked for the "unconditional release of the Scottsboro boys" and presented a "Bill of Civil Rights," designed to put teeth into the enforcement of the Thirteenth, Fourteenth, and Fifteenth amendments.[16]

Rainey told them that he would refer their document to the Judiciary Committee. "As for the Scottsboro case," he said, that was "a matter for the courts. Congress has no authority to direct the release of men charged with a crime."

But "the Scottsboro Boys are absolutely innocent," Bates said to him.

"You testified once they were guilty?" Rainey asked.

"Yes, sir."

"Now you retract?"

"Yes, sir."

"What caused you to change your mind?"

"Well, I didn't want to see innocent boys suffer."

"Because you had perjured yourself?"

"Yes, sir, under duress."[17]

Reporters asked Bates how she felt about herself. She said she was trying "to live it down": "I mean what I told against the colored boys in their first trial. I feel like it's something I've got to live down. I feel like I made up some by telling the truth in the second trial, but I'm still willing to make up some more. Of course I can't make up for the two years I helped cause the boys to suffer in jail—I know that much." Wherever she went, whomever she talked to, she said she was sorry and asked for forgiveness. She found she earned it quickly working for the defense. Janie Patterson had been the first to embrace her. At the Decatur trial, when Bates returned to the witness room after Knight's cross-examination, Patterson jumped up and asked if she had sworn for her boy or against him. "I told the truth on the boy," Bates said. Patterson and Ada Wright smiled and shook hands with her. Bates traveled with them to Scottsboro meetings, spoke alongside them at rallies, corresponded with them when they were apart, celebrated with them, and when Judge Horton ordered a new trial in June, she wrote letters of congratulation to their sons.[18]

As for her future, Bates thought she might like to learn stenography. Before she could commit herself to school, she had to decide what to do about Haywood Patterson's third trial. She wanted to return to Decatur and testify. But she was worried. Since April, hardly a day had passed when she did not receive an angry letter from the South. They called her a "nigger-lover" and said she too should be lynched. She said they had even threatened her mother, simply because she had "told the truth and would not let those innocent boys go to the electric chair for doing nothing."[19]

T W E N T Y - S E V E N

The Thinking People of Alabama

In the South, the greatest effect of Horton's decision was to reinforce convictions previously held. Those who had questioned the fairness of the verdicts in the wake of the 1931 trials finally felt vindicated. Those who had applauded Judge Horton's courageous and conscientious handling of the Decatur trial—including the editors of all three of Birmingham's daily papers—applauded his decision and argued that it was proof that southern courts were not "engines of ruthless injustice to the Negro." Those who had been persuaded by the Decatur trial that the defendants were not guilty had their conclusions confirmed. They cited Horton with pride. And those who had thought that the verdicts were fair and that those who attacked them were enemies of the South now had ample reason to believe, if the betrayal of Ruby Bates and Lester Carter had not been enough, that they had enemies in their own midst.[1]

The editor of the *Lafayette Sun* said that the decision came as a "shocking surprise to those who have been keeping up with the record in the case, especially since Horton was the trial judge and permitted the testimony which now furnishes the technicalities for a new trial." The editor of the *Huntsville Builder,* on the other hand, was not surprised. Horton was the same judge who had "wilted under fire and granted an indefinite continuance of the trials." William Moseley, of Decatur, responded with an angry letter to a

Birmingham Age-Herald editorial praising Horton. The judge had sat idly by while his courtroom was turned into a circus, Moseley wrote. He allowed photographers to take flash pictures and "that Jew lawyer to say and do what he pleased." When Leibowitz ordered Knight to address a Negro witness as "Mister," Horton "sat there and said nothing." Had you been in the attorney general's place, Moseley asked the editor, would you still have called him "brave" and said his "behavior" won "the praise of all thoughtful observers?" Moseley concluded that Horton simply sought notoriety and had "no more backbone than an angle worm."[2]

Moseley was not the only one to question Horton's motives. "Without attributing to Judge Horton any ulterior motive," Files Crenshaw and Kenneth Miller wrote two years later in their book, *Scottsboro: The Firebrand of American Communism,* "it must be pointed out that he had listened intently for seventeen days to witnesses testifying on the stand. After hearing the evidence he charged the jury and after receiving its verdict, adjudged the defendant guilty and sentenced him to death. Several weeks later he came to the conclusion that while the State's witnesses were not credible, the defendant's witnesses were."[3]

Crenshaw and Miller were neither the first nor the last to wonder whether the Communists had had something to do with Horton's decision. Behind every twist and turn in the controversy, behind every instance of black unrest and racial conflict that the controversy spawned, they and many others suspected Communist intrigue. If it wasn't northern Communists, it was northerners who had been blinded and brainwashed by Communist propaganda. By late 1933, two and a half years after the first trials, not all white southerners saw red and only red when the subject of Scottsboro came up. Many big-city southern newspaper editors realized that among those protesting the verdicts there were northerners who were neither Communists, nor fellow travelers, nor even Communist sympathizers. In passing judgment on the protest, they often distinguished between Communists and non-Communists. Some thought of the controversy not so much in terms of politics as of region and religion—South against North, Protestants against northeastern Jews.

In the minds of the majority, the boundaries between politics, region, and religion were blurred. The *Jackson County Sentinel* referred to the protesters and defense attorneys as the "Witzskys, Itzskys and Bitskys." The *Pickens County Herald* called them the

"Leibowitzs and sons-of-witzs from the back alleys of New York to the slums of Moscow." Others simply called them New York Jews. They were all one and the same, for no matter how many different groups had been bought off or duped into supporting them by their lies and misrepresentations, the Communists were behind the defense of the Scottsboro rapists and the agitation surrounding it; and the Communists were behind the ever-widening attack on and subversion of white southern ways.[4]

They produced plenty of evidence to support that sweeping claim. They pointed to the telegrams sent to Judge Horton by Communists around the world. They pointed to the telegrams sent to other Alabama officials; by the end of 1933, Governor Miller alone had received fifty thousand. They pointed to Lester Carter and Ruby Bates. During the trial, they looked and sounded as if they had been bought by the Communists. After the trial, they confirmed every suspicion and fear. Both of them went north and joined the Party, Bates telling numerous audiences, some mixed, some all Negro, that the boys were absolutely innocent. She said she had testified against them in 1931 because she had been "frightened by the ruling class of Scottsboro." "I want to tell you," she said in New York, "that I was frightened by the ruling class, that if I didn't tell the story about these innocent Scottsboro boys, I'd be lynched myself." She led the Communist march to the White House, chanted "Free the Scottsboro Boys" and sang the Internationale. At her side were James Ford, the "Negro vice-presidential candidate on the Communist ticket in the last election," and William Patterson, the "Negro National Secretary of the ILD."[5]

Bates was written off with ridicule, sarcasm, and scorn. The editor of the *Huntsville Times* concluded that she must have found being a "martyr" to the cause of the "Scottsboro Boys" "more profitable than plying the trade she once did in Huntsville." But Bates was the least of white southerners' worries. In December 1932, Tallapoosa County sharecroppers, encouraged by Communists to form a union, picked up guns in resistance to whites who had done nothing more than serve a writ of attachment to cover a bad debt. Several sharecroppers were killed in the uprising. The Communists arranged a "mass" funeral, leading a crowd on a long march through Birmingham to the cemetery. There were hammers and sickles on the caskets.[6]

When the ringleaders of that uprising were tried for attempted murder, union members and sympathizers filled the courtroom and overflowed into the courthouse square. Local officials postponed the hearings, and tried again the third week in April 1933, the week after the end of the Decatur trial. This time whites packed the courtroom, in the county seat of Dadeville, while sheriffs blocked the highways into town. Members of the Sharecroppers Union and their sympathizers came anyway, "along bypaths and across streams and ditches." When the defense protested that Negroes had been excluded from the courtroom and demanded seats, the judge cleared half the courtroom for them, perhaps so they could watch their compatriots convicted and sentenced to long terms in jail. Communist lawyers challenged the indictments on the grounds that Negroes had been excluded from the grand jury that had handed them down, in violation of the Fourteenth Amendment.[7]

The Communists were making trouble among sharecroppers in the country and they were making trouble among mill workers, miners, and even the unemployed in the city. All that upset Alabamans, but what drove them to a frenzy was what they saw as the contagion of Scottsboro. It seemed that whenever and wherever a Negro was accused of rape, Communists rushed to his defense. In July 1933—a month after Judge Horton overturned Haywood Patterson's second conviction—it was in Tuscaloosa. Three Negroes had been arrested for the rape and brutal murder of a twenty-one-year-old woman. Relatives of the accused secured two young local white lawyers, and the court appointed two others. Nonetheless, on August 1, the first day of the hearing, an ILD lawyer stood up in court and insisted that he and his two associates had been retained by the defendants. After calling one of the defendants to the stand, followed by his father and mother, asking them if they had retained the ILD attorneys or any other outside counsel, and hearing them say no, the judge denied the attorneys' request for recognition. Outside the courthouse, a few thousand Tuscaloosans encouraged their speedy, and surreptitious, exit from town. What happened next? From New York the ILD immediately announced it would continue to fight for the defense and sent a telegram to the judge. The telegram warned that "two hundred thousand members" were prepared to expose the Tuscaloosa court's "illegal maneuvers" as another Scottsboro.[8]

The judge scheduled the trials for August 22, but by August 12 reports and rumors—that the ILD would be back and that its first move would be for a change of venue; that the prosecution had made a secret deal and was not going to prosecute the case vigorously—fueled reports that a lynch mob was planning to storm the Tuscaloosa jail. After prolonged discussion, the circuit court judge and sheriff decided to transfer the prisoners to Birmingham, and they assigned three deputies to the job. When they were halfway there, twelve masked men surprised and easily overpowered them; the deputies fled. The men drove the three Negroes seven miles, forced them out of their cars, sent scores of pistol shots their way, and left them for dead. One survived.[9]

"LYNCHED BY CARPETBAGGERS OF 1933" was the headline of the *Tuscaloosa News* the day after the double lynching. The editors argued that just as lynch law was born out of the "ignorance and arrogance" of the carpetbaggers in Reconstruction, responsibility for the recent lynchings fell squarely on the shoulders of the "belled buzzards of the International Labor Defense, spreading their poisoned Communistic propaganda among our contented Negro population" and "pushing their dirty beaks in where they have no business." Others, including the editors of the *Birmingham Age-Herald,* the *Huntsville Times,* and even the *Montgomery Advertiser,* whose editor, Grover Hall, had insisted that "the maggoty beaks of the belled buzzards" of the ILD were "stained with the blood of the three Negro boys," refused to absolve Alabamans of responsibility. But the grand jury called to investigate the lynchings (with the help of Attorney General Knight) did. Tuscaloosa officials were exonerated, and none of the men suspected of taking part was charged. The judge told Arthur Raper that the community had not given the grand jury the support it needed to secure indictments.[10]

In the late summer and early fall of 1933, investigators for the Southern Commission on the Study of Lynching, led by Raper, found "pervasive" fear, "even on the part of the most intelligent people" that Communists were "active in town and country"; that meetings were "being held among the Negroes"; that "itinerant Communists" were "advising Negro men to take liberties with white women"; that Negroes accepted these suggestions and were "eager to act upon them"; and that Negroes arrested for assault would be "shielded from punishment by the I.L.D." Since every gathering of Negroes was suspected to be a Communist gathering, including "every one of the large number of religious gatherings and lodge meetings," white Tuscaloosans designed an elaborate system of espionage.[11]

Espionage gave way to intimidation with the formation of the Citizens Protective League. Hundreds of Tuscaloosans joined, including public officials and members of prominent families. Using the Klan's insignia and techniques, the League "terrorized" the urban black community with "masked parades" and "threatening handbills." In the rural areas it was worse, as automobiles full of masked men roamed the countryside, breaking into homes, beating and shooting Negroes suspected of subversion. "Suspicion and confusion reigned on every hand," Arthur Raper wrote. "People stood about in small clumps—if Negroes, it was to whites a threat of imminent uprising; if whites, it was to Negroes ominous evidence of a murderous mob!"[12]

Judge Horton's decision overturning Haywood Patterson's conviction came in the midst of that black and red scare, yet even his harshest critics understood that he was not a northern judge, not a federal judge, not a Communist judge. He was an Alabama judge, and not a notably liberal judge at that. Although hostility to Horton and his decision was not entirely unrelated to the conflict between southerners and northerners, it was primarily the product of conflicts among white southerners themselves, conflicts between city people and rural folk; lettered and unlettered; middle-class and upper-class; farmers, working people, and professionals. Just as most white Alabamans resented the interference of northerners, many resented the interference (and, even more, the paternalism and condescension) of a minority of white Alabamans and other white southerners who, by virtue of their education, cultivation, and social standing, thought they had a right to tell them how to live their lives.

Scottsboro was full of that conflict, and it had been for some time. Jackson County newspaper editors had been dismayed when Birmingham editors and columnists expressed disappointment in the Alabama Supreme Court decision upholding the original convictions. They'd been furious when the same men applauded the U.S. Supreme Court decision overturning them. Worse than their support for the high court's rebuke was their assumption that they spoke for all thoughtful Alabamans. P. W. Campbell, editor of the *Scottsboro Progressive Age,* singled out the *Birmingham News-Herald*'s John Temple Graves, who had had the "unmitigated gall" to call his column on the Court's decision "Alabama Approves Decision" and then proceed "in his best paternalistic attitude to inform his northern friends that the 'intelligentsia' and the 'really thoughtful people' and leading Alabama newspapers" have "thought all along that the Negroes did not receive a fair trial." Campbell, along with

Scottsboro's other editor, James Benson, responded the same way whenever big-city newspapermen made explicit the belief that Graves implied: that rural and poor white southerners were responsible for prejudice and racial injustice, whether exhibited by mobs, solicitors, or juries.[13]

And then there was the resentment of ordinary Alabamans toward the enlightened few who thought they knew better than Alabama's juries. One of them was the editor of the *Birmingham Post,* who had written that it was "no serious reflection on the Morgan county jury that Judge Horton, experienced in evaluating evidence, should see fit to disagree with their verdict. It is, in a sense, a reflection on the jury system, but thinking people long since ceased to regard the jury system as perfect." Horton himself, the prosperous, highly educated jurist who lived in one of the finest homes in Athens, was another. As one man put it in a letter to the editor of the *Birmingham News,* when Horton overturned the jury's verdict he declared himself "superior to the Supreme Court of his own State" and "by implication accused all who had anything to do with the conviction of these negroes of being too ignorant to know what they were doing."[14]

The day after Horton overturned Patterson's conviction, Birmingham Rabbi Morris Newfield, a member of Alabama's Interracial Commission, speaking to the Conference of American Rabbis, called Horton a "second Lincoln" and said that his decision was the "true expression of the thought of the thinking people of Alabama, backed by the masses." Unfortunately there were not enough thinking people, or the thinking people were not actually backed by the masses, or neither the thinking people nor the masses had their hands on the levers of power. Horton had hoped that his decision would close the case—that the state would decide not to bring new indictments. But moments after Horton finished reading his decision, Attorney General Knight announced his intent to retry Patterson, and the very next day unveiled a new witness. Orville Gilley, the white youth whom Price said had climbed back on the train and witnessed the rape, had returned to Alabama and agreed to testify. Gilley had already submitted an affidavit that corroborated Price's testimony in every detail. Meanwhile former Alabama senator Thomas Heflin sent a telegram to Attorney General Knight to say that he shared Knight's "keen disappointment and resentment" of "the strange and amazing action of Judge Horton in the Scottsboro rape cases." "I will be glad," he said, "to assist you free of charge in having Judge Horton relieved from further consideration of these cases and in having another judge appointed to try the Scottsboro negroes."[15]

Apparently not even the masses in Horton's own election district approved of what he had done. The prosecution's efforts to get rid of him were successful, and shortly after Horton removed himself from the case he announced he would not run for reelection. But when a group of Athens lawyers presented him with a petition, signed by the entire Athens bar, urging him to reconsider, and a half-dozen newspapers endorsed the lawyers' petition and took the opportunity to praise the judge again, Horton changed his mind. He ran hard, and won the endorsements of prominent ministers, businessmen, and lawyers. In the primary, in May 1934, Horton finished second in a field of three, doing worst in Morgan County. In the runoff, a month later, he was decisively defeated. In both primary and runoff his opponents made Scottsboro the central issue. Afterwards, the *Birmingham Post* said that the voters had made "the sort of mistake . . . that makes honorable men eschew politics." Horton's defeat, argued the editor of the *Talladega Daily Home,* was further proof that "popular vote was not the best way to select the judiciary."[16]

T W E N T Y – E I G H T

Reading in the Haymow

In the wake of the Decatur trial, Samuel Leibowitz had nothing but praise for Judge Horton. He called him calm, kind, courteous, judicious, honorable—a "wonderful jurist" who was "sincerely desirous" of according the defendants "a fair chance for their lives." Northern editors and many other observers concurred. Horton had warned spectators and jurors against prejudice, provided the defendants with adequate protection, suppressed the mob, admonished the prosecution for its most unseemly displays, allowed the questions about Price's character that were necessary to discredit her testimony, and charged the jury with the utmost fairness. The *New York Times* said he had done his best "to make Alabama justice worthy of the name."[1]

Ringing praise was not unanimous praise. The *Daily Worker*'s headline three days after the verdict read: "JUDGE HORTON CHIEF LYNCHER." Many black liberals and radicals had reservations of their own. Roscoe Dunjee, editor of the *Oklahoma City Black Dispatch,* argued that if Horton had been fair, he would have declared a mistrial "the moment the defense demonstrated the jury had been drawn in violation of the Constitution." If the judge had been fair, he would have dismissed the charges on the grounds that the evidence was "insufficient," the "testimony too contradictory," and the "integrity and depravity of the witnesses unbelievable." If the judge had been fair, he wouldn't have allowed Attorney General Knight to call Patterson "that thing," or Wade Wright to appeal to racial and religious prejudice.[2]

When Horton overturned the guilty verdict in June, Leibowitz and most other northerners found their faith in the judge confirmed. Some black observers still had doubts. The editor of the *Chicago Defender* admitted that thanks to Horton, the defendants were one step closer to exoneration, but he wondered why Horton had waited two months to do what he had "ample opportunity to have done either during or immediately at the conclusion of the trial." He waited, "preferring to sentence Patterson to the electric chair and to subject him to more months of misery and torture in an Alabama jail." The editor of the *Afro-American,* after noting that Horton overturned the verdict because "Victoria Price was a harlot and her testimony against Patterson was unsupported," asked: "Where was Judge Horton all during the Scottsboro trial? Didn't he know it then? . . . Of course he knew it, but he didn't have the courage of his convictions." By granting a new trial, the editor said, Horton put off, at least for the moment, a Supreme Court review of the jury system.[3]

Judge Horton had lived up to Leibowitz's expectations, but from the moment Knight announced his decision to try Patterson a third time, so did the "bigots" he had seen in the courtroom whenever he turned his eyes away from the judge. First came the machinations that resulted in the removal of Judge Horton from the trial. Moderate and liberal southerners, led by Will Alexander and Bishop McDowell, hoped to prevent it, and had some success in rallying prominent Alabamans behind Horton. They admitted defeat in mid-October, when Alexander found out that Knight had already persuaded the chief justice of the Alabama Supreme Court to ask Horton privately to step aside. The state replaced Horton with the other judge on the Eighth Circuit, William Callahan, and even before the trial began, it seemed to Leibowitz, most northerners, and even some prominent Alabamans, that Callahan had been named not to judge but to impose the majority's will.[4]

The seventy-year-old Decatur resident had been neither to law school nor to college. He was born and raised on a farm, and as Allen Raymond of the *New York Herald Tribune* put it, "after reading plenty of books in his father's haymow," Callahan went on to read Coke and Blackstone in a local law office. In Leibowitz's view, Callahan's ignorance of the law was surpassed only by his intolerance and his prejudice against the defense attorneys, the defendants, and everyone he associated with them. Horton had sent passes to black reporters and provided them with their own press table. Callahan refused to provide a special table for Clarence Mitchell, the *Afro-American*'s correspondent, instead ordering him to buy his own. He was only slightly more generous with white newspeople, banning their typewriters and, when he finally agreed to provide them with a table, insisting it be placed outside the rail.[5]

Defense attorneys returned to Decatur in the middle of November and found it as they had left it in April. "The scene and the atmosphere," Raymond Daniell wrote, were "more tense than at any time in the previous trial." There had been a spate of lynchings, in Alabama and elsewhere, through the summer and early fall, the first of them in Tuscaloosa, after three black men were charged, on the flimsiest evidence, with rape and murder. The Tuscaloosa lynchings were followed by lynchings in Maryland and Louisiana in late October and early November. Leibowitz and ILD attorneys again feared violence, and their first move, which was supported by some prominent Alabamans, was to request the presence of the National Guard. Callahan refused, and persuaded Governor Miller to resist the defense's pleas. Leibowitz appealed to President Roosevelt, who refused to interfere. Callahan assigned two guards to Leibowitz, and the governor, once apprised of the temperament of the town, sent fifteen deputies from Birmingham to keep an eye on the entire defense team.[6]

Leibowitz's sense of security came from having two members of New York City's homicide squad in his retinue, but to him and his colleagues, all of whom concluded from newspaper articles and vivid photographs that a lynching epidemic was spreading all over the country, neither two 250-pound homicide detectives nor fifteen Birmingham deputies seemed adequate. On the last day of pretrial proceedings, newspapers carried the story of the San Jose, California, mob of one hundred who, cheered on by a crowd of several thousand, fought with scores of officers for two hours before smashing the walls of a local jail with a battering ram and lynching two men accused of kidnapping and murder. Afterwards, California governor James Rolph, who had refused calls for troops, said that he would pardon anyone convicted of lynching. On the first full day of the Decatur trial, newspapers carried stories of the lynching of Lloyd Warner, a nineteen-year-old black youth accused of attacking a white woman in St. Joseph, Missouri. There, a crowd of seven thousand fought National Guardsmen and sheriffs outside the county jail where Warner was held, before seizing him, dousing him with gasoline, hanging him from an elm tree, and setting him ablaze. During the trials, there was a lynching in Texas, and near-lynchings in Georgia and South Carolina. Judge Callahan continued to refuse requests for troops.[7]

As in April, the hostility of northern Alabamans seemed to be directed at the defendants' attorneys at least as much as at the defendants themselves. Leibowitz and Brodsky received numerous threats; some appeared in newspapers: "In the face of the feeling which exists at Decatur as well as throughout the Tennessee Valley against any lawyer claiming to represent the International Labor Defense," wrote the editor of the *Huntsville Community Builder,* "we suggest that it would not be well for these lawyers to show up on any soil at any point within the valley. We do not need that type of cattle down here and their further appearance is wholly unnecessary."[8]

The defense moved for a change of venue, and supported its motion with the results of five hundred interviews that had been conducted by ILD investigators posing as soap and brush salesmen. The interviews documented the prejudice against and violent hostility toward the defendants and their Jewish lawyers in and around the town. Hundreds had talked like the proprietor of a lunchroom on Moulton Street who said that "there shouldn't be any trial for them damn 'niggers'—30¢ worth of rope would do the work and it wouldn't cost the County much. . . . If the State don't kill them then the people here will." Several members of the National Guard told investigators that they wanted to see the defendants executed; if a mob went after them and they were called out, they would not even try to stop it. An auto mechanic insisted, with no regret, that "there are no 12 men in Morgan County who will listen to the defense side." Callahan denied the motion.[9]

The defense again moved to quash the indictments on the grounds that Negroes had been excluded from both Jackson County and Morgan County jury rolls, and again fought successfully to have the book in which the rolls were recorded brought into court. This time the monotony of the daylong search for the names of Negroes was broken by the discovery of nearly a dozen. The defense suspected fraud. When Knight turned down Leibowitz's offer to call a handwriting expert of Knight's choosing, Leibowitz asked James Haring, a New Yorker, to rush to Decatur. After studying the books for two hours, Haring confirmed the defense's suspicions. He testified that the names had been added after March 1931. The defense added the charge of fraud to its motion to quash the indictments. Callahan denied the motion. Experts, he said, always confused him—one argued one way, another the other. He couldn't believe that his neighbors, the highly respected officials of Jackson County, would have committed fraud.[10]

In the first Decatur trial, Leibowitz had faced a tough prosecutor in Tom Knight; in the second he faced two tough prosecutors, and one of them was the judge. During Leibowitz's cross-examination of Victoria Price, on the trial's first day, Callahan sustained nearly every one of the prosecution's objections, and when the prosecution did not object, Callahan objected himself, saying "that's enough for me to know," "that is a waste of time," "that's enough on that," "that will do," "treat the lady with more respect."

Knight and Callahan resisted Leibowitz's every effort to give the jury a clear picture of what Price and Bates had been up to in the twenty-four hours before the alleged crime, evidence that Judge Horton had regarded as crucial. Callahan wouldn't let Leibowitz ask Price about the night (two nights before the train ride) that she and Bates had spent in a hobo jungle, making love with Carter and Tiller. Nor about the night before that, which she and Bates had spent in another jungle, this time with Carter and Gilley. Even questions about whom she and Bates had traveled with and where they had stayed Callahan ruled out of bounds. Leibowitz was unable to provide a general picture of Price's long history of lewdness, drunkenness, fornication, and adultery. He was also unable to explain to the jury why it was that Dr. Bridges, who was to testify presently (this time for the defense), had found semen in Price's vagina.[11]

Callahan sustained objections or objected himself just as strenuously when Leibowitz tried to get other witnesses, particularly Orville Gilley and Lester Carter, to tell the jury of their activities in the days and nights immediately preceding the alleged rape. He ordered the words *jail* (Where, Leibowitz had asked Carter, did you meet Victoria Price?) and *hobo jungle* stricken from the record. When Leibowitz asked for permission to explain why he kept asking the questions that so upset Callahan, the judge cut him off, saying, "I can imagine," and told him "to move on to something else." When Leibowitz asked Carter, point-blank, if the two couples had had intercourse in the presence of one another, Callahan exploded and called the question vicious. Leibowitz moved for a mistrial. Callahan denied the motion, but did instruct the jurors to disregard his use of the word *vicious*.[12]

It was not only Price's honor and rights that Callahan worked so hard to protect. He objected to Leibowitz's attempts to highlight improbabilities, inconsistencies, contradictions, and impossibilities in the testimony of every witness the prosecution called to the stand. And even when no one was on the stand he did prejudice's work. Fearing for her life, Ruby Bates had not returned to Decatur. She readily agreed to provide a deposition for the defense. When the taking of that deposition was delayed by her illness and serious operation, the defense moved for a one-day adjournment, the time it was going to take for the deposition to arrive. Callahan denied the motion. He denied a second defense motion for a short delay, this one to allow the expert medical witnesses Leibowitz had called from Chattanooga to travel to Decatur. Callahan said he wanted the trial over in three days.[13]

Callahan refused to declare a mistrial when in his summation the attorney general frankly admitted that his appeal was an appeal to passion. Callahan's charge to the jury, however imperfect from the perspective of criminal law, was a point-by-point refutation of both the defense's case and the grounds on which Judge Horton had overturned the last guilty verdict. And as if the substance of that charge were not enough to let jurors know which way he thought they ought to go, as he read, Callahan frequently paused, lifted his head, turned toward Leibowitz, and glared. And when, in closing, Callahan instructed jurors on the two forms a guilty verdict might take, he neglected to provide the form for an acquittal.[14]

The jurors (nine farmers, one unemployed housepainter, a truck driver, and the operator of a small country store) retired at four o'clock in the afternoon on Thursday, Thanksgiving day, three days after the trial began. At five o'clock the following afternoon, they indicated that they had reached a verdict. Deputy sheriffs brought Haywood Patterson into court, his wrists bound. He smiled slightly as he sat down next to Clarence Norris and listened for the third time in two and a half years to a clerk say, "We, the jury, find the defendant guilty as charged and fix his punishment at death."

Suddenly there was silence and everyone in the courtroom was staring at him. Patterson stopped smiling and stared back. Then leered at the jurors, then at the judge, then at the jurors again. The shortest way out of the courtroom took the jurors right by his chair. He was six feet tall and built like a football tackle. Eight of them took that route, but not one of them looked at him. The other four started out that way but then changed their minds, turning around and taking the long way out of the room. As in April, jurors said they had settled upon a guilty verdict almost immediately and had taken the rest of the time to come to an agreement on the penalty.[15]

Norris's trial was about to begin. Leibowitz had an even harder time than he had had at Patterson's trial trying to find twelve jurors who did not have fixed opinions about the case. Callahan had to excuse seventy-six out of a venire of one hundred even before Leibowitz and Knight began striking. And Leibowitz had a harder time controlling his frustration and anger, both of which grew with each clash with Callahan and with his sense that another conviction was inevitable.[16]

When it came time for the judge's charge, Leibowitz was prepared, and but for a few articles and prepositions, he objected to every word. Pressing the judge as though he were a hostile witness, Leibowitz offered nearly a dozen exceptions. In each of them Leibowitz demanded that Callahan amend a specific part of his charge. When Callahan refused, or amended it in an improper manner, Leibowitz took exception again.[17]

He objected to every word. And every word spoken and every deed done during Patterson's third trial and Norris's second reinforced the images, ideas, attitudes, fears, caricatures, and prejudices that Leibowitz had taken away from Decatur in April. It didn't matter who was speaking—judge, county solicitors, attorney general, the state's witnesses, white spectators in the courtroom, or white Alabamans outside. They all said the same thing. There was only one significant difference between April and November: when Patterson's jury announced its verdict, Leibowitz was not even slightly surprised. Five days later, after deliberating for fourteen hours, a second jury found Clarence Norris guilty. Callahan, sentencing Norris to death, neglected the customary "May God have mercy on your soul."[18]

TWENTY-NINE

Nowhere Are We Safe Today

Judge William Washington Callahan was born on a farm in Lawrence County, Alabama, the last day of June 1863, the eve of the battle of Gettysburg. He went to public school, the Male and Female College, and then read law in the office of W. P. Chitwood, of Moulton. He worked as deputy solicitor of Lawrence County and then as solicitor of Decatur. He served a term in the state legislature and in 1928 he was elected circuit court judge.[1]

Northerners said or inferred that he had little experience and less education, apparently unaware that not even half of his fellow circuit court judges, and fewer of those his age, had taken LL.B.s or even attended law school. Most had just what he had, some college but no college degree. Callahan had learned law by reading law in the office of someone who knew it, and whatever he lacked in formal education, he more than made up for in common sense, shrewdness, and will. Adversaries called him arrogant and stubborn. Friends knew him as straightforward and honest, a man who suffered neither fools nor foolishness, a judge who had strong opinions about the law.[2]

Callahan came right out and said that his goal was to "debunk" the Scottsboro case, by which he meant to diminish it, cut it down to size. He thought the defense and other outsiders had made too much of it, and he wanted to separate the straightforward question of guilt or innocence from the extraneous matters in which it had become entangled. That's why he banned typewriters and cameras and did everything else in his power to make it hard for newsmen to do their jobs. That's why he didn't want troops. That, and the cost of the trials to Morgan County—$1,200 a day, and the county had yet to pay the Lyons Hotel for housing and feeding the jurors in April—was why Callahan announced that he would allow only three days for each trial, though Haywood Patterson's previous trial had taken six.[3]

Callahan came to court eager to rid it of extraneous issues—"lawyers' ways of delaying the proceedings," as he put it—and found that Leibowitz and his associates were interested in little else. First they moved for a change of venue, supporting the motion with statements allegedly made by hundreds of residents—evidence, they contended, of overwhelming prejudice against the defendants in and around Decatur. The prosecution made them look foolish, if not corrupt, by calling to the stand some of the residents whose sentiments the defense had offered as evidence. Each swore that he had never said what the ILD agents claimed he had said. Attorney General Knight also called two undertakers, who testified that a half dozen of the people said to have been surveyed were dead. Defense attorneys, for their part, argued that they themselves had received numerous death threats from white southerners. Callahan was not moved. He and the attorney general had received many more from the Communists.[4]

Next the defense challenged the venire on the grounds that Negroes had been excluded, and charged fraud when names of Negroes were found. They brought in a handwriting expert who agreed with them. Callahan ruled that the defense's contention that Negroes had been systematically or intentionally excluded from the jury rolls was only a "presumption," a presumption undercut by the discovery of the names of Negroes on the rolls. As for the charge of fraud and the testimony of James Haring, the handwriting expert, Tom Davenport of the Associated Press and the *Decatur Daily* expressed the sentiments of a great many in the courtroom when he called it "confusing." Callahan agreed, saying Haring had "made a confusing issue even more confusing." More damaging to the reception of Haring's testimony was the news that the defense was paying the New Yorker fifty dollars a day. In the halls of the courtroom, one man said that he would have done the job for ten.[5]

Callahan soon discovered that the end of the defense's pretrial maneuvers didn't mean the end of extraneous lines of defense. Leibowitz's cross-examination of Victoria Price and every witness after her was full of questions and insinuations that had nothing to do with the case. In Callahan's countless interruptions and interjections—"move on," "that's enough of that," "let's get on to something else," "don't say another word, not another word"—Leibowitz saw an incompetent and prejudiced judge. In the lawyer's persistent questions, Judge Callahan saw an overbearing, arrogant New Yorker, mistreating the state's witnesses. Leibowitz found each of his attempts to introduce crucial evidence thwarted by the judge. Callahan found his interpretation of the law—his ruling that questions about the victim's activities before the crime, let alone general questions about her character and reputation, were immaterial to the case—challenged and ignored. Leibowitz believed that when the judge cut him off he was consciously trying to stymie the defense. The judge, confident that he knew how the jurors felt about Leibowitz's strategy, thought that he was helping Leibowitz, or preventing him from hurting himself: "The more I shut you off," he said at one point, "the better shape you're in."[6]

To Callahan's dismay, Leibowitz continued to ask "illegal" and "improper" questions of Price, then Gilley, then Lester Carter. And then (in Norris's trial) of Price, Gilley, and Carter again. One of Leibowitz's questions to Carter so angered Callahan he lost his composure, saying that since he had "ruled on that very legal point a half dozen times" there couldn't be anything in Leibowitz's efforts but a "vicious attempt to get before the jury evidence the court ruled inadmissible." By the time he excused the jury in the middle of Norris's trial in order to reprimand Leibowitz for his mistreatment of Orville Gilley and his general lack of respect for the bench, Callahan was certain that Leibowitz's disregard for his rulings was a conscious attempt not to win over the jury but to bait him into doing or saying something disrespectful, to force a reversible error: "I'm doing all in my power to see that the State of Alabama and the defense get a fair trial under our laws and the evidence," he said, but "time after time the attorney for the defense has made improper statements to see if I couldn't be nagged into saying something improper. So far I have not done so and I'm not going to do so."[7]

Callahan and Leibowitz argued about everything: the threat of violence, the venue, the venire, the prejudice of jurors. When Leibowitz argued that the difficulty they had had finding jurors without fixed opinions for Norris's trial was irrefutable proof that a fair trial could not be had in Morgan County and renewed his motion for a change of venue, Callahan denied the motion, saying that "the very fact that the jurors have been honest enough to state that they had fixed opinions indicates to me that the defendant can get a fair trial when a jury finally is picked." Most of all, they argued about rape.[8]

Leibowitz called it a "contemptible and dastardly" crime. But when it came to determining just how "contemptible and dastardly" any particular rape was, or whether a rape had occurred at all, he believed the court had to consider the character and reputation of the victim. He had prefaced his characterization of the crime by saying that he wouldn't be arguing the case if the charge had been brought by a decent, respectable, southern white woman. In this case it had been brought by "a lewd woman," by a "girl hobo." The jury had to know that fact and take it into account.[9]

Callahan and like-minded white southerners argued that the question of character had absolutely nothing to do with the question of rape. If a woman has been "unlawfully violated," Callahan said, "she may appeal to the courts with an abiding faith that no accusing finger can be pointed to her erring past or hopeless future, as an excuse for denying to her full and adequate protection of the law." In its 1932 Scottsboro decision, the Alabama Supreme Court had ruled that "previous chastity" was "not an essential element of rape," that "rape may be committed on an unchaste woman." Newspaper editors said it: "The chastity of the two women victims was made an issue," wrote the editor of the *Memphis Commercial Appeal* after the first Decatur trial, "as if this amounted to anything against their right to protection from physical violence." Attorney General Knight and Jackson County solicitor Bailey, frankly admitting that Victoria Price was not all she should have been, said it again and again: "She has erred, but our laws say no man shall lay a hand on a woman against her will."[10]

Knight said it privately as well. "The perpetrators of the crime were negroes," he had written to a friend in September 1933.

> The victims were women of a very low type, and I presume, or concede for the purposes of argument, that they were of more or less easy virtue. The defendants' counsel stressed the circumstances tending to show their lack of virtue and their environment at the time of the commission of the offense and prior thereto,

> and their low station in life. Conceding that they were able to cast numerous aspersions upon the character of the women, there was one little matter they were unable to brush away and I refused to allow them to pass lightly over this: this was the question of their sex. As hard as the defense tried, they were unable to introduce convincing evidence that the victims were not females.[11]

Callahan and Knight were certain that no white "female" would ever allow a Negro to lay a hand on her. That's why Knight thought Leibowitz's repeated attempts to introduce evidence that Price had been convicted of adultery with Jack Tiller were out of order. "We don't care whether this woman has been convicted for forty offenses, the charge is rape," Knight had said in April. "She has never been convicted for living in adultery with a negro." "Unless there is proof of her lack of chastity with the negro race neither her credibility nor the question of consent is at issue; the fact she might have been convicted or had relations with white people does not mean in any sense of the word she would submit to the embraces of a negro." Knight demanded "proof of her lack of chastity with the negro race" because he was certain that Leibowitz would not have it. Without it, evidence of interracial intercourse was evidence of rape.[12]

Callahan argued that the law forbidding rape protected all women, "regardless of race," and in defense of the Decatur verdicts, a few southern writers cited cases where white men had been convicted of attacks on black women. But white men were rarely arrested, let alone tried and convicted, for the rape of black women. In the minds of most white men there was no such thing. Black women were always willing, so they could never be taken against their will. When white southerners turned the image of the pure white woman inside out, they saw a black whore.[13]

Callahan also implied that the law took seriously the rape of white women regardless of the race of the rapist, and he could have pointed to the prosecution of white men for the rape of white women, particularly in cases in which the rape cut across class lines. But no matter how heinous a white-on-white rape, it was seen as a different category of crime. Trials for white-on-white rape proceeded along more familiar lines, with the rules of evidence and standards of proof unique to rape trials—if not the law of rape—in force. Questions about reputation, character, chastity, and resistance—which the prosecution had to prove to win conviction—

were all in order. When white men were tried for the rape of white women (or black women) accusing fingers were pointed at erring pasts and hopeless futures.

The rape that gave the word its terrifying resonance was the rape of a white woman by a black man. It was the lowest and most horrible crime—few thought Alabama Supreme Court justice Knight had exaggerated when he wrote that what had happened to Victoria Price was worse than murder—and it called for the extreme penalty. "If a white woman is prepared to swear that a Negro either raped her or attempted to rape her," the poet John Gould Fletcher wrote in a letter to *The Nation,* "we see to it that the Negro is executed." "It is a heritage of our race and is implanted in us from birth," wrote William Seibels, solicitor of Montgomery County, "that where a white woman is violated there is only one punishment and that punishment is death."[14]

"This dallying about with the Scottsboro rapists is a humiliating insult to the white race in Alabama and the very worst thing that could happen to the law-abiding negroes of this State," former Alabama senator Thomas Heflin said to Attorney General Knight the day after Judge Horton overturned Haywood Patterson's second conviction. "It is putting wicked thoughts in the minds of the lawless negro men and greatly increasing the danger to the white women of Alabama." Five months later, in his closing arguments at Haywood Patterson's third trial, Attorney General Knight told jurors that they were not "avenging" Victoria Price: "What has been done to her cannot be undone. What you can do now is to see that it doesn't happen to some other woman." When Leibowitz protested that Knight's appeal was an appeal to "passion and prejudice," Knight replied, "It certainly is. It's an appeal to passion . . ." Leibowitz interrupted him with a motion for a mistrial, and after Callahan overruled it, Knight finished his sentence: "We all have a passion, all the men in this courtroom, and that is to protect the womanhood of the State of Alabama."[15]

Callahan, Heflin, and Knight believed black men could not keep themselves from raping white women. Where instinct alone wasn't enough, a desire for revenge, nurtured by generations of white-on-black rape, certainly would provide the push. White women, meanwhile, feared for themselves. "Nowhere in the country are we safe today," a New Orleans woman wrote to George Milton, chairman of the Southern Commission on the Study of Lynching. "Even on the public highways, the situation has become so serious that frequently one or more male escorts fail to prevent the Negro highwayman from having his way." Those fears were fed by the perception that black men were getting bolder. Justice Knight himself had remarked that if Price and Bates were to be believed, the atrocity of the Scottsboro defendants' crime was equaled only "by the boldness with which it was perpetrated." And they were fed by the perception that in their boldness and belligerence, their direct and indirect subversion, black southerners had aggressive white allies for the first time since Reconstruction.[16]

White men feared for their women, and they feared for themselves. They were afraid of violent retribution, afraid of the feelings that they knew they would have had, had blacks treated them the way they treated blacks. They imagined what was being thought, and said, and done behind their backs, and it scared them. In Decatur, in April and November 1933, they were angered by what was said right to their faces, what was done right before their eyes. Southern editors ran headlines about Leibowitz's attack on the jury system. Locals talked more about his attacks on people—jury commissioners, prospective jurors, sitting jurors, storekeepers, farmers, clerks, neighbors, and friends.

Callahan delighted his audience by standing up to Leibowitz. He baited him, just as Leibowitz baited Knight. He frowned at him, scolded him, mocked him, cut him off, and more than once told him to sit down. Callahan came to the defense of white men squirming under Leibowitz's cross-examination as often and as decisively as he came to the defense of Victoria Price. Excluding crucial evidence that Judge Horton had allowed, he said angrily, "I don't care a snap what Judge Horton did or how he ruled. You're before me now and I'll do the ruling." Some spectators laughed; others cheered. Hamilton Basso, a southerner sympathetic to the defense who covered the trial for *The New Republic,* heard one man whisper, "We got us a man on the bench this time. He ain't goin' to be free'n easy like Judge Horton."[17]

The image that dominated Callahan's courtroom was evoked less by Victoria Price's description of the rape than by her description of a dozen gun-and-knife-toting black men leaping into the gondola from the boxcar, yelling, ". . . all you white sons of bitches unload." Price used those words. Then Orville Gilley. Then Wade Wright, who bellowed them again and again, so that, as one reporter put it, "they bounded off the walls of the courtroom like tennis balls." Solicitor Bailey used them. So did Attorney General Knight.[18]

According to the prosecution, those words were the battle cry of the defendants in their assault on the white youths, and in the minds of white southerners, that assault was itself a serious crime. It ended with the Negroes bloodying the white youths and throwing them off the train, and it was the fact that made many assume that whatever the other evidence, the defendants must have raped Price and Bates. And for those who were confused enough by the conflicting testimony to have doubts, that assault was evidence enough that whether or not they raped them, they were still dangerous and ought to be put away.

Much to the chagrin of the liberal editor of the *Birmingham Post,* another Alabama editor, writing in defense of the April verdict, had come right out and said it: even if the Negroes were not guilty of attacking two white girls, they were surely guilty of assaulting nine white boys and throwing them off the train. The *Post*'s editor feared that the Decatur jurors, like that editor, had confused what ought to have been two separate issues: the alleged assault on two white women and the admitted assault on nine white men.[19]

They were not alone. The prosecution also confused the two issues, which is part of the reason why, though the charge was rape, at all three of the Decatur trials Tom Knight called to the stand a half-dozen witnesses who could testify to having seen nothing more than a fight on the train. Knight knew that most white southerners would see the rape—as he, Bailey, Callahan, and Wright saw it—as following inevitably from the fight. He knew they would see the fight as both precursor to the rape and proof that it occurred. In his summation to Haywood Patterson's third jury, Wade Wright made the connection as clear as could be, arguing that Price's and Gilley's stories of the fight—the phrase "all you white sons of bitches unload" in itself—proved that the whole incident was a premeditated crime, "a preconceived play by the blacks, who outnumbered the whites, to take the two girls away from them."[20]

Wright—like Callahan, Bailey, and Knight—could no more neatly or easily separate the attack on the white youths from the attack on Price and Bates than he could have separated his ideas about communism and northern interference from his ideas about white supremacy and segregation; his ideas about white supremacy and segregation from his ideas about black women and men; his ideas about black women and men from his ideas about white women; his ideas about white women from his ideas about rape; his ideas about rape from his fear of black women and men; his fear from his hatred and his hatred from his fear; and his hatred and his fear from his understanding (however ephemeral, mistaken, infinitesimal, unconscious, incomplete) of the thoughts and feelings that had to have lurked in black minds, of the answer to a common question: How would I feel if I were in his skin?

THIRTY

A Jury of Twelve Reputable Citizens

From the point of view of the jury, the prosecution's case in Haywood Patterson's third trial, and Clarence Norris's second, was much stronger than it had been in April. At Patterson's trial, Victoria Price took fifteen minutes to tell her story, and as Tom Davenport reported, "her voice carried throughout the court room in which there was not a vacant seat." Judge, jurors, and spectators "leaned forward" to watch her swing an arm forward, point a finger at Patterson, and say, "That defendant over there, Haywood Patterson, was one of them." A week later they saw her point the same finger at Norris. It had been two and a half years since the rape. She had forgotten or was confused about many details. "I don't remember," she kept saying to Leibowitz during his ninety-minute cross-examination. "It's been nearly three years ago." What she did remember was that Norris had raped her.[1]

That was the seventh time she had testified about the rape. Dramatic as she was, she was no longer the star. The previous week she had been upstaged by an eyewitness to the rape, Orville Gilley, the smiling, blue-eyed, radar-eared, almost handsome twenty-year-old who had insisted he was not (as the defense portrayed him) a bought witness and a bum, but rather a wandering entertainer, a poet of hotel lobbies, restaurants, and the streets. Whatever his calling, he was charming and witty. His replies to questions frequently brought laughter from spectators, jurors, and at least once from both Leibowitz and the judge (when Gilley reeled off the "monikers" by which he and his friends were known: Carolina Slim, Kentucky Kid, and Georgia Chicken). He easily wooed the white southerners in the courtroom, who again "leaned forward and to hear better cupped their hands behind their ears."[2]

Although the details of Gilley's direct testimony differed considerably from Price's, he corroborated her testimony, if not in every detail, or in many details, at least in what the *New York Times*'s Raymond Daniell called the "essential fact." On cross-examination, Leibowitz labored for two hours and forty minutes to point up the most telling contradictions. Yet Gilley remained "unruffled," and the most damning contradictions and disparities between his story and Price's were lost in the larger picture he drew of nine Negroes, waving guns and knives, leaping into the car. They shouted "all you white sons of bitches unload," threw him and his companions off the train, and then repeatedly raped both girls. Gilley said he had climbed back on, but found himself at the mercy of a Negro with a gun. The rape ended only when he convinced that Negro to make the others stop "before they killed that woman." Clarence Mitchell, correspondent for the *Baltimore Afro-American,* wrote that Gilley's was "undoubtedly the strongest corroborative evidence the state could have produced." In many ways he was a "stronger witness" than Price.[3]

Lester Carter, the white youth who had been traveling with Gilley, Price, and Bates, returned to Decatur to testify for the defense. But Callahan blocked so many of Leibowitz's questions to him that he left the stand, in Daniell's words, "without having contributed much more than some expert testimony about the proper way to board and alight from a moving freight train." Callahan did not allow "a word from the graphic description" Carter had given in April "of the romantic night he and Orville Gilley spent with the two girls in the hobo jungle near the freight yards in Chattanooga" to "creep into the record of this trial." Nor more than a hint, from Carter or subsequent witnesses, of who, besides the defendants, might have deposited the semen that Dr. Bridges found in Victoria Price's vagina. Whenever Leibowitz succeeded, in spite of Callahan, to get in front of the jury evidence of Price's and Bates's activities in the two days before the train ride, the judge left no doubt in the jurors' minds that he thought it immaterial. Ruby Bates had remained in New York, and Callahan had given

Patterson's case to the jury before her deposition arrived; the defense read to Norris's jury the parts of that deposition to which the judge and prosecution did not object.[4]

Haywood Patterson again took the stand in his own defense. He admitted that he had "cussed" the white boy who had called him "black son of bitches, and nigger son of bitches"—"I called him mother-fuckers, son of bitches, and everything"—but again insisted that he hadn't even seen any women on the train. Knight then introduced as evidence testimony from the trial at Scottsboro, where Patterson had said that although he and his friends hadn't touched Price and Bates, the other five defendants had. When Leibowitz tried to introduce the remainder of that testimony, in which Patterson had said that he hadn't seen any girls before Paint Rock, Callahan cut him off.[5]

The state's case was strong, and its summations were as effective as they had been in April. Morgan County solicitor Wade Wright reviewed Price's story and argued that the state had provided corroboration in the testimony of Orville Gilley, the testimony of "old brother Hill" (the Paint Rock station agent), and the testimony of the white farmers along the railroad tracks who had seen the girls "a-fixin' to get out" and being dragged back by the defendants. Wright told the jurors to keep "in mind that this crime could have happened to any woman, even though she were riding in a parlor car instead of a box car."[6]

Jackson County solicitor Bailey pleaded against passion and prejudice, reminding the jurors that although the story told by Gilley and Price was "as sordid as ever a human tongue has uttered," the defendant was "clothed with a presumption of innocence until" they found him guilty. Bailey said that Carter had come to Decatur "breathing the very atmosphere of a certain strata in that big metropolis up yonder" but he had yet to explain "why he fled and left these defenseless women with a fight going on in the boxcar next to him." As for Price and Bates, Bailey said he didn't care what the defense said about them—"let them say what they want." "Instead of painting their faces and standing on the streets of Huntsville, they were brave enough to go to Chattanooga and look for honest work. They are not as fortunate as some girls, not petted and pampered and raised in the lap of luxury."[7]

All the defense had done, Bailey argued, was "offer the testimony of the Negroes that 'it just didn't happen' " and "cry 'frame up, frame up.' " "They say this is a frame-up! They have been yelling frame-up ever since this case started! Who framed them? Did Ory Dobbins frame them? Did Brother Hill frame them? We did a lot of awful things over there in Scottsboro, didn't we? My. My. My. And now they come over here and try to convince you that that sort of thing happened in your neighboring county."[8]

Knight pulled no stops, but it was in Callahan's charge that jurors heard the most sustained argument for the state's case. He began by telling the jury that rape was "defined by the law to be carnal knowledge of a woman forcibly against her will." The force could be mental as well as physical. The victim did not have to resist; she had only to withhold her consent, and "consent or acquiescence obtained by duress or fear of personal violence" was "no consent at all." If the woman was "overpowered by a display of physical force" or the threat of force and she ceased "resistance through fear of great harm, the consummation of unlawful intercourse" was rape.[9]

"Where the woman charged to have been raped, as in this case, is a white woman, there is a very strong presumption under the law that she will not and did not yield voluntarily to intercourse with the defendant, a Negro," Callahan said. "And this is true whatever the station in life the prosecutrix may occupy, whether she be the most despised, ignorant and abandoned woman of the community, or the spotless virgin and daughter of a prominent home of luxury and learning."[10]

If Patterson was at the scene of the crime for the "purpose of aiding, encouraging, assisting or abetting in any way the commission of the crime," he was "as guilty as the one who committed the offense, although he never moved a muscle or said a word." Conspiracy, Callahan said, "need not be proven by positive evidence"; its "existence and extent" were to be determined by the jury "from the conduct of the parties charged with the conspiracy." "It may be a mere gesture or a mere nod, or it may be inferred that there was a conspiracy by a consideration of all the acts and circumstances and situations of the case at the time."

By way of contrast, and perhaps rebuke, to Judge Horton, Callahan told jurors that the law governing rape did not require corroboration; if they believed Price's story, that was enough to convict. Then he pointed out that the state had offered as corroboration Bates's original accusation, Gilley's testimony, and Price's and Gilley's descriptions of the fight on the train. The prosecution, Callahan said, claimed that both Price and Gilley had given a first-hand account of the fight, and in that account they had been corroborated by other witnesses "who saw the scuffle or alleged scuffle, or fight, and saw some of them jump off or be thrown off, and that blood was on their faces and on their persons."

The defense, Callahan said, admitted that there had been a fight. But it contended that the fight was not a "part" or "forerunner" of "the rape that then and there or afterward occurred." It was simply a fight, a fight between the white boys and the Negroes. The white boys were "put off" and "the blood that was found on them afterward was the direct result of that fight" and "there was no rape in connection with it."

"Well, that is a matter that you have to deal with," Callahan said. "I can't help you on that. That is a matter of weighing evidence," a matter of "drawing conclusions from evidence." He then reminded jurors that they could not consider any questions that he had ruled out of order, or speculate about the answers to questions that he had ruled out of order, or consider any answer that he had ruled out of order, without violating their oath. If "the evidence that the court declared to be illegal and improper" were to "drift into the jury box . . . then we have no law. And when we have no law the government fails."

"When a witness takes this stand," Callahan said, "he himself becomes evidence. You may look at his countenance. God Almighty's hand can be seen in his face by one who can study. . . . You may look at his conduct on the stand. . . . How does he impress you by the way he looks, by the way he acts and by the way he talks? Then, again, you are authorized in looking at him, to apply your common sense, your observation. What sort of a story is it he is telling? Is it reasonable? . . . You may look at a witness's environment . . . his associates, his companions. Has he any bias?"

Callahan noted that "something" had been said "about the defendant's being a Negro." "No man," he said, "is worthy to be in the jury box that would reach the guilt or innocence of a man on any such contemptible grounds." Finally he told jurors that if they were satisfied beyond a reasonable doubt that the defendant was guilty, their verdict should be guilty, and that the guilty verdict could take two forms. They could find the defendant guilty as charged and fix the punishment at death; or find him guilty and fix the punishment at so many years in the penitentiary, but not less than ten.

What he didn't tell them was how they could find the defendant not guilty. Leibowitz rushed to the bench, followed by Knight, and "a whispered conference ensued." When it was over, Callahan said, "I believe I overlooked one thing about the forms of verdict." He then gave them the form for acquittal.[11]

After the April trial, the editor of the *Huntsville Builder* had summed up the case to date by noting that "almost immediately following the incident that happened near Scottsboro, Patterson, along with other Negroes, was tried before a jury of twelve reputable citizens of Scottsboro and sentenced to death. The same Negro, Patterson, was again tried before twelve reputable citizens in Morgan County in April, and sentenced to death." For that editor and many other observers, those facts were among the strongest evidence not only of what had happened in the courtroom but also of what had happened on a freight train two years before.[12]

Eight months later, Patterson's third conviction and Norris's second were more of the same: "With three different juries agreeing on the man's guilt, wrote the editor of the *Strasburg* (Virginia) *Daily* the day after Patterson's trial, "it is reasonable to assume that the evidence to this effect must have been unusually strong. Even admitting that a prejudice against Negroes accused of this particular crime exists in Alabama, few men would care to have the blood of an innocent man on their conscience. It is therefore unthinkable that three juries, of twelve men each, should unanimously agree on a verdict of death unless the evidence abundantly supported the allegation of guilt."[13]

PART THREE

1934–1941

THIRTY-ONE

Our Stories Would Not Be Agreeable

While Norris's jury was deliberating, Leibowitz asked Judge Callahan to postpone the remaining trials. He argued that the constitutional questions raised by Patterson's second and third trials made an appeal to the Supreme Court certain, barring reversal by the Alabama Supreme Court. "These trials may be only an empty gesture after the higher courts have reviewed them," Leibowitz said. Ever sensitive to the cost of the trials, Callahan granted the motion.[1]

After the jury returned its verdict, Callahan sentenced Norris and Patterson, scheduling their executions for February 2, 1934, and immediately suspended those sentences, pending appeals. Sheriffs drove all the defendants to Birmingham. Two days later, Patterson and Norris were moved to Kilby, where the warden put them back on death row. They knew, from newspapers and the sudden ebb in visitors and mail, that few observers were any more surprised by the verdicts than they had been. There was public outrage and indignation—the bigots of Alabama had done it again—but the edges of both were tempered by resignation. With the remaining trials postponed, people turned their attention elsewhere. Defense attorneys, accompanied to the state line by private detectives and special deputies, returned to New York, where they turned to the tedious, unsensational work of preparing bills of exceptions.

"Now lawyer please," Patterson wrote to Benjamin Davis, Jr., in January 1934, "Clarence Norris and myself are in dire need of a little money here." They needed "smokes and other things," for "conditions" were "very very different" from the Birmingham jail, where they had been from the beginning of Patterson's second trial in March to the end of Norris's third trial in December 1933. There, Patterson wrote, "we could make friends and have them to bring us such as we need. but we can't see anyone and we are badly in need. please don't desert me." The next day he wrote to ILD chief William Patterson: "I hardly realize just how to express my appreciations to you and the many friends for the untold happiness you afford we poor Boys while pent up here from the pleasures and freedom that life holds. We are praying and trusting in you all and the good Lord for freedom and salvation." He and Clarence needed newspapers, magazines, stamps, paper, and "something good to eats." Kilby was different from Birmingham, Patterson said, but as in Birmingham, money will "mean much towards our happiness."[2]

One of the chief guards told Patterson he could receive packages and money—prisoners with money meant guards with money—but not letters from Communists. Patterson asked his mother to tell William Patterson to tell his "Friends" to stop sending letters: they angered the guards, and the guards took it out on them. Correctly assuming that the guards read the letters he wrote as well as the ones he received, he closed by reporting: "I like in the way I am being treated here I likes everything that come before me God knows I does. . . . So I am to be real good as good as can Be and obey all of the prisoner's rules here regardless to what they are I am going to obey them all for I wish to be treated right by each and everyone. . . ."[3]

Then a guard got greedy, and Patterson stopped receiving money. In May he wrote to his mother to say that he was "getting along as best" he could "under the circumstances." But the circumstances weren't good. He asked her to tell William Patterson that he was being held "incommunicado": "I sincerely hope that it wont be much longer before someone comes down to see me as I wish for a few things to be known." In August he wrote to Joseph Brodsky to say that he and Norris were in "fairly good health" but that they were "not doing so well under the conditions." "Things are not going so well with us," he said. "We have made several requests asking for someone to come down. I would like to see you or someone else on some very interesting business We are trusting that someone will be down in the near future as early as possible." He asked Brodsky to send magazines. *True Detective* was his favorite, but any "good reading" would help them pass the time.[4]

Patterson and Norris wished they were in Birmingham, but in the spring and summer of 1934, the other seven defendants were in even worse shape than they were. Shortly after their return to the Birmingham jail in December, after the trials of Patterson and Norris, the guards had jumped all over them, as if they knew—everyone else did—that the appeals were likely to take years. Weems wrote at the beginning of January 1934 to say that the guards were "only half feeding" them. The six-foot-four twenty-one-year-old had been losing weight steadily since his arrest. "I ask them for something more to eat," he wrote, but they "put me in the dog house. Please send someone down real soon."[5]

Weems had lost his mother when he was four years old and six of his seven siblings when he was a boy. He began public school at seven, and made it through the fifth grade, quitting to work in a pharmacy when his father got too old to support the family. When his father got sick, Weems was sent to live with an aunt in Riverdale, Georgia. He went to a rural school in Riverdale, and he did his best while he was there. But he wasn't there for long. "I let love get between me and my lessons," he wrote. "Just like a lots of boys do and then I stopped school and went to work, but I have always worked hard ever since." In Riverdale he worked on a farm in the spring, summer, and fall and on a road gang in the winter. He had left home for Chattanooga just a few weeks before he was pulled off the train.[6]

The "doghouse," often called the "hole," was a tiny cell without windows. Weems was given a blanket for a bed and a bucket for a toilet. Shortly after he was returned to his regular cell, guards found him reading literature the ILD had sent him. They fired tear gas at him through the bars of his cell, dragged him out of the cell, and beat him with a gun until he fell on his knees, praying for mercy. The more he prayed, the more they beat him. Months later, his eyes still felt as if they had pepper in them; he couldn't read or write and wondered if he needed glasses. He asked his ILD correspondents not to say "anything about the strikes" in Birmingham's mines and mills.[7]

Roy Wright and Eugene Williams expressed their own frustration with the ILD in a letter to Frieda Brown, of the ILD's Prisoners Relief Fund. In her last letter, Brown had asked them about the holiday season. They replied that they had spent the holidays "somewhat in despare as usual," because nothing had been done to make them comfortable. And Brown had asked them to send her their stories: "Oh! Yes," they wrote, "you said that our stories could be used in your press." Wright and Williams didn't think so: "We do not think . . . our stories would be agreeable with you all, and with the public because we would be letting the public [know] just how we are fairing and just what we think about you all. . . ." Wright said that he had been paying "very close attention to the spaces" that William Patterson had "left in his writings," and "very close attention to Mr. Chamlee's talking and also his writings," and he had come to the conclusion that they were "just as crooked as the rest of them are including our attorneys." It had been thirty-three months since their trials in Scottsboro. Chamlee had said that their cases were "nothing much" and that he "could easily get" them "out." Why didn't he?[8]

In March, all of the defendants in Birmingham were put in solitary confinement after a guard, breaking up a fight in the prison yard, took a knife away from Andy Wright. Wright claimed that another prisoner had attacked his brother with the knife, whereupon he jumped in and wrested the knife from the assailant's hand. The solitary cells were smaller and darker than the regular cells; instead of beds they had shelves that folded down from the wall. Some cells had solid steel doors with peepholes in them; some had bars. In solitary, guards confiscated books and magazines at whim. For days at a time, guards fed them nothing but bread and water and would not let them out of their cells for any reason. They blamed their poor treatment on one particular guard, "Captain Dan Rogers," who got his pleasure waving a pistol at them, beating them, and making them call him "massah." Rogers cursed the Communists and the New York Jews, and he cursed the youths for corresponding with them, and, worse, for receiving them when they came to visit. Rogers promised the boys that their lives would be much easier if only they dumped the "Reds."[9]

The guards' condemnation of the Communists had Olen Montgomery worried—as much for his mother as for himself. Now in her early forties, Viola Montgomery had begun her working life when she was twelve. She had washed, ironed, cooked, cleaned, farmed, and looked after other people's children for twenty-five cents a day. As an adult she had worked for as little as a dollar and a half a week—the most she had ever earned was ten dollars a week. Married at fifteen, she had had five children, one of whom was born dead. A second died of pneumonia at two. Her husband gambled, drank, and chewed tobacco; he worked only now and again. Olen's parents had quarreled often and split up when he was nine.[10]

Olen was born in Monroe, Georgia, in 1913, began school at seven, and went through the fifth grade. He did third grade twice because he "messed around, got lazy and played too much." He quit when he was about fourteen, to help his mother. He delivered groceries, then worked for a construction company, then at a fertilizer plant; he left the plant when one of the bosses "cursed" him. "Some folks would have put up with it," he said, "but I just could never stand to be cussed at." Badly nearsighted in both eyes, and going blind from a cataract in one, Montgomery left Monroe for Memphis in March 1931 to find a job that would provide money for a new pair of glasses. (The pair he had was broken the day he was arrested, and he went without a new pair for two years. After a visit to the Birmingham jail in May 1933, Benjamin Davis reported that Montgomery could not "see a match stem in his own hand.")[11]

Viola Montgomery took to the ILD early, and three years of Party work had only increased her enthusiasm. In one week in the fall of 1932 she had obtained signatures on six hundred protest postcards, addressed to the justices of the Supreme Court. "I am with the Party as long as I live," she wrote in February 1934. "I don't care who likes it or who don't like it. . . . I like it because it believes in every man or woman to have a right to a decent living. . . . I tell the world I want to be somebody but I can't under this government. This so called government has put many a good woman in the garbage can, and put the lid on it, but I tell the world I will fight like hell to stay out and I want the rest of my comrades to do the same."[12]

Writing from solitary, Olen had another view. On May 3 he wrote to tell his mother that she shouldn't worry about his asking the ILD for money and things: "The I.L.D. don't send me enough money to buy 3 package of cigarettes hardly. And I got my shoes in pawned and my hat and I want them out before the fellow get tried and go off and I want my shoes and hat. I had to pawn them so I could smoke." He wrote again the next day, after receiving a letter in which his mother had asked him if he had heard or read about the recent May Day meetings in Birmingham. "Listen," he wrote, "I don't care anything about it. Other words I didn't see it and I didn't want to see it. Such as that ain't no good. It only making it hard on me here in jail and I know it. That thing they had here on May Day what good did it do. Not any at all. I'm still locked up in the cell. Instead of the I.L.D. trying to make it better for me here in jail they are making it harder for me by trying to demand the people to do things. Listen, send me some money. Send me three dollars like I told you in my first letter."[13]

Inmates ordinarily remained in solitary for fourteen days, and confinement for more than twenty-one days was rare. The defendants had been in for four months when representatives of the National Committee for the Defense of Political Prisoners, led by the playwright John Lawson, visited them in July. They told Lawson they had recently gone an entire week without food.[14]

Along with bad treatment, 1934 brought bad news. First came word that Attorney General Knight and Judge Callahan had tricked the defense into missing a deadline for a motion to Judge Callahan for a new trial. Then an airplane carrying the bill of exceptions for Patterson's appeal to the Alabama Supreme Court crashed, causing the defense to miss that court's deadline also. At the end of June, the Alabama Supreme Court upheld the convictions, ruling that Patterson's bill of exceptions hadn't been filed in time and that Norris's rights had not been violated in any way: not by the selection of an all-white jury; not by Callahan's conduct of the trial; and certainly not by Callahan's refusal to admit evidence of Price's sexual relations the night before the crime.[15]

The Alabama Supreme Court scheduled the executions for August 31, and Patterson and Norris had to live with that date ahead of them until July 9, when the defense filed a motion for a rehearing and Callahan suspended the executions. The court denied the motion on October 4 and rescheduled the executions for December 7. Norris and Patterson lived with that day until November 16, when the state Supreme Court granted a sixty-day stay, time for appeals to the U.S. Supreme Court. It was a difficult year, and it ended in the worst possible way, with another protracted struggle for control of the defense, this time between Leibowitz and the ILD.[16]

All the defendants knew for sure was that Brodsky and Leibowitz and each man's friends were at one another's throats. Both sides argued vehemently and persuasively; both sides insisted on their undivided allegiance. ILD people told them that Leibowitz, hungry for fame and bitter because they hadn't picked him to argue the appeals before the Supreme Court, had joined the lynchers. Leibowitz told them that the ILD's shenanigans—the latest, he said, was an attempt to bribe Victoria Price—only stiffened the resolve of the Alabamans who wanted to execute them. Even sympathetic southerners turned against them when they saw red. If having Leibowitz and his aides talk into one ear while ILD attorneys and their aides talked into the other wasn't confusing enough, the youths' parents also had strong opinions, opinions which, like their sons', were subject to change. And even when they were alone in prison, the youths were not free from advice. Wardens and guards cursed the ILD and Leibowitz alike and urged them to find themselves an Alabama attorney.[17]

"So here we were," Clarence Norris recalled, "stuck in the middle again. The people who had our lives in their hands were fighting among themselves. The press had a field day, the Southern press loved it." Editors smugly quoted Leibowitz's criticisms of the ILD and its criticism of him, concluding that both sides were right and that they had been saying the same things all along. The northern press, moderate and radical, castigated both sides and begged for peace in the interest of the defendants. "We signed papers for Leibowitz that he was our lawyer and nobody else," Norris said. "Then we signed papers to the same effect with Joe Brodsky. We didn't know what to do."[18]

"I am half-crazy," Haywood Patterson wrote one October day, explaining that he could no longer remember which affidavit he had signed for whom and when he had signed it. The next day he said he was completely crazy—"crazy all the time." They were crazy with confusion, especially Patterson and Norris, who were at the center of the fight, and few blamed them. They were pushed and pulled in so many different directions and the strain was made all the more painful by a wish in the form of a question that nagged at them at all times and that neither side's explanations could allay: Why do I have to choose?[19]

Norris told Brodsky that he did "not think anyone could find any greater friend." "I will always have the highest respect toward you. Every living thing that you have did for me since the dawn of this frame up against me are appreciated." Yet he had signed up with Leibowitz, and his "intention" was "to stick with him." "I prefer having him above all others. I feel like he is able to defend me in any court in the land."[20]

Haywood Patterson simply could not choose one or the other. "We are looking forward with great Confidence that you all will put forth every efforts possible onward in getin the Cases before the supreme Court of the united states where I Can rest assure that I will receive justice outright," he wrote to Osmond Fraenkel, the constitutional lawyer retained by the ILD to argue the appeal before the Supreme Court. "Now I am greatly sorry there was a little Disagreements between Mr. Leibowitz and you and of his dissent to agree to you all attitudes and opinions well as you may understand He is always that way about things and in Deference to you all opinions I am with the hopes that Mr. Leibowitz will change his attitudes and be agreeable."[21]

Patterson understood that an inflexible organization was doing battle with an inflexible man. Still he couldn't quite understand why each side had to agree to everything the other side thought and said in order to work together. Along with his parents, he believed the Party's meetings and marches had saved his life. Yet Leibowitz had been at his side through two difficult trials. Having sensed the depth of Leibowitz's belief in his innocence, having seen the determination with which Leibowitz fought for his freedom, Patterson had a faith in the lawyer that neither the year and a half in prison since Leibowitz had taken over the defense nor two guilty verdicts could shake. "I love him more than life itself," Patterson wrote to the playwright John Wexley, in a letter thanking him for *They Shall Not Die,* Wexley's play about the case. "He is such a mighty great man I think such a lot of him in case I should live 19 years from today I will remember him. Now Mr. Wexley you will excuse my expression which it are a little different from yours now I wish the play will bring forth good results."[22]

Patterson put his opinion of the fight most bluntly in a letter to Brodsky at the end of October: "As I have alred say I dont care who represent me before the United States Supreme Court and whosoever intend to present the appeal wish they would go right along and stop so much talks about it."[23]

T H I R T Y – T W O

Jobs You Want to Do

Leibowitz had a fit when he learned, from a reporter who had called to find out what he knew about the story, that two lawyers associated with Joseph Brodsky and the ILD had been arrested in Nashville on October 1, 1934, and charged with attempting to bribe Victoria Price. Police said that the men had tried first in August, offering to pay her $500 to sign an affidavit repudiating her testimony. Price feigned interest and then reported the offer to the police. The next time the lawyers approached her, this time with an offer of $1,000, she set them up. Leibowitz summoned Brodsky to his office and demanded an explanation, and Brodsky explained: the men hadn't approached Price; she had approached them. Had she kept her word, she would have broken the prosecution. Leibowitz was not satisfied. He didn't care who had approached whom. He did not want people to think he bribed witnesses. He told Brodsky in "brutal English" that he had "assassinated the Scottsboro boys with that sort of business." It was high time for the ILD to get out of the case. Brodsky, now angry himself, warned Leibowitz not to make a fuss. "If you do," he said, "I will put you out."[1]

After Brodsky left, Leibowitz called Walter White, William Davis (publisher of the *Amsterdam News*), and several Harlem ministers. He met with White and the NAACP's assistant secretary,

Roy Wilkins, at four that afternoon. He told them he would have to quit the case if the Communists didn't, but that he wouldn't go without first trying to oust them. He suddenly recalled every reservation he had had when William Patterson first approached him in January 1933, every regret in the two years since, every criticism or angry word he had kept to himself, either because he wanted to keep the peace or because during those difficult days in Decatur his sense of solidarity was greater than his annoyance. He had thought that at least in this case the Communists had done more good than bad—until they tried to bribe Price.

Speaking to reporters the next day, Leibowitz charged that Party officials had made a circus of the case. In the middle of the first Decatur trial, they sent telegrams to Judge Horton. After the trial, they paraded witnesses around the country, raising huge sums of money to free the Scottsboro Boys and then using that money to fund Communist Party election campaigns. In private meetings with Walter White and his associates, Leibowitz spoke angrily of the Party's idiotic use of Ruby Bates. He had warned Party people not to bring her to New York, not to dress her up in New York clothes, and not to have her barnstorming around the country after the trial. He told them to let her tell the truth where she had told the lie. Most southerners believed that Bates's sudden disappearance, reappearance, and recantation had been arranged by the Communists and paid for with Moscow gold. Now that the ILD had been caught trying to bribe Price, what fool would waste one breath trying to persuade them they were wrong?

Leibowitz dispatched two of his assistants and two ministers to Kilby Prison; they secured pledges of support from Haywood Patterson and Clarence Norris. ILD officials responded by firing Leibowitz and sending Ben Davis and Ida Norris to Kilby to tell Patterson and Norris the same thing that *Daily Worker* editors told their readers: the bribery charge was one more Scottsboro frame-up, and Leibowitz had fallen for it. Davis and Norris returned with affidavits repudiating Leibowitz and supporting the ILD. Leibowitz sent John Terry, his secretary, to meet with George Chamlee in Chattanooga and together the two men traveled to Montgomery. ILD people were visiting the boys when they arrived and tried, unsuccessfully, to keep Terry and Chamlee away from their cell. Terry returned to New York with the defendants back on his boss's side. The ILD turned to the boys' parents. Leibowitz himself traveled to Alabama to appeal to the boys. The tug-of-war went on until January 1935, when the Supreme Court agreed to review Norris's and Patterson's appeals. With Norris wanting Leibowitz and Patterson wanting the ILD (and Leibowitz), the two sides agreed to a cease-fire and a division of the legal labor. Leibowitz, officially representing Norris, would argue the facts, after which Walter Pollak (who had argued *Powell* v. *Alabama* in 1932) and Osmond Fraenkel, officially representing Patterson, would connect them to constitutional law.[2]

February 15 was the day, and partly because he was nervous, partly because he knew that this wasn't the place for histrionics, Leibowitz's delivery was as plain as his argument. Alabama law didn't exclude Negroes from juries, he said. But the people who administered the law did. The practice was so widespread, and had been for so long, that it was no longer a subject of great controversy. As the jury commissioners themselves had said: it was not even discussed. Only when he got around to explaining the names forged on the jury rolls did Leibowitz let himself get carried away. The forgery was fraud, he cried, a crime against the defendants, a crime against the Supreme Court itself.[3]

Chief Justice Charles Evans Hughes interrupted to ask if he could prove that. Leibowitz said he could. A page brought in the jury roll and a magnifying glass. Hughes looked first and then passed the book to Justice Van Devanter, who passed it to Justice Brandeis. Brandeis passed it to Justice Butler, who used the glass, Butler to Justice Roberts, and when Roberts signaled that he was through, the page carried the big book to Justice Stone at the other end. None of them said a word, but Leibowitz saw disgust on their faces, and apparently Thomas Knight did too. Knight, who was now the lieutenant governor of Alabama (having been elected to that office a year earlier, in the spring of 1934, in the same election in which Judge Horton was defeated), defended the process of jury selection before the Court. But he told the justices he honestly couldn't say whether or not the names had been forged.[4]

A month and a half later the court delivered *Norris* v. *Alabama*, reversing the Alabama Supreme Court and remanding Norris's and Patterson's cases to Alabama. "I am thrilled beyond words," Leibowitz said. The decision was "the culmination of the hopes and ambitions of 15,000,000 Negro souls in America." Leibowitz said that the defendants could not be reindicted or tried except by a grand jury and a petit jury drawn from rolls with Negroes on them. He doubted that they would be retried. When Lieutenant Governor

Knight announced that he would seek new indictments immediately, Leibowitz tried to go over his head, traveling to Montgomery to meet with Alabama's new governor, Bibb Graves. Graves, who was in the middle of the all-important first legislative session of his term, said he couldn't spare the time to meet with him. So Leibowitz sent a messenger to the State House with a letter asking for an unconditional pardon. Leibowitz called Graves's attention to Horton's opinion—"an indictment of the prosecution of these defendants as a dastardly frame-up germinating out of the depraved mind of a veteran harlot and jail bird." He noted that southern as well as northern journalists had thought the verdict a mockery of justice, and he reminded Graves that the longer the state kept the case alive, the more profitable it would be for Communists using it to gain recruits among southern Negroes. Leibowitz urged Graves to use his pardon power before Alabama wasted thousands of dollars on another round of senseless trials. Put an end to "the mad pursuit of these boys," he wrote; stop the "carousel of hate."[5]

Leibowitz had called *Norris* v. *Alabama* a "triumph for American justice" and an answer to all the "subversive elements" who sought to "engender hatred against our form of government." The Communists thought it a victory for mass protest over American injustice, and with their clashing interpretations of the Court's decision the war of words between Leibowitz and the Party began anew. But by the summer, little more than habit and enmity drove it along. All the defendants had drifted to Leibowitz's side, or were on their way, and the Comintern had made Popular Front coalitions and cooperation the order of the day. In September 1935, the ILD's Robert Minor asked the NAACP's Walter White if he was interested in forming a united defense. When White said no, Minor approached Norman Thomas, asking him to use his influence to get White and other liberals at least to talk.[6]

Negotiations began in October and lasted three months. Walter White, White's closest aides, and most of the black leaders who a year earlier had organized the American Scottsboro Committee to back Leibowitz in his fight with the ILD, could not have been warier of cosponsoring any defense organization in which the ILD was involved. Battered and bruised from four years of Communist abuse, they asked: How many times, and how disingenuously, had the Party talked of cooperation before? Others, led by Roger Baldwin and Morris Ernst, thought the Communists could be contained in a broadly based defense committee headed by non-Communists.

But what, Baldwin and his allies wondered, was to be done with Leibowitz?[7]

Leibowitz knew that most of those talking of a united defense wanted him out of the case. For some, he thought, it was a matter of ideology; they didn't like that he wasn't a radical and couldn't stomach the idea of allying themselves with a man who defended gangsters and anyone else willing to pay his fee. For others, it was a matter of expediency: they didn't think that a New York Jew, let alone a Jew who had called jurors "lantern-jawed morons," could win the case. He knew that they wanted him out. He also knew that many of his critics, once they had flashed their anti-Leibowitz credentials, had to go on to explain why, if he did not withdraw, he was better suited to lead the defense than anyone they were likely to find. "He wasn't their choice," they would say. "He should withdraw voluntarily." "The ILD should never have brought him into the case." Then, as much as it pained his critics to admit it, they would add: "He has the complete confidence of the defendants." "He knows the case better than anyone." "He works without a fee."[8]

Confident that his critics would be as unhappy without him as they were with him, and unconcerned about being wanted so long as he was needed, Leibowitz kept aloof while White, Wilkins, Baldwin, and Minor negotiated and several times nearly called it quits. Then he readily agreed to a compromise worked out by Norman Thomas. Leibowitz would remain in charge of the defense, but he promised to allow a local lawyer, retained by the committee, to examine prospective jurors and the state's complaining witnesses. It wasn't much of a compromise; he himself had thought that at the next trial he ought to lie low. The last week of December 1935, five groups—the ILD, the NAACP, the ACLU, the LID (Norman Thomas's League for Industrial Democracy), and the Methodist Federation for Social Service—joined together to form the Scottsboro Defense Committee, under the direction of a minister named Allan Knight Chalmers.[9]

Around New York, meanwhile, Leibowitz did nothing to discourage talk that his days as a criminal lawyer might be numbered. A reporter mentioned to him that those who followed his career were surprised when he had agreed to lead the Scottsboro defense, a job that involved principles and publicity a long way from home—but no other remuneration. "It didn't seem to be in your line," the reporter said. "Where will you be going from here?"

"It's not bad to get where you can take on jobs because you want to do them," Leibowitz said, adding that someday soon he might like to switch sides of the aisle: "Well after all I've learned as a criminal lawyer in this town, I'd make a tough District Attorney." The reporter asked what the crooks he had defended would think of that. Leibowitz replied: "There would be flocks of them leaving town."[10]

T H I R T Y – T H R E E

Blessed and Damned

When a guard arrived at his cell on April 1, 1935, with news of the Supreme Court decision, Haywood Patterson assumed the man was teasing him, taking him for an April fool. He refused to come to the bars: "You must think I'm drunk if I believe that," he said. Even before a second guard arrived with a telegram from Leibowitz, something in the first guard's face or tone of voice made Patterson realize he was for real. He laughed loudly and began to shout, "A new trial. A new trial. A new trial."[1]

Clarence Norris called the news to death-row neighbor Willie Winton, who ten days earlier had received an execution-eve reprieve from Alabama governor Graves. Winton had been convicted of the murder of two white men, but at his final interview with the pardon board and the governor he held so tenaciously to the claim of self-defense he had made at his trial that Graves decided to take thirty days to study the case. Norris asked Winton to write a letter to Leibowitz, dictating down the row: "Dear Sir. Your telegram was received and it is beyond words how I felt and feel over being granted a new trial. I am a happy person to know that the grand argument which you made for this new trial was a great success." Norris expected that the "high courts opinion" would "pave an avenue" for his complete freedom in his next trial. Until then, he wondered if Leibowitz could get him out of Kilby: "If it is possible

I would like very much to be transferred back with the other boys in Birmingham, where I can get some exercise. I am in need of it in the worst."[2]

Only Patterson and Norris would have gone to the chair if, for whatever reason, the Court had ruled the other way. But *Norris* v. *Alabama* touched many other black Americans profoundly, in ways that lawyerly talk of precedents and rights (rights that the person talking usually enjoyed) could not convey. It touched black Americans as mothers and fathers and sisters and brothers, for they knew that the blight that had struck those boys could just as easily have struck their kin. They celebrated the decision as if it had been their own boys the Court had spared and given another shot at justice.[3]

The decision also touched them, particularly black southerners, as citizens without legal power. They experienced the law not as something that black and white people did to one another, as Constitution and democratic common sense said it ought to be, but as something that white people did to black people. White champions of the defendants and white advocates of civil rights understood that the South's laws and criminal justice system were unjust and could list a dozen reasons why. But to know that injustice as black people knew it, it was necessary to know it in the parts of the body that produce nausea, chills, sweat, and tears, to have it knock the wind out of you and triple the beat of your heart.

Knowledge of southern justice came in part from fear of it, and fear came from the knowledge that the color of your skin made you a suspect—a suspect that looked just like the prime suspect—every time the police were looking for a black man. It came from the knowledge that if arrested, you were likely to be subjected to the third degree; if indicted, you were likely to be unrepresented; if convicted, sentenced to a longer term in prison or on the chain gang than a white man convicted of the same crime. The fear came from the near inescapability of the danger, the sense that no matter how careful and deliberate your every expression, word, and deed, no matter how unblemished your past, how fine and widely recognized your reputation, no matter how prosperous you were or how well placed, no matter how unshakable your alibi, you were not immune from false accusation, mistaken identity, wrongful conviction, and punishment.

The fear of southern justice came from the knowledge that in the organized hysteria that so often followed reports of assault, murder, riot, insurrection, and rape, you might be beaten or killed because white men suspected you committed a crime. Or because, in the absence of a suspect, they thought the punishment of any black person, as an example to all, would be better than the punishment of none. The fear, in thinking about Scottsboro, came from the knowledge that in the course of two weeks, nine boys, two of them pathetically ill, had been pulled off a freight train at gunpoint, accused by complete strangers of a crime they knew absolutely nothing about, badgered and beaten for confessions to a rape that did not happen, brought before a white judge, defended by one white lawyer who was scared and didn't want the job and by a second who didn't want the job and may have been drunk, examined and cross-examined by hostile white solicitors, and finally found guilty and sentenced to death by an all-white juries. Afterward, when the boys complained, or others complained on their behalf, they were told they were lucky to be alive.

In a unanimous opinion written by Chief Justice Charles Evans Hughes, the U.S. Supreme Court agreed with the defense that Negroes had been arbitrarily and systematically excluded from Alabama's jury rolls in violation of the equal protection clause of the Fourteenth Amendment. Equally encouraging was the resolution with which Hughes dismissed the state's claim that the absence of Negroes did not prove exclusion. Lieutenant Governor Knight had argued that the names of colored citizens had been included on the lists from which the rolls were made; the defense, he said, couldn't prove—hadn't even offered any evidence—that the commissioner or anyone else had told the county clerk to be sure that no Negroes were put on the rolls. In *Norris* v. *Alabama,* Chief Justice Hughes said it didn't matter. He acknowledged that the law itself did not discriminate; he insisted that between the letter of the law and the jury rolls someone did. Testimony showed that there were hundreds of black men qualified for jury service; testimony showed that in the memory of the living, not one black man had been called. Those facts and the testimony of the jury commissioners—which Hughes characterized as "so sweeping, and so contrary to the evidence" that it "destroyed" its intended effect—pointed to "unvarying and wholesale exclusion" based on the "violent presumption" that Negroes en masse were "utterly disqualified by want of intelligence, experience or moral integrity to sit on juries."[4]

The white jury system the Court attacked was a symbol and a source of concrete misery in the lives of black Americans, and not only in the South. The white jury was just part of the legal system (and the legal system just part of their misery). But it was an unchanging and nonnegotiable part, close to the lives of all those who had been in court and all those who had a stake in the trials of others. Ordinary black Americans knew that if the Supreme Court suddenly ordered an end to segregation and exclusion, it would be some time before they would become lawyers, solicitors, and judges. But if the court suddenly ordered black people, in proportion to their numbers, on every jury, they and almost everyone they knew would be eligible to take their seats the day after the decision was made.

Some radical black southerners—for example, the delegation of Alabama women who responded to *Norris* v. *Alabama* by marching to the Jefferson County Courthouse to ask the circuit clerk to put their names on the jury rolls—believed that the same mass pressure that won the reversal could win the right to sit on juries. The *Southern Worker* expressed confidence that "more and more such delegations, going from every neighborhood, church, union auxiliary, and shop" would force court officials to add the names of black men to the jury rolls.[5]

Most black southerners were more cautious. They watched, eager to see how white southerners would respond to *Norris* v. *Alabama*, and they cheered when Governor Graves sent copies of the decision to every solicitor and judge in Alabama and reminded Alabamans that Supreme Court decisions were the "supreme laws of the land." "Whether we like the decision or not," Graves said, "it is the patriotic duty of every citizen and the sworn duty of every public officer to accept and uphold them in letter and in spirit. . . . This decision means that we must put the names of Negroes in jury boxes in every county in the State." And some commissioners complied. The *Chicago Defender*'s Alabama correspondent reported that "the names of Race citizens" had been added to the jury list of Etowah County for "the first time since the stirring days when carpet-baggers held forth back in the sixties." Black Americans were heartened also by the editorials in some influential southern dailies, in which editors repeated and praised Graves's words, insisting that the decision couldn't be challenged and that people would only make a complicated matter more complicated by trying to get around it.[6]

Black Americans realized that not all white southerners agreed with Graves. Many others suggested with varying degrees of subtlety that Alabamans would find constitutional ways to keep the

South's juries (if not its jury rolls) white. The editor of the *Raleigh Times* was confident that the South that had survived Lincoln and then, by tacit repeal, two of the three Civil War amendments could live with "such a minor matter as letting a Negro take a seat in a jury box if, under all the circumstances, it is not too uncomfortable a roost." The editor of the *Jackson Daily News* called the decision "a stiff blow" and said he expected it would keep jurists and lawyers up late into the night figuring out how to evade it. He suggested making it harder for people to qualify for jury service.[7]

Alabama state senator J. Miller Bonner, of Wilcox County, proposed legislation that would have prohibited jury commissioners from adding to the jury rolls the names of people who were not qualified to vote. Bonner noted that many states had similar laws. The bill died in committee, but court watchers noted that southern whites didn't have to take such drastic action to keep their juries white. All they had to do was relieve black men of duty when they asked to be excused. It was not, as whites often claimed, that blacks didn't want to serve. But rather that they knew they risked losing their credit, jobs, or more if they insisted upon taking their seats.[8]

So the news and outlook were mixed. In light of the history of the Supreme Court, that was as much as could be expected, if not better. Only the very oldest black Americans could remember *Dred Scott* v. *Sanford* (1857), when the Court, in a decision written by its eighty-year-old chief justice, Roger Taney, ruled that the word *citizen* in the Constitution did not refer to black men. More would have been familiar with Taney's most infamous phrase, handed down in disgust from generation to generation, that at the time of the writing of the Constitution, Negroes were regarded as beings of "so far inferior" an order that "they had no rights which the white man was bound to respect." (Taney then inferred that in the years between 1789 and 1857, white sentiment had not changed.)[9]

The Supreme Court had played a part in starting the Civil War, and it played an even larger part in its resolution. In the *Slaughter-house Cases* (1873), the Court ruled that the framers of the Fourteenth Amendment had intended to protect only the (by and large meaningless) rights of national citizenship, thereby wresting from the realm of race relations the amendment designed to guarantee the civil rights of former slaves and signaling the beginning of the end of Radical Reconstruction four years before President Hayes withdrew federal troops from the South. In *U.S.* v. *Cruikshank* (1876), the Court ruled that the Fourteenth Amendment, though meant to protect the rights of black citizens against encroachment by states, was not meant to protect them against encroachment by private citizens, as, say, a mob. In the *Civil Rights Cases* (1883), the court struck down the section of the Civil Rights Act of 1875 meant to give black people equal access to public accommodations. In *Plessy* v. *Ferguson* (1896), the Court ruled that the framers of the Fourteenth Amendment had not intended to abolish distinctions based on color or enforce commingling of the two races, thereby giving states the right to compel segregation. In related turn-of-the-century decisions, the Court sanctioned or legitimized segregation in schools, prohibitions of intermarriage, and various forms of disfranchisement, most notably the grandfather clause.[10]

Not every major Supreme Court decision since the Civil War had gone against the interests of black Americans. In *Strauder* v. *West Virginia* (1880), the Court ruled that a statute expressly limiting jury service to white men violated the equal protection clause of the Fourteenth Amendment. In *Neal* v. *Delaware* (1881), the Court ruled that even in the absence of an exclusionary statute, the deliberate practice of excluding Negroes violated the Constitution. (*Strauder* and *Neal* were important precedents for *Norris* v. *Alabama.*) In *Guinn* v. *U.S.* (1915), the Court struck down the grandfather clause, and in *Moore* v. *Dempsey* (1923) the Court overturned the conviction of the Elaine, Arkansas, sharecroppers, and in so doing restated its responsibility to protect the right to a fair trial when state courts could not or would not do it themselves. In fact, an optimist, taking the long view of the Court's civil rights decisions, might even have been inclined to see in *Moore, Powell,* and *Norris* a gathering momentum, a Court moving slowly but steadily in the right direction.[11]

Black people had to take the long view. There was no other way for most to maintain their sanity in the midst of the racial insanity of their day-to-day lives. But they were not permitted to be unequivocal optimists, not even for half a day. Moments after the court reversed the convictions of Patterson and Norris, it upheld, in *Grovey* v. *Townsend,* the Texas Democratic Party's right to exclude black people from its membership, which meant from its primary election—even though, in the absence of a viable Republican Party, the primary *was* the general election. The party, the Court ruled, was a "voluntary association," fully "competent to decide its membership."[12]

The Court had "blessed and damned" Negroes, wrote NAACP

field secretary William Pickens, and "the damnation in the Texas primary case" outweighed "the blessing of the Scottsboro decision." Those who voted ruled, Pickens argued. With the vote, southern Negroes could put themselves not only on juries but on judges' benches and in legislatures, where they could "defend their still more fundamental rights to economic opportunity." Without the vote, *Norris* v. *Alabama* would not save them. Grand juries required only a majority vote to indict; whites could change the laws governing trial juries so that a majority could convict. Then, without worry, they could put a few Negroes on their juries and comply with the law. Of course they didn't have to go that far. The Court had not guaranteed Negroes seats on any jury; it said simply they should be on the jury lists—not systematically, blatantly, obviously barred. "If we did not know the great court to be above such motives," Pickens concluded, "it would look to us as if it had made a trade, giving the nine million Negroes a kick downwards, as an apology to the race's enemies for favoring the nine Scottsboro boys with another precarious chance for their lives."[13]

Hours after the Court reversed the convictions of Norris and Patterson, Thomas Knight announced that the state would seek new indictments. Seven months later, a Jackson County grand jury that included one black man, Creed Conyers, a farmer from Paint Rock and chairman of the board of trustees of the town's Negro schools, returned indictments charging the defendants each with two counts of rape.[14]

THIRTY-FOUR

He Couldn't Get Us to the Chair Fast Enough

The Supreme Court saved their lives, but it didn't get Patterson and Norris out of the death house. It didn't get the others out of the Birmingham jail. It didn't even end, once and for all, the fighting among their friends. That went on for eight more months, ending in late December 1935 with the formation of the Scottsboro Defense Committee (SDC). The youths had not met or even heard of the committee's chairman, Allan Knight Chalmers, and they had no sense of the dramatic shift in the Communist Party program that made it possible for the ILD to work with him and other liberals in the SDC. But insofar as it meant peace among all of the people who thought they were in jail for something they didn't do, the boys were pleased. The defense committee had less than a month to prepare for trial, and, as might have been expected, Judge Callahan was in no mood for delays. On January 6, 1936, he angrily dismissed the defense's request to transfer the case to federal court, and on January 20, the day Callahan said the trials would begin, Haywood Patterson's fourth trial began.[1]

Patterson and the others noticed some differences between this trial and the last ones, back in December 1933. There were no crowds outside the courthouse, and at times there were empty seats inside; only a handful of guards brought them to and from court. Among the prospective jurors there were Negroes, many of whom seemed eager to be disqualified—one said his boss couldn't do without him at work; another that he was too old. A few were excused when they said they opposed capital punishment. Reporters wrote with sarcasm and condescension about the uneasiness of the prospective black jurors. The defendants understood the difficult position those black men were in, but they weren't always sympathetic. Patterson, for one, was happy to see the judge dismiss the ones with excuses: "I didn't want no scared Negroes judging me."[2]

Wade Wright was gone, replaced as Morgan County solicitor by an equally nasty-looking man named Melvin Hutson. Orville Gilley was missing, said to be in jail in another state. Samuel Leibowitz, in keeping with his promise to the SDC, spent most of the trial in his seat behind the defense table, right beside Haywood Patterson. Leibowitz quietly coached, while Clarence Watts, a Huntsville attorney who, Leibowitz assured the boys, had come with a strong recommendation from Judge Horton, did most of the talking. Southerners advising the defense committee had hoped Leibowitz would stay away from the courtroom; that was the only way, they thought, the defendants would have a chance. Patterson wanted him right where he was.

Lieutenant Governor Knight led the prosecution. The first thing he did was ensure an all-white jury by striking, with peremptory challenges, the half-dozen black men who wanted to be on the jury. Callahan hadn't changed either. He refused to let prospective black jurors take seats in the jury box during jury selection and when one walked in by mistake, he pointed to the chairs he had ordered set up near the box and growled, "Here, boy, sit over there." He dismissed the motion for a change of venue as mechanically as he had dismissed the petition for a transfer to federal court, though both were supported by the affidavits of a Huntsville detective and an officer in the Alabama National Guard. Callahan told prospective jurors that their belief in the inferiority of the Negro race was no barrier to service. He prevented Watts from removing a prospective juror who admitted he had been present for closing arguments at the last trial and had formed an opinion prejudicial to the defendants at that time. "It would take a very dumb man," Callahan ruled, "not to get some kind of impression."[3]

Callahan did not allow Knight to wave Victoria Price's panties around the courtroom. Otherwise he gave Price great leeway in telling her story, and then he did everything he could to obstruct Watts's dogged attempt to contradict her. He allowed the prosecution, short on corroboration without Gilley, to call to the stand a prison guard named Golden, who said that Patterson had confessed to him—more than a year before. Leibowitz cross-examined him, and the defendants enjoyed watching Golden squirm. Patterson had a pencil and paper in his cell: Why, Leibowitz asked Golden, didn't you ask him to write his confession down? The warden lived a mere three hundred yards away and had a telephone: Why didn't you try to call him that night or even the next day? Why didn't you record the confession in the prison log?[4]

Callahan ran the trial ten hours the first full day, overruling a motion for an adjournment at five o'clock in the afternoon, when the state suddenly rested its case. He was in a hurry, and the defense attorneys were in his way. He hardly let them talk, not just interrupting them, as in 1933, and sustaining Knight's objections, but making sarcastic comments about the defense's witnesses, evidence, and lines of argument: "Never mind about that." "You have gone over that." "What is the use of that?" "What is your point?" "Enough on that." "We are magnifying things that are not very important." "I don't see the importance of that."[5]

Callahan again refused to let defense attorneys ask Lester Carter anything about the hours preceding the rape, which meant that Watts was unable to show jurors why they should not necessarily conclude, from evidence of sperm in Victoria Price's vagina, she must have been raped. Callahan would not even give Watts the chance to justify his questions, explain where he was going with them, before he ruled them out of order. He said he knew. At the end of the first day, Watts moved for a mistrial, citing Callahan's impatience and irritability, his comments indicating he thought the defense was wasting time on trivial matters. Watts charged that Callahan's conduct, whether calculated or not, tended to minimize the evidence offered by the defense in the eyes of the jury. As Haywood Patterson put it years later: "He couldn't get us to the chair fast enough."[6]

Patterson, Montgomery, Roberson, Powell, and Andy Wright took the stand the next day. They came to court smartly dressed, hair greased and combed, hoping to make a good impression. They were getting good at testifying, and Montgomery, Wright, and Patterson resisted Knight's and Hutson's attempts to unnerve them. But their anger grew with their confidence, and it became harder to control. Ozie Powell, who the others said had been going nuts in jail—sitting alone most of the time playing a small harp, now and then jumping up and cursing everybody and everything—seemed to be cursing Melvin Hutson with his answers as he told him he did not remember the things Hutson wanted him to remember, did not say the things Hutson insisted he had said, did not see the things Hutson seemed to think he had seen. Powell said he boarded the train alone, and he rode alone.[7]

Watts did his best. "I am your friend and neighbor," he told jurors in summation. "I have never stood before a jury and defended a man I believed guilty of an attack. I was convinced of the innocence of this man before I ever consented to come into this case." But considering the predisposition of the jurors, he was no match for Solicitor Hutson, who was almost as effective as Wade Wright. Hutson spoke of the jury's duty to uphold the law and to save the pure womanhood of Alabama: "Women red, white, black or green," whether in "overalls or furs," depended on them. Unless they found Patterson guilty and sentenced him to death, Alabama women would have to "buckle six-shooters around their middles" in order to protect "the sacred parts of their bodies." More unbelievable than that, Hutson told the jurors "not to go out and quibble over the evidence: Say to yourselves we're tired of this job and put it behind you. Get it done quick and protect the fair womanhood of this great State."[8]

Callahan's charge was virtually unchanged, that same old one-sided diatribe about rape, interracial sex, conspiracy, and guilt written all over the defendant's face. The trial was over in two and a half days. Patterson told Leibowitz he knew a guilty verdict was coming, and it came after eight hours of deliberation. The court clerk read the verdict, and the first seven words—"We the jury find the defendant guilty . . ."—were so familiar that it would have been understandable if Patterson and everyone else in the courtroom had missed the shocking twist at the end: ". . . and fix his punishment at seventy-five years imprisonment."[9]

But no one did. Patterson had been spared the chair. One juror, thirty-five-year-old John Burleson, a devout Methodist who neither smoked nor chewed tobacco, and who had never even tasted liquor, had gone into the jury room determined to prevent an execution, even if it meant blocking a verdict. Burleson had graduated from Morgan County High School, spent two years at the Gulf Coast Military Academy, left there to play professional baseball, and eventually quit baseball to return to his family's 3,000-acre farm. He said he had traveled widely—once to New York to see Babe Ruth play—and read widely, including a dozen journals of current affairs and the arts.[10]

Burleson had expected the state's attorneys to strike him from the venire. His brother was the National Guardsman who had testified, in support of the defense's motion for a change of venue, about hostility toward the defendants in Morgan County. They missed the chance, and he set himself to the task of seeing "justice done no matter whether a man is black, yellow, red or white." Callahan told jurors to use their knowledge of men and affairs, and Burleson took his words to heart. Knowing that "a Nigger's going to stay in his place as long as you let him alone," Burleson doubted the prosecution's contention that it was the defendants who started the fight on the train. He did not doubt that Patterson committed the crime, for the Negro had "more animal in him than white folks. The beast in him overrides him and they go temporarily insane and do things they swear they never would do." But considering that the white boys started the fight and Price and Bates tempted him, Burleson didn't think Patterson deserved to die. He was alone in that conviction at the start of deliberations and remained so for hours. Once Callahan made it clear he wasn't going to let them call it a hung jury and go home anytime soon, he was able to persuade the others to settle for seventy-five years.[11]

Patterson looked across the aisle and saw that Knight and Hutson were stunned. He turned to Leibowitz, who, though restrained in his response and reluctant to call it a victory, was pleased. Leibowitz promised Patterson that he would not give up until he was out of jail, and tried to explain to him why he thought the verdict was a great break, the first since Judge Horton's decision two and a half years earlier, and the first ever to come from an Alabama jury. They had finally broken the prosecution's puppeteer-like hold on the jury, even if he and Watts had only severed one of twelve strings. Patterson would come to see what he meant. At the moment the verdict was announced, however, he saw it exactly as the editors of the *Daily Worker* did; their editorial ran under the headline, "A LIVING DEATH." Patterson said it first: "I'd rather die," he told reporters, "than spend another day in jail for something I didn't do."[12]

While Patterson's jury was out, Clarence Norris's was chosen. His trial was set to begin the next morning, but it didn't, for Leibowitz and Knight could not agree on the form of a "showing" of the testimony of Dr. Bridges, who was gravely ill. At Patterson's trial, Knight had allowed the defense to read Bridges' previous testimony into the record. Now Knight, smarting from a verdict neither he nor Callahan had even mentioned to the jury as a possibility, refused. When Leibowitz asked for a postponement, Callahan offered to postpone Norris's trial and proceed with Andy Wright's. Leibowitz insisted the testimony was as important to one as the other, and Callahan reluctantly postponed all the remaining trials until Bridges was well enough to take the stand. Watts left for Huntsville. Leibowitz boarded a train for New York. The defendants were loaded into three cars for the trip back to the Birmingham jail.[13]

Handcuffed together in one car were Clarence Norris, Roy Wright, and Ozie Powell. Sheriff Sandlin drove, and Deputy Sheriff Blalock sat beside him in the front seat. Twenty miles outside of Decatur, one of the sheriffs said something about Leibowitz that the boys didn't like, rekindling an argument they had had on the ride to court that morning. A few minutes into it Powell "sassed" the deputy, and Blalock reached back and smacked him in the head. Powell pretended to take it without complaint, but with his free hand he pulled a knife out of his pants. ("They searched us coming and going and they never found our knives," Norris said later. "We used to cut the lining in the fly of our pants and put the knives in there. They would never pat that part of us.") A few minutes later, Powell reached forward and slashed Blalock's throat. Blalock hollered, Sandlin reached back to grab Powell, and the car careened from one side of the highway to the other for a hundred yards before Sandlin was able to stop it. Sandlin threw open his door, pulled his revolver, and leapt out of the car. Norris and Wright threw up their hands, which meant that one of Powell's hands was also up when Sandlin turned and shot him in the head. Either Norris or Wright cried out, "Boss, we haven't got anything on us. You can search us."[14]

The sheriffs called it an escape attempt and claimed that Powell had tried to grab the deputy's gun. Leibowitz rushed back to Birmingham and fought his way into Hillman Hospital and then the Birmingham jail by threatening, with court orders, those who tried to keep him out. He found Powell "tossing in delirium" but talked with Norris and Wright, who persuaded him that the official version of the incident was nonsense. The three defendants, he reminded reporters afterwards, were "shackled together in the rear seat of a rapidly moving automobile." The car had only two doors, and the sheriff and his deputy were leaning against them, armed to the teeth.

The car in front of them carried two armed officers. The car behind them carried armed guards and a highway patrolman. "Under those circumstances," Leibowitz asked, could the sheriff of Morgan County claim that "the defendants, armed with a pen knife, attempted to escape?"[15]

Norris and Wright told reporters that even if their odds had been better they would not have risked an escape attempt in the wake of Patterson's seventy-five-year sentence. "We wouldn't try now that things look better for us," Roy Wright told reporters. "We don't believe we'll ever get sentenced to death in these cases, but we believe we will be turned loose." Olen Montgomery told the ILD's Anna Damon that he wasn't in the car and didn't know why Ozie did it. But, he added, "he hasn't real good sense no way." On the way to the operating table, Powell said that he had slashed the deputy because he had cursed his lawyer, told him to let an Alabama lawyer defend him, and talked about killing them all.[16]

Powell was twenty-one, born in a rural town in Georgia, not far from Atlanta. His "real" father had been mean to his mother and they had "busted up" when he was small. His mother had remarried and worked for white people in Atlanta. He had only one year of school, when he was eight, and couldn't write much more than his name. He did odd jobs when he was very young but by the age of thirteen began doing "rough jobs," at sawmills and camps. He ran away from home for the first time at fourteen, joining a highway camp, where he was paid two and a half dollars a day. He liked to travel and never stayed at one job more than a few months. At fifteen, he left home again, hoboed to Chattanooga, and from there headed toward Memphis. That's when he was arrested. Powell described himself as "quiet," "shy" and "bashful," not much for crowds, and living "without a definite goal in view."[17]

A doctor closed Deputy Blalock's wound with ten stitches and released him the same day. Powell was less fortunate. The bullet had entered the side of his head, penetrated the upper part of his skull and lodged itself an inch into his brain. Doctors removed it in two pieces and gave him a fifty-fifty chance of surviving.[18]

He was hardly out of the operating room when sheriffs resumed their talk about Leibowitz. Ozie's mother, Josephine Powell, drove from Atlanta with one of Ozie's brothers, three of his sisters, and a girlfriend, but sheriffs let only his mother see him, and only after she convinced them, with a furniture receipt with her name on it, that she was his mother. When a Negro nurse approached Josephine

Powell at the door to Ozie's room, one of the sheriffs told her not to talk with her or any of the other nurses. Powell was lying there "like asleep," she said, "most likely doped up sleep." The deputy said, "Here's your mother," and he sat up and fell back and started crying. She asked him how he was. He said, "Very well." She asked if anything hurt; he said, "Not now." She asked him what had happened, why this thing had happened now. "I don't feel that there's no need for me to express any further cause," he said. "I done give up." She asked why. "Cause," he said, "I feel like everybody in Alabama is down on me and is mad with me." He didn't want to talk more, but added: "Momma, ain't but one thing I want to tell you right now. Don't let Sam Leibowitz have anything else to do with my case." After "about a minute," sheriffs made her leave the room.[19]

A few days later, Josephine Powell met with Joseph Gelders, a radical white Alabaman working with the Scottsboro Defense Committee. She described the pressure the sheriffs had put on her and her son. On the car ride to the hospital they told her what they wanted her to say to him, and what they didn't want her to say. She was alone with the deputies in the room, with more deputies out in the hall, and she said she just gave up. "I haven't got the strength to fight," she told Gelders. "They all had guns and blackjacks and I was scared I didn't know what they were going to do to me." And Ozie was scared and said only what they wanted him to say.[20]

Ozie Powell survived, but those who had known him, including Clarence Norris, said he was never the same again.[21]

THIRTY-FIVE

Not Boys but Men

Sheriff Sandlin said Andy Wright pulled a knife on him at the same moment Ozie Powell pulled one on Deputy Sheriff Blalock. Sandlin put his foot on the brake, let go of the steering wheel and grabbed Wright, pinning him to the back of the front seat. Then he realized that Powell had slashed Blalock's throat and was going for his gun. Sandlin threw open his door, turned toward Powell on his way out, drew his gun, and "dropped him." Blalock was rushed to the hospital in nearby Cullman; Powell, to Hillman Hospital in Birmingham. The sheriff ordered a guard of six outside Powell's room and additional men on the eighth floor of the Jefferson County Courthouse, the Birmingham jail. Governor Graves sent his adjunct general to the jail and put fifty National Guardsmen on alert. He told surgeons to use "every effort known to medical science" to save Powell's life; they operated as soon as X-rays revealed the extent of his wound. Graves also ordered an investigation, as did the Morgan County solicitor.[1]

All that, and yet even before Alabama editors had a chance to print their first editorials on the latest "chapter in a bitter tragedy," Scottsboro sympathizers "began to howl." Telegrams came from the "East, West, North, and as far south as Kentucky." The most temperate demanded a complete investigation of the attack on the Scottsboro Boys; others demanded the removal of Judge Callahan, the arrest of Blalock for murderous assault, and, to ensure their safety, the immediate and unconditional release of the defendants.[2]

So far from the facts was the version of the event recounted in those telegrams, so absurd the demands for the release of prisoners as a reward for an escape attempt, white Alabamans might have been amused by them, in a perverse sort of way. After five years, they were used to the distortions. What disturbed them was the thought that the radical account was the one most northerners would take for the truth. *Montgomery Advertiser* editor Grover Hall wasted no words in saying that despite the viciousness of the attack, the sheriff and deputy had displayed nothing but coolness and self-restraint, preventing not just an escape but loss of life: "They might have drilled all three prisoners and left them dead." Yet Hall and the other Alabama editors and officials—including at week's end Governor Graves, who praised the lawmen for their "presence of mind" in a "desperate situation"—praised without any confidence that the sheriffs' story would be believed outside the South. To make his point, Grover Hall reprinted a *Baltimore Evening Sun* editorial entitled "Poor Alabama." Even if an archangel came down from heaven and swore to the truth of Sandlin's story, the *Sun*'s editor complained, "there are people who would still believe that the affair was an attempt to murder Powell; and to date, there are no archangels in sight."[3]

The archangel could not have convinced Alabama's critics that Sandlin and Blalock's story was true. Nor, despite the bandage on Blalock's neck, could the archangel have convinced them that the defendants were responsible for the trouble they were in, and had been responsible all along.

Nothing had upset white Alabamans as much in the early days of the controversy as northern descriptions of the defendants as the innocent victims of southern racism. In Communist literature, in the fund-raising letters of fellow travelers, and in reports in southern newspapers of radical activities, Alabamans read about nine poor, ragged, ignorant boys from poor but respectable families, living in clean but very poor working-class homes. Boys who had left home to find work so they could help support their parents and siblings, or, failing that, so they could, simply by leaving, lighten their parents' load.

Not every northern writer imagined the defendants as spotless and pure. Hollace Ransdall had said they were "undoubtedly members of a rough, undisciplined gang." Walter White had heard that their reputations were exceedingly bad. Dorothy Van Doren, writing in *The Nation,* had reminded readers that they were not noble characters: they all had "unsavory reputations"; they all had been accused of various petty crimes. "It was safe to guess that not one of them" would "ever amount to much." Nonetheless it was the northerners who ignored or were blind to the defendants' characters and reputations who had had the most to say about them. And as time passed and northern outrage grew, northern talk of the youths' shortcomings, whatever they were, shrunk in comparison with northern talk of the poverty that had characterized their lives up to the day of the fateful train ride and the injustice that characterized it after. If by 1936 there were still northerners who saw the defendants in any way resembling the way Alabamans did, Alabamans would have had no way of knowing it. Northerners who didn't have something good to say about the defendants, didn't say anything at all.[4]

White southerners were not of one mind about the youths. Some thought the defendants' vices, however great, were not the cause of their troubles but the consequence of their miserable backgrounds. In a letter to Arthur Raper, the CIC's James Burton wrote about the poor housing, the absence of playgrounds, the uninterrupted association with the worst types of people in the Chattanooga neighborhood where some of the boys had lived. "The work for these boys," Burton concluded, "should have begun twelve years ago." And when the defendants chose Communists to defend them and stuck with them in spite of pressure from all quarters, or when they rioted in jail, even the southerners who, in the days after the crime, had talked about the defendants' bad characters as if they were inherent and all-determining—the southerners who had called them beasts, savages, and diabolical fiends as if that were all that needed to be said—concluded that they were being manipulated by others. Few could imagine the defendants making the decisions they made on their own, including, in January 1936, the decision to try to escape. "White persons," Sheriff Sandlin charged, "were responsible for the plot to kill us." Yet when set alongside northern views of the defendants, the differences among southerners didn't seem so great. Even the southerners who saw the defendants in the best light were astounded and annoyed by the sentimentally warped images of the defendants in northern minds.[5]

By January 1936, most white Alabamans had given up trying to change that image; most despaired of convincing northerners of anything having to do with the case. They were tired of it, on the verge of exhaustion. As John Temple Graves noted shortly after Haywood Patterson was indicted for the fourth time in November 1935, Alabamans were divided about the merits of the case. They were divided about the question of guilt. But, Graves said, they were of "one mind and heart" in their "desire to be rid of the case forever," to be free of the "passion," "ill-fame," and "expense," as well as the "racial," "sectional," and "class feeling" that went with it. When Patterson was sentenced to seventy-five years instead of death, few complained that the sentence was light. Many liberals quietly cheered.[6]

One was William G. McDowell of Birmingham, the Episcopal bishop of Alabama. Born in Virginia in 1882, McDowell was educated at Washington and Lee University and the Virginia Theological Seminary. He led churches in his home state before the war, served as a chaplain during the war, and was called to Auburn, Alabama, in 1918. A tireless leader, revered by clergy and laity alike, McDowell had been following the Scottsboro case for the CIC since 1933; at the time of Patterson's fourth trial he was busy organizing a group of Alabama ministers, attorneys, and industrialists to work with Allan Knight Chalmers and the Scottsboro Defense Committee. In a letter to the ACLU's Roger Baldwin, written the day after Patterson was sentenced to seventy-five years, McDowell said he thought the verdict indicated "a remarkable change of sentiment," perhaps even revolutionary in that it was the first time in anyone's memory that "a negro convicted of criminal assault on a white woman was not sentenced to death." It was impossible, McDowell predicted, that any of the others should get the chair.[7]

McDowell's optimism was shattered by the slashing of Blalock. "If Patterson were tried today," he told Chalmers, "he would get death." "There is a new tenseness that bodes ill for the future trials." But the incident on the road to Birmingham gave McDowell and his allies in Alabama new strength for debate. With almost no trace of the defensiveness that had begun to infect their discussion of the case in 1933, they spoke confidently about their desire to take the defense out of the hands of Leibowitz and the ILD. Their confidence came from their renewed conviction that they had been right about the controversy, and especially about the defendants, all along.[8]

When Baldwin wrote to McDowell to ask about Powell's safety, having been alarmed by reports he was going to be moved from

Hillman Hospital, McDowell reminded him that most of the reports in the papers were "sensational." "You must not be so easily upset by rumors—there is considerable sense and decency in the South for which you might give us credit." It was going to be hard to figure out what had happened:

> You must realize these Negroes are vicious and ignorant; they are not innocent victims of a frame up, but were a gang of petty criminals running from the Chattanooga police when they got into trouble on the freight train. It must be remembered that at the first trial they all accused one another, and that, as much as the testimony of Price and Bates, led to their conviction. They are entirely unreliable, as shown by their widely varying tales of any given event, and their revised versions from time to time. They have from the first fought among themselves and have also created several disturbances, once wrecking the plumbing in the new jail and attacking keepers. It is hard to get the truth out of them, because they belong to a low grade of intelligence and moral conception which does not know what the truth is.

McDowell said he and his friends wanted to see the defendants' rights protected. But to protect them, they had to resist getting "sentimental about them." There was no doubt that some of their problems were beyond their control. They had been hurt by racial prejudice and Communist prejudice; they had been used for propaganda and politics by northern radicals and southern reactionaries. "But," McDowell insisted, that "must not blind us to the fact that the chief hazards are of their own making: they got into this trouble by fighting, throwing the white men off the train and annoying two women, if some of them didn't do worse; by lying and accusing one another; by showing themselves unreliable; by creating trouble in jail; and now by this cutting affair and their variant versions of it."[9]

Alabama editors made the same point, with the same confidence. "If law officers were half as bad as Alabama's critics charge," wrote the editor of the *Birmingham Age-Herald,* "at least two negroes would be dead." The editor of the *Birmingham News* reminded readers that the defendants' violence, past and present, had nothing whatsoever to do with the question of their innocence or guilt. But he too thought that this "latest act of violence on the part of some of the Scottsboro defendants should convince all their sympathizers everywhere that, whether these Negroes are guilty or innocent of the charge on which they are being tried, they are—or at least some of them are—vicious men, and not the lamb-like victims of circumstances which the more irresponsible and prejudiced champions of their cause have pretended to believe them to be."[10]

So great were the differences between most northerners and southerners that they could not even agree about whether the defendants were men or boys. To Alabamans, they were men, and they had been from the start. That was partly because in March and April of 1931 local newspapers got most of their ages wrong, reporting them to be older than they actually were. But as the managing editor of the *Montgomery Advertiser* put it, literal age didn't have much to do with it: "The age of a Southern Negro [was] purely relative. Rare—almost nonexistent—is the negro who knows his own age. Eight of those arrested were grown, mature. The ninth, Roy Wright, was obviously a boy somewhere in his middle teens." To northerners, by contrast, they were all boys, two of them thirteen, one fourteen, the oldest nineteen. And when they weren't boys, they were youths or children, Negro children in prison, or the unfortunate sons of the Scottsboro mothers.[11]

Alabamans argued at first, insisting that the defendants, at least the eight who had been sentenced, were men, "full grown and responsible," old enough to know better. They sent letters of protest to northern editors who continued to call them children or boys. When reasonable and dispassionate argument and protest failed them, they tried ridicule. After the Supreme Court delivered *Norris v. Alabama,* Grover Hall asked if the Court would have overturned the convictions "if negroes had served on Jackson County court juries every year for 29 years before the 'Scottsboro' infants came into the court in their diapers and shaking their baby rattlers but for some reason—any reason—had not been drawn to serve on the jury that tried the infants aforesaid." Three weeks later, the *Decatur Daily*'s editor asked northern critics of the South's jury system to put down their copies of *Uncle Tom's Cabin* and visit Alabama for some "first-hand information regarding negroes and whites in general and the case of the Scottsboro babies, muling and puking in their mother's arms in particular."[12]

They did visit. And they went home talking about the Scottsboro Boys.

THIRTY-SIX

How Can I Feel Up Lifted?

Judge Callahan postponed the remaining trials after the shooting of Powell. The defendants were taken back to the Birmingham jail to wait, but the wait was wearing them down. Nearly five years had passed since their arrest. The youngest, Roy Wright, was now eighteen; the oldest, Charlie Weems, twenty-four. For five years they had tossed endlessly and uneasily between confusion and understanding, suspicion and trust, hope and despair. It was five years of torment, conflict, exhausting calculation, and delicate negotiations, five years of figuring how to get what they needed, how to get along with one another, with other prisoners, with guards, with Leibowitz, with the ILD. Five years of never knowing for sure yet always wondering what difference, for better or worse (they were still alive, but also still in prison), their decisions had made. And all they saw when they looked ahead was more uncertainty, more figuring and more wondering about what the consequences of all that figuring would be.

"I feel sad and depressed most of the time," Norris said. "I just think and worry about being in this place. I feel and hope that I will get out. Sometimes I feel down-hearted and sometimes I feel a little up-lifted." Norris complained about his health—ruined, he thought, by bad food and a lack of exercise—and he complained about being back in solitary: "I am alone," he wrote, "out to my self No one to say a Kind word to Me just listen to the other people away from me."[1]

Others complained about the ILD. When Anna Damon, a charter member of the Communist Party who in 1936 was both head of women's work for the Central Committee and organizational secretary of the ILD, asked Andy Wright why he didn't write more often, he told her it was because she usually ignored his letters: "I figured that you wasnt interested in nothing I say. . . . I have tried every way I possibly no how to interest you in my letters but it seems that I am a failure so I decide to give up trying but it actually hurted me to the depths of my heart and I would appreciate knowing just why you're so rude to me?" He thanked her for his monthly check, which he appreciated "to the highest."[2]

Willie Roberson's hurt was even greater, for he fell easily in love by mail. In 1934 he began calling the woman corresponding with him "Darling," telling her that she couldn't imagine how much he enjoyed corresponding with her, asking her to tell him more about herself and about how she was feeling. He said he wanted to be with her in New York after he was released. He described himself as almost nineteen years old, five feet four inches tall, with brown skin, brown eyes, and black, wavy hair. And he described his interests: dancing, shows, parties, swimming, the piano, the guitar, and tennis. But he felt blue when she wouldn't send him a picture or answer even his least intimate questions. When she stopped writing, passing his case on to another correspondent, he stopped writing too.[3]

In 1936, Olen Montgomery had the most gripes. "This is a matter of Business no fun," he wrote Anna Damon in July. He needed an advance on his next check so that he could buy a night with a woman. There was a new warden on night duty who would arrange it for five dollars. "Now listen you realize how long I have been cut off from my Pleasure dont you? And you realize it hard on me dont you? especially me being a young man." He knew his request might offend her, but said he had no choice: "Because if I dont get to a woman it will soon run Poor me crazy. I really have stood it long as I can. I Just got to get to one. I have Been in Jail over five years. And its a shame."[4]

Throughout the spring and summer, Montgomery asked for shoes. He wanted "Friendly Five shoes . . . size 7½ real keen toes with a plain cap across the toe and color real light tan, and leather heels." When they hadn't come by the end of September he wrote an angry letter that began: "Anna what is the matter with you? I need a pair of shoes real Bad and I have written and ask you Just as nice as I could to send me a pair." He explained why he couldn't use his regular monthly allowance: "Its all I can do to keep up in smokes and other little things that I need and you know it."[5]

It wasn't just the shoes that were bothering him. He was angry to discover that Rose Baron, head of Prisoners Relief, had told his mother he was getting along fine. Yet he hadn't written to Rose "in three months" and she knew it:

> I am not getting along fine. I am not doing any good at all. You all got sense enough to know I am tired of being in Jail. And you could have done got me out too I do Believe. the longer I stay in Jail is the richer you get and Better you feel. But yet we are staying trying to keep faith and you all wont do a damn thing to encourage us you wont do a thing we ask. You know I am not able to Buy no shoes and clothes. But yet you will sit up there like something dumb wont even answer my letters.[6]

In October, Montgomery wrote to say his health was good except for his bad eye, which gave him "a little trouble" at times, and to ask when his case was coming up. He had received a letter from his mother, who was "all worried and up set" about him. "I feel so sorry for my poor mother she needs my help and I know it." He asked once more for the shoes, new ones: "I dont want any one old clothes and shoes." "Anna," he wrote, "I am honest and you know that I am and always willing and glad to help my own self as much as I can." But, he reminded her, he was in prison and couldn't get what he needed on his own.[7]

What he wanted most was a six-string guitar. He had been writing songs—in July, the lyrics to one of them, "The Lonesome Jailhouse Blues," had been published in the *Labor Defender*. Now he wanted to play them. He wanted to make records, thought he could make his first one in jail, and when he hadn't received the guitar by the end of October, he complained bitterly:

> You all wont do nothing to help me. I wrote you and Begged you like a dog to send me one and you wouldnt even answer my letter. But that's alright. Just take my next $8.00 and get one. dont get such large one if you can help it. You can get some small six string guitars and send it rite away please I need it. if I live I am

> going to Be the Blues King. I want to surprise every Body some day Anna please dont wait a minute send it rite on to me so I can Be practicing on these too songs that I have made up.[8]

"Olen, you know that I try to make things as comfortable and as pleasant as possible for you," Damon replied nine days later. "You asked for an 8 string guitar last time and you remember that we tried so hard to get it for you but couldn't because these guitars are so expensive. I will try to get you the kind you want now." Damon said she was very sorry she hadn't answered sooner, but she was very busy. She was sorry also that she had nothing new to report about his trial; she had told him a few weeks earlier that it had been postponed again, this time because Callahan was ill. He was still ill: "Now I want you to be patient, and I will try to get your guitar for you as soon as possible. I hope this letter finds you well and in much better spirits."[9]

"Listen woman," Olen replied, "I aint ask you for no 8 string guitar I told you plain as I could speak to take my $8.00 and get me a 6 string guitar. And I cant see why you aint done sent it to me. Woman you will run a person Crazy. I Begged you like a dog once Before to send me one. And you wouldnt even answer my letter. do you call that making things comfortable for me?"[10]

Unlike Montgomery, Haywood Patterson almost always tempered his demands and complaints with thanks and fulsome praise. Patterson was shrewd and enterprising, and in prison he discovered how to get the most from friends just as quickly as he discovered how to take the least abuse from foes. He was also defiant, and the combination of shrewdness and defiance made prison easier for him to bear. Of all the defendants, the ILD considered him the most spirited, the most militant, and the most loyal. Most of the time he was. But in the year following his fourth conviction, even his spirit and his loyalty showed signs of wear.[11]

He stopped writing in the summer of 1936, and at the end of August he wrote to say that he was "ashamed" for the "long silence." The "truth is," he wrote, "I Have felt so unhappy and Horribly Disappointed and resentful over the outcome of my last tiral and the way the case are now Being conducted." He felt misrepresented by lawyers and reporters, and he despised the picture of him that the ILD used in its publications. He wondered why Damon didn't write more, why she wrote such short letters, and why she left so many of his questions unanswered.[12]

Again there was a long silence, again Damon wrote to ask why, and again Haywood wrote to explain. He knew he had "innumerable" friends and supporters and he knew they all wanted to know how he and the boys were getting along. But he found it hard "to describe" his feelings and therefore "rather Hard to tell just How" he was "getting on." There was "no Happiness nor pleasure" in jail and never would be. The days were "very very long" and tedious and "dark." The "wearisome nights," he said, were full of "nightmares and restless Moments. . . . Why I am full of tossing to and fro unto the better of each Day before I can be able to get much sleep." Nonetheless, Patterson said, he tried "to take whatever Hardness" there was "with a smile" and he was "overconfident that all good things" would come.[13]

Anna Damon wrote again on October 14, saying that she was glad to receive his letter, glad also that he was not going to let himself get depressed: "Your attitude is a very intelligent one and will do a great deal to preserve your health and resistance." He wrote back the same week, "thankful" for her "very short note," thankful also for her "great Kindness and courtesy," glad she still liked and enjoyed his letters. "Hereafter," he promised, "I shall press forth my uttermost and try as I might an make my letters more amusingly an interestedly like . . . I use to. . . ." But, he added, it would be hard for him to say anything encouraging to the workers and his countless friends who had been "wonderfully kind and generous and considerate" and who were "forever doing something great" for him and the boys even if they didn't "know about it." He closed by asking Damon to have "Lawyer Powell or some other good christian white person" escort his parents and siblings on all their future visits to Kilby. A few days earlier his "baby sister" had traveled all the way from Chattanooga only to be turned away at the gates by guards who made indecent comments, leaving her hurt worse than she had ever been hurt before and leaving him "badly grieved and disappointed," feeling sorrier for his sister than he felt for himself.[14]

The next week it was Roy Wright who made him feel blue. Once again that "most Disagreeable" and "unreasonable foolish" boy had given him a hard time. Wright, Patterson said, was a "piece braker among the boys and myself." He had abused him terribly on many occasions, taking money away from him, and setting their hearts against him by saying things about him. Patterson didn't wish to harm him, but he would have to if he was harmed by him.

Two days later he was feeling better. Damon had written with news of the trials of the other boys and his appeal, and the news "brought some comfort and joy and gladness." Without it, he had to "depend solely upon the Local newspapers to obtain any information concerning the case." It was "wonderfully kind," he said, but he wasn't surprised, because she had "always been Heavenly good and considerate constant." He said he expected "some good candy for christmas," like the candy she had sent last year, which he had split with his "most beautiful girl friend." He reminded her that his birthday was on December 12. "I wonder Do people gets presents on their birthdays?"[15]

That was October 30. Sometime between then and November 6 he had been angry again and had said so. On November 6, he wrote to apologize: "Didn't mean the nasty things I said when in a foul mood and I wanted you to know it. I'll make sure it doesn't happen again." Guilt about the heartache he had caused his parents had made him feel low. "You know all of my family are good people except me and my 2 brothers and we wasnt so bad Boys." His mother was "a good warm Christian hearted mother," "a faithful church worker most of her whole entire life." His father was "a loving and kind daddy" whom he liked so much it hurt. His father had tried to bring him up right, going so far as to beat him sometimes when he found out that he had not been going to school. Now, he said, "I have again reformed. some goodness that have been lying latent with in me have came already to the front, and I have made a sacred vow to god. that if only I am freed again . . . I shall never gone away and leave my mother so she would never again feel sorry on account of me." He was, of course, "absolute innocent of any wrong-doing," but admitted: "I supposed I be convicted in men minds."[16]

A month later, Haywood had a list of complaints. He was annoyed because it was December 11, the day before his birthday, and yet no one but "one little Beautiful girl of Birmingham" had sent him a present. Was it because "all of the Boys would want one if they knew"? And he was angry because they had paid no attention to his complaints about the horrible picture of him they had sent all over the world: "I dont like it. And I beg of you all not to place another one like it In the paper or magazine. . . ."[17]

The presents and pictures troubled Patterson less than a simple question he couldn't answer: Why am I still here? Some said it was the CP and New York Jews, but he doubted that, for he had spent his life among "the Jew race of people," understood "them all too well" and liked them. They had never caused him "to grief or to suffer any misfortune." What, then, could it be? The facts that proved his innocence had been in the newspapers. He had "recapitulated" the "calumnys" of all the witnesses who stood waiting "to declare the different stories" against him. Witnesses against him had recanted. Others had contradicted themselves. "So," he asked Damon, "see if in your opinion the jury awarded the just proper verdict in my former trial?"[18]

Suddenly he remembered who he was writing to: "But I need not to comment on these matters because by now my innocence Have appealed to everybody" and everybody knew it was "a most dreadful situation." He simply wanted to assure them it was a "just cause to carry on continually purposely to gain" his "freedom."[19]

Patterson's moods changed not just by the month, week, and day, but by the letter, the paragraph, the sentence, the breath. So too with all the others; they condemned in one paragraph or in one letter and then apologized in the next. Each had his own way of saying what Eugene Williams said in December 1936: "Sorry about my last letter—hope it didn't make you angry. didnt mean any harm whatever. only telling you how I felt towards you and whats more I could not help it."[20]

When, in January 1937, a Tuskegee Institute physician, Dr. G. C. Branche, came to see them, they had been in solitary for a year. Branche found Patterson on a bad day. "Every day just seems the same to me," he said. "They just come and go. I don't have a mind for anything." He was worried about his mother and family. He was angry at the ILD: "They look you right in the eye and then go right back to New York and scandalize my name. They haven't did anything for me but just got me in deeper trouble. If I thought you would scandalize my name I wouldn't let you examine me. You don't know how it hurts my heart when somebody scandalizes me." He charged that the Communists had misused money raised in his behalf. He complained that his lawyers wouldn't let him talk at his trials, though he could barely control himself at his last one, having "just about lost all hope of getting out." The Communists didn't want him out. Leibowitz, who had once told him he was going to put him "in Hell with the Communists," was just in it for "fame and publicity." Patterson wished "they would hurry up and do something," reminding the doctor that he had been "sentenced to die three times." Considering the beatings and the food,

The defendants with National Guardsmen outside the Scottsboro jail. From left to right: Clarence Norris, Olen Montgomery, Andy Wright, Willie Roberson, Ozie Powell, Eugene Williams, Charlie Weems, Roy Wright, and Haywood Patterson. March 26, 1931. UPI/BETTMANN

Ruby Bates (left) and Victoria Price, in a photograph that appeared in a few southern newspapers shortly after the alleged crime.

The crowd on one side of the courthouse square in Scottsboro on the first day of the first trials. April 6, 1931. AP/WIDE WORLD

Scottsboro demonstration organized by the Communist Party. 1931.
SCHOMBURG CENTER, NEW YORK PUBLIC LIBRARY

The defendants with Samuel Leibowitz in the Decatur jail. Haywood Patterson is sitting with Leibowitz. Behind them from left to right: Olen Montgomery, Clarence Norris, Willie Roberson, Andy Wright (directly behind Roberson), Ozie Powell, Eugene Williams, Charlie Weems, and Roy Wright. March 1933. UPI/BETTMANN

Victoria Price testifying at Patterson's second trial. April 1933. UPI/BETTMANN

Judge James E. Horton, Jr., listening to the testimony of Dr. R. R. Bridges at Patterson's second trial. April 1933. AP/WIDE WORLD

Beatrice Maddox, sister of Andy and Roy Wright, testifying at Patterson's second trial. Standing at the prosecution table (behind the court stenographer) is Attorney General Thomas E. Knight, Jr. Sitting next to Knight is Morgan County Solicitor Wade Wright. April 1933. UPI/BETTMANN

Haywood Patterson sitting between defense attorneys Samuel Leibowitz and George Chamlee during his second trial. April 1933. UPI/BETTMANN

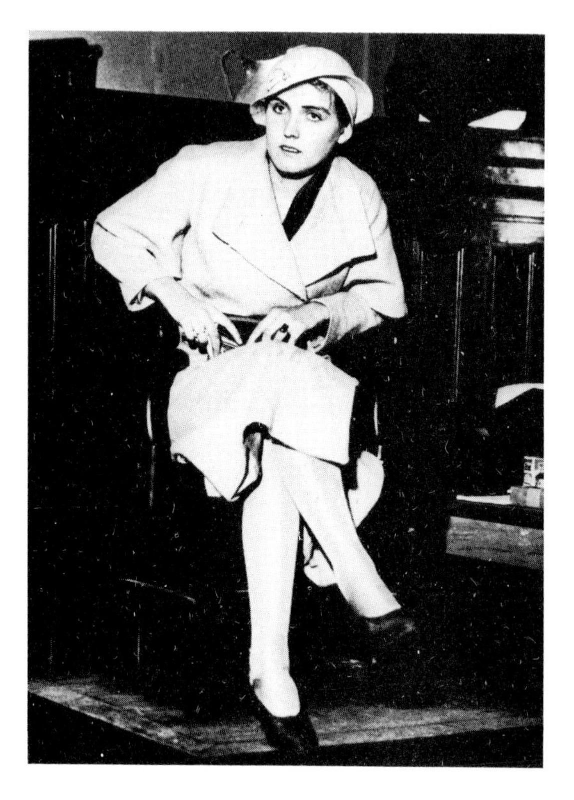

Ruby Bates testifying at Haywood Patterson's second trial. April 1933. AP/WIDE WORLD

Jurors in Haywood Patterson's second trial, behind the replica model train made for Leibowitz by the Lionel Corporation. April 1933. AP/WIDE WORLD

A Harlem street corner as news of the verdict in Haywood Patterson's second trial reached New York. April 9, 1933. UPI/BETTMANN

Ruby Bates with five of the mothers of the defendants in the 1933 May Day Parade in New York City. Bates is sitting between Ida Norris and Ada Wright. Behind them from left to right: Viola Montgomery, Mamie Williams, and Janie Patterson. AP/WIDE WORLD

Janie Patterson (directly in front of the banner) in the Scottsboro march on Washington. May 1933. UPI/BETTMANN

The defense team returns to Decatur. From left to right: Joseph Brodsky, George Chamlee, two bodyguards, and Samuel Leibowitz. November 1933. UPI/BETTMANN

Victoria Price and Jack Tiller, a few minutes before Price took the stand in Haywood Patterson's third trial. November 1933. AP/WIDE WORLD

Eight of the defendants in the Decatur jail during Clarence Norris's second trial. Against the bars: Charlie Weems and Haywood Patterson. In front of them: Clarence Norris and Ozie Powell. On their right: Andy Wright, Olen Montgomery, Willie Roberson, and Roy Wright. December 1933. UPI/BETTMANN

On Mother's Day, 1934, Ida Norris, Janie Patterson, Ruby Bates, Mamie Williams, Viola Montgomery, and Richard Moore (of the ILD) went to the White House. President Roosevelt said he could neither receive them nor intervene in the case. AP/WIDE WORLD

The grand jury that reindicted the defendants after *Norris* v. *Alabama*. In the upper left: Creed Conyers, who was said to be the first black man to serve on an Alabama jury since Reconstruction. November 1935. BIRMINGHAM NEWS

HAYWOOD PATTERSON
Four juries found him guilty

A photograph from *Scottsboro: The Firebrand of American Communism*, written by Files Crenshaw, Jr., and Kenneth Miller and published in 1936.

A photograph from *Scottsboro: The Firebrand of American Communism*, written by Files Crenshaw, Jr., and Kenneth Miller and published in 1936.

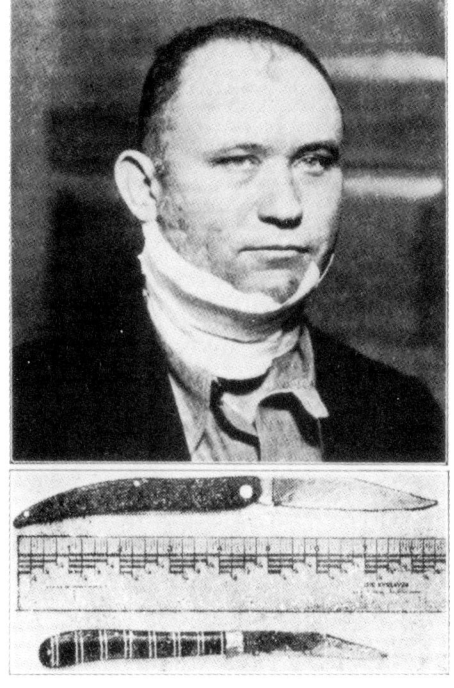

Deputy Sheriff Edgar Blalock of Morgan county, whose throat was slashed by Ozie Powell. Below—The "pen" knives used by Powell and Roy Wright in the attack.

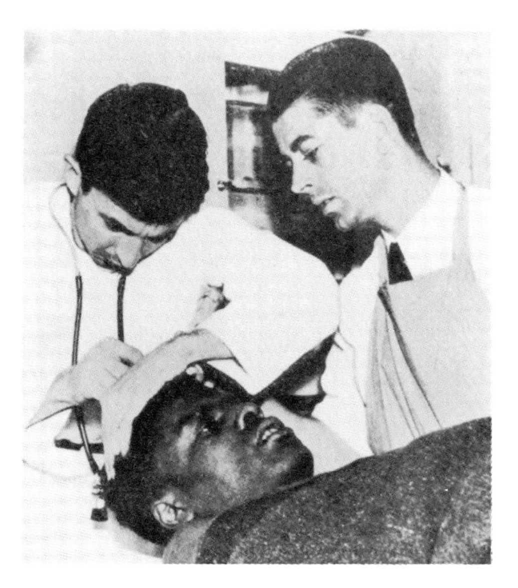

A photograph of Ozie Powell, taken just before doctors at Hillman Hospital in Birmingham operated to remove a bullet from his head, from *Scottsboro, The Shame of America: The True Story and the True Meaning of This Famous Case*, published by the Scottsboro Defense Committee in 1936. PRINCETON UNIVERSITY LIBRARIES

Haywood Patterson, 24, the best-known of the Scottsboro Boys, is vain, publicity-loving, unpopular. A onetime Chattanooga grocery-store helper, he now corresponds regularly with expatriate Author Kay Boyle, British Negrophile Nancy Cunard.

SCOTTSBORO BOYS ONCE MORE ON TRIAL

Alabama now hopes for an end to this old case

On July 6 at Decatur, Ala., two young Negroes named Clarence Norris and Charlie Weems were arraigned on a charge of raping two white women, held for trials on July 12 and 15 respectively. The courtroom was sparsely filled. The Birmingham *News* had sent no reporter. Most Alabama newspapers buried the story on inside pages. No reason of obscurity or unimportance accounted for this apathy. It was simply that Alabama has grown heartily sick and tired of its world-famous Scottsboro Case.

Since the March day in 1931 when Clarence Norris, Charlie Weems and seven other stripling blackamoors were taken off a freight train at Paint Rock, Ala., near Scottsboro, and accused of raping two white female vagrants named Victoria Price and Ruby Bates, the Scottsboro Case has wound through an expensive and apparently interminable series of trials. All of the Scottsboro Boys except Roy Wright, the youngest, have been condemned to death at least once, and the lives of Norris and Haywood Patterson have twice been saved by the U. S. Supreme Court. From the beginning the Boys themselves were obscured in the miasma of old hatreds which arose when Northern liberals and Communists rushed down to defend them as martyrs to Southern injustice and intolerance, and Alabamians struck back at the malicious interference of Yankees, Reds and Jews. But after six years, tempers on both sides have cooled. The longtime prosecutor, Lieutenant Governor Thomas E. Knight Jr., died last May. The defense attorney who so infuriated the South, famed Samuel Leibowitz of New York, made no appearance at the arraignment. Last month the Montgomery *Advertiser*, which long howled for the Boys' blood, spoke for many an Alabamian when it called for a compromise which would end the case for good, declaring: "'Scottsboro' has stigmatized Alabama throughout the civilized world."

The current series of trials is scheduled to progress at the rate of two Boys per week for four weeks. (Patterson, tried last year, is under a 75-year sentence.) Whatever their fate, the Scottsboro Boys whose Birmingham jail portraits appear on these pages, are already assured of a place in U. S. history.

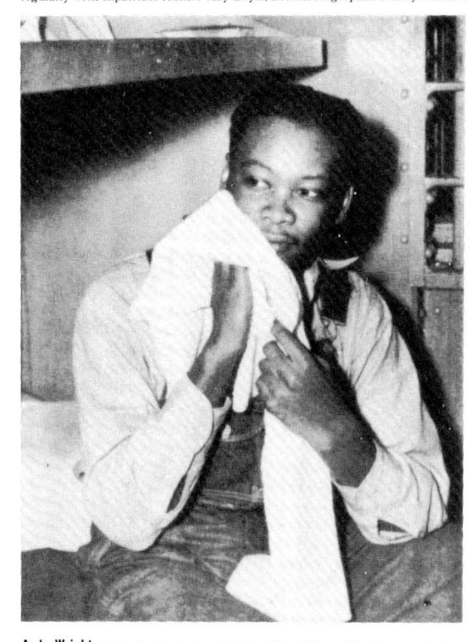

Andy Wright, 25, is the best-natured of the Boys. He confidently expects to go free and get back his old job as truck driver for a wholesale grocer named Talley in Chattanooga. He enjoys girl correspondents in California and Florida.

Clarence Norris, 24, who was raised on a farm and worked as a stonemason's helper in Atlar the dandy of the outfit. He plasters his hair with strong-perfumed grease, keeps his shirt and ov neat and clean. His illiterate mother sends him letters when she can get somebody to write

A photo essay on the Scottsboro case that appeared in *Life*. July 19, 1937.

Willie Roberson, 21, has been cured of a disease since he went to jail. Like the rest of the Boys, he gets newspapers from friends and $10-per-month pocket money from the Communist International Labor Defense and Scottsboro Defense Committee.

harlie Weems, 26, whose parents are dead, gets a letter every week from his ınt Gussie McElroy. Tall and ungainly, he used to be deliveryboy at Watson's ·ug store in Atlanta, says that if he gets out of jail: "I wants to fly a airship."

Eugene Williams, 21, a sullen, shifty mulatto, used to be a dishwasher in Chattanooga's Dixie Café, usually tries to impress interviewers with his piety. Behind the barred door which he clasps (*above*) is Andy Wright's brother Roy, 20, youngest and smartest of the Boys, who refused to be photographed.

Olen Montgomery, 24, is frail, gentle and half-blind, spending most of his time singing and twanging a one-string tenor guitar. He has composed a *Lonesome Jailhouse Blues*, which begins: "All last night I walked my cell and cried, Cause this old jailhouse done get so lonesome I can't be satisfied."

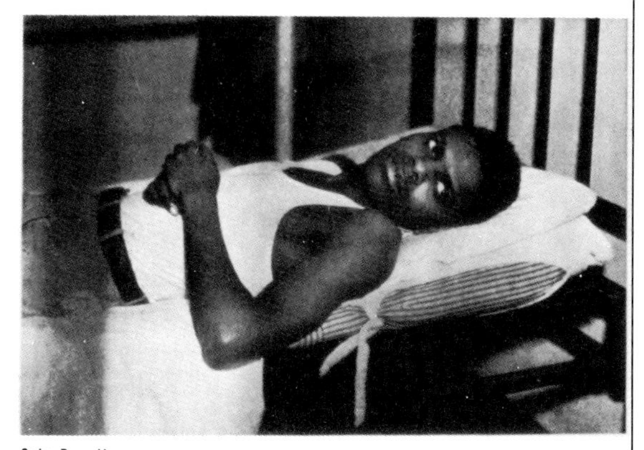

Ozie Powell, 22, is under indictment for assault with intent to kill, as well as for rape. Returning from Patterson's fourth trial last year, he stabbed a deputy sheriff and got a blast of buckshot in the head. Powell went through the first grade but he can barely spell out words. Nobody writes to him.

From left to right: Eugene Williams, Olen Montgomery, Willie Roberson, and Roy Wright with Samuel Leibowitz in Nashville the day after they were released. July 25, 1937. AP/WIDE WORLD

In Pennsylvania Station in New York the following morning. July 26, 1937. UPI/BETTMANN

Alabama Governor Bibb Graves
ALABAMA DEPARTMENT OF ARCHIVES AND HISTORY

Montgomery Advertiser editor Grover C. Hall. ALABAMA DEPARTMENT OF ARCHIVES AND HISTORY

Clarence Norris leaving Kilby Prison. September 27, 1946.
AP/WIDE WORLD

Andy Wright receiving $13.45 in parole pay from the clerk at Kilby Prison moments before he was released to New York. June 9, 1950.
AP/WIDE WORLD

Haywood Patterson with Civil Rights Congress attorney Ernest Goodman after Michigan Governor Williams refused to extradite him to Alabama and a federal judge ordered Michigan officials to release him from prison. July 13, 1950.
AP/WIDE WORLD

Clarence Norris at a news conference at NAACP headquarters in New York shortly after he learned that Alabama Governor Wallace had granted him a full pardon. October 25, 1976. AP/WIDE WORLD

he said he thought he and the other boys had "held out nicely." He also said: "This place is killing me. I don't see why we innocent boys should be kept here all this time for nothing."[21]

Patterson's bad days were no worse than those of any of the others, and better than some. Branche found Montgomery gloomy and depressed. "I just think about getting out of here. That's all I want to do. That's the only thing that will bring happiness to me. I'm just being held here because I'm a Nigger. That's why I'm in jail; not nothing I've done." Andy Wright told the doctor that he had nothing to do but think about his condition. "Sometimes I think about my case, sometimes I think about my mother, and sometimes I think about how I'm being treated; first one thing and then another. How I'm being treated I think about most." His brother Roy thought most about being young and being in jail. He wondered how much more time he was going to have to serve: "If I have to spend more than one or two years longer, I just as well spend the rest of my life. If I was an old man perhaps I wouldn't mind it so much but that's what's against me; I'm young and innocent of the crime. I was put in solitary confinement in January, 1936 and got fresh air once out of the thirteen months and that was last Friday. Some may count it a year but I count it thirteen months."[22]

Roy was able to get hold of a newspaper now and then, and he kept his Bible with him at all times. He liked to read, but he thought magazines like *True Story* would be "ruination" to his mind: "reading and thinking of the pleasure that others were having, that would run me crazy, and I'm here in solitary in jail." He had been in jail for six years without a new trial, and he didn't "know of any law in the United States that holds a man in jail for six years" without a trial. The ILD and the NAACP collected money to help him, but "if they were doing so much they would free some of us before now." It was a "government affair" because he and his friends had been taken from a moving train; the case ought to be "transferred to a federal court." He had spoken to Brodsky about that in 1934, and the defense had raised the issue at the last trial, but he didn't "see where they have done anything about it." "The presidents been knowing about it but has not done anything about it. I don't think you could stand what we've been through here in this jail. I've been knocked in the head, tear-gassed, and the like, but I just laugh at it because it was small to what I've been through."[23]

Eugene Williams and Charlie Weems thought a lot about

women. Williams thought about his "girl friend and the things he used to do when he was out" and the women he had met while he was in jail. If it were not for the girls who wrote to him, he didn't know what he would do. "Getting out is the main thing I think about," he said. "We're in here because of lies." Weems thought about "the ladies out there in the world and I'm shut in here. The reason I'm in trouble is prejudice against colored people; nothing but a frame-up."[24]

Ozie Powell had suffered brain damage when he was shot. His memory was impaired and he was having trouble speaking and hearing. His right side, both the arm and leg, though not paralyzed, were weak. After Powell, Dr. Branche found Willie Roberson in the worst shape. Roberson was born on July 4, 1916, in Columbus, Georgia. His parents separated shortly after his birth and his mother died when he was two. His father died while Willie was in jail. He was brought up by his mother's mother and two of her sisters.[25]

Roberson began school in Atlanta when he was five and reached the seventh grade. Except for math, which he had to repeat, he did well. He quit at twelve: "I just got lazy and did not care any more for school." He hoped to go back if he ever got out. He worked as a bus boy in a hotel as soon as he was big enough to work, then left the hotel to seek a better job in Chattanooga, and when he couldn't find one he headed toward Memphis, by train. Besides work, he had been hoping to find a free hospital, for he was suffering from a severe case of gonorrhea. He wasn't treated by injection until 1933. The doctor calculated Roberson's IQ at 64-plus (the same as Powell's), and his mental age at nine (again the same as Powell's). He concluded that Roberson (along with Montgomery, Patterson, and both Wrights) had developed a prison neurosis. Nevertheless, Roberson was able to recall that when his third great aunt died from poisoned ice cream, "Woodrow Wilson was President." And he was able to tell the doctor how he felt and what was on his mind:

> While out in the street I suffered with asthma. Some nights I can't catch my breath. This steel and concrete just kills me. No outlet, no exercise, no window in front of cell; some nights I just can't get my breath. I have a hurting in my left side and right side of my head. . . . Would like to know the cause of that. How is my mind Doc? . . . Doc., I tell you the truth I am just lucky to be living I been through a heap. Its bad to say I just as soon be dead as living. I know you hate to hear the truth but I just as soon be

> dead at time as to be living. . . . Doc. I just got to say I think I am doing well to keep the mind I got now. . . . These people make wise cracks talking about somebody in Alabama to defend us, say I would get out better. They won't let the New York people come around, no paper. . . . Another feller came around and said will you be willing to take life? . . . If I don't get free I just rather they give me the electric chair and be dead out of my misery because I sure don't want no time for something I haven't did.[26]

Every day's mail brought letters. But because ILD officials and defense attorneys knew that the warden read the defendants' mail before the defendants did, letters never brought important news. So every day's mail hurt. "Dear Anna," Olen Montgomery wrote in March 1937,

> I rec'd you little short letter. nothing said about trial. you always want to know how I am getting along. you ought to know just how I feel with out asking. if you stay in Jail six years how would you feel. you wouldnt even want no one to ask you that. in other words you people up there will help run a person insane the way you all act. I writes you and ask you to do things and you wont even answer. But yet you always wants to know how some Body is feeling and getting along. how can I feel up lifted?[27]

THIRTY-SEVEN

Loving One's Enemies

Allan Knight Chalmers was born in Cleveland, Ohio, in 1897. At sixteen he enrolled in Johns Hopkins University, where he played football and lacrosse, put the shot, managed the baseball team, joined ROTC, worked on the school newspaper, earned an A average, and was on his way to completing degree requirements in two departments when, in April 1917, he quit school to join the army. It was three days before the United States declared war, but much to Chalmers's dismay, the eye doctor concluded that his vision, though good enough for him to be the goaltender on Hopkins's championship lacrosse team, was not 20-20. He was turned away, and when he tried the navy, the result was the same. A call came for a Hopkins ambulance corps, and Chalmers helped to organize it. This time he memorized the chart and passed the eye exam, only to fail the physical when the doctor discovered a heart murmur. Chalmers went back to school and by June had completed all the requirements for his degree. He took a summer job with the forestry service, leaving when the YMCA hired him to supervise construction at Camp Meade. Soon after, the YMCA asked him to go to France to aid the French Army, whose generals, by late 1917, were not inclined to turn away volunteers simply because they had heart murmurs or less than perfect vision.[1]

By Christmas, his first ever away from home, Chalmers was

acting as a second lieutenant in the Second French Army, living under enemy fire in a dugout in the side of a hill near Verdun. For eight months he had wanted nothing more than to get there. Once there, he wondered how he could have been so naïve. When the skies were clear, he walked along the narrow-gauge railroad track that ran from Fort de Belrupt to Fort Douaumont, the air thick with the smell of the rotting bodies of both side's soldiers buried in the mud beneath his feet. In the dugout, shortly before Easter, he narrowly escaped death by a shell that killed nine of his new friends.[2]

The son and grandson of Protestant ministers who were themselves the grandsons of ministers, Chalmers naturally turned to the church for guidance. He had been sent overseas with a khaki-bound Bible, but he found that the "Star-Spangled Banner" printed inside the front cover and the pledge to fight well for Jesus and the U.S.A. on the back did not "jibe with the words inside." Nor did army routine fit with the admonition to "love one's enemies" and "do unto others as ye would that they would do unto you." Worst of all was the discovery, in a holiday letter, that the church had changed the wording of a poem he knew, from "I would be friend to all—the foe, the friendless" to "I would be friend to all—the poor, the friendless." War, he decided, though supported by the church, was incompatible with the teaching of Christ.[3]

After ten months in that trench and four more with the U.S. Army, he came home a pacifist, unsure of what he was going to do with the rest of his life. At Johns Hopkins he had thought he would be either a doctor or a history professor, and when he returned from Europe he gave teaching, at the Gillman School, a try. But the war had kicked up spiritual needs that were not satisfied by teaching or history, so notwithstanding his disgust with the hypocrisy of the church and the cowardice of so many ministers—or perhaps because of it—he decided to go to divinity school, enrolling at Yale and graduating in 1922. He had parishes in West Springfield, New Haven, and Buffalo, before being named, in 1930, pastor of New York's Broadway Tabernacle Church, a cauldron, a century earlier, of abolitionism and other antebellum social reform.[4]

Chalmers's initial encounter with the Scottsboro defense came in 1931, a month after the first trials. On his way to Talladega College for a trustees meeting, he was asked by George Haynes, secretary for race relations of the Federal Council of Churches, to see what he could find out about the case. He met with Robert

Moton at Tuskegee, and as it happened, Irving Schwab of the ILD was scheduled to speak at Moton's house that night. As Schwab spoke, there was a stunned silence, broken only by skeptical questions about the Communists. Moton's guests wondered how the Party and its plans—Schwab had spoken of a worldwide tour—would possibly help the boys. Chalmers listened more than he spoke, but he left with a sense that his feelings about the Communists, or the consequences to him personally of working with them, should not have anything to do with his attitude toward the defense. To serve justice was also to serve love, Chalmers wrote in *Tidings,* a church journal he edited, and both required him to participate in the defense. Justice and love were "beyond the communists' power to add or detract from them." So why shouldn't he join with them in a common cause?[5]

He would work with anyone for the boys' freedom, but he had his own ideas about how it ought to be achieved. He thought it an axiom of social reform that only the people living *in* a community could change it; the best efforts of outsiders were, in the long run, likely to fail. Chalmers believed the Communists understood that axiom in theory, but didn't practice it. Leibowitz didn't understand it at all, hadn't anticipated that his being a Jewish lawyer from New York would make it difficult for him to obtain racial justice in Alabama. Chalmers thought Leibowitz's defense of the boys was brilliant and his personal courage inspiring; though many friends of the defense merely endured Leibowitz, Chalmers was fond of him, enjoyed being with him. Nonetheless, by 1935 he was convinced that Leibowitz was more of a liability than an asset.[6]

Happily, by the time Chalmers was asked to lead the Scottsboro Defense Committee (SDC), in December 1935, Leibowitz had agreed to let Clarence Watts, a Huntsville attorney, do most of the dirty work at Haywood Patterson's upcoming trial. Chalmers thought the logical next step was the establishment of an Alabama branch of the SDC, and a few days after Patterson was found guilty for the fourth time and sentenced to seventy-five years, he took the idea to his committee. ILD representatives protested immediately. The Alabamans who could help, they said, couldn't be trusted. A number of non-Communists on the committee agreed with them. It had been tried before, too many times to make it a top priority. Chalmers carried a bare majority on an argument that he admitted was weak: it would cost nothing but his time to try once more.[7]

He himself knew the odds were long. He knew no one with

any power in Alabama, and his church responsibilities prevented him from making the long trips necessary to establish meaningful ties. To make matters worse, it was just days after the slashing of the sheriff and the shooting of Powell, and Chalmers was receiving contradictory reports about public opinion. Birmingham's Bishop McDowell and *Chattanooga News* editor George Fort Milton believed that the "cutting" had "re-intensified all the old feelings." Yet Joseph Gelders, a native Alabaman working as an advance man for Chalmers, reported that he found it easier than ever to get white Alabamans to talk calmly and reasonably about the case.[8]

In the middle of February 1936, Chalmers flew to Birmingham. He met first with George Fort Milton. It took him an hour and a half to satisfy Milton that he was neither a Communist nor "window dressing for the Communists," after which Milton persuaded a reluctant James Chappell, editor of the *Birmingham Age-Herald,* to give him a few minutes of his time. The five minutes Chappell promised Chalmers turned into two hours, and by that time it was Chalmers who insisted that he had to go. He told Chappell he intended to talk with everyone: labor leaders, Ozie Powell's mother, the officers of the local branch of the NAACP, Communists, and "whites of all political stripes." Chappell told him to go ahead, so long as he returned the following afternoon to meet a group of his friends.[9]

The people he met that afternoon found Chalmers even-tempered, easygoing, and gracious, not at all what they had expected of the chairman of the "Scottsboro Defense Committee." He was burly but soft around the edges, with dark eyes and a head full of thick dark hair. When others were speaking, his eyes and mouth gave assurances of seriousness and sympathy without solicitousness or alarm. When he spoke, Alabamans who had agreed to talk with him grudgingly, expecting not to be moved, found his determination infectious. He left people with the impression he not only understood their point of view but agreed with it, and he used it to get people to compromise, if not to do exactly as he wanted.

His personality was irresistible, but he was the first to acknowledge that on this visit to Alabama he had good luck. First there was the Birmingham newsman who had been uninterested, even hostile, until Chalmers mentioned that one of his grandparents was from Kentucky and that he was a trustee of Berea College and an alumnus of Johns Hopkins. Not "Hank" Chalmers, the legendary lacrosse goalie, he asked. Suddenly, Chalmers became an athlete from a southern university—as opposed to a Yankee on suspect business, and, Chalmers said, the editor suddenly became human. Then there was the prison warden. He had been reluctant even to let Chalmers meet with the defendants, until his secretary, who had been in the audience earlier in the year when Chalmers had addressed a conference of the Methodist Episcopal Church South, recognized him and told the warden that Chalmers was the minister she had been talking about ever since. From then on, Chalmers visited the defendants whenever he wanted to, and the warden, at Chalmers's suggestion, read the concluding paragraphs of Judge Horton's opinion.[10]

The next day, Chalmers met with the men Chappell had rounded up, including John Temple Graves of the *Birmingham Age-Herald*; James Mills of the *Birmingham Post*; Forney Johnston, who was the son of a former governor and a leading Alabama attorney; Donald Comer, owner of the Avondale Mills and also the son of a former governor; Guy Snaveley, president of Birmingham Southern College; and Bishop McDowell. The meeting got off to a rough start when one of the southerners suggested the boys plead guilty in exchange for reduced sentences and immediate release. Chalmers stood up and said: "Gentlemen I don't want to seem arbitrary but on this point there is no question in our minds. We believe the boys to be innocent and we are not open to any compromises on this point. Do you want me to stay or not?"[11]

They did, and by the time the meeting broke up, Chalmers had a blueprint for an Alabama committee under the direction of Henry Edmonds, founder and minister of Birmingham's Independent Presbyterian Church and head of the CIC in Alabama. (As early as 1933 Edmonds had addressed a public meeting of blacks and whites called to promote a fair trial.) Back in New York, Chalmers reported to his committee that the Alabamans had agreed to advise the SDC, work to create a climate of favorable public opinion, and procure local counsel to cooperate with the defense at the next trial. The Alabamans understood that the SDC opposed guilty pleas, and they promised to retain only attorneys who were convinced of the defendants' innocence. Chalmers hoped that members of the Alabama committee would also be convinced of the defendants' innocence. But if they were not, he insisted they at least be convinced of their right to acquittal on grounds of reasonable doubt. For its part, the SDC promised to prevent radical organizations from using the case for propaganda and to encourage Leibowitz to keep a low profile if not stay out of Alabama altogether.[12]

It was a terrific start, yet Chalmers's presence was so powerful that agreements had a way of collapsing shortly after he left a room. He took stenographic notes, which he referred to when people insisted that his perceptions of negotiations were skewed toward his desires. The notes rarely helped, for people agreed to things or made promises when sitting in a room with him that they couldn't keep when he wasn't there. Within days of his return from Alabama, it became clear that his and McDowell's understanding of the agreement was different at several crucial points. Or as Chalmers put it, the Alabamans "got cold feet."[13]

Part of the problem was that when Chalmers sent McDowell an annotated copy of the "plan of co-operation," based on his discussions with his committee upon his return to New York, he had no choice but to note in parentheses that the SDC had itself balked at the idea of putting the defendants' lives in the hands of anyone not willing to commit himself to the proposition that they were innocent.[14]

McDowell wrote back immediately to say that no one in his group was willing. McDowell and the others believed that it was "most probable" that most were not guilty of any serious charge, and "quite possible" that all were. But, unconvinced themselves of the defendants' complete innocence, they were unwilling to ask others to commit themselves to more than justice. (And even if they had been willing, they said, they would not have been able to find more than a handful.) McDowell insisted that their conclusions had nothing to do with "racial or sectional prejudices" but came from careful study and close observation, "not from a long distance but from close up, not from a sentimental but from a very practical and personal interest" in justice. That said, he and his friends had a different idea of justice. They believed the defendants were entitled to acquittals, especially considering the characters of their accusers. But because they did not think it likely that all the defendants would be acquitted, they didn't think acquittal or death the only alternatives. Prison sentences, like Patterson's, for example, could be modified later.[15]

In light of the distance between the Alabamans and the SDC, McDowell concluded that he and the others could continue to help the committee as individuals, behind the scenes, but ought not take an active public role in the case. Chalmers didn't think that was enough, and so, in order to keep the conversation going, he planned another trip to Alabama. He went down thinking that differences about innocence and outcomes made the chances of success thin, only to discover that it was worse than that. The Alabamans were angry that Chalmers had been unable to muzzle the ILD and other anti-Alabama propagandists. Nor had Chalmers been able to persuade Leibowitz to quit the case. Now he was not even saying that he could.[16]

Chalmers returned to New York discouraged, but he was as stubborn as he was shrewd. He persuaded his committee to drop its demand that members of the Alabama committee swear to their belief in the defendants' innocence. That concession, he argued, was likely to get the Alabamans moving, particularly in the area of public opinion, without in any way committing the SDC to put negotiations with the prosecution (or the trial work) in hands they didn't trust. Chalmers spent the next six weeks working out the other sticking points, and by the end of his third trip, late in April, the formation of the Alabama Scottsboro Fair Trial Committee seemed imminent. At the insistence of the Alabamans, it was to be a wholly indigenous organization, without organic connection to the SDC. Edmonds and the others planned to work with the Alabama Bar Association to assemble a team of outstanding Alabama attorneys who would take over only after they received the approval of the SDC. (Until then, they would be patient about the removal of Leibowitz.) And they planned to go public in a letter, signed by one hundred prominent white Alabamans, mentioning neither guilt nor innocence but the Alabama committee's goal of an unprejudiced trial.[17]

Then, in the first week of June, a gloating Tom Knight called a press conference to share private correspondence, leaked to him by a member of the Alabama Bar Association, between the Alabama committee-to-be and the Bar Association, correspondence about southern attorneys for the next trial. Knight hoped to embarrass the Alabamans, create mistrust between them and Chalmers, and infuriate Leibowitz—in short, to kill the Alabama committee and the new alliance at birth. And he almost did. But once Edmonds, Chalmers, and Leibowitz realized what had happened, they were as one in their desire to prevent Knight from getting his way. Edmonds got his first real taste of Knight's unscrupulousness and it sickened him, leaving him more determined than ever to undo him. Chalmers, relieved to discover that the Alabamans hadn't double-crossed him, dispatched a flurry of letters and telegrams, restating the confidence of his committee in Edmonds and the growing spirit of understanding and trust.[18]

He also had a long talk with Leibowitz, rushing to his office to explain that the committee had never intended to remove him against his will; once he had pacified Leibowitz, Chalmers got further than ever in persuading him that once good and trustworthy counsel were secured it would be best for him to stay in New York—a development that Chalmers was able to report "confidentially" to Edmonds.[19]

The Alabama committee survived, but as 1936 wore on, Chalmers was disappointed, though not entirely surprised, to find that despite all the good feelings, the Alabamans were slow in getting about their work. The committee was racked by internal divisions, particularly between the eagerness of its youngest members and the caution of its oldest. Nearly two months passed before Edmonds issued the press release announcing its formation. The Alabamans' educational campaign was extremely cautious; they weren't even willing to saturate the state with Judge Horton's opinion. Each time Chalmers tried to hurry them along, Edmonds replied with testier questions about his own progress with Leibowitz and the Communists, tasks that Edmonds thought no more difficult than those the SDC had asked of them: namely, to remove Knight and Callahan and arrange a change of venue. In Edmonds's eyes, the northerners did nothing but make demands and set deadlines. When they met them, the northerners demanded more, as if trying only to string them along.[20]

What could Chalmers do about it? The Alabamans were sure to move gingerly until Leibowitz was out; Leibowitz would not get out until the Alabamans met the committee's demands. The Alabamans complained about every bit of SDC publicity; yet Chalmers's associates, especially the ACLU's Roger Baldwin and the ILD's Anna Damon, felt muzzled. They believed agitation had spared the defendants the chair and would in time bring Alabama to the bargaining table. It couldn't be separated from negotiation.[21]

Throughout the fall and summer of 1936, Chalmers met regularly with Edmonds, Johnston, and Chappell, leaving for Alabama after Sunday services. After those meetings, he usually visited the defendants. On one of those visits, he was surrounded by a group of armed men and told to leave town. After another visit, he was cornered by the lieutenant governor, Thomas Knight.[22]

"Plead the boys guilty," Knight said, "and I'll see to it that they get only seven years." Chalmers's first instinct was to say no, flat out; his second was to remember that they had already served five years and that it was their lives, not his, that were passing in cells half the size of a nine-by-six rug. Chalmers told Knight that the boys were innocent and he could have nothing to do with guilty pleas. But, he added, it was their decision not his: "Put it to them yourself." Knight told Chalmers that he had already put the offer to them, but that they had rejected it, because (he thought) they didn't believe that it was a "straight deal." Reluctantly Chalmers went back to the see the boys. He spoke first to Andy Wright. Wright said, "No, Doc., I'll rot here till I die before I'll say I did something I didn't do just to get myself out of here."[23]

Chalmers returned to New York without even mentioning Knight's offer to the others, but things moved so slowly that summer and fall that he feared that the defendants very well might rot in jail. The Alabamans finally selected a lawyer to work with Watts, Congressman Archibald Carmichael, of Tuscumbia, but neither Leibowitz nor anyone on the SDC was happy about the choice and negotiations broke down shortly after Carmichael set his fees: a five-thousand-dollar retainer and five thousand more for the first trial. (Watts charged half that—and Chalmers considered *his* fee high.) The trials were postponed once more, this time because Judge Callahan was sick. In the meantime, letters from the defendants, reports from visitors, and his own visits convinced Chalmers that the defendants were deteriorating in mind and body. He tried to get Edmonds to do something about it, writing to say that their confinement was driving them insane. The great danger, Chalmers said, was that when the case was finally resolved we will have "destroyed something which cannot be restored."[24]

Edmonds visited the defendants and was visibly shaken, but he concluded there was nothing his committee could do. Chalmers hired A. A. Brill, a student of Jung and translator of Freud, and G. C. Branche, the Tuskegee doctor, to conduct an extensive series of neuropsychiatric exams. And he wrote to Governor Graves, insisting that whatever the reasons for the defendants' close confinement for nine months, and the guards' refusal to let them exercise, the treatment had driven several of them "into such mental decline and physical disintegration (sometimes called prison psychosis)" that they were being "executed without a fair trial." As in his letter to Edmonds, Chalmers warned that even the most conservative members of his committee were pressuring to protest publicly. If the governor did not do something, he would have to act.[25]

Graves did not respond, and all seemed lost when in late December 1936 Knight, without notice, arrived in New York. He had come to talk to Leibowitz about a deal.

T H I R T Y - E I G H T

You Ought to Know Me Better Than That

After the sheriff shot Powell and Callahan postponed the remaining trials, Leibowitz turned his attention back to clients who paid for his services. He won an acquittal for Laura Parr, a beautiful Manhattanite in her late twenties, charged (then tried and convicted in the press) with the murder of her lover, a charming, highly educated, and cultured German businessman. Leibowitz was also involved in the Lindbergh case, conducting a series of prison interviews with Bruno Richard Hauptmann, in an unsuccessful effort, in the months before Hauptmann's execution, to get him to reveal the full story of the kidnapping and murder.[1]

Leibowitz paid only occasional attention to the work of the Scottsboro Defense Committee, and when in May 1936 he learned that Allan Knight Chalmers had recruited a group of prominent Alabamans, under the direction of a liberal minister, to work with the SDC, he was pleasantly surprised. With Alabama public opinion, they needed all the help they could get. When Tom Knight leaked correspondence between the Alabama committee and the Alabama Bar Association, Leibowitz was not so pleasantly surprised to learn one of the reasons for Chalmers's success. Apparently he and Edmonds had strongly suggested, if not promised, that Leibowitz would be replaced; in the meantime the Alabamans were shopping around for a new attorney.[2]

Leibowitz issued an angry statement to the press. The boys wanted him to defend them. What's more, talk of Alabama attorneys was little more than a diversion and had been from the start. Where, he asked, was the prominent Alabama attorney who would have raised the question of adequate counsel? Where was the Alabaman who would have challenged the jury system? Most of the so-called southern liberals regarded life imprisonment as a fair resolution of the case. Leibowitz said he bore full responsibility for the defendants and would step aside only when he was certain the youths were truly in safe hands.[3]

In a long meeting with Chalmers, he made it clear that he was ultimately in charge and retained the right to veto anyone's choice of attorneys to assist him—let alone replace him. He was satisfied by Chalmers's explanation that Knight had quoted private correspondence out of context, and he was reassured by letters from Edmonds and Clarence Watts, who said, as Chalmers had, they had never intended to force him out of the case. They had simply been trying to determine who among Alabama's best attorneys would be willing to help if, in the event of great progress, Leibowitz were to decide to remain in New York.[4]

The Alabama Scottsboro Fair Trial Committee went back to its work and so did Leibowitz, but he was not satisfied with its progress. Before leaving for a vacation in Europe at the end of June 1936, he wrote to Clarence Watts to express his disappointment and to say that for him to step out at this point would "constitute a desertion" of the defendants. When he returned two months later, it was as if the committee had also been on vacation—they hadn't circulated Horton's opinion, they hadn't persuaded Knight and Callahan to step aside, they hadn't even found counsel that met Leibowitz's criteria. And to Leibowitz's further dismay, Edmonds was still talking about his withdrawal and strongly suggesting that Chalmers was too. Leibowitz gave them an ultimatum: if there was no progress in two weeks, he would begin to prepare for the trials as if there were no Alabama committee and no Alabama counsel.[5]

The deadline passed and Leibowitz began to prepare for the trials he expected Callahan would schedule any day. Then, in the last week of December, he received a telephone call from Thomas Knight. Knight said he was in New York, wanted to see him, and asked him to stop by his hotel. Leibowitz said no, inviting him instead to dinner at his home and promising not to talk about the case. Knight said he wanted to talk about the case—but didn't want anyone to know he was there. When Leibowitz arrived at the New Yorker the next morning, he found Alabama Attorney General Albert Carmichael there too (no relation to Congressman Archibald Carmichael). Knight got right to the point. The case was bleeding Alabama financially, and it was a nuisance, politically and every other way. He was sick of the Scottsboro Boys, and he was prepared to make a disposition satisfactory to all. He offered to end the prosecution of Roberson, Montgomery, and Williams, to give Roy Wright and Powell ten years for simple assault, and Andy Wright and Weems ten years for rape.

Leibowitz got up and walked to the window of the hotel room, motioning for Knight to follow him. He pointed down the block, in the direction of the Fourteenth Precinct police station. The sergeant behind the desk, Leibowitz said, probably received a dozen complaints a day, many of them from crackpots, publicity seekers, and liars. He was no genius, but years of experience had given him some ability to tell, on the spot, when complainants were lying. "Had Victoria Price and Ruby Bates walked into that station house to complain to the sergeant on duty that nine Negro boys had raped them, that sergeant, after questioning them for five minutes, would have known them to be two liars. He would have tossed them out of the precinct and that would have been the end of the whole affair."

"What's the point?" Knight asked.

"Even the dumbest cop on the force would have spotted those two as tramps and liars. You know damn well they lied that day at the Paint Rock station and the Price girl has been lying ever since. Now you want me to plead three or four of the boys guilty of something they never did. The State of Alabama finally realizes that it has made a horrible mistake. You want me to pull your chestnuts out of the fire. You want a chance to save face. Tom, you ought to know me better than that."

"They fought with those white boys and threw some of them off the train," Knight said. Leibowitz reminded Knight that assault carried a five-year sentence and that not all of the boys had been in the fight.[6]

The three of them met several times at Knight's hotel and subsequently in Washington, and after considerable argument reached an agreement: the state would release Olen Montgomery, Willie Roberson, Eugene Williams, and Roy Wright at once. Leibowitz would advise Clarence Norris, Charlie Weems, and Andy Wright to plead guilty to simple assault, for which they would receive a sentence of not more than five years, with the possibility of parole after two more years in jail. Haywood Patterson would be released whenever they were. The state would drop rape charges against Ozie Powell and charge him only with assaulting the sheriff. Leibowitz was not entirely satisfied with the agreement; it left the fates of Patterson and Powell to the good faith of Alabama officials—and he didn't trust them. But considering the unlikelihood of the successful appeal of subsequent convictions on constitutional grounds, it was a better bet than new trials and long prison sentences, if not death. Knight had come to New York looking, nearly begging, for a way out, but for a prosecutor he begged from an unusually strong position: he knew that if the case went to trial the jury would give him most if not all of what he asked for.[7]

Knight and Carmichael promised Leibowitz they would take the proposal back to Alabama, get the approval of Judge Callahan and local solicitors, and get back to him; Leibowitz, meanwhile, promised to take the proposal to the SDC. Neither Chalmers, whom Leibowitz had kept informed of the negotiations, nor Morris Shapiro (SDC secretary and Chalmers's closest ally), nor any other SDC official wanted to be party to a deal. Their position was that the boys were innocent and, as Norman Thomas put it, an admission that they were guilty of simple assault would surely be interpreted by the public as admission that they were guilty of a sex crime.[8]

But Shapiro was an attorney, as were committee members Roger Baldwin and Whitney North Seymour. They understood as well as Leibowitz that the boys' legal lifelines were frayed. They also understood that Leibowitz, whatever else they thought of him, was not one to settle for anything less than he thought he could get. Leibowitz assured Chalmers and Shapiro that he had pushed the state as far as he could. And he assured them he would not proceed without consulting with the boys and their relatives, letting them know that the SDC, holding fast to its belief in their complete innocence, would continue to defend them whether or not they decided to go along with the proposed settlement. The SDC endorsed the compromise, reluctantly: "I say yes," Shapiro told Chalmers's secretary, "but with a very heavy heart, and feel very badly about it." Leibowitz made plans to travel to Alabama and present the proposal to the boys.[9]

Then, as suddenly and unexpectedly as Carmichael and Knight

had appeared, and even before Leibowitz was able to leave for Alabama, they broke off communication. Carmichael didn't get back to Leibowitz, and when Leibowitz called him, his secretary said he was not in. He returned neither the calls nor Leibowitz's telegrams. Leibowitz cursed them; it was shabby treatment, particularly when they had come to New York asking him to help them out of their own mess. He worried that Carmichael wanted stiffer sentences, a harsher plea. Chalmers and Shapiro assured him that Henry Edmonds and Forney Johnston were busy trying to determine what had happened and why, but what followed was a circus of uncertainty. One day Chalmers would report that he had learned that Callahan had reacted angrily ("No fifty-dollar fines for rape!") to Carmichael's proposal, at which time Carmichael backed down. Two days later it would be Carmichael who was holding things up, simply using Callahan as an excuse. Both Callahan and Carmichael denied they stood in the way of compromise and each hinted it was the other.[10]

The sudden death of Thomas Knight, in the third week of May 1937, only added to the confusion. Few friends of the defense mourned; Leibowitz assumed that the defendants had cheered. But he himself had a sense that, unlikely as it seemed, the lieutenant governor's death was bad news for a compromise. Having prosecuted the case so stubbornly for so long, Knight didn't have to worry about anyone calling him soft on rape. He could retreat without significant political sacrifice. The same could not be said for his attorney general, Albert Carmichael, who struck Leibowitz as spineless. Carmichael's assistant attorney general, Thomas "Buddy" Lawson, was up for reelection in a year.[11]

A week after Knight died, Callahan announced that the trials would resume on July 12. Carmichael denied that a compromise was in the works and said the state was ready. When reporters asked Leibowitz for a statement, he joked that it would be hot down there—the nation was in the grip of a heat wave—and then added that he knew for a fact that all sorts of prominent Alabamans were in favor of compromise. Chalmers and Morris Shapiro continued to say, though not always with infectious confidence, that their Alabama allies, old and new, including prominent attorneys unconnected with the defense committee, were putting pressure on Carmichael and Callahan.[12]

There were some encouraging developments: Birmingham editors reported that a compromise was in the making and supported it wholeheartedly. The editor of the *Post* suggested that the prison terms agreed to by defense and prosecution ought to take into account the time the defendants had already served, which put him out in front of some members of the Alabama committee. Calls for compromise came also from editors who had heretofore supported the prosecution without even the slightest reservation, most notably Grover Hall, editor of the influential *Montgomery Advertiser.* Chalmers admitted that Hall's editorial calling for compromise, which came in the middle of June, wasn't perfect. But, he said, "in light of the paper's past attitudes," it was "almost a miracle." Hall, Chalmers told Leibowitz, was a close friend of Attorney General Carmichael and Governor Graves. On June 26, Chalmers's tireless Alabama ally, Forney Johnston, reported that Carmichael and Callahan were willing to go through with the compromise outlined in February just as soon as the cases were called for trial.[13]

Leibowitz thought such assurances should have come to him directly from the attorney general, who still refused to call or answer his calls. He had a hard time "squaring" Carmichael's insistence that he was sticking by the agreement with his public talk of preparations for trial. Leibowitz told Chalmers and Shapiro he wanted confirmation of Carmichael's attitude and intentions from Grover Hall. Until he heard from Carmichael or Hall, he would assume that on July 12 he would be in court, in Decatur, for the first day of Clarence Norris's third trial.[14]

THIRTY-NINE

Lay Down This Body of Death

Grover Cleveland Hall was born in Haleburg, Alabama, in 1888. His grandfather's grandfather, an Englishman living in Northern Ireland, had emigrated to the colony of Georgia in the 1760s. Eighty years later, shortly after Congress opened up half a million acres of public land for settlement, Hall's grandfather moved his family to Henry County, Alabama—in the wire-grass region of the southeast corner of the state. In 1860, Hall's grandfather owned 2,000 acres and thirty-five slaves, and he and his neighbors were enthusiastic about secession. Two of Hall's sons enlisted in the Sixth Alabama Infantry; James was killed in action, and William, one of three in his company to survive hand-to-hand combat at the Battle of Seven Pines, was seriously wounded at Gettysburg. Fifteen years later, William Hall named his sixth and last son after the first Democratic president since Buchanan.[1]

The family's fortunes declined fast after the war, and by the time Grover was born, his father owned a mere 160 acres. Although closer in land and income to the poor farmers of the postwar South than to the planters and landlords, the Halls were not Populists; in 1892, Hall's father and brother Samuel went armed to their polling place to cast the only Democratic votes in their precinct. The Halls had memories of the old days that made it difficult for them to identify with the raggedy bunch bolting the party. And they didn't think farming the only honest way to make a living. Hall's father, an amateur veterinarian, encouraged his sons to try something else, and Grover followed his brother William into the newspaper business, taking a job as a printer's devil at the *Dothan Eagle*. He moved on and up quickly. Within three years he was the editor of the *Daily Siftings,* though he lost that job shortly after he defended a traveling song-and-dance troupe, a brother and a sister who were under attack, as salacious, by the minister of the Methodist Church. The church terminated its business with the paper and stockholders forced Hall to resign. In 1910, three years and at least three newspaper jobs later (he was fired from one when his boss tired of the smoke from his cigars and his refusal to sweep the office floor), he was invited to be the third man on the editorial page of the *Montgomery Advertiser,* a paper he held in such high regard that he had never even considered applying there for a job.[2]

In politics the eighty-two-year-old *Advertiser* had always been in the Democratic Party's mainstream, vigorously opposed to populism and, more recently, wary of progressivism. That suited Hall. Although at twenty-two he shared many values with the southern progressives, he detested Prohibition and every other form of progressive moral proscription. His first notable *Advertiser* editorial was a defense of Alice Roosevelt Longworth's right to smoke, and by the time he became editor-in-chief in 1926, the paper had become a powerful voice for his idiosyncratic blend of traditionalism and unorthodoxy, which he defined, abstractly, as a belief in absolute freedom of the human spirit. In practice it meant support for small government, balanced budgets, and interracial cooperation; faith in science; skepticism toward religious fundamentalism; and insistence upon individual liberty and the complete separation of church and state. Hall cheered the defeat of an "antievolution" bill in the state legislature two years before John Scopes challenged a similar law in Tennessee. Hall's idol was H. L. Mencken, his very model in substance and style. He had begun reading him in the *Smart Set,* corresponded with him in the early 1920s, and, after Mencken married a Montgomery friend of his in 1930, he and Mencken became friends.[3]

The resurrected Ku Klux Klan was the embodiment of all Hall thought wrong with the South, but until 1926, when three Klan-backed candidates—none of whom Hall thought had a chance—were swept into office, he seriously underestimated the Klan's political threat. Charles McCall became Alabama's attorney general;

Bibb Graves, its governor; and Hugo Black, one of its U.S. senators. Liberal southern journalists, including Julian Harris (who had just won a Pulitzer Prize for his editorial war on the Klan in Georgia), encouraged Hall to go after them, and the *Advertiser*'s owner gave his permission, on the condition that Hall focus on Klan violence. All Hall needed was provocation, and that came on the first of July, 1927, when Klansmen abducted and flogged an Oneonta man they had seen drinking near a church. Two days later Hall ran his first anti-Klan editorial; by the end of August he had run half a dozen.[4]

He called Klansmen the "drill-sergeants of hatred, the go-getters of intolerance, the high powered salesmen of bigotry, aided and abetted by the Machiavellis of politics." Hall ridiculed the governor and attorney general for not using their prestige and power to stop Klan lawlessness, comparing the state's hands-off policy toward the Klan with its vigorous enforcement of Prohibition. He asked Klansmen to give up their hoods voluntarily and proposed strong antimask legislation if they refused. Governor Graves eventually ordered state police to investigate the flogging, and Attorney General McCall, after quitting the Klan, prosecuted the accused. But Graves also responded to Hall's attacks by supporting legislation that would have allowed fines for libelous criticism of public officials, prompting Hall to compare him to Trotsky and Mussolini. The Klan boycotted the paper and circulation increased by 4,000. Hall was praised by liberals nationwide and, in 1928, won a Pulitzer Prize.[5]

Earlier in 1928, Hall had endorsed Al Smith for president, thereby drawing fierce criticism from Alabama's other U.S. senator, Tom Heflin, a man so unembarrassed by his prejudices that he glibly admitted to a Senate investigating committee that he received money from the Klan for anti-Catholic speeches. Hall struck back, and was not surprised when, after Smith's nomination, Heflin bolted the Democratic Party and openly campaigned for Hoover. Hall and his loyalist allies managed to keep the state in the Democratic column—by 7,000 votes—and as soon as the election was over, he set out to use the issues of disloyalty and Klan affiliation to unseat Heflin and defeat William C. Davis, the Klan-backed candidate to succeed Graves in the election of 1930. Against Heflin and Davis, Hall supported John Bankhead, an old ally, and Benjamin Meeks Miller, a new one. Miller was a former state supreme court justice whose quiet courage and dogged determination had earned him the nickname "The Sturdy Oak of Wilcox." Miller said he was "neither pro-Klan or anti-Klan" but for the best interest of all, Jew and Gentile, Protestant and Catholic. Yet he ran against Klan control of state government and the profligate government spending of the progressive Graves. He invited voters to "Save Millions with Miller" and won by a wide margin, as did Bankhead. Hall was ecstatic. He considered the election a greater vindication of his politics than the Pulitzer.[6]

It was less than six months after that election that news of the mass arrest at Paint Rock and the averted lynching at Scottsboro came across the wires. Hall "applauded lustily," praising the sheriff and governor and also the "grim mountaineers" of Jackson County who, newly blessed with self-restraint, had let the law take its course. Persuaded by wire-service reports of the trials that the defendants were guilty, and by the posttrial investigations of Birmingham journalists that the proceedings were fair, Hall concluded that the Communists were driven by expediency and opportunism alone. He called them buzzards, likened them to the Carpetbaggers, and insisted they couldn't care less about justice. Their aim was political thunder; Scottsboro and sharecroppers' unions, ways to make it. There was no point in arguing with them, trying to point out the facts of the case. Nor was there any point in worrying about the possibility—nonexistent—of Americans, black or white, going red. Yet Hall believed the Communists had to be confronted. The real danger of communism was the very real possibility that Klan politicians and other reactionaries, so recently driven from office, would seize upon its specter and use it to return to power by way of fear and hate.[7]

Hall thought he understood the Communists. But the liberals baffled him—Dreiser, Steffens, Dos Passos, as well as the editors of a "surprisingly large number of eastern newspapers, many otherwise intelligent and enlightened journals." He respected them and considered them his intellectual allies, and he was stung by their attacks. He had assumed that with their intelligence they would have thought twice before lending the weight of their names to reckless denunciations of Alabama and, worse, to threats against men like Governor Miller, who had fought the Klan at every turn, saved the Scottsboro defendants' lives by calling out the militia, and never in his life said a nasty word about a Negro.[8]

Hall tried to reason with them, explaining to those protesting the "legal lynching" that instead of lynching the nine Negroes who beat up six white men and then assaulted two white girls, Alabama had given them as fair a trial as possible. The case against them, which included their own confessions, was "overwhelming in its force." Hall got nowhere. The northern intelligentsia not only "swallowed the stuff broadcast by the radicals," making a "race problem" of a criminal trial. They took the radicals further, insisting that grown men were "boys" and common criminals "political prisoners," shedding crocodile tears for their poor mothers. Having tried persuasion and found it useless, Hall lashed out at the "indecent" and "outrageous" conduct of "idiots." But he never stopped trying to figure them out. A year after the trials, the Alabama Supreme Court upheld the convictions, leaving no room for doubt, Hall thought, about the defendants' guilt. Yet the "calumnies" and "harangues" of professional liberals went unabated. Perhaps, Hall wrote, Alabama's critics were simply opponents of capital punishment in disguise.[9]

Throughout 1933, Hall remained steadfast in his defense of the state. He took Ruby Bates no more seriously than the jurors did, and he had nothing to say about Judge Horton. He believed that his own criticism of the South gave him the right to criticize the South's critics when they were wrong. He believed his attacks on anti-Semitism wherever it appeared gave him the right to attack Leibowitz without being tarred with that brush. He exercised those rights liberally, and in 1934 the continuing controversy encouraged him to break an old *Advertiser* tradition. In the past, editors had endorsed only candidates for governor and the U.S. Senate. He endorsed Thomas Knight in his race for lieutenant governor, urging voters to cast their vote "as a rebuke by Alabama to the outer world for the contumely and slander that it had heaped upon our state because of the Scottsboro cases."[10]

When at the end of 1934, Leibowitz feuded with the ILD, Hall ridiculed both sides. When in April 1935, the U.S. Supreme Court reversed the convictions for a second time, he ridiculed the justices. He granted the technical point—that in practice, Negroes were excluded—and he urged jury commissions to put the names of reputable Negroes on the roles, making it possible for Alabama to win a case involving a Negro in the Supreme Court. Otherwise, he thought Chief Justice Hughes's "pontifical deliverance" was "a lot of baloney." He simply couldn't stomach the idea that the Supreme Court, "reviewing the trial of two men charged with an offense that stands first among felonies in this State," reversed the verdict of "an oathbound jury" because it did not like the "color scheme of that jury." Was the Court saying that it was more concerned with the "academic political 'rights' of a politically dispossessed race" than with the "otherwise credible evidence demonstrating human depravity"?[11]

Admitting that he might be thick, Hall could not see what the political rights of Negroes in Alabama had to do with the guilt or innocence of "the gorillas" charged with rape. Either they did it or they did not. If they did, the jury, though white, knew the truth and reported it faithfully. If they did not do it, the jury would have said so. In a subsequent editorial he asked if the Supreme Court was qualified to rule on the case, since it too had "systematically excluded Negroes" for 140 years. Hall urged Thomas Knight to prosecute the Scottsboro "sucklings" to "the bitter end." The dignity of a self-respecting state demanded no less.[12]

With the exception of his editorials in January 1936 praising sheriffs for their restraint after Ozie Powell slashed Deputy Sheriff Blalock, Hall wrote nothing about the case for two years after *Norris* v. *Alabama*. What was the point? Alabama's critics were no more likely to find truth in his words than he was to find it in theirs. Then in May 1937, Thomas Knight died. The case had been Knight's case to win or lose. Hall thought he had deserved to win it, and he had been prepared to assist him, regardless of the cost to the state in cash and prestige. With Knight's death, Hall began to wonder if there was another way out. Now that the honor at stake wasn't Tommy Knight's, perhaps it made sense to sacrifice a bit of it in order to salvage the state's reputation. But how? He had been asked, the previous year, to join the Alabama Scottsboro Fair Trial Committee, but he refused, preferring to "remain aloof from all organized propaganda agencies." Within a month of Knight's death, he agreed to meet with Chalmers.[13]

It was admiration and affection at first sight. After six years of disingenuousness and delusion, here was a man who made sense. And what a difference just one man talking sense could make. Hall suddenly discovered that there were all sorts of facts about the case that he ought to have known before. He still thought the evidence showed unmistakably that Price and Bates had been attacked. But he hadn't realized that in 1931 one of the accused was twelve and another thirteen—"mere children." Nor that there was so much doubt, some coming from evidence of physical disability, that all of those on trial were the culprits. In the middle of June 1937, after a meeting with Chalmers, Hall sat down to write an editorial on the case, which he called "Lay Down This Body of Death." He had been reading Thomas Gray.[14]

Hall used the first half of the editorial to remind readers of his credentials as the prosecution's most stalwart defender. He refused to apologize for anything. He knew all about southern sentiment about the crime and the law, all about the whole sickening, sordid story. He also knew that "the 'Scottsboro Boys'—now approaching middle-age—committed whatever crime they might have committed in extraordinary circumstances, and against two women who by all accounts never before had put a high premium upon their virtue." Scottsboro had injured Alabama immeasurably. There were grounds for reasonable doubt about the positive guilt of all of the men now in jail. Considering that they had been in jail for six years, considering that they were "doing more than all other citizens of Alabama combined to injure the whole people of Alabama before the world," Hall urged the state to move for a decent, dignified compromise. "Nothing could be gained by demanding the final pound of flesh."[15]

Hall telephoned his friend Albert Carmichael, the attorney general, and read him the editorial. Carmichael applauded "enthusiastically." Hall asked if he had any suggestions for revision; Carmichael advised him not to change a word. Then, to get his editorial to readers in northern Alabama, where the *Advertiser* had almost no circulation, Hall telephoned the editors of the *Birmingham News* and the *Birmingham Post* and asked them to report his call for compromise. Forney Johnston telephoned them too, and both papers reprinted the entire editorial. Hall also called the editors of the *Huntsville Times* and the *Decatur Daily,* asking them to comment upon his editorial or reprint it. The *Daily* did neither; the *Times* did both.[16]

Hall then joined Johnston in his efforts to determine why the movement toward an out-of-court settlement, initiated by Knight and Carmichael six months earlier, appeared to have stalled. Johnston met with Carmichael on June 18. Carmichael said he was willing to go through with the agreement as long as it was acceptable to Callahan. Johnston told Carmichael that he himself had met with Callahan and Callahan was willing. That made a noticeable impression on him, but Carmichael still appeared to be concerned that it would hurt him professionally and politically, and the next day he backed off: he said he was willing to discuss a settlement, but only after the cases were called. Carmichael expressed bitterness about press interviews and reports from New York, and Johnston feared that he intended to make heavy demands based on the state's readiness. Hall and Johnston each visited Carmichael a few days later. On June 22, Johnston reported that everything that could be done was being done: "We are simply dealing with an obstinate official." Carmichael had finally admitted that Callahan was agreeable, but he himself was afraid that negotiations before the call of the case might break down and result in embarrassing and costly postponements. Hall urged Carmichael to uphold his end of the deal.[17]

On July 2, Johnston received a call from Chalmers, who was leaving for Europe the next day. Months earlier, thinking that the case would be settled long before July, Chalmers had agreed to be a delegate to an international conference of church leaders at Oxford. Now Chalmers was disturbed by the confusion in Alabama and by Leibowitz's skepticism that the deal would go through, skepticism based primarily on Carmichael's refusal to negotiate with him.[18]

Johnston tried to reassure Chalmers. Grover Hall, he said, had been to see Carmichael a few days earlier and had learned that both the attorney general and the judge were ready to go forward with a settlement. Nothing had changed since then. In Chalmers's absence, Johnston promised to do his best to reconcile all the different viewpoints, to try to keep Leibowitz and Carmichael cool, to ensure that there were no guilty pleas, and to see to it that the six years the defendants had already served counted as their sentence. Johnston and Hall were especially interested in the last point. The case wouldn't be closed, the propaganda eliminated, until all the defendants were out of jail. It was in Alabama's interest to rid itself of all the defendants at once.[19]

The first of the trials that had been postponed in February 1936, after Powell slashed the sheriff, was set to begin in ten days. Johnston promised that he and Hall would use that time to assemble a committee of lawyers to be on hand in Decatur when the cases were called, in the event that the prosecution and judge decided to back down or try to sweeten their end of the deal.[20]

F O R T Y

After Six and a Half Years in Jail

In the first week and a half of July 1937, there were reports and rumors of compromise almost every day, followed by official denials. On July 6, the day he arraigned Clarence Norris, Judge Callahan told reporters there would be no compromise—nor would there be soldiers or cameras at the trial. Two days later, Solicitor Hutson was more vehement. The defendants, he said, were either guilty or not guilty of rape. When editors and friends of the defense tried to reach Attorney General Carmichael, the former to confirm Hutson's denials, the latter to try to get him to change his mind, they were told that he had yet to return from North Carolina, where he had gone for vacation the last week in June. The case, they were informed, was in the hands of his assistant, Buddy Lawson.[1]

Morris Shapiro, who was on the scene, told Leibowitz that it was his impression that Carmichael had not set out to double-cross him, though he couldn't rule out the possibility entirely. Rather, Shapiro believed that Carmichael had "really thought" he could get the compromise by Callahan, and disappeared when he realized he was mistaken. Shapiro himself had met with Callahan, but couldn't move him. Shortly afterwards, another attorney, an old college friend of the judge, had tried his hand and was "unceremoniously repulsed."[2]

On Monday, July 12, Leibowitz and Lawson began interviewing

prospective jurors. Three out of one hundred were black. One black man was excused when he said he didn't believe in capital punishment; the other two were struck by the state. Not even the start of jury selection stilled talk of a negotiated settlement, and when Leibowitz left for Birmingham in the middle of the day, reporters assumed it was to meet state officials, driving up from Montgomery, halfway.[3]

On Tuesday morning, after Judge Callahan denied the defense's motion for a transfer to federal court, Clarence Norris's third trial, the ninth Scottsboro trial, began. Price told her story quickly, and after cross-examination by Clarence Watts, the prosecution proceeded with its corroborating witnesses. A few said they thought they had seen the fight on the train; a few said they had seen Price swoon at the depot. Watts cross-examined them. Then Leibowitz, who was on his best behavior, impressing friend and foe alike with his humility and restraint, together with Buddy Lawson reenacted the direct and cross-examination of Dr. Bridges, who had died shortly after Haywood Patterson's last trial. Watts called a few new witnesses, including Ruby Bates's mother and two Huntsville deputy sheriffs. The sheriffs told the court they would not believe a word Price said, not even under oath.[4]

Callahan rushed Watts along, though in this trial he seemed less interested in frustrating the defense than in beating the heat. It was ninety-five humid degrees outdoors at noon, and hotter than that in the horribly ventilated courtroom. The whir of fans made it hard to hear the quieter witnesses, and the air was so thick that Callahan himself, seventy-four and said to have a bad heart, climbed down from the bench more than once, explaining that up near the ceiling he couldn't breathe.[5]

In closing arguments, Watts talked of his southern roots and pride. He wanted to believe Alabama was a state where "even-handed justice was administered to black and white alike." Yet he was absolutely certain that no white man would convict another of rape on the testimony offered by Price. Lawson summed up for the prosecution, and Leibowitz was pleased that only once did he stray from a calm analysis of the evidence. If guilty, he asked, should Norris be "turned loose upon the people of our state"? Of course not: he should be executed, not only as a punishment but also as a warning to others similarly inclined. When Leibowitz's turn came, he pitted the late Dr. Bridges against Victoria Price. One of them had lied. Price said repeatedly that she had been beaten black and blue, rapped on the head with a pistol butt, smashed on the nose by a fist. Bridges examined her the same day and found no evidence of such treatment, nor the wounds she described. Price was more to be pitied than blamed, Leibowitz said, but not to be believed at all.[6]

For the first time in five trials, Leibowitz argued that the verdict need not be a matter of all or nothing. He discussed in some depth the law of rape: the Alabama statute, he said, left juries wide latitude in fixing penalties. If the jury wanted to send Norris to the chair, it could. If the jury wanted to send him to prison, it could. In providing that flexibility, the lawmakers had to have intended to take into account the difference between a decent woman and a train-riding bum. When Leibowitz was through, Solicitor Hutson asked the jury for a guilty verdict and a death sentence that could be written in golden letters across the Alabama sky to discourage outsiders from meddling in Alabama's affairs.[7]

Callahan charged the jury Wednesday morning and the jury deliberated an hour and three-quarters in a cubicle no larger than a sauna and almost as hot—it was 101 degrees outside—before finding Norris guilty and sentencing him to death. It was the quickest verdict since the trials in Scottsboro in 1931. Norris, who hadn't even been asked to stand, did not flinch and seemed not even to blink. Leibowitz, tired and disgusted, told reporters he would appeal the conviction "to hell and back." Callahan was about to start the next trial when Clarence Watts stood up and, obviously unsteady on his feet, said he was too ill to go on. The long hours Callahan insisted upon and the heat were more than his "constitution" could bear. Others said it was more than the weather: he was paralyzed by the thought that his very best efforts had failed to save an innocent man from the chair.[8]

Callahan, though suspicious of all requests for delays, was anxious to escape the heat, and agreed to postpone Andy Wright's trial for a week. Talk of an imminent settlement somehow survived Norris's conviction. On Saturday, Leibowitz met with Hutson, who said, "You have talked with everyone else down here but you have not talked with me. I am the boss. We will not give in to less than rape." Leibowitz said he would not give in to rape. But the next day Hutson announced that he was eager to dispose of all the cases as quickly as possible so long as the ends of justice were served. When reporters asked him how the cases could possibly be speeded up, all he would say was that the ringleaders had been convicted.

"One can never tell what may happen." Leibowitz, who had learned from Watts's doctor that Watts would not be well enough to return to the courtroom anytime soon, said he was prepared to go it alone.[9]

Monday morning, the three prosecution lawyers held an unusual closed-door conference with Victoria Price; it lasted two and a half hours, and afterwards Leibowitz learned that they had told her she could retract the charge she had made against the Negroes awaiting trial without fear of prosecution for perjury. She stuck to her story, but immediately after the conference, Lawson and Hutson summoned Leibowitz and announced their willingness to waive the death penalty in Andy Wright's case. In exchange, Lawson asked Leibowitz to waive his right to the special venire—a panel of sixty-five prospective jurors—required by law in capital cases, as opposed to the regular panel of thirty-five. The prosecution wanted to begin the trial immediately, but couldn't even begin jury selection without that waiver, for heavy thunderstorms the night before, while mercifully lowering temperatures, had washed out roads and turned others into swamps. Fewer than half the prospective jurors made it into town. Leibowitz agreed. One twelve was as good as another, he said. How could he say no? "It was like being asked to swap a turkey for a horse."[10]

Andy Wright's trial began after the last few jurors were selected Tuesday morning, July 20, and testimony took half a day. Leibowitz watched in straight-faced fury as Solicitor Bailey opened the state's summation with one more attack on Ruby Bates's traveling companion Lester Carter and New York. When his turn came, Leibowitz said as calmly as he could that he had had enough. In every trial the prosecution had turned to the New York business at the end, and he couldn't help but conclude they used it as a "knockout punch." It had worked every time. He reminded them that he was entitled to try cases in any state but admitted he couldn't fight that kind of thing. If, before hearing the evidence, jurors had made up their minds that the trial was a matter of us against them, he might as well go home. "I'm entitled to an acquittal," he said, and he went on to make the case for reasonable doubt. He asked the jurors to do the job they had sworn on the Bible to do.[11]

Melvin Hutson asked the jurors to give Andy Wright life in prison, and told them not to interpret the prosecution's waiving of the death penalty as evidence of its uncertainty about Wright's guilt. It was not the jury's job to ask why the state did what it did. Its job was to decide whether Wright committed the crime. He said that if he had any doubt about Wright's guilt, he wouldn't be prosecuting him. He praised Price for her six-and-a-half-year fight "to vindicate the laws of Alabama against the onslaughts of powerful forces in the North aided by skillful and resourceful counsel."[12]

Callahan charged the jury Wednesday morning, July 21, and Leibowitz took exception to all forty-eight minutes of it on the grounds that he had reviewed the prosecution's case at length without even once mentioning the testimony of defense witnesses, the notion of reasonable doubt, or the possibility of acquittal. The jury retired at half past ten, took lunch from noon until a quarter past one, and a few minutes before two announced it had agreed on a guilty verdict and a sentence of ninety-nine years. The jury foreman said afterwards that jurors had not seriously debated the question of guilt or innocence; for a while one juror had held out for a seventy-five-year sentence, to match Patterson's.[13]

Callahan asked Wright if he had anything to say before sentencing. Andy Wright said, "I ain't got justice here." Callahan told Wright that he had nothing to do with that and then turned to the sentencing of Norris, who had just been brought to court and learned, from Wright, how Wright's trial had come out. They both laughed. Callahan told Norris the jury had found him guilty and fixed his punishment at death, adding that he had "nothing to do with that." Was there any reason, Callahan asked Norris, "why that sentence should not be carried out"?

"Yes Sir," Norris said. "They didn't find me guilty. They just thought they did. I am accused of a crime I never even thought about committing."[14]

Charlie Weems's trial began Thursday morning. Price testified. Leibowitz rose to cross-examine her, and within minutes of his first question he had her contradicting herself and so angry at him for pointing out the contradictions that she began shouting answers at him. He kept her on the stand all morning, repeatedly putting before her two or more of her own versions of a particular part of her story and asking her which one she wanted the jury to believe. Judge Callahan and Assistant Attorney General Lawson tried their best to help her, cutting off lines of inquiry, demanding that he show her respect, and, when Leibowitz persisted in his attack, threatening him with contempt of court. She needed more help than they could give, and so pathetic were her attempts to stick to her story that she began to dispute not just Leibowitz but the stenographic record of the previous trials. At one point, with the jury removed from the courtroom, Leibowitz asked Callahan to strike Price's testimony from the record on the grounds that it was so "rampant with perjury" that the court could not use it. Callahan cut him off in mid-sentence and denied the motion.[15]

Bailey delivered the first of the state's closing arguments, reminding jurors that when Weems told Price he was going to take her up north and make her his woman, he had "hurled a challenge against the laws of the state, sovereignty of the state, and sanctity of white womanhood." Then he talked about New York.[16]

Leibowitz followed. Four days behind on sleep, believing he had absolutely nothing to lose, he looked from judge, to jury, to prosecution table and said he was "sick and tired" of the "sanctimonious hypocrisy" of the state and the people of Alabama. Weems wasn't on trial, he said, he was: a Jew lawyer from the state of New York. Leibowitz called the string of farmers the prosecution had called at every trial to bolster Price's testimony "trained seals." He flatly accused Jackson County Solicitor Bailey of suppressing evidence. He characterized the prosecution's contention that northern Alabama courts treated black men no differently from white men as "so much poppycock." He had examined more than one thousand prospective jurors and not one admitted that he harbored any prejudice or would treat a Negro any differently in court. Yet out on the street, white men had told him that "a Negro's life was as worthless as a burned match stick."[17]

Lawson left the courtroom long before Leibowitz was through. Callahan paced along the bench. Hutson scribbled notes, and when his turn came, he accused Leibowitz of deliberately seeking to inflame the jury and make an acquittal impossible. Hutson asked jurors how they would have liked to have had their own daughters on that train. Leibowitz asked for a mistrial. Anticipating his critics, he insisted that if his arguments in Morgan County had ever made a difference they certainly didn't make a difference now: the jury would give the prosecution exactly what it asked for. After deliberating for three and a half hours Friday afternoon and two and a half hours Saturday morning, that is exactly what it did. A few minutes before eleven, the jury foreman signaled to the judge by knocking on the jury room door. The judge had guards retrieve Weems from jail. The jurors filed in and handed their verdict to the court clerk, who read the guilty verdict and the sentence: seventy-five years. Callahan thanked the jurors, dismissed them, and sentenced Weems.[18]

Moments later, Birmingham sheriff Sandlin brought Ozie Powell into the courtroom and Thomas Lawson announced that the prosecution had dropped the rape charge against him. Powell was charged only with assaulting the deputy. Leibowitz told him not to plead guilty if he wasn't guilty. Powell replied, "I'm guilty of cutting the deputy." Leibowitz pleaded for leniency, pointing to the six years Powell had already served. The state insisted on the maximum, twenty years. It was Saturday afternoon and spectators were on their way out of the courtroom, which didn't bother Lawson, who had his eye on the attorney general's chair and was happy to say what he had to say next to an empty courtroom.[19]

Lawson announced that the state had decided to drop the charges against the remaining four defendants: Willie Roberson, Olen Montgomery, Eugene Williams, and Roy Wright. After eleven trials, the prosecution was convinced "beyond any question of a doubt" that the defendants already tried were guilty of rape. Price's testimony, Lawson said, was "corroborated by reputable witnesses so as, in our opinion, to convince any fair-minded man that these defendants did participate in throwing these white boys off the gondola car and raping" her. But, he continued, "after careful consideration of all the testimony, every lawyer connected with the prosecution" was "convinced that the defendants Willie Roberson and Olen Montgomery" were "not guilty." The late Dr. Bridges had testified that Roberson was suffering from a severe venereal disease; it would have been very painful for him to commit the crime, and "he would not have had any inclination to commit it." In addition, Roberson had "told a very plausible story from the beginning: that he was in a box car and knew nothing about the crime." Olen Montgomery had also been sick, "practically blind," and he had "also told a plausible story," one which "put him some distance from the commission of the crime" and which remained "unshaken all through the litigation." Only Victoria Price had testified that Montgomery was in the gondola. In this identification, Lawson said, she must have been mistaken. The two other defendants, Roy Wright and Eugene Williams, were on the boxcar when the crime was committed, but in view of their ages at the time, twelve and thirteen, and the six and a half years they had already served, the state had concluded that the ends of justice would be met "by releasing them, on the condition that they leave the state, never to return."[20]

Leibowitz was already out of the courtroom and on his way

across the street to the jail, where he retrieved the four whom Lawson had just freed and led them, hands in the air, into two waiting cars. Sheriff Sandlin, thinking that the prisoners were on their way back to the Birmingham jail, cursed Leibowitz as he led them to the car. "Why don't you get in there with your clients, you bastard," he said, having no idea that Leibowitz was about to, or that they were free. With an escort of state troopers to the Tennessee border, Leibowitz and the defendants were driven to Nashville in cars supplied by Dr. Newman Sykes, the Morgan County dentist who had testified in 1933 about the exclusion of Negroes from juries. In Nashville all of them, including Sykes (who had driven one of the cars), boarded a train for Cincinnati.[21]

Speaking to newsmen in Cincinnati, Leibowitz said that it was "nothing short of a miracle" that the boys had been spared the chair. He characterized the state's last move as completely illogical and said he was impatient to know by what reasoning prosecutors had decided to believe Price when she accused Patterson, Norris, Wright, and Weems, and not believe her about the others, when she had charged, at eleven trials, that all of them had raped her. He described the freed defendants as "problem children" and demanded restitution for their ruined adolescences. Alabama, Leibowitz said, would pay damages to a farmer whose mule had been run down by a state truck. Well, Alabama had just admitted that for nearly seven years "it caged four innocent Negro boys without any evidence against them." In the name of fairness and justice, ought not Alabama award them "some measure of compensation for the injuries it has inflicted upon them?" "These boys just can't be turned loose after nearly six and a half years in jail," he told the Associated Press later the same day. "I hope they can be placed in some vocational school where they can learn a trade."[22]

At nine-thirty the next morning, the train arrived in New York. Leibowitz led the boys out to the platform, punched out the crown of his straw hat and tossed it to the crowd that had gathered to greet them, saying that he had to get rid of some Alabama grime. A few minutes later, at his office at 225 Broadway, Leibowitz reiterated what he had said in Cincinnati: "There will be no exploitation, no barnstorming, no theatricals of any kind. In a day or two we're going to put them in charge of some responsible and respected agency with a view of giving them a chance to resurrect lives almost crushed out of them by the relentless persecution of Alabama."[23]

Three days later, Leibowitz and the boys joined Roger Baldwin,

Ruby Bates, Norman Thomas, Viola Montgomery, Joseph Brodsky, and Ada Wright at a mass meeting called by the SDC to welcome the defendants to New York and demonstrate the SDC's determination not to rest until all nine were free. The meeting was held at the Hippodrome; 4,500 people attended. In an address that was broadcast over the radio, Leibowitz revealed publicly for the first time the "pact" that he had made in January with Knight and Carmichael, the pact that assistant attorney general or judge or both had broken. He called on Carmichael to use his influence, as attorney general and a member of the pardon board, to see that the terms of the agreement were carried out: "Come forward like a man and a true American citizen who loves liberty and justice and fair dealing, and say to the Governor of Alabama: 'I have given my word that these boys should be given their freedom within two years, and I ask you to honor my promise.' "[24]

F O R T Y - O N E

I Felt I Had to Say It

Chalmers had just returned to his hotel from an afternoon at Wimbledon when he learned that six months of negotiations had been for naught. Don Budge had come back from match point, two sets down, to beat Baron von Cramm. There was a cable on top of his mail, and it read: NORRIS SENTENCED TO DEATH. The words took him back to Verdun, the end of a twelve-day German bombardment, when he heard pieces of a German shell "chug" into the body of his friend Duvergne. A few weeks earlier, on a four-day leave, he and the Frenchman had played soccer together, and Chalmers had marveled at the confidence with which he leapt into the air to head the ball. Now, in the trench, his body rose in an arched spasm and then tumbled into the mud where he lay like a kicked rag doll.[1]

Afterwards Chalmers felt an "indescribable loneliness," which he had thought only a man in battle could know. He found the loneliness that followed the news of Norris's third death sentence even worse. He lost all interest in the conference—the learned discussions; the preparation of pronouncements about economics, education, politics, Germany, and war; the delicate negotiations over the exact wording of the agreement that led ultimately to the establishment of the World Council if Churches. At an ecumenical worship service that evening he sought to pray, but couldn't, and when, on his way out of the church, a close friend greeted him, he couldn't reply. Outside, he leaned against a wall and began to cry.[2]

At the conclusion of the conference, Chalmers went on to Switzerland to climb the Jungfrau. Upon his return to New York, he tried to figure out what had happened in Decatur and told everyone who cared to listen that, notwithstanding some of the headlines they'd seen, the case was not closed. The committee had to look after the four boys who had been released, as well as free the five still in jail. Chalmers was buoyed by the thought that the prosecution had thrown away its case when it released four of the defendants after insisting for six years that each one was as guilty as every other. Editors in Baltimore, Raleigh, Birmingham, New Orleans, and Baton Rouge had the same thought, and the SDC decided it could do no better than to prepare a pamphlet full of editorial opinion on the absurd turn of events: *Four Free, Five More in Jail—on the Same Evidence*.[3]

Chalmers's next step was to make sure Alabama governor Bibb Graves knew the prosecution had scuttled a negotiated settlement and encourage him to make good on it by pardoning Patterson, Norris, Andy Wright, and Weems. He spoke to Graves for the first time in September. Graves expressed his desire to do whatever he could to resolve the case. The following month, after the U.S. Supreme Court declined to review Patterson's appeal, Chalmers asked Henry Edmonds and Grover Hall to arrange a meeting with Graves, warning that there was no time to waste: "The elements in my committee that enjoy agitation are quite frankly going out to agitate as soon as they can gather their forces together."[4]

It took two months, and late in December Chalmers went to Montgomery. He went prepared to argue, but found that Graves was way ahead of him: he planned to act as soon as the appeals were exhausted. When Chalmers offered to withdraw the appeals currently before the Alabama Supreme Court, Graves said he would prefer to wait: "I cannot make any promise which would look like a deal," he said. "I have already stated my feeling that the position of the state is untenable with half out and half in on the same charges and evidence. My mind is clear on the action required to remedy this impossible position. When the cases come before me I intend to act promptly. I cannot be any clearer than that, can I?"[5]

Chalmers's delight was tempered only by the thought that he was running out of time. Graves made clear that disclosure of his intentions would put him in an impossible position. That meant

Chalmers had to go back to his committee and report, vaguely, that things looked good—"The Governor was receptive," he told Roger Baldwin—then ask Baldwin and Anna Damon, who was now acting national secretary of the ILD, to trust him when he insisted that, for reasons he couldn't elaborate on, even the slightest bit of publicity would spoil everything. Chalmers worried about his committee, and he worried about the defendants. The longer Graves took, the more likely the four in and around New York would embarrass the SDC in one way or another, as they had in August when, ignoring the committee's advice, they took to the vaudeville stage, appearing at the Apollo Theatre alongside the Harlem Playgirls Band and the All-Girl Revue ("Fifty Fascinating Females"). The longer Graves took, the more likely the five in jail would do something to hurt their own chances.[6]

Damon, Baldwin, and the other SDC officials and sponsors who wanted to take the case back to the streets pressed hard in early 1938, but Chalmers was able to hold them back. Chalmers, in turn, pressed Hall and Forney Johnston, asking if they thought they could get Graves to act sooner. Their answer was no. The third week in March, when Charlie Weems was stabbed by a prison guard, Chalmers couldn't have prevented the SDC from sending letters of protest and Morris Shapiro to investigate, even if he had wanted to. Nor, a week later, could he have prevented the committee from issuing a statement calling attention to the seventh anniversary of the Scottsboro trials. In part to smooth over any bad feelings created by that publicity, in part to try to prod him along, Chalmers wrote to the governor at the beginning of April. Graves wrote back, repeating what he had said in December: so long as matters were in the hands of the judiciary, it would be improper for him to act.[7]

In May, Graves reaffirmed his intention to pardon the defendants, adding one detail he had not mentioned before. He had to put the defense committee's pardon application before his Pardon Board. After the board ruled—a ruling he was not bound by—he would act. Two weeks later, on June 16, the Alabama Supreme Court upheld Norris's death sentence. Three weeks after that, on July 5, without advance notice, Graves commuted Norris's death sentence to life in prison. Shapiro and Chalmers weren't sure what to make of the commutation. Why did Graves bother to commute the sentence of a man he was about to pardon? Edmonds thought it was a trial balloon, to test public opinion, and, judging from the positive reaction in the press, it was on a good flight.[8]

In the middle of August, Chalmers and Shapiro appeared in person to present pardon applications to the Pardon Board. Attorney General Carmichael, the board's chairman, opened the hearing by announcing that the board would consider only Patterson's and Powell's applications—it was two months too soon for the others to apply. Chalmers was startled, but Graves came to his aid, suggesting he proceed as if the board were considering pardoning them all; the board could then make use of his argument when the time came to consider the others. Chalmers began his presentation, but was interrupted by one of the board members, former attorney general Charles McCall, the first time he referred to the defendants as boys. Those remaining in custody, McCall said, were men. Chalmers went on to say he hoped they would be able to work things out before the Communists tried to regain control of the case, and he promised that his committee would prevent anyone from exploiting the boys upon release.[9]

The following day, the board announced it had voted unanimously to deny Powell and Patterson's applications. Chalmers had expected that, though he had hoped one of the board members would make Graves's job easier by voting in favor. Nonetheless, in meetings with Shapiro and Hall in September and early October, Graves gave every indication that as soon as the Pardon Board had rejected the last three applications, he would "act favorably." On October 11, the board acted as expected, and the next day Graves told Shapiro and Hall he had decided to release all the defendants but Ozie Powell. Graves told them the SDC should be ready to pick them up on October 24.[10]

Chalmers was ready. Eugene Martin, an Atlanta insurance executive and the brother-in-law of Walter White, had arranged for a limousine—"a seven passenger car, good, powerful, but not too conspicuous in looks"—to pick up Shapiro, Chalmers, and the four boys in Montgomery, and he had mapped out a route to Atlanta, carefully avoiding towns whose citizenry was prone to mob violence. If, on the day of release, no auto route seemed safe, they planned to pay the driver, send him on his way alone, and take the train. In Atlanta they would spend the night at the parish house of a church, as guests of some of the most respected members of the black community, including the head of the Atlanta School of Social Work. The next day they would all go by train, in drawing rooms reserved under unfamiliar names, doors locked, under supervision for the entire trip, to Cincinnati, where relatives of one of the boys were prepared to take him and, with the help of the committee, find work for him or a place in a trade school. The others would go on to Cleveland, where an uncle of one of the boys had agreed to take charge of his nephew and trained social workers had agreed to supervise the readjustment of the other two.[11]

On October 17, Chalmers received a telegram from Graves. He had yet to receive the applications from the Pardon Board and his legal adviser was critically ill. He had to delay the release until October 31. On October 29, as Chalmers sat in a barber's chair at the University Club, airplane tickets in his pocket, a messenger delivered another telegram from Graves. He was still not ready to act. Chalmers rushed back to his office and spent three desperate days trying to figure out what had happened. There were reports that former senator Thomas Heflin had made a last-minute appeal against pardons, threatening Graves with political ruin; that Graves had been angered by telegrams and phone calls from Communists; that Haywood Patterson had come with a knife to a pre-pardon interview with Graves; and that the other defendants had made equally ominous impressions.[12]

The only good news Chalmers received was that Grover Hall had persuaded Graves to delay announcing his decision until after Chalmers had had a chance to talk with him once more. Hall had arranged for Chalmers to meet with Graves the following week. In the meantime, Chalmers wrote long letters to Edmonds, Johnston, and James Chappell, putting forth the argument with which he hoped to change Graves's mind. He would admit that the defendants were cocky and had caused trouble, that some of them had developed homosexual characteristics, and that in general they were not in an ideal mood for release. Yet, he insisted, none of that was news, and none was relevant. "Maladjustment" was inevitable in prison. None of them had exhibited homosexual characteristics before incarceration. Most prisoners carried knives. Psychiatric examinations showed, without question, that the four released were less prepared for freedom than the four in jail, and they were doing fine.[13]

Neither Chalmers nor Shapiro believed that Graves's interviews with the defendants could have, in and of themselves, changed his mind. Political considerations must also have come into play—though it wasn't obvious what they were, since the sixty-five-year-old Graves was a retiring second-term governor. Chalmers went to Alabama prepared to make clear to Graves a few of the political implications of his hesitation. Chalmers planned to remind him that he had restrained the radicals who for years had argued that the Alabamans with whom he was negotiating couldn't be trusted. He had kept his committee in the dark and quiet for nearly a year. Graves had set a date and a time for the defendants' release and Chalmers had made elaborate plans to remove the boys from the state and begin their rehabilitation. Far too many people had been brought in on those plans to keep Graves's turnabout a secret. Chalmers told his Alabama allies that he would tell Graves that time had run out; it was now or never. He also told them that he hated to contemplate the "vials of wrath" and the "vitriolic bitterness" that would follow their failure and the return of control over the defense to those who believed that justice could be obtained only by "denunciation and violence."[14]

Chalmers and Hall met with Graves on Thursday and succeeded only in persuading him to defer action temporarily. Afterwards, Chalmers left for Birmingham, where he met with Chappell, Johnston, and Edmonds. They talked about the options that remained in the two months before Graves left office. The phone rang, and Chappell picked it up. "My God, it's Eleanor," he said, handing the phone to Chalmers. Actually, though Chalmers never let on, it was Walter White, who had appealed to Eleanor Roosevelt when Graves balked and who now had her on another line. The president and Mrs. Roosevelt, White told Chalmers, wanted to see him.[15]

Once before, Chalmers told the Alabamans, he had seen the Roosevelts about Scottsboro. Chalmers asked if one of them could get him on the night plane.

While Chalmers was en route, the Roosevelts decided he should present a brief, an extensively documented chronology of the case since the last trial, focusing on the SDC's negotiations with Graves. In a memorandum accompanying that brief, Chalmers urged FDR to meet with Graves when he was in Warm Springs at Thanksgiving and to try to make him see what a catastrophe it would be if he did not carry through on a promise so many reputable people thought to be "definite and final." In the meantime, Chalmers asked Johnston and Hall to appeal to Graves themselves. If he showed no inclination to come around, they should let him know that the president was interested. Roosevelt wasn't demanding anything, of course, but simply hoping that Graves would delay his final decision and announcement until they had had a chance to talk.[16]

Johnston spoke with Graves, but Graves refused to wait, and

the following day, November 15, his press secretary announced that Graves had marked the pardon applications denied. Two days later, Chalmers met with Eleanor Roosevelt, presented the memorandum and supporting documents, and afterwards reported her "sold" on his point of view. She expected her husband would be too. While in Washington, Chalmers also met with Supreme Court Justice Hugo Black, who said he would do whatever he could to help.[17]

The president invited Graves to meet with him in Chattanooga, and when Graves said he had a previous engagement, invited him to Warm Springs. Graves again turned him down, and so on December 7, Roosevelt wrote to him, not as the president but as "a very old and warm friend." He called Graves a "grand Governor" and praised the work he had done "for the cause of liberalism in Alabama." Roosevelt said he wanted Graves to leave office without losing the many friends he had made across the nation. There was, he wrote, "a real feeling in very wide circles" that Graves had said "definitely and positively" that he would commute the sentences of the remainder of the "Scottsboro boys." Roosevelt acknowledged the possibility that the defendants' records in prison were not good. He noted that many people thought the knife found on Patterson had been planted. But the president said he neither wanted nor thought he was able to go into the details of the case. He simply thought it would be a good thing if, before the end of Graves's term, the boys could be taken "at least a thousand miles away from the State of Alabama," with guarantees from their sponsors that they would not return.[18]

The president's plea had no obvious effect on Graves, so Chalmers did not have much hope that he would be able to change his mind. Nevertheless the following week he tried once more, alone. Graves said he could not release the defendants. He looked old to Chalmers, and tired and frightened. He said he would be finished if he released them. Chalmers told him he would be finished if he didn't. He had affidavits, minutes of meetings, and letters on Graves's own stationery, all of which he would have to publish. The governor told him to do what he had to do.[19]

For a year now, the SDC had given Chalmers carte blanche. He had promised that he would either produce results or turn over the records that would show why his confidence (and their trust in him) had been justified. He collected the documents, and on December 19 sent them, with a letter, to Governor Graves. Chalmers charged that in giving his word and then going back on it Graves had committed a shocking "betrayal of all honor and decency." Men might differ in their convictions about the case, but there could be "no appeal before men of honor from a Governor going back on his given word."[20]

Then he waited, assuming, as did most of those who waited with him, that Graves would come around. Sitting with Chalmers in his office, Raymond Daniell of the *New York Times* kept saying, "He must break, he will break." He didn't, and three days later Chalmers released the letter and the complete record of the negotiations to Daniell and a reporter for the *Herald Tribune*. He held a press conference the next day. Newspaper articles and editorials ran under headlines like the ones that appeared in the *Birmingham World* and the *Richmond Times-Dispatch*: "CHARGES GOV. GRAVES DOUBLE-CROSSED LAST OF THE SCOTTSBORO BOYS" and "GOVERNOR GRAVES WELCHES." The SDC published the letter and documents in a pamphlet, *A Record of Broken Promises*.[21]

Chalmers was surprised to find that his Alabama allies were upset by his letter to Graves. He received letters from Hall, Chappell, and Birmingham industrialist Donald Comer the day after he released it. Hall questioned his moral interpretation of Graves's action; all doubted the strategic wisdom of the release. Chalmers responded by citing the names of people, including Hugo Black, who thought he had had no choice but to release the documents. And by noting that compared with the editorials he had read, his comments were restrained. As for the moral interpretation, he insisted that it was not "his" moral interpretation. Graves had given his word, and Chalmers believed there was "a judgment among all men, good and evil, about a man" who "goes back on his word." He admitted that it may have been a mistake to say it so bluntly, but he thought there was "no question that a man would think it." "For good or ill," Chalmers wrote, "I felt I had to say it."[22]

FORTY-TWO

Saving Alabama

In his lead editorial on July 25, 1937, the day after the state dropped charges against four of the defendants, Grover Hall thanked Attorney General Carmichael and his colleagues for "a good day's work" and then reminded them there was more work to be done. A few weeks later he predicted that the state would reduce Norris's sentence to "nothing of consequence" and pardon the other four "boys" before they had served much of their time. "Alabama," he wrote, "merely wanted to have its own way." The prosecution had asked for Norris's last death sentence "largely to show what Alabama, unintimidated, could do." Now Alabama had "had its own way, if at a greater cost . . . than it had anticipated." Having made that prediction, Hall worked hard on Bibb Graves to see that it came true.[1]

Hall and Graves had clashed throughout Graves's first term as governor, which ended in January 1931. When in 1934, after three years out of office, Graves decided to run for a second term, Hall recruited Frank Dixon to run against him. Graves won, succeeding Benjamin Meeks Miller, and the *Advertiser* was once again on the outs. But the Klan was no longer a player in Alabama politics. Governor Miller had wrested the county jury system from Klan control and reformed the election laws that had made it possible for Klan candidates (or any other) to win elections in multicandidate contests without a majority of the votes or a runoff election. Without the Klan between them, Hall got to know Graves and found they had much in common. He was bright and good-humored, as fond of teasing as Hall was, and as unable to hold a grudge. Hall thought him the rare politician who truly cared for the people he governed, and by the beginning of Graves's second term, two years into the New Deal, Hall generally approved of the initiatives in education, transportation, conservation, and public health that marked the second Graves administration. Bibb Graves made "a good governor," Hall wrote, "but an expensive one." In 1936, Graves named Hall vice chairman of the Alabama delegation to the Democratic National Convention. By late 1937 they were close friends.[2]

Hall was instrumental in arranging the December 1937 meeting between Graves and Chalmers. In Graves's hand when Hall and Chalmers walked into his office was the letter sent to him ten days earlier by Forney Johnston and Chalmers's other Birmingham allies. It was "a peculiarly opportune time," they wrote, "for the Chief Executive of a Southern State to give consideration to a request for clemency preferred on behalf of a group of darkies." The Costigan-Wagner (antilynching) Act was again before Congress; Graves's own wife, Dixie, sitting in the unexpired Senate seat of Supreme Court Justice Hugo Black, was in Washington arguing against its "unsound theory" and "drastic provisions." If the governor were to review the facts of the Scottsboro case and conclude that logic and evidence pointed to reasonable doubt, what better way than clemency would there be to demonstrate that, contrary to the opinion of so many northerners, opposition to national antilynching legislation was not based "upon prejudice or indifference to the negro in his long road to enlightenment." Clemency would also increase the governor's "prestige and national reputation" at a time when he had "assumed an important role in connection with the freight rate controversy." Johnston knew Graves would not "make a gesture in this notorious Scottsboro affair" to strengthen his position on another issue. But, he said, there was "a timeliness about all things."[3]

Graves promised to release the defendants as soon as the case was in his hands. When early in 1938 Chalmers asked Hall what he thought he could do to speed things up, Hall advised him to relax. The governor was a humanitarian, without exceptional racial prejudices; he had said all they had "any right to expect him to say." If the "impetuous agitators" couldn't be satisfied with that, it was too bad. Hall said he could not possibly approach Graves again before the Supreme Court had acted. It was gubernatorial election season in Alabama—Hall's choice to succeed Graves, Frank Dixon, was the front-runner in a large field—and they had to get past a primary and probably a runoff without allowing anyone to inject Scottsboro pardons into the race.[4]

In early May, Hall himself went to work on Graves, writing to say that he believed in Dr. Chalmers and was "glad to vouch for him." Chalmers, Hall wrote, was a "moderate," who wanted to close the case "without embarrassment to anyone." He wanted to save the "boys," and he had to keep his committee satisfied, but he also wanted to "save Alabama." Before leaving Alabama for a vacation in July, Hall wrote again. For all the familiar reasons, he said, but especially for the damage being done to the state's reputation throughout the civilized world, Graves should not "hesitate to *pardon outright* the remaining Scottsboro culprits." Hall reminded Graves of the kudos he had received for his editorial calling for compromise, and predicted the same for Graves. No one whose opinion he valued would object. Alabamans would applaud. The nation would applaud. The Negro race especially would be moved. Neither justice nor courts would suffer; it was simply a matter of public policy: "Let's accept an imprisonment of 7 years and 3 months as sufficient penalty for men who injured our State more than they injured the alley cats that they found on a gondola in High Jackson."[5]

In August 1938, after the Pardon Board turned down the first pardon applications, Hall wrote an editorial calling on the governor to pardon the defendants. He emphasized the presence and pleas, at the pardon hearings, of Donald Comer and Forney Johnston, the sons of former Alabama governors and themselves among the best men the state had ever produced. He noted that neither Comer nor Johnston had argued the question of the defendants' innocence or guilt. How could they have when the attorney general dropped charges against four, when Judge Horton and Judge Callahan were hopelessly divided? Instead they had argued about the honor, dignity, and good name of the state. As Johnston had noted at the hearing, the governor was the "final repository of justice" in Alabama. "Without prejudice to the intelligence or the integrity of the three gentlemen" on the governor's advisory committee, Hall urged Graves to broaden their perspective. After writing that editorial, Hall telephoned editors around the state, asking them to give Graves their support. Editors in Anniston, Eufaula, Selma, and Birmingham followed his lead.[6]

In September, after a meeting with Graves, Hall wired Morris Shapiro to say that Graves planned to release all the remaining defendants, including Ozie Powell. A month later, Graves set the date, though he had changed his mind about Powell. Hall wrote Chalmers to explain: "We saved one defendant so as to insure ourselves that you and Shapiro would have occasion to make numerous other visits to Alabama and thus afford your hookwormy friends down here the pleasure of seeing you." "Seriously," Hall wrote, Graves's plan was "sound psychologically and philosophically." Powell would remain in jail for stabbing a peace officer: "However deeply he may have been provoked," he stabbed him with "the intent to kill, and murder has never been the issue in the Scottsboro case." Hall urged Chalmers not to make an issue of it.[7]

Two weeks later, Graves changed his mind about the others. Hall made an appointment to see him as soon as he learned, and three days later they had a long talk, after which Hall went back to his office and called Chalmers. Hall told Chalmers that Graves was "passionate and adamant about his decision," but not for the reasons Chalmers thought. Graves "scoffed" at and "ridiculed" Tom Heflin. He had been annoyed by the "absurd" telegrams urging him to protect the defendants from Heflin, but also amused. He knew the committee had nothing to do with them. Graves's prepardon interviews with the defendants had changed his mind, and to make sure Chalmers and Shapiro understood that, Hall wrote them a graphic account of his meeting with Graves the moment he hung up the phone.[8]

Graves told Hall he had interviewed the prisoners on Friday morning, three days before he planned to release all but Powell. He routinely interviewed prisoners before making important decisions about them. He interviewed them separately, was gentle with them, assured them he was in the mood to help them. He told them they didn't have to say anything they didn't want to, but—reminding them that he was the governor and that they had been in a lot of trouble—expressed his hope that they would confide in him and assure him that, once released, they would pursue orderly lives.

Graves interviewed Patterson first, and as Graves began to tell Hall about their talk, he opened his desk drawer and pulled out a knife with a five-inch blade made from a file. Prison guards had taken it off Patterson when they searched him at the gate. Graves questioned Patterson about the knife, asking him where he got it and whom he had planned to kill. Patterson "evaded and dissembled." Graves didn't think Patterson meant to kill him; he probably meant to attack his driver and guards and escape. But he couldn't be sure.

Powell was next, and his interview was short. Graves said, "Tell me only what you wish." Powell sneered at him and said, "I don't want to say nothing to you." Wright and Weems were more forthcoming, but Graves found their answers to his question about the alleged crime and their trial testimony so similar and parrot-like that he concluded that they had been coached. They kept saying: "I didn't say that—if I did I was in fear of my life. They wusn't no women on that car." And, Graves told Hall, the moment Weems was returned to prison he violated Kilby's strictest rule, strutting across the no-man's-land separating white and black prisoners and reporting that he had just seen the governor and would soon be saying goodbye. One of the white prisoners knocked him down.

Norris was last. From prison officials, Graves had learned that he and Patterson were feuding bitterly, perhaps over a "gal man." Patterson was an "aggressive sodomist." Norris had threatened to kill Patterson at first chance, and so, after Graves asked Norris about the alleged rape, he asked him about the death threats, mentioning the principle of forgiveness. Norris looked Graves in the eye and said, "Yes, I'll kill him! I never furgits."

By this time in his conversation with Hall, Graves was up out of his chair, standing over Hall, pleading with him to see "the picture as he had come to see it." Releasing these men, Graves said, would be calamitous: "They will humiliate you, they will humiliate Dr. Chalmers and Mr. Shapiro. They will humiliate Comer and Johnston and all other decent sponsors. They are anti-social, they are bestial, they are unbelievably stupid and I do not believe they can be rehabilitated in freedom." Graves said he had drawn that conclusion "without regard" for the evidence by which they were repeatedly convicted. He had his own theory about what had happened on the gondola. Now he had to decide what was best for the state, the defendants, and their sponsors. He said, "I have decided against clemency at this time."

Hall thought that Graves was utterly sincere. As he sat there,

Patterson's knife in his hand, Hall wondered what he would do if he were in Graves's position. He wondered what Chalmers would do. He left Graves's office resolved not to challenge him.[9]

Hall sent copies of his letter to Chalmers to the entire Alabama committee. Forney Johnston wrote back to Hall to say that his account of the meeting between Graves and the "African cro-magnons" had at first affected him, and also Donald Comer and Henry Edmonds, precisely as Graves's account had affected Hall. The defendants themselves, Johnston said, "made out a perfect case for perpetual imprisonment."[10]

Chalmers's lengthy reply to Hall's letter turned each of them around. Johnston acknowledged the validity of every one of Graves's reservations: as individuals the men were "manifestly subnormal." They showed "ugly natures," "complete ignorance of the catastrophe" of which they were part, and an "incapacity for citizenship and the responsibilities of freedom." But, Johnston said, all that had nothing to do with the real question before Graves: reasonable doubt and Alabama's public interest in parole. He wondered why the state would even think of "keeping them here to proliferate and exude like cancer cells their sordid jungle reactions" when the "benevolent North" was "baring a bosom for them."[11]

Birmingham Age-Herald editor James Chappell was also "considerably shaken" by Hall's account. He was equally disturbed by Johnston's letter to Hall, and wrote to Hall to assure him that although he and Johnston had reached the "same general conclusions," they had reached them by different routes. Chappell reduced Chalmers's elaborate argument to a few essential points: first, "whatever the psychological condition" of the Negroes, "the State of Alabama had created it." The longer they were in prison, the worse off they would be. Second, whenever they were released, they would need rehabilitation. No one would ever be able to match the arrangements for rehabilitation Chalmers had made. Third, if they were ever to make "any real progress" in solving their "biggest problem, race relations," they would have to strengthen the alliance "between men of good will in the North and South." A refusal to release the defendants would "break" that alliance and "render it practically impossible to establish it for some years to come."[12]

Chalmers and Chappell changed Hall's mind, and Hall agreed to accompany Chalmers to his meeting with Graves on Thursday,

November 10. It didn't go well, particularly after they were interrupted, twice, by phone calls from Athens, Alabama, fifteen miles north of Decatur, where a mob chanting "No more Scottsboro" was threatening to lynch a Negro rapist. Hall left the meeting "crestfallen," feeling that they were licked, but Chalmers revived his spirits and together they decided to go all out, to get Comer and Johnston to lean on Graves, and if that failed, to call out Eleanor and FDR.[13]

Then, on the afternoon of November 14, Johnston had an "earnest talk" with the governor. Graves told him his interview with the defendants and the disturbance in Athens had convinced him he should deny the application. Johnston mentioned the president's interest. Graves said he would be happy to talk with him. He also said he planned to mark the application denied, "without prejudice to future action" and without comment, the next day. He appeared to be under tremendous pressure to act, perhaps, Johnston thought, before he had to say no to the president.[14]

Johnston sent a telegram to Chalmers and called Hall. Hall called Graves; he wouldn't budge. Sitting at his typewriter at 2:00 A.M. the next morning, just having finished a batch of business letters, Hall decided to appeal to Graves one last time. He told Graves he knew he was licked but didn't like to quit. He admitted that he had been in on all the harassment of the last week. His only regret was that he had not asked Hitler, Mussolini, and Stalin to give him hell. If he thought it would do any good, he would have the telephone operator call him "out of bed at 4 am," especially if he could send "a staff photographer to his home to report how the governor looked "in a night gown and foot warmers."

Hall didn't care if Graves got mad, for he knew he couldn't stay mad, knew he couldn't even hate his enemies. Hall told Graves he liked him as much as any other politician he had ever known, despite the "extraordinarily large operating capital" he needed to perform his wonders. He trusted him even more, "even though God in his wisdom" had advised him not to vote for him on the three occasions he "ran for King." He risked a few hours of Graves's ire because he thought his friend was about to lend his hand to "one of the most fateful decisions" of his life. The governor was in the mood to do the wrong thing: his chin was set and he was resolved not to weaken. Hall said he knew that mood. And he said he knew that everything Graves had said about the remaining Scottsboro "children" was true. It was simply beside the point:

> Who cares whether Norris kills Patterson? I don't. Who cares whether Weems picks fights with all and sundry? I don't. Who cares whether Patterson loves long knives and "gal men"? I don't. Who cares whether Powell is impolite and sullen? I don't. I don't care if they kill off one another. I don't care what they do—so long as they do it in another state, preferably Ohio or New York. I don't care if they eat one another without benefit of pepper sauce. I do not know whether they are guilty or innocent of the rape of two cut-rate prostitutes. I do not care.

Throwing Graves's own words back at him, Hall said the defendants could not be half innocent and half guilty. "Half of them—the worst half—are now free and apparently deporting themselves acceptably." The clamor resulting from the rape in Athens would die out and be forgotten. Graves's unhappy memory of his interview with the "morons" would pass. Hall asked Graves to consider the advice of his friends, and the appeal of the president, and to wait. "Now go ahead and cuss me and all the rest," he closed. "I'd like to write 20 pages more, but I am awfully tired and sleepy. I just do not want you to err in the last great days of your administration, and this is my final appeal to you for delay and reconsideration. You do not have to act now!"[15]

F O R T Y – T H R E E

The Facts Were Enough

A messenger delivered Hall's letter to the governor's office. Graves didn't respond, and later that morning his secretary announced that he had denied the pardon applications. Then, though Graves adored FDR, he dodged the president's invitation to meet in Chattanooga. Chalmers believed there was time left: FDR could still invite Graves to Warm Springs; there were six weeks left before the end of Graves's term. Hall knew they had been beat, done in by one bad break after another: the "poor showing" of the "fool niggers" in Graves's office; the mob in Athens; the lobbying by Heflin and (rumor had it) political figures even more formidable; and, finally, in the last week in November, by the Southern Conference on Human Welfare.[1]

Alabama's liberals had turned to the Birmingham conference as enthusiastically as liberals elsewhere in the South. They saw it as a chance to celebrate the achievements of the New Deal and rally their forces for an assault on the region's most pressing problems, the problems that made the South, in the words of the recently released National Emergency Council report, the "nation's number one economic problem." Governor Bibb Graves and Senator Dixie Graves topped a long list of sponsors, which included former attorney general Carmichael and Donald Comer. Justice Hugo Black was coming from Washington to receive the conference's first

Thomas Jefferson Award. President Roosevelt himself sent greetings, reminding the "liberal leaders of the South" that their program had been "implemented on an unprecedented scale these past five and one-half years by Federal help." Yet, the president said, that was just the beginning, and he was heartened that the delegates planned to face the difficult human and economic problems created by the "South's unbalance" in a "united front."[2]

Then the day came, and Governor Graves and most of the other moderates and liberals who lent their names were aghast to find that the gathering of 1,500 had been hijacked by radicals, who used it as a platform to publicize their support for the rights of labor, federal antilynching legislation, and universal suffrage. Most embarrassing of all was the attack on segregation. Conferees met in mixed sessions for a day and a half, until Birmingham police chief Eugene "Bull" Connor sent fifteen policemen into the Municipal Auditorium with orders to move whites to one side of the auditorium and blacks to the other—and then to arrest those who crossed the line. Except for Eleanor Roosevelt, who moved her chair to the center isle, everyone complied. But that evening, without much debate, the delegates voted to condemn the police and resolved never again to hold a segregated meeting.[3]

The backlash was immediate. Opponents of the New Deal leaped at the opportunity to associate it with communism and the subversion of white supremacy. Moderates and liberals immediately distanced themselves from the conference, and Forney Johnston, James Chappell, and Grover Hall all agreed that in its wake subsequent appeals to Governor Graves were futile. Johnston told Chalmers that the "so called Southern Welfare Conference," which included "a counterproductive call for the release of the Scottsboro prisoners, distinctly prejudiced racial understanding" and "froze the matter." Chappell reported that all the people who regarded "improvement in race relations in the South as essential to the welfare of the section" believed that since the conference "progress had been rather definitely blocked." Had "this welfare conference taken place thirty or sixty days earlier," Chappell told Chalmers, Graves would "not have made the promise he did." He would have "refused flatly" to release the defendants.[4]

Chalmers met once more with Graves, got nowhere, and shortly afterwards released the record of the negotiations with Graves. Hall knew, from Chalmers, that the release was coming. He was nonetheless disturbed and embarrassed to discover that in his letter to

Graves, Chalmers had accused Graves of duplicity and bad faith. To make matters worse, the early editions of several newspapers reported that he had signed Chalmers's letter. Hall wrote to Graves to assure him that he didn't subscribe to Chalmers's sentiments. He agreed with the "historical facts," but not Chalmers's moral interpretations of those facts: "I think your final decision was wholly wrong, but I believe it to have been honest."[5]

Then he wrote to Chalmers to say that he had found his personal criticism of Graves unnecessarily harsh and had felt compelled to distance himself from it. Hall was angrier at Chalmers than he let on in that letter, angrier even than he let on in the letter he wrote a week later, refusing Chalmers's request to ask the incoming governor, Frank Dixon, for an appointment to talk about Scottsboro. There was "a bitter feud between Graves and Dixon," Hall explained. Graves was still powerful, and Dixon would be foolish to touch the case "in the honeymoon days of his administration." Alabamans would see it as "a slap at Graves" and Graves would be "less than human if he did not retaliate." Hall also refused to send a reporter to prison to interview Patterson and Powell: "That is a type of work that does not appeal to me." Hall said again he was "terribly sorry" Chalmers had "abused Graves" in his review of the facts. "The facts were enough."[6]

For six months Hall kept his distance, but by August 1939 he was back in the fray, urging Chalmers to be patient while gingerly approaching Governor Dixon and introducing him to Chalmers's point of view. Dixon reminded Hall that the Alabama legislature had recently reorganized the Pardon and Parole Board, creating a new board and putting the decision-making power entirely in its hands. Nonetheless, Dixon agreed to use his influence without being pushy.[7]

In January 1940, Hall delivered five pardon applications by hand and spoke with two of the three board members, Judge Smith and Judge Hill, who were "most cordial and most sympathetic." They expressed their respect for Chalmers and their desire to do the right thing, and afterwards Hall wrote to Chalmers: "The sap is flowing again, Yankee!" Hall said Hill and Smith were as "unprejudiced" as Forney Johnston, Henry Edmonds, or himself. "If the latter three persons were on the board they could not appear to be better disposed toward all issues involved!" Hall reminded Chalmers that "no human being" had made a commitment. Patience and tact were essential. Yet, he reported, when he mentioned that the SDC intended to take the prisoners out of Alabama forever, Judge Smith, the chairman, said, "If I thought that was true I'd put half of them in my car and drive them across the border."[8]

The board set aside February 15, 1940, for the open hearing, and Hall and Chalmers decided that Edmonds, Comer, and Johnston ought to appear and that Chalmers ought not—except in an emergency. Then Thomas Heflin announced that he would appear, and there were reports that Attorney General Thomas Lawson and his former boss, Albert Carmichael, would appear too. Hall approached Judge Smith privately to ask how he thought the SDC should handle Heflin, and he received more advice than he expected. Judge Smith told Hall that the "smart" thing to do would be to ignore Heflin. He couldn't speak well without an audience; not having one would upset and confuse him. Smith suggested that the Alabamans working with the SDC simply write to the board, "setting forth their views on the question of parole." Edmonds liked the idea, and Hall wrote Chalmers to report enthusiastically on the meeting, assuring him that it wouldn't be necessary for him to come to the hearing. "So cancel all plans. . . . Hold everything. We can't be licked when even members of the Board are coaching us!"[9]

On February 15, all went as planned. F. D. Patterson, who had succeeded Robert Moton as president of Tuskegee Institute, submitted a written statement and bowed out of the room. Patterson had written to assure the board that every "self-respecting" Negro detested the heinous crime of rape and most would agree that the behavior of these boys in jail placed them with the "lowest class of human beings." If the only consideration were "society's loss," Patterson wrote, it would probably be "of little importance" if their lives were taken. But the problem before the board was larger: the question of reasonable doubt and the reputation of the state and its courts, particularly in the minds of the "other 900,000 black citizens whose loyalty and devotion" would be "ruthlessly trampled upon" if the board failed to grant clemency. Thomas Lawson had also put his thoughts in writing, which left only Heflin asking for the floor. The moment the chairman recognized him, he began reading from the transcript of the first trial. Smith asked if he thought it important to read testimony the committee had easy access to. Heflin said it was. An hour later Smith asked if Heflin was aware that Ruby Bates had recanted the testimony he was reading. Bates was a bought witness, Heflin said, and "clemency would encourage lynch law."[10]

That was that and Hall was thrilled, until three weeks later when Judge Smith informed him privately that the board had voted unanimously not to grant pardons. Each board member had studied the entire record of the case and written a separate opinion. All agreed that the crime was as serious as could be. All agreed that the defendants were guilty (though the third board member, Edwina Mitchell, wasn't sure who did what). All agreed that they were not yet properly penitent. All agreed that the prospects for their rehabilitation were not good. Judge Hill paid special attention to the suspicious circumstances surrounding Bates's repudiation and the attempt to bribe Price. Edwina Mitchell quoted from one of Chalmers's letters, in which he had acknowledged the boys were "cocky" and had "caused trouble," that "some" had "developed homosexual characteristics" and none were in an "ideal mood for release." In his introduction to the three opinions, Judge Smith declared that from that moment on, the defendants would be dealt with as individuals, each on his own merits: subsequent reference to the Scottsboro men would be inaccurate. In her conclusion, Mrs. Mitchell asked "the well-meaning people" interested in the defendants' "welfare" to "back off," freeing the prisoners "from the unfortunate excitements that have distorted them." Alabama might then be able "to restore them to normal, law-abiding lives."[11]

Hall expressed some of his disappointment in an editorial on March 9, 1940, the day after the decision was formally announced. The decision may have been technically sound, he wrote, but it wasn't philosophically sound. Chalmers had done a good job rehabilitating the four defendants released by the attorney general two and a half years earlier. He was prepared to do an even better job with the remaining five. There was no reason not to give him the chance. Hall praised the board's decision to deal with the defendants as individuals, then criticized as inconsistent Judge Hill's suggestion that they all needed at least four more years in prison. He closed by saying that although he disagreed with the board's decision, he believed that it was "worthy of respect."[12]

Hall knew Chalmers wouldn't be so understanding. Chalmers likened the result to Graves's betrayal and said he could not believe the "colossal naivete" of the board in thinking it could "by fiat" separate the parole applications from the Scottsboro case. Hall protested, reminding him that no promises had been made: board members had approached the applications with open minds and concluded the men were not ready for parole. But Chalmers argued that in warning Chalmers and Hall away from the hearing, Chairman Smith had strongly implied that things would go their way. Chalmers told Hall that he had come as close as ever to losing control of his committee. Roger Baldwin and others wanted a nationwide campaign to call attention to Alabama's recalcitrance, and if he didn't get results immediately he wouldn't be able to prevent them from going back to the old way: "Don't let anyone kid you into thinking that this feeling up here can be ignored."[13]

Chalmers asked Hall to put one more proposal to the board: ask them to release one of the defendants, the best or the worst, whichever one they want, and he would show them what he could do. Hall took the proposal to Smith, Hill, and Mitchell, and they responded sarcastically, making no attempt to conceal their resentment at Chalmers's failure to accept their decision as final. In six to eight months, after the warden's next report, they might reconsider, but not before then. Shortly after Easter, Chalmers went to Alabama to meet with them. They kept him waiting for three hours, at the end of which they would say no more than: "We have made our decision and you must abide by it."[14]

Hall knew Chalmers had lost his patience, and with it his strongest weapons, understanding and tact. In letters to board members—the same letters in which he swore his belief in their integrity and sincerity—he spoke of his being fooled, of their taking a narrowly correct point of view but missing the real point, of his hope that they were not being influenced by little people who could not see beyond the borders of their state. In letters to Hall, he reported the editorials—in one paper after another—expressing shock at Alabama's ways. He spoke of volcanoes building and old flames firing in his committee, never suspecting that Hall too was losing his patience, particularly with these thinly veiled threats of agitation.

When Roger Baldwin wrote, in Chalmers's absence in June 1940, to ask Hall about the possibility of persuading the board to release one of the Scottsboro Boys sometime soon, Hall typed his blunt reply on the bottom and back of Baldwin's own letter. The board, he reminded Baldwin, had said in February that henceforth the men would be treated as individuals. He himself was through with the case for the time being, for unlike Baldwin and Chalmers, he had accepted the board's decision to try its hand at rehabilitation. He said he would be wholly out of sympathy with any outside crusade to break the board's will and purpose. He signed the letter, and then scribbled a coda, asking Baldwin to forgive the informality of his letter. It was late at night and he had no stenographers, and "Besides France is dying as I write."[15]

Hall was never through with the case for long. He believed in Chalmers and stuck with him, despite their differences. He continued to deliver documents and messages from northern parole officers and other experts, to take the Alabama board's pulse and report it to Chalmers, to keep Edmonds, Johnston, and Chappell involved, and to help Chalmers keep the faith despite his own increasing and uncharacteristic frustration. "I do not know anything more to say," he wrote to Chalmers in early January 1941, "except to reassure you of my high regard and of my hope that all is not lost except for the present. If we don't quit, we can't be licked. Keep plugging, as I know you will, and have fun on the way."[16]

A few days later, Hall suddenly died, of a bleeding ulcer. Ten years later, Chalmers dedicated his book about Scottsboro to him and observed in it, by way of eulogy: "You would have liked Grover Hall."[17]

PART FOUR

1937 – 1989

FORTY-FOUR

We Are Our Own Men Now

"How do you feel?" a reporter asked Olen Montgomery, Roy Wright, Eugene Williams, and Willie Roberson on July 24, 1937, as Leibowitz ushered them into one of the two cars waiting outside the Decatur jail. Montgomery, grinning, said he hadn't been so happy since he was two years old. They were so happy it didn't occur to any of them to worry when their car broke down in Tennessee. They were out of Alabama. Or to be bothered when they had to spend the night in a day coach on the train from Nashville to Cincinnati. They were too excited to sleep, they told reporters, and would have stood all night, so long as the train was traveling north. After baths and a brief rest in Cincinnati, they were taken sightseeing and to a movie by local Negroes. Still dressed in prison overalls, they attracted well-wishers and the curious wherever they stopped. Hats were passed; at one restaurant patrons raised $4.20 in less than ten minutes.[1]

In New York early Monday morning two thousand people gathered in Pennsylvania Station. An even larger crowd had gathered the previous afternoon before being disappointed by the news that the train would be half a day late. Scores of men and women, having found their way around police barricades, were on the platform when the train arrived. Some wept, some tried to touch them (which they didn't like), and everyone cheered as police led them to the nearest escalator, out of the station, and into a cab. At his office a few minutes later, Leibowitz introduced them to reporters. One asked Roy Wright if he had been scared. "No," he said, "not even in 1931." Had they minded the commotion at the station? "It sure was noisy. . . . We were so glad to be free we didn't mind." Did they have plans? Not yet. Someone asked Roberson if he planned to return to the South. He shook his head no, looking tired and sad, and Leibowitz interrupted, saying that the boys had been up for most of three days and had not been eating well. They needed a hot meal, and rest. They got the meal, but after it Leibowitz's assistant took them to the dentist and then clothes shopping in the Red Hook section of Brooklyn. Crowds gathered at every store.[2]

The four of them were back in Leibowitz's office the next morning, and the reporters were back too. Williams told them he wanted to play in a jazz orchestra; Wright wanted to be a teacher or a lawyer as famous as Leibowitz; Roberson, an airplane mechanic; Montgomery, a lawyer, physician, or musician. Leibowitz said he hoped the boys could be placed in vocational schools. They spent part of every day that week in Leibowitz's office, smoking cigarettes and cigars, drinking orangeade, and talking to reporters. They spent the evenings at the home of Thomas Harten, a Brooklyn minister. Thursday they attended their first Scottsboro rally, at the Hippodrome, in Manhattan, organized by the SDC to raise money and celebrate their release. Roy Wright addressed the crowd, and afterwards the singer and dancer Bill "Bojangles" Robinson presented the defense committee with a check for one hundred dollars and announced that, on top of that, he was going to pay for Wright's education. The following afternoon, Robinson took them all to Yankee Stadium, where they enjoyed their first hot dogs since 1931.[3]

After a week of freedom their only big complaint was with Leibowitz. He would hardly let them out of his sight, and he treated them no differently from the way he had treated them when he first met them, when they were boys. Even before they arrived in New York they had received numerous commercial offers, from agents, theater groups, and political organizations. The ILD itself had offered to pay them to go on a speaking tour. Leibowitz turned down every offer, without even asking them what they thought.[4]

In the first week of August 1937, they confronted him, at his office. They charged that he had made money and a worldwide reputation on the case. They pointed out that their mothers' "Scottsboro tour" had been a great success. Now it was their turn. They wanted the chance to go out on their own, to help their mothers, to help Roy's brother and Clarence and Charlie and the others. Leibowitz wasn't moved. The Communists would use them, he said, and then dump them, leaving them right where they were now, which was nowhere. What they needed was some kind of schooling and jobs. They said they wanted to go to school. But school wouldn't start for at least a month. In the meantime, they wanted to make some money.[5]

As they turned away from Leibowitz, they turned toward Thomas Harten. The ILD people tried to warn them away from him. They said he was shyster who had never accounted for the funds he had raised on their behalf. The defendants liked him. He didn't boss them around, and he understood their desire to get on in the world. When, over Leibowitz's and Chalmers's objections, they accepted an offer to appear at the Apollo Theatre—to sing, play music, and take part in a reenactment of one of their trials—Harten agreed to be their manager. Montgomery told reporters he was "his own man" now. He would choose his own career. The others felt the same way. They all liked the idea of a career in show business. Harten admitted they might get themselves in trouble: that's why he had agreed to look out for them. But "idle hands were the devil's workshop," Harten said. Any work the boys could get—and would take—was better than none. If the boys were truly to be free, they had to be free to think and act for themselves.[6]

They appeared at the Apollo but quit the stage shortly after their first payday. They made a decent salary, but it was reduced by Harten's share and the fees they had to pay the theater for their outfits and accessories. It was, they complained, just like sharecropping, and it made them sick. Morris Shapiro invited them to a special SDC meeting to discuss their futures. Eugene Williams chose to go to St. Louis, where he had relatives and where, Chalmers hoped, he would enroll in the Western Baptist Seminary. Willie Roberson chose to stay in New York and take one of the job offers that had come in. Montgomery and Wright agreed to go on a national tour sponsored by the committee, on behalf of Haywood, Charlie, Ozie, Clarence, and Andy. It took a few weeks to work out the details, such as where they would go and how much they would be paid—they wanted thirty dollars a week but settled for ten plus expenses. In the end, they spent two and a half months on the road, speaking in more than forty cities, from coast to coast. Christmas week they visited Tom Mooney in San Quentin.

(Mooney was a radical trade unionist who had been in jail since 1916, when he was convicted, on perjured testimony, of planting a bomb that killed several people.) Afterwards, Roy told reporters that he had hated to leave Mooney standing there, knowing how it was to have visitors come and go: "I felt sorrier than I've felt about most anything else."[7]

F O R T Y - F I V E

I Am in the Same Shape I Was in in 1931

On July 24, 1937, the day Montgomery, Wright, Williams, and Roberson were released, Clarence Norris wrote to Rose Baron of the Prisoners Relief Fund to say that he was "awful Sorry" he had been out of touch. "I was in good hopes of Bein out where I could talk with Each and Every one of my friends face to face." He was not out with his friends, and the following day, he was no longer in prison with his friends: Andy Wright, Ozie Powell, and Charlie Weems were transferred from the Birmingham jail to Kilby Prison. Norris, the only defendant still facing the chair, was held in Birmingham pending appeal, at the request of Leibowitz, who knew that if Norris were transferred he would be put back on death row.[1]

When Rose Baron wrote back to reassure him that the SDC would not give up the fight and that she was sure that he would soon be able to speak to every one of his friends face to face, he wrote back to ask her what she meant by "soon." "Rose I wonder what do you all call soon, a month or two or a year or so. I can't understand what some people call soon. Rose I only call a few days soon." Norris said he hoped to be out of jail before Christmas and asked her to tell him if she knew how long he would have to be in jail.[2]

He wanted to know when he was going to get out. He wanted to know why the others were out and he wasn't. He wanted to know why the ILD and SDC couldn't get him out of solitary, even though he reminded them in every letter that he was without light and exercise, so stiff half the time that he could not walk or digest the horrible food. Or why, though he begged them, they couldn't get the warden to allow him visitors: "the colored only have one visiting day. and Every day is visiting day with the white. And no day is No Visiting with Me." A friend came down from Ohio, and the "dirty sheriffs" cursed her and drove her from the jail, just because he was "a Negro man and she were a Negro woman." He was thankful for the money and packages the ILD and SDC sent. Without clothes and shoes between him and the concrete he was not sure he would survive the winter. But he wondered if they thought money and clothes were all he needed to survive.[3]

In October 1937, Norris told Shapiro he was losing his faith in his friends, as well as his courage. Every week he asked for news about his case. No one said a word. He asked for a visit from Leibowitz or another attorney, reminding them that he hadn't seen a lawyer since his trial in that "Kingaroo Court in July." He used to have visits all the time. Something was crooked, and he was beginning to suspect that the SDC and ILD had helped "the State frame me out of the Best of my life Just to Get those Four Boys Free." He was glad the boys were free; they got what they deserved. But he also deserved to be free. A month later, he complained that everything the committee did seemed to be done for "Show and for the Benefit of Some one Else." He was tired of being used. He wanted to see Leibowitz. He accused the committee of not understanding what it was like to be in jail and unable to get information. Morris Shapiro wrote to assure him that if only he knew the latest developments, he would feel much better.[4]

Norris said he hoped what Shapiro said was true. He didn't believe it, didn't believe the committee was doing all it could, and in the middle of January, when Shapiro sent his monthly two-dollar check with a note saying that Norris would be pleased to know that Roy and Olen were on tour, working very hard on his behalf, Norris had a fit. He told Shapiro that instead of helping, the SDC was holding him in prison, using him as "a tool trying to make things good for the generation to come" and to make the reputations of lawyers and other "higher influence peoples." Shapiro and the others never stopped talking about how many friends he had and how hard they were working. He now thought he would rather be dead than treated as he had been treated by his friends: "I Believe all of you all Just as much against me as that old lying woman. . . . I Don't Believe I have a white friend in the world." If the committee didn't mean to get him free soon, he wished that it would stop "agitating and tantalizing" him, telling him "a whole lots of things isn't so: You all Must think that I want to Stay in Jail the Rest of my life Just to Receive two Dollar a month."[5]

Nothing bothered him as much as the thought that he had been done in by a "dirty deal" between the committee and the state, that Leibowitz and Shapiro had "come down" and "picked' the boys that they wanted free. Norris told Shapiro he knew he would say he was "ignorant and crazy" for holding such "light ideas" about the case, for wanting to "look at it the Dark way." He would insist the SDC had made no such deal. But the newspapers had said it, and what was more, if a deal hadn't been made, the four others would also still be "in prison Serving time for Something they didn't do." "I am in the Same Shape that I was in in 1931."[6]

All five of the defendants thought that their continued imprisonment was the price paid for the others' freedom. They had heard "talk of a deal" since the time of Haywood Patterson's last trial, in January 1936. In May or June of that year, Chalmers had come to prison with an offer from Thomas Knight. Andy Wright said no so emphatically that Chalmers didn't even bother to ask the others. Nonetheless, there were newspaper reports of a compromise in the making from the moment Knight and Leibowitz began negotiating in December 1936. In May 1937, Haywood Patterson sent Shapiro a newspaper clipping reporting that he and the others would plead guilty to felonious assault instead of criminal attack. It was "inconceivable," he said. He committed neither crime and would "plead guilty to nothing."[7]

Considering that not even Leibowitz and Morris Shapiro knew for sure what had happened (Who blocked the agreement Leibowitz and Knight worked out in January 1937? Who made the decision to release the four in July?), it was no wonder that Wright, Patterson, Norris, and Weems were confused, or that, in their confusion, they suspected the worst. It didn't help when, at the end of August 1937, in response to motions by defense attorneys for new trials, Callahan insisted that a "hard and fast agreement" had been made in July. With the release of the four, he said, the case was closed "for good."[8]

In every press release and pamphlet and at every meeting, Leibowitz and Chalmers insisted that they never would have agreed to a deal that meant a death sentence for Norris and "virtual" life sentences for the other four. Leibowitz told reporters he would take the appeals to hell and back. Shapiro, Chalmers, and Anna Damon told the defendants the same, in their own words: "We will not give up." "We got four boys out." "We can get you out." Norris and the others usually believed them over Callahan. But on bad days, the defendants didn't know whom to believe. The fact was that they were still in jail and the others were free.[9]

For a time, toward the end of January 1938, letters from Chalmers and visits from Henry Edmonds lifted Norris's spirits, but between February and May both his spirits and his physical health deteriorated day by day. Haywood Patterson had been with him in the Birmingham jail since late September, but he and Patterson didn't get along. He needed news, and he told Chalmers that if he couldn't trust the prison's mail he should visit. Chalmers and Shapiro did visit Norris regularly in the late spring. They told him to expect bad news from the Alabama Supreme Court, but not to worry. They were confident Governor Graves would come through. True to their words, three weeks after the court affirmed Norris's death sentence and set another date for his execution, Graves commuted his sentence to life. Shapiro promised more good news, but as usual, he said he couldn't be more specific, and at the end of August 1938, without notice or explanation, Norris was transferred to Kilby Prison.[10]

F O R T Y - S I X

Slow Cold Blood Murder

On July 24, 1937, the day his brother Roy and the other three were released, three days after the end of his own trial, Andy Wright wrote a long letter to the ILD. He had been reading the newspapers, wondering how the newsmen could be so mean or dumb. They reported that he, Norris, and Weems had listened without emotion as the clerk read their verdicts. They reported that he and Norris joked as Callahan was about to sentence him to ninety-nine years and Norris to death—as if that meant they didn't care. Wright was "quite Sure" that his friends would know the trial was a "miscarriage of Justice" and that he was furious about it. But because not "all the facts" were "published in the papers," he felt it was his duty to write. Once again, he reminded his friends, he had been "framed, cheated and robbed" of his freedom. He asked how he could receive justice in Alabama when perjury was used against him and his attorneys, when Judge Callahan failed to mention a single one of the defense's arguments or witnesses. He was innocent, and he was tired of the "slander" being thrown at his "race of people." He begged his friends to "pull and Struggle together and see that Justice be done." He hoped the ILD would publish his letter in its newspaper, and closed: "Now in you all spare time I wish you will drop me a few lines frequently as possible."[1]

The next day, Wright, Weems, and Powell were transferred

from Birmingham to Kilby Prison. They were assigned to the day shift at the cotton mill, the largest of Kilby's industries. Wake-up bells began ringing at four in the morning and forty-five minutes later they had better be in line for work; their first break came at one in the afternoon. They worked at least twelve hours a day, and after three weeks Wright wrote to his mother and sister to say he was being treated like a dog and couldn't take it. He had stomach trouble and a bad case of the "piles." When he complained to guards that he was too sick to work, they beat him unmercifully. Upon his arrival at Kilby the warden had made a point of telling him that he was no longer a special prisoner; he and his friends would be treated like the rest. It seemed to Wright that he was being treated worse.[2]

Guards "carried" him "Before the Warden night and day to Be Beat up." The mill foreman moved him to the night shift and put him in the middle of a bunch of white convicts who had orders to work him as hard as they saw fit and do what they wanted with him if he didn't keep up. He feared there was nothing but his letters between him and death. "I have Sit Day after Day with pencle and paper and called on you all." When he didn't hear back, he wondered if the SDC had forgotten about him. Or else had not received his letters. Forbidden to write, he had to have them smuggled out of jail.[3]

At the end of October 1937, a prisoner who said he was a stranger to the SDC but a friend of the Scottsboro Boys wrote to ask the committee to send someone down. Wright was sick and taken to the prison hospital for treatment after "two of the officials and Six convicts . . . Beat him up." He hadn't had a pair of shoes since he arrived, and guards were "driving him Every way that a White Man can do a poor Negro." "I am a Life Timer My Self," the prisoner wrote, "But i Do Say if these Stump Jumpers Bat they Eye i Will Be With the Boys that you Freed." Charlie Weems was also in the hospital, suffering from tuberculosis, which killed many more prisoners each year than the electric chair, or any other disease.[4]

There were better days than those that winter, days when Wright found the time and presence of mind to write to the SDC and ILD requesting money, cigarettes, letters, visitors, a sweater, socks, and news. There were times when his enemies—the guards and white prisoners—left him alone long enough for him to get angry at his friends. When, on one occasion, Shapiro scolded Wright for accusing him and Chalmers of lying, Wright apologized. He had been expecting a visit from his mother, and when she didn't come, he thought it was because the SDC had not sent her money. He later learned she was ill. But Wright himself was ill more than he was healthy, and illness that slowed him down or prevented him from working enraged prison guards.[5]

At the end of March 1938, the mill foreman went after Wright with a knife. He got Charlie Weems, who happened to be working at Wright's station that night. A friend of Wright's sent the SDC a letter of distress: "Help Help, its lashing it slashing its slow cold blood murder down here at Kilby for we." Weems, the writer said, was near death, and there was no truth to the report that he had attacked the guard. Charlie worked hard day and night and he and the others hadn't given "one minet troble" since they arrived. Prejudice, he said, was the cause of it all. Blacks and whites knew that "Charlie didn't not atack this man in no way." The boss came at him with a hammer and knife; Weems backed away from him and picked up the stick only to try to deflect some of the jabs and blows.[6]

The newspaper reported an investigation, but it was no more than a meeting between the bosses and the warden behind closed doors. The inmates who witnessed the attack weren't allowed to make a statement. Wright was put in solitary before he was able to send a letter, and he wasn't let out until after the warden met with reporters. Wright's friend went on to list the names of "race men" and "whites" who would make a statement and said there were lots more: "I am asking you to come at once with a federal agent and a news reporter also a noterepublick and a lawyer."[7]

Weems survived, but Wright had a feeling his own days were numbered.

FORTY-SEVEN

I Am a Double Murder

Haywood Patterson's father died in February 1937. Haywood's hope for release by out-of-court settlement was dashed when Clarence Norris was sentenced to death the second week of July. Two weeks later, he was transferred from Birmingham to the hospital at Kilby Prison for an operation on his right leg, which was swollen and infected, complications of a bone disease he had suffered from since childhood. His mother visited him there, and on her way back to Chattanooga she suffered a stroke. Six weeks after his operation, though still in the hospital, sixteen pounds lighter and barely able to walk, Patterson was transferred on only a moment's notice from Kilby to Atmore, a prison farm in a "lonely Deslate stretch of land and Woods" near Mobile. So many dangerous prisoners were sent there, and so many died there, that Atmore was known to prisoners all over the state as "murderers' home."[1]

Patterson's troubles at Atmore began with registration, when the bookkeeper began calling him "all sorts of names." Patterson asked another prisoner what he had done wrong, and he was told that the clerk was from Scottsboro. Sure enough the next thing he said to him was, "You missed the Hot seat but will never get a way from atmore alive." Patterson was assigned to the rice fields and put out there the next day. When he complained that he had just been released from the hospital, guards said they didn't want any trouble out of him and would not give him any—provided he worked. They sent him to the doctor, who gave him two horse pills and sent him back to the farm. When he complained again, the captain asked him to choose between work and the strap. He chose work, but wrote letters to Chalmers and Anna Damon and smuggled them out with a prisoner who had just been released. Within a week, after a visit by one of Chalmers's Alabama friends, the warden gave him a job in the yard.[2]

Annoyed to see that Patterson had not been worked to death, the bookkeeper tried murder, offering two black prisoners fifty dollars apiece to kill him. Fortunately, they were "good Hearted fellowers" who knew about Scottsboro and didn't want to see him harmed. They warned him, and tried to protect him, but told him it was unlikely they would be able to protect him for long. He wrote half a dozen distress letters and paid a trusty a dollar to mail them in town. Again Chalmers came through, and Patterson was transferred back to Birmingham. At the end of September, he wrote from solitary to say thanks and to ask each of his friends to write "a nice letter" to the warden asking him to allow Patterson to exercise and mix with other prisoners. He also asked them to do something for Ozie Powell, who was still at Atmore, bearing the double burden of being a Scottsboro Boy and having stabbed the sheriff two years before. Patterson said he appreciated the committee's help and he was happy to see the four boys gain their freedom. Still he could "not help but to feel that" he had "received a rotten deal."[3]

The U.S. Supreme Court delivered the next blow. Twice the Court had saved his life, and Patterson considered the justices among his most loyal friends. He was sure that they would agree with Leibowitz's "great" argument that his rights had been violated when Judge Callahan refused a change of venue or transfer to federal court in spite of affidavits demonstrating the utter impossibility of a fair trial in Morgan County. The justices didn't, and at the end of October 1937, they upheld his fourth conviction by refusing, without comment, to review it. Patterson called the decision "unjust" and "unfair" and thought it threw a revealing light on the characters of the justices, who had to have known that he and the others were "the unfortunate victims of circumstances." His heart was "broken and bleeding every day."[4]

Locked up on the back side of the jail, denied exercise and visitors, Patterson spent much of November and December writing letters. He wrote more about the Supreme Court (the justices held "the power of life and Death over us Negro people" and "ought to be just enough to give a Negro equal rights according to law"). He wrote about the frame-up, "the full extent of the horror," and the unspeakable outrage experienced by him and his fellow defendants. He wrote about the "hate against Negroes that was the cause of it all."[5]

Shapiro was impressed and told him so, and Patterson acknowledged that he was a pretty clear writer when he had "perfect control" of his nerves. But, he added, since the Court's decision he seldom did, for the thought of the decision "haunted" him "day and night." One day, in an attempt to go over the justices' heads, he wrote to the president:

> I suppose you are president of this Country and If So you are president of the state of alabama as well. . . . I am a citizen of america that has always Been Square toward every man and paid My Bills as they accrued. I now ask you in return . . . to entervene and protect Me in My rights. I Have Never been guilty of any bad crime or open defyance off the law and yet I am unable to get a square deal.

A pardon attorney in the Department of Justice wrote back to inform him that he had been charged with a violation of Alabama law, and the president had no jurisdiction.[6]

Throughout December 1937 Patterson was expecting a visit from Chalmers. Chalmers was so busy with Scottsboro business—including the meeting where Graves promised to release the defendants—that he repeatedly postponed the visit and finally had to cancel it. On December 29, Patterson wrote to say that he needed to talk to someone, even if it was not Chalmers. His mother was seriously ill, and he couldn't sleep or eat for worrying. He asked the SDC to see she got the best doctors and care. A quick response, he said, assuring him that the committee would take care of her, would set his mind at rest. But a few days later, he was "terribly shocked" to learn, from his sister, that his mother had died.[7]

He blamed the state. Like his father, he said, his mother had been "worried to death by the state of Alabama." And he blamed himself: "I am a double murder. I was the cause of my father's death about 10 months ago and my darling mother now." He didn't know if he would ever regain his "sanity" and "balance of power." What hurt most was the thought that he could no longer "ask them to forgive for all the miserable heartaches and sorrows and Heavy Burdens I caused them to bear." It hurt him to think about his parents, and for months he couldn't think about anything else.[8]

By the summer of 1938, Patterson had regular visits from Chalmers and Shapiro. They were hopeful, but, as always, vague. But they were more hopeful, Patterson thought, than ever before. In the middle of August, after the Pardon Board denied Patterson's application, Shapiro told him that the ruling was predictable. The governor would have the last say. Two weeks later, Patterson was suddenly transferred to Kilby Prison. He hoped, as Shapiro and Chalmers did, that the governor was about to pardon him, that Kilby was going to be the last stop on his way out of Alabama. He got along "all right" for a week, but it turned out that Kilby was just one stop on the way back to Atmore. Patterson begged the warden to keep him at Kilby. He refused.[9]

F O R T Y – E I G H T

The Governor Made a Fool Out of You All

Seven weeks later, on October 28, 1938, Patterson and Powell were driven from Atmore to the statehouse in Montgomery. Andy Wright, Charlie Weems, and Clarence Norris were already there. They all knew that Chalmers thought Governor Graves was going to release them, but none of them had any idea why they were there. No one had said anything about interviews.

One by one they were taken, in handcuffs, into Graves's office. He looked even larger in person than he did in pictures, with broad shoulders, large head and hands. Graves greeted Norris cordially, and the interview went smoothly until Graves started asking about the events on the train, at which time he stopped liking Norris's answers, though Norris told him only what he knew. He had been in the fight with the white boys; he hadn't seen the other boys rape Price and Bates; he hadn't even seen Price and Bates before Paint Rock. The more he said, the angrier Graves got: "I am trying to help you," he said. "I saved your life. . . . I could have let you go to the electric chair. I don't believe you have told me the truth." By the time Graves abruptly ended the interview, Norris felt "his knowledge" did not allow him to answer the governor's questions the way he wanted them answered.[1]

Andy Wright's interview went the same way. Graves asked Wright where he was from, where he had caught the train, where he had been going and why. Then he asked him where the fight had taken place, who had started it, and who had had the gun. Wright told Graves the white boys had started it and he hadn't seen a gun.

"Wright," Graves asked, "didn't you say at your first trial in Scottsboro that Haywood had the gun?"

"I did not."

"Didn't you say that all the boys except you and your brother attacked these girls?"

"I did not."

"What do you take me to be, a fool?"

"No sir. I do not. But the same statement I made at Decatur I made in Scottsboro."

Just as Wright was about to say it again—he was sure he had never said that anyone had a gun or attacked the girls—the governor turned to the guard. "If that's all he's got to say, take him away."[2]

By late afternoon, they were all back behind bars. For two weeks they heard nothing. Then, on November 16, Andy Wright read in the papers that Graves had denied their pardons. He wrote to Morris Shapiro to ask what had happened and what the committee was going to do next: "I would like very much for you to write an tell us something at once. Why is it none of you all don't come down? Hoping to hear from you soon." Two more weeks went by. Then each of them received a letter from Chalmers: "I have been so busy in trying to overcome the very bad impression that was made on the governor by his interview with you boys that I have not had a chance to write." Chalmers went on to say that the good prospects for their release, which he had told them about in person, were "entirely ruined by the impression" they had made upon Graves. Whose fault that was, Chalmers didn't know. He assured them he was working as hard as he could to fix things, pursuing every possible angle. In the meantime, he said, their attitude and behavior in prison would be of the utmost importance.[3]

Wright wrote immediately, complaining to Morris Shapiro that Chalmers was talking "like he has been drinking whiskey." Wright said he didn't appreciate Chalmers "faulting" him for Graves's ruling. He guessed that Chalmers was angry at Graves for making "a monkey out of him" and had taken it out on him. Wright didn't understand why Chalmers and Shapiro were so surprised by the governor's decision. If he had wanted to free them, he could have done it long ago. "I'm no fool," he said, "I just can't help my self no protect my rights." He asked Shapiro to use his Christmas gift of three dollars for a new pair of shoes. Two days later he wrote to Chalmers.

> Dr. Chalmers. You seem to think I am the cause of the Governor ruling, but I am absolutely not. The governor just made a fool out of you all. If anyone thinks that I am going to say I'm guilty when I am not and tell a lie on myself or anyone else he's crazy. If that's the way I will have to get out of prison, I will always be here. I am hoping that you will look into the matters and see that I am right. Because you don't know the question that was asked me. Hoping you don't think hard of me for writing as I have.[4]

Norris also wrote to Chalmers:

> Your disencourging letter was received. Listen Dr. I would like to know what kind of impression was that I made to the governor for him to denie giving me my freedom. . . . I have told the Governor just what I have foretold others who have asked me question concerning my Case. I told him I was innocence of the crim that I am accused of an I wasn't going to tell no lie on myself or . . . any of the rest of the boys to get my freedom the Governor ask me for the truth and I told him the truth. So, Dr., if I have to tell lies on myself or the other boys for him to act in my favor he will never do anything for me.

"Of course Dr.," Norris added, "you should know that I am not satisfied to be in prison serving time for a crime that I really did not commit."[5]

Chalmers wrote back immediately, thanking them for their letters. He said he had thought there was something "fishy" about Graves's explanation for his decision. Chalmers asked Wright to send a more detailed report of his interview, and to beat the prison censor, Wright sent a short transcript out of Kilby with a visitor. He closed by telling Chalmers he was expecting "a nice Christmas present" and hoping he could get out soon because prison was driving him "crazy": "I don't believe my health will hold up much longer because I am going down each an every day."[6]

Wright, Weems, and Norris put all the blame on Graves. Haywood Patterson knew he had made "one big mistake." He forgot to leave his knife behind, and guards searching him on the way into

Graves's office found it. "That was the kind of thing they were looking for," he said. "They worked up a big story about it, saying I would have killed the governor." He insisted he carried the knife because he always carried it, and had to carry it. His life had been in danger since the day he arrived at Atmore. His knife was his only defense.

Graves opened the interview by quoting something from the Bible, about truth. He warned Patterson that this was his last chance to tell it. Patterson told Graves he always told the truth, then tried to move the governor by showing him his sore and blistered hands, full of cuts and bruises from digging ditches at Atmore. Graves wasn't moved, and didn't recognize the truth when he heard it. Back at Atmore, Patterson was taken directly to the warden's office, where four guards held him down and another gave him twenty-one lashes with the strap for carrying the knife—"I have been Beaten so terribly that I can not sit Down and So Have ozie."[7]

F O R T Y – N I N E

I Want a Chance in Life

Olen Montgomery and Roy Wright completed their "Scottsboro tour" the third week of January 1938, with stops in Kansas City, St. Louis, Indianapolis, Cincinnati, and Columbus. By the beginning of February they were back in New York. Wright enrolled in vocational school, with Bill Robinson paying his way. Montgomery wanted to study music, and one music school had offered him a scholarship. The problem was that, unlike Wright, he had no one to pay his room and board. Part-time work was one possibility, but not a good one, considering that he was completely blind in one eye and severely nearsighted in the other. He was qualified for few jobs and interested in even fewer. For a few weeks, it seemed the SDC might send him back down south to live with his mother.[1]

Anna Damon didn't like that idea, and she brought the others around to her idea of supporting Olen with committee funds until they could find a sponsor or he could support himself with his music. He bought a saxophone and began classes. Later in the year he bought a guitar. Now and then he traveled around New York and New Jersey to speak at defense committee meetings. He was glad to do it when he felt the committee was treating him right, and until February 1939 he had few serious complaints. It was then that SDC members agreed it was time for him to find a job. They promised to help him find one, but said that if he wasn't willing to work, they would have no choice but to send him back to Georgia.[2]

For a week, Montgomery couldn't eat or sleep. He knew what jobs the committee had in mind: porter, dishwasher, laborer. Leibowitz had wanted him to take a job delivering clothes two days after he got out of jail. He couldn't stand the thought of wasting his days that way when he could be practicing his music. Montgomery went to see Roy Wilkins at the offices of the NAACP and told him he was resigned to leaving town but disgusted with the way the SDC was treating him. Just when he had straightened himself out and settled down to his music, the committee was cutting him off. Six months more and he would be able to support himself. He deserved a chance and the committee was not giving him one.[3]

Wilkins reminded him that the committee had given him a chance, a very good one: twenty dollars a week for nearly a year. Montgomery said he appreciated what the committee had done for him, and realized he was lucky. But if the committee sent him back to Georgia he would have to interrupt his study, and his life would be in danger. Atlanta police would harass him as soon as they discovered who he was. When Wilkins mentioned the possibility of part-time work in New York, Montgomery said he had tried but couldn't find it, adding that he didn't really have time. He had to practice every day. He couldn't practice at night without disturbing the neighbors. If he worked days, he would have no time to practice.[4]

Wilkins agreed to speak to Damon, Chalmers, and Baldwin, and he persuaded them to extend the SDC's support—though not indefinitely. They reduced his allowance in the spring, and in August informed him his time was up. They gave him bus fare and pocket money, and he arrived in Atlanta with his head high, happy to see his mother, heartened by the warmth with which he was greeted by Eugene Martin, the man Roy Wilkins had said he should look up as soon as he arrived. Montgomery told Martin he hoped to get a job pressing clothes.[5]

Four days later he left town. His brother had "jumped all over him" the second day he was home, and the next day, as he and his sister sat on his mother's porch, a policeman stopped in front of the house and asked, "Aren't you one of those G-d D-m Scottsboro Niggers?" Montgomery said he was. The policeman said he had better be careful: "They may find you yet." Montgomery decided to leave Atlanta for Detroit, where he had an aunt. Eugene Martin bought him a train ticket and gave him spending money, and together with Olen's mother he drove him to the station. After driving Mrs. Montgomery home, Martin reported to Roy Wilkins that Olen had made the right decision: his mother lived on one of the worst blocks on the west side of Atlanta, a few doors down from a "disreputable joint." There would have been nothing for him at home but trouble.[6]

No one bothered Olen in Detroit. No one was much help to him there either. After a few weeks he wrote to Chalmers to ask if he could return to New York. Chalmers urged him to stay put; if he did, he would have a better chance of finding a job. Chalmers told Olen he was busy negotiating with the Pardon Board for the release of the other boys, and he wanted to continue to be able to point to his and Andy's adjustment, Andy's schooling and Olen's music, and to both of their fine spirits. But Montgomery couldn't find a job, and his spirits weren't fine. In early December he wrote to explain why. The city was a "stranger." It seemed like the "colored people" were just like the white people, "only interested in their own selves." If a man did not have "some one to look out for him," he was "just out." He wanted to return to New York, and said he was going to return. Again Chalmers urged him to stay. Montgomery agreed to stay, but he wasn't happy about it, and he wrote Chalmers a long letter to make sure he knew:

> God in Heaven knows I wouldnt do anything in the world to hurt those other boys chance of getting out, or discredit what have already been done. But you all must realize some body got to have some interest in we boys who are free, because we havent had a possible chance in life. Thats what hurt me so bad. A lot of people dont like us because we the Scottsboro boys. The same way here. I dont have very many friends here. If I had friends here I would be working, and Dr. Chalmers, if we boys who are free have to be a bum, and a tramp, in some city, some body are going to be sorry, and those other boys will never get out. Dr. Chalmers, I want to be a man, and I want a chance in life. Something I have never hade.[7]

He had worn down his only pair of shoes. Everything he owned was in hock. He owed money to more than one landlord, and he spent many nights in bus and train stations, theaters, and the dark corners of taverns. In January 1940, he finally got a job, as a laborer. He hated it, breaking his back from four-thirty in the morning until eight-thirty at night for $7.50 a week: "I have to do three mens jobs. This aint nothing but a big dump and they works me to death." He quit and told Chalmers he was afraid of what would happen if he stayed in Detroit. He was on his way back to New York.[8]

Chalmers begged him to stay, at least for another month. The members of the Pardon Board had Patterson's, Weems's, and Norris's applications before them at that very moment, and they took a dim view of the influence of New York. On top of that, there was no one in New York with the time, energy, or money to help him. Montgomery agreed to stay until the others got out. The others didn't get out, and when Montgomery finally left Detroit six months later, he left in a hurry. A young Negro girl he had occasionally been seeing had invited him to her room, and the two of them were drinking with her landlady, who didn't particularly care for Montgomery. The landlady left, and at some point, he and the girl passed out on the bed. When the landlady found them there the next morning, she called the police, charging that Montgomery had raped the girl. The local branch of the NAACP hired a lawyer, and two days later the police dropped charges. Montgomery's friend couldn't remember what had happened, and her landlady admitted she had been angry at Montgomery and knew he would be vulnerable to a charge of rape.[9]

Montgomery returned to New York, hoping to get along "nicely," as he had when he was in New York in 1938. But in every way he was in much worse shape than he had been in 1938, drinking most nights and many days, his hangovers costing him even the rare jobs he liked. In October he decided to return to his mother's, and Wilkins gave him bus fare and spending money. It took him two buses to get there—he was thrown off the first when he refused to give his seat to some soldiers—and he couldn't find work when he arrived. Still looking, two months later, he heard that a packing house by the rail yards was hiring. He walked out there, and on his way home was stopped by two railroad detectives. They slapped him around and searched him; they found a letter from Chalmers on him, and after questioning him about it, discovered who he was. He decided to return to New York. On his second day back, he was robbed at knifepoint in Harlem.[10]

When he wasn't working, he had no money, and when he had no money he couldn't pay his rent. When landlords got tired of waiting, tired of his excuses, they evicted him and he lived on the street until he found the money to get himself another room. Not even steady work meant better days. Montgomery was in the habit of spending paydays at bars and clubs, where he drank and told stories about who he was and what he had been through and flashed his money around and ended up in fights and, when he sobered up, often found that he had been robbed.[11]

He went to Chalmers and Roy Wilkins for help, knowing that when they were through lecturing him—reminding him that they had been supporting him for four years, telling him it was time he learned to take care of himself, urging him to keep out of bars, stick with a job, and stop complaining and feeling so sorry for himself—they would help him, if only, he thought, because they feared the trouble he would get into if they didn't. They found him jobs. They gave him money for rent, money to repair his glasses or buy new ones, money for laundry, money to get his clothes and possessions out of the pawnshop, money for transportation to jobs outside the city. Each time they said it was the last time, said that he would be better off on his own. He, in turn, reminded them he had been through a lot, was nearly blind, rarely physically well, had done everything he could do to get and hold a job, and hadn't been "such a bad fellow."[12]

In September 1941, he decided to move to Connecticut, having heard there were jobs there paying four or five dollars a day. He found one on a tobacco farm and kept it until the season ended. But he didn't stop drinking, fighting, and losing his money, and before long he was back in New York, looking for help from the NAACP. Wilkins found him a job as a dishwasher and set him up with a social worker at the Bureau for Men and Boys. He didn't like the job or the social worker's ideas about work and spending money. In June he returned to Georgia.[13]

He moved back and forth between New York and Atlanta, drinking himself into the drunk tanks in both towns, swearing off liquor forever, living in rags and run-down boardinghouses when he was not living on the street. At least once he found himself in New York's Bellevue Hospital, where doctors concluded he was neither dangerous nor sick enough to be committed. Every once in a while in New York he ran into Willie Roberson. They would have a drink, and talk. Roberson seemed to have steady work, but from the bad luck that had landed him in prison in 1931 to the asthma that was so aggravated while he was there, he too found himself haunted by his past. He told of the night, in 1942, when he was in a crowded social club in Harlem and a fight broke out. Although he was not in the fight, he ended up among those the police arrested and charged with disorderly conduct. "I guess a whole lot of people think I've let them down," he wrote from jail, "but just the opposite. I am again a victim of almost inconcievable maglinity and though I hartily dislike the role of myrter I have been cast in that role and it seems impossible to escape it."[14]

As time went on, Montgomery turned less often to Wilkins and Chalmers. He hated the lectures and the threats. He knew they thought he had let them down, and the part of him that agreed with them felt bad about it. They did not understand him, and that hurt too. Only one person associated with the SDC understood him, a social worker named Frances Levkoff. She had written to him in prison and visited him occasionally in New York. She knew why he was revolted by the only work he was qualified to do, knew why he refused to do it. She alone seemed to agree with him when he said the committee hadn't done all that it could do. However often she tried, she couldn't get Chalmers or Wilkins to understand—they told her they had no money and didn't know of any school that would take him—and in the end, besides understanding him, she was not much more helpful than they were.[15]

Still, Montgomery had to admit that whenever he really needed them, his old friends were there, as in April 1952, when he was arrested for sleeping on a subway and charged with disorderly conduct. He asked a guard at the Tombs to call the NAACP, and an Association attorney got the charge dismissed.[16]

F I F T Y

I Knew I Was a Devil

Once Haywood Patterson lost his mother, he lost his faith. God had let him down. The president had let him down. The Supreme Court had let him down. Governor Graves had let him down. The ILD had let him down. Leibowitz had let him down. The defense committee let him down. Fellow prisoners let him down. Half the time, Chalmers let him down. He had come "face to face with the fact that in an ultimate emergency" there was "but one living person" he could rely upon "for sincere assistance," one living person who could act. Yet half the time, he let himself down.[1]

"I got to change inside," he said. To describe that change, he would tell about the snakes at Atmore. The place was full of them, and at first he was as afraid of them as anyone else. He had always been afraid of them. Then one day, stopped suddenly by the sight of a black snake, he asked himself what that snake could possibly do to him that had not already been done. He picked it up and looked it in the eye, and he was never afraid of a snake again. He learned everything he could about them, and when other prisoners and guards saw him wearing black snakes like necklaces, or saw half a dozen blue runners, coachwhips, or rat snakes wiggling around in his shirt, they figured he was "bedeviled," or crazy, or both. When they saw him hunting and handling poisonous snakes, they knew he was a devil, and he knew he was a devil too.[2]

Atmore's inmates were men whom the wardens at Alabama's other prisons couldn't handle, and only those who were respected and feared survived. Patterson thought two-thirds of them ought to have been in mental hospitals, though he was quick to acknowledge that the joint could drive the sanest man insane, making it difficult, and often unfair, to distinguish between the two. To illustrate he would tell the story of Merle Myers, a prisoner who "cold-watered Negroes for serving God." Myers taught fellow prisoners black history and told them to give praise to Frederick Douglass: "That's my god," he would say. Myers, Patterson said, was brilliant. And also very dangerous. To cross him, insult him, even to out-argue him was to invite a knife to your throat. He had killed a dozen men.[3]

Prisoners who wanted to get out of Atmore alive had to leave their sense of trust at the gate. Prisoners killed other prisoners while they were sleeping, washing, and eating—anywhere and anyway but face to face. Guards ordered prisoners to walk up to them and then shot them for attempted assault; ordered them to walk away and shot them for attempted escape. Every prisoner had to assume every other prisoner was out to get him, had to learn to anticipate danger, read faces for thoughts and emotions, imagine what someone might do to you, or have done to you, even before it occurred to him to do it. The tougher you were, inside and out, the better you were treated. Patterson's knife came to mean more to him than religion. "I had faith in my knife," he said. "It had saved me many times."[4]

Much of the violence at Atmore was over sex. It started when a "wolf," usually an older man, went looking for a "wife." Young new prisoners were the likeliest prey; the recent graduates of the Mt. Meigs Reformatory, prized possessions. A wolf sweet-talked a new boy, told him that to survive he would need someone to live with and take care of him. He bought him gifts at the commissary, warded off other wolves, fought for him, then propositioned him. If the boy didn't like the idea, the wolf would beat him to submission. Often "the other prisoners just looked on," Patterson said. "They knew a young woman was being born." If another prisoner took the boy's side, "there would be a murder. Often there was. After the boy was beaten up and lying on the floor the old wolf picked him up and brought him to his bunk. The covers went up over the old wolf's double-decker bed. The wagon was covered, the hunk set. The boy was broken."[5]

A "gal-boy" was a wolf's slave, to be loaned, rented, traded, or sold to the highest bidder. Once broken, some gal-boys carried on like prostitutes. One wolf might kill another for messing with his gal-boy. Wolves killed gal-boys for cheating. Gal-boys killed wolves—there was no other way to get free. Trusties sold Vaseline cut with lard. Some guards liked to watch. Most looked the other way, as the warden did, believing that "devils" with "wives" worked harder, killed fewer prisoners and guards, and rarely tried to escape. The gal-boys did the work of women, and with their wolves watching over them, they, too, behaved better.[6]

Prisoners who did not prove that they were men were in danger of becoming "women." As soon as Patterson was propositioned, he began to patronize the "weekend whores." He didn't like it at first, but grew to like it, and before long he had a gal-boy himself. But he was still young by prison age, and one of the tougher wolves, John Peaseley, continued to come on to him, and to his gal-boy. Patterson went after him, switchblade in hand, and found him talking to "his kid," in his kid's bed. Patterson beat him "like he was a snake" until he crawled out of the cell grateful to Patterson for not using his knife: "He didn't try to take my gal-boy from me after that. Nobody did. And he didn't try to make a girl out of me no more. Nobody did. I had taken a gal-boy, whupped a wolf, and set myself up as a devil."[7]

Wardens came and went, and Patterson found that some were better and some worse. But not even the best of them could do much with the guards. Patterson presumed they were "the poorest grade of white men in the South," willing to spend their lives on an 8,000-acre prison farm in exchange for a piddling salary and the title "Captain." They hated Patterson not only because he was a Scottsboro Boy but also because he cursed whites and refused to take their abuse without a fight.[8]

"Captain" Si Gumpert was the worst. He had been trying to get someone to kill Patterson since the day Patterson arrived. In February 1941, he nearly succeeded. He sent a prisoner named Milford, an old friend of Patterson's, the last prisoner Patterson thought would turn on him for a few dollars. Even when Patterson knew that something bad was about to happen, he didn't suspect Milford. That made it easy for Milford to sneak up on him with a knife. Milford stabbed him twenty times, puncturing one of his lungs. The doctor said Patterson was as good as dead. The warden said he wanted him to live. The doctor did what he could do, and afterwards said it was a miracle that he survived.[9]

Soon after Patterson was released from the hospital he had a visit from his sister. Although he had not seen her in eleven years, the warden allowed them only fifteen minutes, and refused to leave the room. After she left, a guard taunted him about his sentence: You may live seventy-five years, he said, but you'll be with us till the day you die. Before, it had been easy for Patterson to ignore the guards, or to throw their words back in their faces. This time there was something in the words, or something in the way the words felt after his sister's visit, that made him think that perhaps the guard was right. Perhaps he knew the state's plans, or the warden's plans—for the warden too could make the guards' words come true: "Every time they learn about my case is supose to go up before the board," Patterson wrote to Chalmers, "they goes about getting ignorant negros here to adgitate me and to pick upon me so trying to get me in to something . . . these guard here even urges negros up to kill one another."[10]

He knew what he had to do now: play "good nigger," work hard, appear to have learned his lesson, take whatever filth spewed out of the guards' mouths with his head down and without a reply. He had to play flunky, pretend to be resigned to a life at Atmore, gain the trust of the warden and guards. It wasn't going to be easy. But he was a good actor, and he had a lot of time. Sooner than he expected some of the guards began to soften. They put him in charge of a squad of men, and he began spending unusually long periods of time near the perimeter of the prison farm. Just as the captains began to wonder where he was, he would return, with a perfectly legitimate explanation, expressing astonishment that the guards thought he might have fled: "Oh no boss, this is my home. I likes it here." Guards began to test him, sending him off on errands from which he easily could have run. By early 1943, he was in a squad of prisoners the guards thought they knew so well they didn't think they needed to carry guns around them.[11]

Patterson ran one afternoon in April. He and a dozen others (some of whom figured that the guards would want Patterson back more than all of the rest of them combined) took to the woods at the same moment from different parts of the farm. Patterson stayed free five nights, then walked right into Si Gumpert, who probably would have killed him on the spot if he hadn't thought the dog boy (a prisoner who tended the prison's dogs) accompanying him would inform on him. The guards and warden knew they had been fooled and let him know how they felt about it with a hose pipe. Shortly after he was released from the hospital, Patterson reported the beating to Chalmers in a letter, asking for a hundred dollars to finance another break: "If I keep waiting for the parole board to turn me loose, I will never be free doctor."[12]

The guards had had enough: one sent two gal-boys to kill him; another sent two dog boys. Each time, friends tipped him off. He didn't "dare sleep," afraid his "skull would be crushed during the night," and he could not contain his bitterness. "Your mammy was a bitch for birthing a bastard like you to grow up and mistreat people," he shouted at one guard. The guard threatened to shoot him. "You would be doing me a favor," Patterson said. The guard went to the warden, complaining that if Patterson got away with that, there would be no controlling the others. "Send him to Kilby," the guard said. "Put him behind walls he can't get over." And that's just what that warden did.[13]

F I F T Y - O N E

Without Hope a Man Is Nothing

Chalmers told Charlie Weems, Clarence Norris, and Andy Wright that the better they behaved in Kilby, the sooner they would get out, and they took his words to heart. Their behavior had been good—they knew it, he knew it—and even in the difficult months after Graves broke the promise he had made to release them, they managed to steer clear of the devils and wolves and do nothing to give guards an excuse to demote them or put them in the hole.

Weems worked hard and kept to himself. He lived for the radio sent to him by the ILD's Hester Huntington, and reluctant as Weems was to ask his friends on the outside for anything but the bare necessities—soap, toothpaste, slippers, and socks—he couldn't help asking to have that radio fixed or replaced when it "burned up." Norris liked to gamble, and there was always a game, but his monthly checks from the SDC and ILD helped him keep out of the fights to which gambling and gambling debts so often led. Of the three of them, Andy Wright had the hardest time beating back despair. Writing helped him "be brave," and he wanted to be brave. But, he wrote, "a person can be brave for a certain length of time and then he is coward down. that the way it is with me. for It seems as though I have been in here for century an century."[1]

Most of their days were rotten, and some were worse: Norris lost a finger to a machine in the mill in 1939. "I will really be glad when you all do something for me," he told Morris Shapiro, "because something might happen worst than that after a while." That same year, Wright suffered persistent pains in his chest, back, and stomach; the cotton mill, he said, was "against" him. Doctors took X rays for tuberculosis, but didn't find it or any of the other diseases common among inmates. Nevertheless by October he had been sick for three months and in and out of the hospital four times. Whenever they weren't well enough to work, they were at high risk of abuse from the guards, but Wright and Norris managed to keep out of serious trouble, and now and then even enjoyed a few moments of their lives. One of them was the mid-March day when Andy Wright sat down by the window in his cell to write to Hester Huntington to thank her for some recent gifts—some stamps, a fountain pen, and a radio: "I takes the golden opportunity in addressing you these few lines while . . . inhaling the cool breezes as they slowly Pass by and listening to the sweet music as it softly sing the song of you is my sunshine, frankly you is my sunshine."[2]

Along with gifts, Huntington, Shapiro, and Chalmers gave them hope. They gave them enough to keep them alive and out of trouble but, not wanting to set them up for severe disappointment, they tried not to give them too much, tempering the hope they gave with candid appraisals of their prospects. It was impossible to get the mixture right. When ILD and SDC people told Wright it was going to take them time to get him out and asked him to be patient, he complained he was getting to be an old man: "all I can hear the same old theme about it takes time and I have been listening at that song for 12 long years." When they told him to keep his chin up, he asked, "What Do you think i am a iron Man?" When they hinted of good news to come and he did not think, from his careful reading of newspapers, that there was cause for optimism—he accused them of "building up false hope." When they evaded questions about his prospects, he accused them of trying to distract him with small talk: "if you are not going to answer my question dont waist any of your time telling me things I dont care to hear."[3]

Wright, Norris, and Weems were disappointed by Graves in 1938. They were disappointed by the Pardon Board in February 1940, in November 1941, and again in July 1942. At the end of 1942, Wright pleaded for news. He was having trouble with his kidneys. Norris was having trouble with his left eye after surgery to remove a tumor that had grown around it, making his whole head hurt. Chalmers responded with as pessimistic a letter as he ever wrote to them: conditions brought on by the war had destroyed what goodwill there was in the South. There was no hope for consideration of their pardon applications anytime soon. By "conditions" Chalmers meant the agitation for civil rights in the military and war industries, but he wasn't specific, leaving Wright suspicious: "Just what the war got to do with my case? I got sense enough to know that I have been bargain off in this prison?"[4]

"Without hope," Norris wrote, "a man in prison is nothing," and by 1943 he had lost his. He fought twice with a prisoner who owed him money and refused to pay up. Guards broke up the second fight, only to hand each of them a belt and order them to continue until one of them dropped. They both went right down. Guards made them drink castor oil, locked them up in the hole, and kept them there, with nothing but a blanket and bread and water, for ten days. (The toilet in the hole was a hole in the floor, which guards flushed several times a day from the outside, often causing it to back up onto the cell floor. When the drain was completely out of order, prisoners were sent to the hole with a bucket.) The next time Norris was caught fighting, he received his first official whipping, ten lashes with the leather strap. He narrowly escaped a second whipping after a white prisoner, tired of pestering him about Price and Bates, accused him of sabotaging one of the machines Norris was in charge of in the mill. Norris happened to be working with a white mechanic at the time (a "mechanic" was a white prisoner who did what Norris did in the mill). The mechanic stuck up for him, insisting Norris had not touched the machine, and his accuser went to the hole. But later that winter, Norris was among those punished for a prison riot that grew out of a protest over food. Norris had nothing to do with starting the riot, but, he said, when an uprising comes along, "you are just in it. It doesn't matter if you want to be or not, because there are only two sides, the inmates and the officials."[5]

Wright and Weems kept their records clean, and in August 1943 the Pardon Board announced its willingness to release them as soon as their paroles could be arranged. Norris's turn, board members told Chalmers, would come after six months of good behavior. All three of them wanted to get out of the South, and Chalmers wanted them out of the South, but the northern states to which the board was willing to parole them rejected Chalmers's requests: Michigan authorities, still in shock from thirty hours of race riots in Detroit in June, didn't want to add Scottsboro to their troubles. Ohio refused to accept Norris after Cleveland parole officers discovered his mother was of "low type." Negotiations dragged on for months, and Andy Wright had a hard time handling the delay: "Why must you continue to write more things that is untrue?" he asked in September. "Do you realize how long it has been since August?" he asked in November. "It do not take God in Heaven to make a decision. Now just what is you waiting on? . . . I have got tired of waiting. I have lost my health and most of my mind." No matter what state he ended up in, Wright thought that Alabama should help support him: "The state have got my youngest and very best days. Let them carry my burden also."[6]

Charlie Weems was paroled the third week of November 1943. He walked out of Kilby with a Bible in his hands and told reporters he was going to forget about "the part of his life just past, work hard, and make a man" of himself. He was off to Atlanta, where the board had arranged a job in a laundry. Soon after he arrived he wrote to the ILD to thank them for "the hard and long fight" for his freedom. A month later he wrote again, apologizing for not writing more. He was busy working, and though he thought it a shame to be working so hard for so little pay, he promised to stay put for the sake of the other boys: "I want to See them free and do not wish to do anything that would harm them. . . ." He complained that he had gained a "mean and unruly temper" in prison. So far he had been unable to control it. "Please tell all the young mens to try hard and not go to prison for my Sakes."[7]

By the time Chalmers and the board worked out the details of Andy Wright's parole, the board was also prepared to release Norris, and both of them got out on January 8, 1944. Their parole officer, Jack Lindsay, a former deputy warden at Kilby, drove them from Kilby to the Foshee Lumber Company, on the outskirts of Montgomery, where he had found them jobs. They were paid thirty-five cents an hour and required to live in company housing, sharing an eight-by-ten room, a bed, and even a pillow. Their boss charged them each seven dollars a week for the room, then deducted a few more dollars for insurance and laundry. When it rained, or when they were sick, they didn't get paid but still had to pay all their bills. Their foreman drove them hard and, worse, was looking for a fight from their first day on the job, when he asked them: "Didn't you have those women?" They would have quit after a week but Lindsay wouldn't let them. Having arranged the job, he received a kickback while they worked there.[8]

Wright was terrified of the ripsaw. He quit for the first time at the end of January, going back only after Lindsay told him he could choose between Foshee and Kilby. He quit again at the end of February, fed up with being treated "like a dog in every respect." He had asked permission to go visit his mother, who was sick, in Chattanooga, and Lindsay told him to wait until Mother's Day. This time it was Chalmers who persuaded him to go back, for the good of Patterson and Powell. "I wants to prove to the world I am worthy of the many sacrifices they made for me," he told Chalmers. But it was not going to be easy: "I Will never be happy not until I am out of the state of Alabama I dont feel safe here I cant knowing how I am hated and every body acts a towards us ase we are in human."[9]

In the spring, both Norris and Wright got married, Norris to a Montgomery woman named Dora Lee, Wright to a Mobile woman named Ruby Belle. Norris and his wife rented a two-room house off company grounds, but even with Dora Lee cooking in white people's homes they couldn't make do, and when Chalmers visited shortly after their weddings, Norris urged him to help them get their paroles transferred. Failing that, perhaps he could persuade the board to allow them to find other jobs. There were lots of them because of the war, the worst of them paying seventy-five cents an hour, Norris had heard. Chalmers said he would do everything in his power to find a northern state willing to accept them, and he urged them to persevere until he was able to work something out.[10]

The winter weather was miserable and their health was miserable and the work was miserable and neither their boss nor their parole officer was even the slightest bit understanding. "You do not realize just what I am forced to endure in this state and I am really sick of it," Wright wrote. "My chance here is just like a rabbit when he jump up in front of a marksmen." Lindsay finally allowed Norris to switch to the Marshall Lumber Company, where he received "a big fat nickel raise" and was treated as if he were on a chain gang. Wright said most of his days were "twice worse than prison," but even on the best days, like the day in June when Norris wrote that he was "doing fine and working every day" and "so proud of that," they simply were not as free as they wanted to be. In September 1944, they left Montgomery in violation of their paroles.[11]

Wright went to Mobile, where his wife was staying with her mother. He stayed there until E. D. Nixon, a Pullman porter and head of the Montgomery chapter of the NAACP, persuaded him to return, promising to appear before the Pardon Board in his behalf. Nixon persuaded the board to allow Wright to switch jobs, on account of his health, and Nixon found him a position as a helper on a grocery delivery truck. Norris went straight to New York, where he stayed with a Harlem attorney while Shapiro and Chalmers tried to figure out what he should do. Thinking of Patterson and Powell, and also Weems and Wright, they advised him to go back—but only after the Pardon Board promised them that Norris would not be sent back to Kilby and would, like Wright, be allowed to look for a new job.[12]

The board didn't send him back to Kilby, but it did send him back to Lindsay, who ordered him to return to the Marshall Lumber Company. His boss continued to taunt him about Price and Bates, threaten him, and work him like "a slave." At the end of October 1944, after talking it over with his wife, Norris decided to appeal to Lindsay once more. He kissed Dora Lee goodbye, promised to be home by dinner, and went to Lindsay's office. Lindsay said he was sick of his complaints and called the warden at Kilby, telling him Norris wouldn't work. Fifteen minutes later the deputy warden walked through the door: "They slapped the handcuffs on me, shoved me in a car, drove to the prison and put me back behind the walls." The Parole Board informed him that he would not be eligible again for two years. "I could have killed every cracker in Alabama," Norris said later, "and been joyful doing it."[13]

For a year Dora Lee came to see him every visiting day and sent him two or three letters a week. Then suddenly, without explanation, she stopped. Instead, she sent him packages full of cigarettes, toothpaste, and face cream, the kind of things she used to bring him—but without even a note. At the end of September 1946, the board granted him a second parole and Lindsay arranged a job for him with the gas company, digging ditches with a pick and shovel. This time Norris remained in Montgomery only long enough to confirm that Dora Lee was going with another man. On September 30, he took a train to Atlanta, where he spent a happy evening with Charlie Weems. Weems was now married, living in federal housing, still working hard, healthy except for some trouble with his eyes from the tear gas bomb that guards threw into his cell in 1934. The next evening Weems and his wife put Norris on a train bound for Cleveland.[14]

Wright kept his job with the grocer for nearly two years, the two years Norris was back in jail. Then he got in "some trouble" with a hotheaded white man and fled to Chicago. When he returned to get his wife—his second wife; he and his first wife had split up—he was picked up and sent back to Kilby. He asked about Clarence and learned that he had been released a month before. Two months later, the week before Christmas 1946, Wright himself was released again, but for the next six months he was in and out of Kilby more times than he could keep track of. He was sent back once after a prospective employer found out he was a Scottsboro Boy and refused to hire him; another time after he was fired from a job because the "white" people he worked for insisted he "steal from the Jews for them," and he refused; a third time, in the summer of 1947, after a truck accident on the job. He was charged with reckless driving and driving without a license. After that it took Chalmers three years to persuade the board to give him another chance—his first chance in the North—and on the afternoon of June 9, 1950, Wright walked out of Kilby with $13.45 in parole pay and "no hard feelings" for Victoria Price. "I feel sorry for her because I don't guess she sleeps much at night," he said. It was nineteen years, two months, and fifteen days since his first night in jail.[15]

Wright had been promised a job in a hospital in Albany, New York, and when that job fell through for the usual reason—the director discovered he was one of the Scottsboro Boys—friends of Roy Wilkins helped him find another one, at a candy company. The boss ran the company like a family, and Wright was expected to be one of the boys. The problem was that Wright didn't want to be one of the boys. He didn't trust anyone. He didn't want to talk to anyone. He wanted to be left alone, and when he wasn't he could get mean. After a week, the boss let him go.[16]

Wright disliked the constant surveillance by his parole officers. "I am sick and tired of this whole things," he wrote Wilkins. "People in Alabama didnt treat me quite this Bad even if they did try to take my life I knew in front they were my enemys and not my friends and they didnt Pretend to be." The very sight of police sent him into a panic. He hated wearing the same cheap clothes he had worn out of Kilby. He missed his wife and daughter. He told Chalmers he was "proud" of his decision not to bring his family to New York until he had steady work, but that without them, freedom didn't mean a thing to him. And he told Chalmers he wanted to see him real bad: "Now I am just like a rabbit in strange Wood. and the dogs is after him and no Protection."[17]

Wright's prospects brightened at the end of July. He had mentioned to his parole officer, almost in passing, that he knew how to operate a loom, and it turned out that his parole officer had a friend who ran a rayon mill. The man asked Wright to show him what he could do, and hired him as soon as he had an opening. Wright kept that job and lived quietly for a year, losing it and the quiet when a woman he had known since he first arrived in Albany accused him of raping her thirteen-year-old foster child. The woman told police she had discovered a dress Wright had bought for her daughter hidden under the bathtub. When she questioned her daughter about the dress, the girl confessed that the week before she had willingly had sex with Wright. The woman called the Welfare Bureau, and the Welfare Bureau called the police.[18]

On the morning of July 11, 1951, Wright was hauled down to the police station, taken into a back room, read a warrant, and asked if he was guilty or not guilty. When he said not guilty, three officers began to beat him with their fists and a red rubber hose. They knocked him to the ground, and then stomped on him some more. One of the men stepped on his neck. Another told him to get up, and when he didn't move, drew a pistol and threatened to shoot him. They pulled him up, put him in a chair, wrote out a confession, and asked him to sign it. He was charged with first-degree rape.[19]

Wright said he had done nothing but buy a dress for the girl, a graduation present. He had been going out with her mother and they had recently broken up. Private detectives hired by Thurgood Marshall, the NAACP's special counsel, confirmed Wright's version of the story. So did Jawn Sandifer, the attorney Marshall hired to defend Wright. Sandifer charged that his client was the victim of "a fantastic plot" and would not have been arrested, and certainly would not have been indicted, if he had not been one of the Scottsboro Boys. Wright went on trial in February 1952. An all-white jury deliberated for an hour and twenty minutes before finding him not guilty. By that time, Wright had spent nearly eight more months in jail, and he couldn't help feeling that he had been jinxed the day he was pulled off that train. "Everywhere I go, it seems like Scottsboro is throwed up in my face. . . . I don't believe I'll ever live it down."[20]

Wright moved to New York and took a room at the YMCA, with the NAACP picking up the tab and helping with occasional expenses until November, when they told him he was on his own. He chased work back and forth between New York and Albany for the next three years, holding jobs when there were jobs to be held. He brought his wife and daughter to Albany, only to find that he and his wife hardly knew each other and couldn't get along. In a fight one night, he stabbed her. She wasn't seriously hurt, and he received a suspended sentence—on the condition that he leave town.[21]

He left Albany for Cleveland in March 1955, but by November he was back in New York City. He told Wilkins and Chalmers he had tried his best to make good in Cleveland. The cost of living was high and the only regular job he could find was at the Republic Steel Coke Plant. He had to leave it, having twice been burned and once knocked out by smoke and gas. In New York he found that the only employment offices that had any jobs were the ones that sold them. He was broke and hungry, having pawned most of his clothes to pay rent. "Now I am dumbfound," he wrote, "really dont no what to do as I realize I have Been a big burden to the NAACP since I been out But I really dont means to be I honestly tries hard it seems as though Bad luck just follows me I am forced to ask you again for help, if you no where I can find a job. or the money to buy me one and little change for transportation."[22]

F I F T Y - T W O

I Trusted Neither Wind Nor Tree

Back in Kilby in June 1943, Patterson was assigned to the cotton mill—the prison's prison. The superintendent kept his job only so long as his prisoners produced; it was not in his interest to let go of inmates who worked hard or well. Patterson schemed and bullied his way out of the mill's dye house, and then the spool room, pretending he knew nothing about the work and could not learn. He told guards he would be nothing but trouble if forced to do work he didn't want to do, and the guards, having heard of his reputation at Atmore, believed him. They didn't let him out of the mill, but they gave him the easiest and safest job in it, sweeping the main floor.[1]

For over a year he kept his record clean. Guards kept their distance, both because they were more afraid of him than he was of them, and because he abided by most of their rules. Fellow prisoners left him alone or liked him, because he treated them right at his "store." He ran it right out of his cell, selling food, cigarettes, candy, stamps, and paper—virtually everything the commissary sold. Unlike the commissary, he was open at all hours, he bartered and gave credit, and he rarely pressed hard when payments were past due. With his considerable profits, he helped out prisoners in trouble, bought off some enemies, and made many friends.[2]

That good year ended when two of his friends set fire to the spinning room. As guards rushed to put it out, they beat on the machines in the weave and spooling rooms with heavy iron rods. The warden assumed Patterson was in on it. He denied it. They didn't believe him but couldn't prove he was lying, so they accused him of a crime of which they had proof, theft and possession of state property: meat. In fact he hadn't stolen it; he had bought it, paying the guard in charge of cold storage. Not wanting to rat on him, Patterson took ten licks with the lash and a demotion to "Class C," which meant a shaved head, a striped suit, and loss of privileges—prison entertainments, exercise, letters, and visitors—for sixty days.[3]

The deputy warden took away his broom and put him in the mill's weaving shop. Patterson refused to work there. The warden sent him to the doctor to see if his heart could take another dozen stripes. Kilby's regular doctor was out of town, and a few inmates reached his substitute before the warden did, appealing to him in Patterson's behalf. Guards were "hard-timing" him, they said. The doctor kindly reported that Patterson might not survive. The warden put him in solitary, for two months, then asked him if he was ready to work in the mill. Patterson said no. The warden made him drink a can full of castor oil and sent him, with a bucket and a blanket, to the hole for fourteen days. From the hole he went straight to the hospital—most prisoners did. When he was well enough to work, the warden asked once more. "I am not working in the mill," Patterson said. "You might as well just shoot me." The warden assigned him to the cell block, where he swept and mopped, made beds, and, after executions, carried out the dead.[4]

The guards wanted him dead, though they didn't have the guts to try to kill him with their own hands. Throughout 1945 he was in and out of solitary, in and out of the hole, in and out of stripes. In October he told Chalmers that after four months in "Class C" he was "as mad as a dog with a can tied to its tail," "confused and shaken and about as badly rattled as any man you ever seen." The following year was more of the same, although Patterson stayed out of solitary long enough to reopen his store, eat his way back to health, and enjoy a few prizefights on the radio. (Guards tried to prevent black inmates from listening to Joe Louis's fights but inmates usually found a way.) In the spring of 1947, after the warden closed down his store, Patterson decided it was time to get on the good side of the wall. He purposely got himself caught with "julep" (the liquor prisoners made out of sorghum) and then played "Br'er

Rabbit" with the chief of the guards, pleading with him not to put him out on the prison farm. A guard gave him fifteen lashes and the warden put him right where he wanted to be. He worked in the cotton and corn fields until October and for the rest of the fall and all winter canned vegetables, dug ditches, and cleaned creeks.[5]

Chalmers visited that winter and they talked about his prospects. Ozie Powell had been out of Atmore since June 1946, living in Georgia and said to be getting along. Norris was a fugitive. Weems was out. Wright had been in and out, though he was in at that time. Patterson was the only one of them who had never been paroled, and Chalmers, who ordinarily tried to put bad news in a good light, had nothing encouraging to report. The Parole Board continued to characterize Patterson as "vicious," "sullen," and "incorrigible." The best Chalmers could say was that if Patterson maintained a good record, he would have more leverage with the board.[6]

In Patterson's mind, there was only one way out, and he was halfway there. He had only to wait for the warm weather, when the corn would be high enough to hide in and the trees and vines full of fruit. The first hitch in his plans came with spring, corn planting time, when he was transferred back to the devil's squad, under "Shotgun" Smith. Nobody had ever escaped from him, and at least half a dozen men had died of gunshot wounds trying. But in June that glitch turned into a godsend: Smith retired and was replaced by a rookie.[7]

Patterson talked eight other prisoners into going with him—"for bait." He paid a friend who worked in the laundry to keep street clothes ready for him—"I'm giving myself a pardon," he said—and at dinner on July 17 he picked them up, put them on under his uniform, and went back out to the farm. He worked until shortly before sunset, when the dog boys usually ran the dogs on the far side of the grounds. The moment he heard them, he gave the signal. He and the others bolted through the corn. As soon as Patterson was out of the captain's sight, he stopped and stripped off his uniform. One boy stopped with him. They ran a bit farther, then circled back, through a cane field. He hoped the dogs would follow the others, which they did, but only until they captured a few of them, at which time they came back for him. He and the boy darted through the fields and between fields, farm buildings, gardens, and woods. The boy started talking about stealing a car. Patterson told him he was crazy; there were guards and dogs all over the grounds and search planes overhead. But the boy persisted, and Patterson ditched him.[8]

At dusk Patterson slipped into the woods, knowing that once it was completely dark the guards would leave the dogs in there alone. They might order the dog boys to stay behind with the dogs, but in the dark the dog boys would mainly be watching out for themselves. Sure enough, the first three dogs to track him down were untended. Patterson walked toward them slowly and called to them—"sweetened them"—pretending to be a dog boy. When he had hold of all three of them, he tied them together with his old shirt and tethered them to a tree.[9]

He walked away and had waded through a stream for about a mile before the same three dogs, having somehow gotten free, caught up with him. Patterson grabbed the first one to swim out to him, "carried him under the water, and held him there till he ceased kicking." He died easy. The second one fought for his life, but not as hard as Patterson fought for his own. The third ran away. Patterson continued on down the stream, to the end of the prison grounds, where he climbed out of the water, walked west, and then "stopped and studied," wondering where the guards were least likely to be looking for him. He walked all the way back to the field he had left from, took two watermelons from a garden, and spent the night and most of the next day under a bridge, within "hollering distance" of the prison.[10]

Late in the afternoon he went back to the woods, walking east until he reached the rail yards in Madison Park. He walked all night, lay low all day, wide awake, and walked ten miles more that night. After sunrise he rested for a few hours, but, still unable to sleep, decided to walk all that day. By nightfall, hungry and thirsty, he took a chance on a black family that lived in a small house near the tracks. The people fed him and, once they discovered who he was, offered to do whatever they could to help. He asked them to show him the safest way back to the tracks. He rode in the toolbox of a freight train, barely escaping a raid near Tuskegee and another near Opelika, when the train's fireman tipped him off. He hid out all day in the basement of a refrigerator warehouse, picked figs for dinner, walked right by the dog warden from Kilby Prison, who didn't recognize him in civilian clothes, and decided he had better stay off the trains until he was out of Alabama. He walked until he was weak with hunger, then dined on watermelon under the moonlight, all ears and eyes: "When the wind blew a tree I looked at it. I trusted neither wind nor the tree."[11]

The next day he crossed the state line, and in West Point, Georgia, feeling bold, he jumped into the blind between the engine and first coach on a Pullman bound for Atlanta. In Atlanta, he switched trains for Chattanooga. In Chattanooga, he tracked down cousins, who gave him money for the rest of his trip. He got himself a meal and a hotel room, but stayed in the hotel only long enough to wash up, shave, and drink half a pint of liquor. He headed straight for the freight yards, riding all night, happy finally to be moving out of the South. He took a bus from Cincinnati to Detroit, and went straight to his sister Mazell's house. Two other sisters, Sebell and Louise, rushed over, as did his brother Julian. The next day they had a "great home-coming meal." At the age of thirty-six, Patterson had his first beer.[12]

Within two weeks of his arrival, word leaked out that he was there. He went underground, and for two years he lived a fugitive's life, helped along by the Civil Rights Congress (an organization established in December 1946 through the merger of the National Negro Congress, the National Federation for Constitutional Liberties, and the ILD). He took jobs, but left them as soon as he suspected anyone had figured out who he was. He took some night courses, met women, gave up men. He made friends, then dropped them, not knowing who would turn him in. On one visit to New York, he met the writer Earl Conrad, author of *Jim Crow America*. Patterson liked him, and they talked about the possibility of a series of newspaper articles about Scottsboro—useful weapons in the event of arrest and an extradition fight. I. F. Stone thought Patterson's story ought to be "told in full, and in his own way." With Stone's encouragement, and an advance from an editor at Doubleday, Conrad and Patterson took a place in the country to do the book.[13]

Scottsboro Boy was published the first week of June 1950, much to the chagrin of Allan Knight Chalmers, who was awaiting word from Alabama governor Jim Folsom about the pardon of Andy Wright. Folsom approved Wright's pardon, but two and a half weeks later, the FBI arrested Patterson in Detroit and charged him with fleeing Alabama to avoid imprisonment. Bail was set at $10,000. The Civil Rights Congress fought to have it reduced, then put up the money and sent letters and telegrams to the governors of Alabama and Michigan and to President Truman. Alabama asked

Michigan to extradite Patterson, but when Michigan governor G. Mennen Williams refused, Alabama gave up the attempt to get him back.[14]

Patterson was finally free, but only until December, when he was arrested for questioning after a barroom brawl in which a man was stabbed to death. Five witnesses identified him as the man who had fought with the dead man. He was charged with first-degree murder. At first Patterson claimed that he had not been in the bar and did not carry a knife. Then that he had been in the bar, selling copies of his book, but not in the fight. Then that he had been in the fight but had acted in self-defense. His first trial, in May 1951, ended in a hung jury; his second in a mistrial, when two witnesses were seen talking to jurors. He was tried again in September, convicted of manslaughter, and sentenced to six to fifteen years. He served less than a year. Shortly after his last trial, doctors discovered cancer. He died in the state penitentiary on August 24, 1952, at the age of thirty-nine.[15]

FIFTY-THREE

I'm Just So Glad to Be Free

On October 1, 1946, Clarence Norris said goodbye to Charlie Weems and his wife at the Atlanta station and boarded a train for Cleveland. He had not seen his mother in thirteen years. She returned home from work a few minutes after he arrived. "We were both crying, tears falling everywhere," Clarence said. He used his brother Willie's birth certificate to get a Social Security card, and found work in the furnace room at Pharaoh's Machinery, shoveling coal. He took his first paycheck to a whorehouse, where he asked for a pretty white girl, wanting to know once and for all what all the fuss was about.[1]

Before long, FBI agents began dropping by. They never found him, but when they began threatening his mother with arrest for harboring a fugitive, he moved out. He remained in Cleveland, where in addition to his mother, two sisters, and numerous nieces and nephews, he soon had a girlfriend. He moved in with her, but left a year later when he discovered she was cheating on him. He took a room in a house and became involved with the woman who owned it, Mary Pierceson. When she asked him to marry her, Norris told her that after his troubles with Dora Lee he had promised himself never to marry again. He didn't love Pierceson, but he didn't want to give her up, and considering he was already living with her, he figured he had nothing to lose. He hadn't figured that she would take a different attitude toward his gambling once they were married, and when he could no longer tolerate her complaints and suspicions, he left her.[2]

Norris kept his job at Pharaoh's for three years, losing it after a row with a new foreman, a southerner. He had some money, saved from work and gambling, and took it easy for a while, sleeping days and partying at night. When he got tired of that, he went back to work, moving from one job to another until 1953, when he won three thousand dollars playing the numbers. He gave some of it to his mother, telling her he had done some carpentry (she wouldn't have taken it otherwise), and left Cleveland for New York.[3]

With the help of Roy Wilkins, he found a room at the 135th Street YMCA. For a few days he just walked the streets. The words *New York* had been part of his life for twenty years, sometimes spit at him, other times held out like a lifeline. Yet he knew so little about the city that the first time he got lost in Spanish Harlem he thought the people who tried to give him directions, in Spanish, were putting on airs.[4]

For a man who could not fill out his own job application, steady work was hard to find. He worked in sweatshops, on loading docks, and in warehouses—"stacking, hauling, lifting, pushing, pulling," all for "less than nothing in salaries." He worked in Harlem, Brooklyn, Queens, Yonkers, upstate, and New Jersey. At one place he made pipe fittings. Among his favorite jobs was a moonlighting gig at a Harlem restaurant, baking cakes and pies.[5]

Unemployed in 1956, Norris went to see Samuel Leibowitz, who since 1941 had been a judge of the Kings County Court in Brooklyn (and who would soon be a justice of the New York State Supreme Court). "I'll be damned, it's Clarence," Leibowitz said, as he shook his hand. They talked for hours. Judge Leibowitz had a reputation for being tough on hardened criminals, and Norris told him that he too believed in capital punishment and long sentences, so long as the accused were guilty and black people received the same sentences as white people for the same crimes. Leibowitz made a few phone calls and one of them led to an interview with the union that organized cafeteria workers. Norris was hired as a dishwasher on South Street. The pay was decent and there was lots of overtime, but for reasons he never discovered he was laid off after five months.[6]

Norris was arrested numerous times: for gun possession (badly beaten and robbed late one night in 1959, Norris carried a gun from then on, believing the fine a small price to pay for his life); for gambling; once for stabbing his girlfriend with a knife. Yet Norris was doing no worse than many others and better than some, including Olen Montgomery, whom he saw around town now and then. One Saturday, not long before Montgomery returned to Georgia for good, he took Norris to see Willie Roberson in Brooklyn. They arrived at Roberson's apartment only to discover that he had died, following an asthma attack, the week before. Norris also saw Andy Wright from time to time. Wright lived in Connecticut in the late 1950s, but often came to town to visit his brother Roy.

Roy had finished school, served in the army, and married. He had a good job, in the merchant marine. Andy promised to take Norris to see Roy sometime when Roy was in town, but he never got the chance, for in 1959 Roy returned home from a stretch at sea to trouble with his wife. Convinced that she had been unfaithful, he shot and killed her, and then, with his Bible by his side, shot and killed himself. Norris never saw Andy again.[7]

In 1960, Norris married for the third time, a woman named Melba Sanders, whom he had met through a friend of Allan Taub, the first ILD lawyer to visit him in the Gadsden jail in early April 1931. Melba had a two-year-old daughter, and she and Clarence had two more, Adele and Deborah. The family moved to Brooklyn, living as quietly and privately as anyone could live in New York. Norris turned down numerous requests for interviews by writers and reporters who had discovered who he was and wanted to write about his life.[8]

Every now and then in the late 1960s the Scottsboro case was in the news. Norris's children were growing and he knew that before long they would hear that he had served time for rape. He wanted to be sure they knew that he had been convicted of something he had not done. He wanted to free himself and his wife from the fear that one day the FBI would show up and take him away. He wanted to visit his sisters and his mother, with whom he had not even spoken since he left Cleveland, seventeen years earlier, for fear of FBI surveillance. He approached the NAACP, and Nathaniel Jones, the Association's chief counsel, wrote to Fred Gray, a prominent black Montgomery attorney (he had been Rosa Parks's lawyer), to ask about the possibility of getting Norris's parole violation lifted.[9]

In the meantime, Norris got a new job, with the city, operating a vacuum sweeper at a warehouse in Queens. He got along well with his supervisors and most of the time he was his own boss; he never had a job he liked more. Two and a half years passed. In visits to NAACP offices in 1972 and 1973 he learned of the deaths of Allan Knight Chalmers, at the age of seventy-four, and Judge Horton, at ninety-five. He heard nothing from Alabama, and he grew tired of waiting.[10]

One day he called the governor's office and asked to speak to George Wallace. The woman who answered said the governor wasn't in. He asked for the next in line, and a man came on and asked how he could help him. Norris identified himself as one of the Scottsboro Boys and briefly told his story: "I was arrested in Alabama in 1931 and sentenced to the electric chair three times. The governor commuted my sentence to life in prison. I was released on parole twice, once in 1944, and I broke my parole and went back to prison until I got out in 1946. I broke my parole again and I have been free ever since. I want to know if Alabama still wants me."[11]

The man said he couldn't help him, and gave him the number of the Department of Corrections. Norris called, a man answered, and Norris told his story again. The man asked him to hold, and when he came back on the line said, "Yes, we want you and I will do everything in my power to get you back." The man asked for his phone number and address. Norris gave him phony ones and hung up.[12]

Norris went back to the NAACP, and Roy Wilkins assigned a young attorney named James Myerson to help him. Myerson discovered that Fred Gray's law firm, overwhelmed in 1972 and 1973 with work on the Tuskegee Syphilis Case, had made no progress. Myerson kept after Gray, and in 1974 Gray put one of his associates, Donald Watkins, on Norris's case. In late 1974, Watkins arranged a meeting with Governor Wallace's legal adviser and the chairman of the Pardon and Parole Board, Norman Ussery. Ussery reminded Watkins that under current Alabama law a person whose death sentence had been commuted could not be pardoned unless all three board members were convinced that he was innocent of the crime. The board's unanimous decision then had to be approved by the governor. A pardon, Ussery said, was unlikely. A transfer of parole to New York was possible, but only after Norris surrendered.[13]

Norris had no intention of surrendering, and for about a year he figured he was out of luck. But Myerson had not given up, and after kicking around the idea of a new trial he decided to approach Alabama's attorney general, William Baxley. Baxley was making a name for himself nationwide by vigorously prosecuting whites suspected of violence against blacks. Even more to the point, just that year, at a trial in Federal District Court resulting from a class action suit brought by two prisoners, Baxley had admitted that Alabama's prisons grossly violated prisoners' Eighth Amendment right to protection from cruel and unusual punishment. Donald Watkins knew one of Baxley's assistant attorneys general, a black man named Milton Davis. Davis asked Watkins for a summary of the case, and in April 1976, the two of them met with Baxley. Baxley said that a full pardon was the least Alabama could do.[14]

Davis prepared a lengthy report for his boss, and in early August 1976 Baxley wrote to the Pardon Board. He did not want to appear to be pressuring the board. Nonetheless, his thorough review of the case revealed that Norris should never even have been "charged with any offense." The repeated death sentences and fifteen years of incarceration could only be called "tragic," "indicative of a time when men were judged by the color of their skin and not the content of their character." Pardon and Parole Board chairman Ussery responded by saying that as long as Norris was a fugitive and there was an outstanding warrant against him, he could not consider a pardon.[15]

Myerson, with the full support and cooperation of NAACP executives, decided it was time to rally public opinion behind Norris's application. Wilkins sent a telegram to Governor Wallace. Myerson sent Wallace copies of letters of support Wilkins had solicited from New York City mayor Abraham Beame, New York senator Jacob Javits, and New York State Supreme Court justice Harold Stevens. They issued a flurry of news releases, and the next thing Norris knew there was a *New York Times* reporter at his door. The story ran on October 9, on the front page. The next day it was a camera crew; CBS broadcast the interview on the evening news. Before the week was out, Norris had been interviewed by a dozen editors and reporters, and editorials calling for a pardon appeared in the *New York Times,* the *Washington Post,* and the *Montgomery Advertiser.* Wallace and Ussery received letters, telegrams, and phone calls from people in every state.[16]

On October 13, after Ussery again insisted that Norris would have to surrender, serve three years on parole, and then apply for a pardon, the NAACP stepped up its campaign, mobilizing its ninety-two branches and 14,000 members in Alabama and encouraging them to work closely with Alabama's Black Political Caucus, an organization of more then 200 black elected officials. With phone calls coming from reporters at all hours of the day and night, and phone calls from Myerson and Watkins, and phone calls from friends and total strangers, and with everyone at the warehouse wanting to know what was going on, Norris decided to take a vacation and hide out at a friend's house in Harlem.[17]

On Friday, October 22, Sara Sellers and William Robinson, the two other members of the Pardon and Parole Board, deserted their chairman, voting to withdraw the "delinquency" warrant for Norris's arrest and reinstate his parole—without supervision. Norman Ussery met with Governor Wallace later the same day, and immediately afterwards asked Attorney General Baxley to submit a brief in support of the pardon. Baxley and Davis's brief was essentially a synopsis of Judge Horton's opinion. They closed by "vigorously" appealing to the board to grant a "full and complete pardon," thereby freeing Norris from a living nightmare and removing "the unjust stigma of conviction for a crime which the overwhelming evidence clearly shows he did not commit." The board reviewed the evidence over the weekend and voted to grant Norris a pardon. On Monday, when George Wallace approved it, Clarence Norris was officially not guilty as well as free.[18]

James Myerson had called Norris from Alabama the night before to say that Wallace was likely to sign his pardon sometime the next day. When the morning passed without any news, Norris went to a bar at Seventh Avenue and 123rd Street, from which he kept calling the NAACP. "I was nervous, and I had two hookers—White Label Scotch—and I called and got the word. I was free! Then I went back quick and had two more." When he got down to NAACP headquarters, at 1790 Broadway, reporters greeted him at the door.

"Are you going to bring suit against the state?"

"I don't know."

"Are you bitter?"

"No . . . I'm just so glad to be free. They had said I was a nobody, a dog, but I had stood up and I said the truth."

"Where were you when you found out?"

"I went to a bar . . . I know it doesn't solve anything, but you need something to keep you from thinking sometimes. Sometimes you feel worse afterward, but you need something, don't you?"[19]

It had been forty-five years; someone asked him what he had

learned. "The lesson to black people, to my children, to everybody, is that you should always fight for your rights, even if it cost you your life," he said. "Stand up for your rights, even if it kills you. That's all that life consists of." His voice broke, and he cried, "thinking of those other eight boys who grew to manhood in the penitentiary." Later that day he spoke to his sister Virginia for the first time in twenty-three years and learned that his mother had died the year before.[20]

Two days later, Norris learned from reporters of the death of Ruby (Bates) Schut. Bates had moved to Washington State in 1940 and married a carpenter, Elmer Schut, returning to Alabama in the 1960s when Schut was admitted to a Veterans Administration hospital there. She had emerged from obscurity earlier in 1976, when she filed a $2.5 million suit against the National Broadcasting Company for libel, slander, and breach of privacy. NBC's crime, in her mind, was a docudrama called "Judge Horton and the Scottsboro Boys," which Bates's lawyer charged portrayed his client as a bum, a liar, and a whore. A few months later, lawyers for Victoria (Price) Street, who was living in rural Tennessee, stepped forward. They filed a separate suit, asking for $6 million in damages.[21]

Norris agreed to go on a speaking tour for the NAACP. The third stop, at the end of November, was Montgomery, Alabama. A few hundred people gathered at the airport. Until Myerson assured Norris that they were either reporters and photographers or well-wishers (and that he had arranged security), he refused to get off the plane. Another crowd gathered outside the offices of the Pardon Board, where Norris received his pardon certificate and board members wished him well. Next was a rally and press conference at the Dexter Avenue Baptist Church. The church was "wall-to-wall people, black and white." Norris said he was proud to be at Martin Luther King's church, wishing only that the others were with him—"their lives were ruined by this thing too."[22]

The following day, Norris traveled to Tuscaloosa to give a speech at the University of Alabama. The day after that, he returned to Montgomery for a meeting with George Wallace. The governor asked him to take the chair next to his, and when Norris sat down, Wallace "grabbed" his hand and "just held it for a while." Wallace said he had been a boy when Norris was arrested and in the service when he was first paroled. He was happy to be the one to sign his pardon. Alabama had come a long way, he said, and now it was one of the best places in the country for whites and blacks to live.[23]

Many observers noted the irony of George Wallace's signing the pardon. With one eye on a Senate seat in 1978, and the other on Alabama's 400,000 registered black voters, the man who had once said that segregation was forever seemed now to have got religion on race. After leaving the governor's office, Norris was asked if he cared to comment on Wallace's motives. He said he didn't: "I'm grateful to the governor, and I told him so. I'll tell him every time I see him."[24]

In July 1977, a federal judge dismissed Price's suit against NBC. In January 1978, Samuel Leibowitz died. In 1979, Norris published his autobiography, *The Last of the Scottsboro Boys*. In 1982, Victoria Price died. Around the same time, Norris's own health began to decline. Doctors discovered Alzheimer's disease, and he died on January 23, 1989, in the Bronx Community Hospital. He was seventy-six years old.[25]

F I F T Y - F O U R

How Can You Judge a Man?

The NAACP arranged the memorial service. It was held at the Abyssinian Baptist Church, the site of many Scottsboro rallies in the 1930s, when Adam Clayton Powell, Sr., was pastor. With Norris's body lying below him in an open casket, the pastor, Dr. Calvin O. Butts, gave the invocation and read from Ecclesiastes and John. The soloist, Joan Faye Donovan, sang "When I've Done the Best I Can" and "Just a Closer Walk with Thee." Dr. Gloster B. Current, former director of branches for the NAACP, told the story of Clarence Norris's life and of his and the NAACP's contribution to the early struggle for civil rights.[1]

Reverend Butts thanked Current for refreshing his memory. "I have no other way of understanding the Scottsboro case," he said, "except as it is told to me by those who were there." Butts said he could not judge Clarence Norris: "How can you judge the behavior of a man who has lived through living hell?" Considering how often he heard people judging the Clarence Norrises of the 1980s, he imagined that there were people, black as well as white, who had judged Norris back in 1931. He could hear their voices: "They shouldn't have been on that train anyway." "What were they doing sitting with them white women?" "Something must have been wrong with them boys."

Butts's faith assured him that God would judge Norris, as God would judge those who caused his misery. "We must believe," he said, "that those who were responsible for the horrible indignities heaped upon the Scottsboro Boys will be, if not in our lifetimes, brought to justice." Along with faith went struggle, and Butts, addressing those who were not in the church that January morning as much as those who were, insisted that "the same kind of injustices that claimed the early vigor of Clarence Norris" were "still a part of the fabric of our society today."

There were about a hundred people at the service. Butts wished there were more. He thought there would have been—"this church might be packed," he said—if memories weren't so short, "if connections could be made between the Scottsboro Case and indignities today." Butts thanked God for the people who remembered, the people who understood that they were much better off because of Norris's suffering, and who realized that hand in hand with their "good fortune" went the "responsibility to continue the struggle and the fight for justice." The soloist sang "Amazing Grace."

The struggle to save Norris and the others had helped revive the great struggle for freedom and equality waged by white people and black people together from the beginning of abolitionism to the end of Reconstruction. White southerners with a sense of history had understood the connections as well as anyone, and they had understood the danger, understood that in their part of the world a little agitation might lead to revolution. Clarence Norris's death came at the end of two decades of stalled revolution and counter-revolution. It was not surprising that in thinking about the meaning of his life, Reverend Butts was struck by how little had changed.

Norris himself, in the last decade of his life, could talk about things being the same. When, in 1976, Norman Ussery kept insisting that he would have to surrender, Norris was reminded of the Alabama Pardon Board in the 1940s, its members simply unable to grasp the big picture. When in 1977 the Judiciary Committee of the Alabama House of Representatives killed a bill, sponsored by Representative Alvin Holmes, that would have awarded him $10,000 in compensation, Norris was reminded of the decision of the Alabama Board of Adjustment in 1943, denying him compensation for the finger he lost in the mill. When Norris looked around New York City and saw teenagers in the streets, in court, and in jail, he was reminded of himself at eighteen. "The crowds in Scottsboro hated us because they were afraid of our black skins," he said in 1985. Kids all over New York were hated for the same reason.

He was not sure if America would "ever learn that even poor street kids have as much right to live as those with plenty."[2]

Yet Norris knew that to understand how bad things were you had to understand how bad they had been, and in 1976, when he returned to Alabama for the first time in thirty years, he was struck by change. It was a cold day, not unlike the day he had hopped that freight, but when he stepped off the plane, wearing a blue topcoat over a gray suit, he did not look like a hobo. There were crowds, but now there were black people in them as well as white people, and they were cheering for him. There were women. They all seemed to want to kiss him. Attorney General Baxley and his wife took Norris out to lunch at a "big fancy restaurant." Joining them were two black assistant attorneys general, one of them a woman, two prestigious black lawyers, a black member of the Alabama House of Representatives, and a black judge. They all sat at one big table, with Norris at the head. In Tuscaloosa, Norris saw black students and white students walking together, sitting together, talking. The governor welcomed him to his office, and wished him a long life. And everywhere he went, everyone wanted to shake his hand.

Chronology

1931

March 25	The fight on the freight train and the arrest.
March 30	Jackson County grand jury indicts nine black youths for rape.
April 6–7	Clarence Norris and Charlie Weems tried, convicted, and sentenced to death.
April 7–8	Haywood Patterson tried, convicted, and sentenced to death.
April 8–9	Olen Montgomery, Ozie Powell, Willie Roberson, Eugene Williams, and Andy Wright tried, convicted, and sentenced to death.
April 9	Trial of Roy Wright ends in a mistrial when some jurors hold out for death penalty though prosecution asked only for life imprisonment.
April–December	ILD and NAACP fight for control of the defense.
May	Hollace Ransdall's trip to Alabama.
July	Violence at Camp Hill, Alabama.

1932

January	NAACP withdraws from the case.
February	Ruby Bates, in a letter to a friend, denies that the defendants raped her.
March	Alabama Supreme Court affirms the conviction of Olen Montgomery, Clarence Norris, Haywood Patterson, Ozie Powell, Willie Roberson, Charlie Weems, and Andy Wright and reverses the conviction of Eugene Williams—on the grounds that Williams was a juvenile in April 1931.
May	U.S. Supreme Court agrees to review Scottsboro convictions.
November	U.S. Supreme Court reverses the convictions of Olen Montgomery, Clarence Norris, Haywood Patterson, Ozie Powell, Willie Roberson, Charlie Weems, and Andy Wright in *Powell* v. *Alabama*.
December	Violence at Reeltown, Alabama.

1933

January	ILD retains Samuel Leibowitz.
March	Judge Hawkins grants change of venue to Decatur, Alabama.
March–April	Haywood Patterson tried for the second time, convicted, and sentenced to death.
April	Ned Cobb's trial and conviction.
June	Judge Horton sets aside Haywood Patterson's second conviction and orders a new trial.
November–December	Haywood Patterson tried for the third time, convicted, and sentenced to death. Clarence Norris tried for the second time, convicted, and sentenced to death.

1934

June	Alabama Supreme Court affirms Haywood Patterson's third conviction and Clarence Norris's second conviction.

October	Two lawyers charged with attempting to bribe Victoria Price, triggering a fight between Samuel Leibowitz and the ILD for control of the defense.

1935

January	U.S. Supreme Court agrees to review Patterson's and Norris's convictions.
April	U.S. Supreme Court reverses Norris's conviction (and, effectively, Patterson's) in *Norris* v. *Alabama*.
November	Jackson County grand jury, with one black man on it, reindicts the defendants.
December	Scottsboro Defense Committee formed.

1936

January	Haywood Patterson tried for the fourth time, convicted, and sentenced to seventy-five years. Sheriff Blalock slashed; Ozie Powell shot.
February	Allan Knight Chalmers's first trip to Alabama on behalf of the Scottsboro Defense Committee.
December	Thomas Knight meets with Samuel Leibowitz in New York.

1937

January	Alabama Supreme Court affirms Haywood Patterson's fourth conviction.
July	Clarence Norris tried for the third time, convicted, and sentenced to death. Andy Wright tried for the second time, convicted, and sentenced to ninety-nine years. Charlie Weems tried for the second time, convicted, and sentenced to seventy-five years. Ozie Powell pleads guilty to assaulting sheriff and is sentenced to twenty years. Alabama drops charges against Eugene Williams, Olen Montgomery, Willie Roberson, and Roy Wright.
October	U.S. Supreme Court declines to review Haywood Patterson's fourth conviction.

December	Meeting between Allan Knight Chalmers and Alabama governor Bibb Graves.

1938

June	Alabama Supreme Court affirms Clarence Norris's death sentence.
July	Governor Graves commutes Clarence Norris's sentence to life imprisonment.
August	Alabama Pardon Board denies pardon applications of Haywood Patterson and Ozie Powell.
October	Alabama Pardon Board denies pardon applications of Clarence Norris, Charlie Weems, and Roy Wright. Governor Graves interviews the defendants.
November	Governor Graves denies pardon applications of all five of the remaining defendants.

1943

November	Charlie Weems paroled.

1944

January	Clarence Norris and Andy Wright paroled.
September	Clarence Norris and Andy Wright leave Montgomery in violation of their paroles.
October	Clarence Norris is returned to Kilby.

1946

June	Ozie Powell paroled.
September	Clarence Norris, paroled a second time, leaves Alabama.
October	Andy Wright is returned to Kilby.

1948

July	Haywood Patterson escapes from Kilby.

1950

June	Andy Wright paroled to New York. FBI arrests Haywood Patterson in Detroit. Michigan governor Williams refuses extradition request. Alabama abandons extradition proceedings.

1952

August	Haywood Patterson dies.

1959

August	Roy Wright dies.

1976

October	Clarence Norris pardoned.

1989

January	Clarence Norris dies.

Abbreviations

AC	*Atlanta Constitution*
ACLU Papers	Papers of the American Civil Liberties Union, Seeley Mudd Library, Princeton University
AD	Anna Damon
ADAH	Alabama Department of Archives and History, Montgomery, Alabama
AKC	Allan Knight Chalmers
AKC Papers	Papers of Allan Knight Chalmers, Mugar Memorial Library, Boston University
AN	*Amsterdam News* (N.Y.C.)
ANP	Associated Negro Press
ASF	Alabama Scottsboro Files, Alabama Department of Archives and History
ASWPL Papers	Papers of the Association of Southern Women for the Prevention of Lynching, Robert W. Woodruff Library, Atlanta University Center (Microfilm, 1983)
AW	Andy Wright
BAA	*Baltimore Afro-American*
BAH	*Birmingham Age-Herald*
BG	Bibb Graves

BN	*Birmingham News*
BP	*Birmingham Post*
BR	*Birmingham Reporter*
BW	*Birmingham World*
CDT	*Chattanooga Daily Times*
CIC Papers	Papers of the Commission on Interracial Cooperation, Robert W. Woodruff Library, Atlanta University Center (Microfilm, 1983)
CNS	*Chattanooga News*
CN	Clarence Norris
CD	*Chicago Defender*
CC	*Christian Century*
CW	Charlie Weems
DW	*Daily Worker*
DD	*Decatur Daily*
EJ	*Equal Justice*
EM	Eugene Martin
ER	Eleanor Roosevelt
EW	Eugene Williams
GCH	Grover C. Hall
GCH Papers	Papers of Grover Cleveland Hall, Alabama Department of Archives and History
GFM	George Fort Milton
HH	Hester G. Huntington
HME	Henry M. Edmonds
HP	Haywood Patterson
HR	Hollace Ransdall
HT	*Huntsville Times*
ILD Papers	Papers of the International Labor Defense, Schomburg Center for Research in Black Culture, New York Public Library
JB	James Burton
JC	James Chappell
JCS	*Jackson County Sentinel*
JDA	Jessie Daniel Ames
KCC	*Kansas City Call*

LD	*Labor Defender*
LSB	Clarence Norris and Sybil Washington, *The Last of the Scottsboro Boys*
MA	*Montgomery Advertiser*
MS	Morris Shapiro
NAACP Papers	Papers of the National Association for the Advancement of Colored People, Library of Congress (Microfilm, 1986)
NJG	*Norfolk Journal and Guide*
NM	*New Masses*
NCDPP	National Committee for the Defense of Political Prisoners
NR	*National Republic*
NYDM	*New York Daily Mirror*
NYDN	*New York Daily News*
NYEJ	*New York Evening Journal*
NYEP	*New York Evening Post*
NYHT	*New York Herald Tribune*
NYP	*New York Post*
NYT	*New York Times*
NYWT	*New York World-Telegram*
OCBD	*Oklahoma City Black Dispatch*
OM	Olen Montgomery
OP	Ozie Powell
PC	*Pittsburgh Courier*
RB	Rose Baron
RNB	Roger N. Baldwin
RNO	*Raleigh News and Observer*
RS	Rose Shapiro
RTD	*Richmond Times-Dispatch*
RW	Roy Wilkins
RWR	Roy Wright
SB	Haywood Patterson and Earl Conrad, *Scottsboro Boy*
SCSL	Southern Commission on the Study of Lynching
SDC	Scottsboro Defense Committee

SPA	*Scottsboro Progressive Age*
SSL	Samuel S. Leibowitz
ST	*Savannah Tribune*
STJ	*Selma Times-Journal*
SW	*Southern Worker*
TEK Papers	Papers of Thomas E. Knight, Jr., Alabama Department of Archives and History
TINCF	Tuskegee Institute News Clipping File, Tuskegee Institute, Alabama (Microfilm, 1976)
TM	Thurgood Marshall
TN	*The Nation*
TNR	*The New Republic*
TSBF	Allan Knight Chalmers, *They Shall Be Free*
VM	Viola Montgomery
WFW	Walter White
WGM	Bishop William G. McDowell
WNS	Whitney North Seymour
WR	Willie Roberson
WW	*Washington World*
WWA	Will W. Alexander

The Scottsboro Case legal documents (records, petitions, briefs, motions, bills of exceptions, and court decisions) cited in the notes are all available, in ten bound volumes, in the Cornell University Law Library, Ithaca, New York.

Notes

CHAPTER I

1. This account is based on *SB,* 3–7; Record at 51–54, *Weems* v. *Alabama,* U.S. Supreme Court (No. 100; Oct. Term, 1932); Record at 39–46, *Patterson* v. *Alabama,* U.S. Supreme Court (No. 99; Oct. Term, 1932); Record at 36–40, *Powell* v. *Alabama,* U.S. Supreme Court (No. 98; Oct. Term, 1932); *LSB,* 17–22.
2. OM to "My Dear Friend Mr. George [Chamlee]," 25 May 1931, ILD Papers.
3. *SB,* 7–8; *LSB,* 20–21; *DD,* 26 March 1931; *HT,* 25–26 March 1931; Carter, *Scottsboro,* 7–10.
4. *SB,* 9–11; *LSB,* 17–26; *CDT,* 14 June 1931; *JCS,* 26 March 1931; Record at 130, *Weems* v. *Alabama,* U.S. Supreme Court (No. 100; Oct. Term, 1932); Report of Douglas McKenzie, 14 April 1931, ILD Papers; Affidavit of CN, quoted in *ST,* 25 June 1931; Roderick Beddow to WFW, 3 June 1931, NAACP Papers.
5. *SB,* 10–14; *LSB,* 23–25.
6. AW to Ada Wright, printed in *DW,* 11 April 1931.
7. *SB,* 18–19; *LSB,* 26.
8. *NYT,* 24 April 1931; *LSB,* 57–61; Carter, *Scottsboro,* 56–57.
9. *DW,* 27 April 1931; Carter, *Scottsboro,* 58.
10. *LSB,* 58–59; *DW,* 16 May 1931.
11. WFW to Robert R. Moton, 19 Aug. 1931, CIC Papers; Carter, *Scottsboro,* 92–99; *CDT,* 24 April 1931; *DW,* 25 April 1931.
12. RWR to George Maurer, 6 Sept. 1931, printed in *DW,* 14 Sept. 1931; *SB,* 25, 48; *LSB,* 23, 30–32, 59.
13. *SB,* 15–24; *LSB,* 59.
14. *LSB,* 50–51.
15. *SB,* 25.

CHAPTER 2

1. *HT,* 25 March 1931.
2. *HT,* 25 March 1931; *JCS, SPA, DD, CDT, CNS,* and *MA,* 26 March 1931.
3. *SPA,* 26 March 1931.
4. *HT,* 26 March 1931; *CDT,* 27 March 1931.
5. *HT,* 30 March 1931; *CDT,* 29 March 1931.
6. *HT,* 26 March 1931; *CDT,* 26 March 1931; *SPA,* 9 April 1931.
7. *HT,* 26–27 March 1931; *JCS,* 26 March 1931; *SPA,* 26 March 1931; *CDT,* 26–27 March 1931.
8. Record at 22–28, 43, *Powell* v. *Alabama,* U.S. Supreme Court (No. 98; Oct. Term, 1932); Record at 21–30, 50, *Patterson* v. *Alabama,* U.S. Supreme Court (No. 99; Oct. Term, 1932); Record at 22–33, 42–48, 59, *Weems* v. *Alabama,* U.S. Supreme Court (No. 100; Oct. Term, 1932).
9. Record at 28–30, *Weems* v. *Alabama,* U.S. Supreme Court (No. 100; Oct. Term, 1932).
10. Record at 30, *Patterson* v. *Alabama,* U.S. Supreme Court (No. 99; Oct. Term, 1932); Crenshaw and Miller, *Scottsboro,* 32; Record at 48–50, *Weems* v. *Alabama,* U.S. Supreme Court (No. 100; Oct. Term, 1932); *CDT* 8 April 1931; Carter, *Scottsboro,* 31n.
11. Record at 56–58, *Weems* v. *Alabama,* U.S. Supreme Court (No. 100; Oct. Term, 1932); *HT,* 7 April 1931; *CDT,* 8 April 1931.
12. Record at 35–38, *Patterson* v. *Alabama,* U.S. Supreme Court (No. 99; Oct. Term, 1932); Crenshaw and Miller, *Scottsboro,* 35–38.
13. Crenshaw and Miller, *Scottsboro,* 38–39.
14. Record at 33–44, *Powell* v. *Alabama,* U.S. Supreme Court (No. 98; Oct. Term, 1932); Record at 42–50, *Patterson* v. *Alabama,* U.S. Supreme Court (No. 99; Oct. Term, 1932); Record at 51–54, *Weems* v. *Alabama,* U.S. Supreme Court (No. 100; Oct. Term, 1932); *JCS,* 2 April 1931.
15. *HT,* 25–27 March 1931; *JCS,* 26 March, 2, 9 April 1931; *SPA,* 26 March 1931; *CDT,* 12, 17 April 1931; *Fairhope Courier,* 9 April 1931; *CNS,* 27 March 1931; *MA,* 27 March, 14 April 1931. See also Dollard, *Caste and Class,* esp. 134–73; Fredrickson, *Black Image in the White Mind,* 255–82; Collins, *The Truth About Lynching.*
16. Hall, *Revolt Against Chivalry,* 59–65, 167–71, 180–86; CIC, "The Crime of Mob Murder"; CIC, "The Mob Still Rides"; SCSL, "Lynchings and What They Mean"; Raper, *Tragedy of Lynching,* 40–54; *DD,* 26 March 1931; *HT,* 27 March 1931; *JCS,* 26 March, 2 April 1931; *SPA,* 26 March, 2 April 1931; *CNS,* 6 April 1931.
17. Raper, *Tragedy of Lynching,* 480–81; Dollard, *Caste and Class,* 314–62; Hall, *Revolt Against Chivalry,* 145–49.
18. Raper, *Tragedy of Lynching;* Work, *Negro Year Book;* CIC, *The Mob Still Rides; HT,* 26–27 March 1931.
19. Daisy F. Morris to JDA, 27 April 1931, CIC Papers; Thomas E. Anderson to Benjamin M. Miller, 13 July 1931, ASF; *Fairhope Courier,* 9 April 1931; *HT,* 27 March 1931.
20. *DD, HT,* and *CNS,* 10 April 1931; *CDT,* 10–11 April 1931; Crenshaw and Miller, *Scottsboro,* 52.

CHAPTER 3

1. *CDT,* 27 March 1931.
2. Price said she was twenty-one; her mother said she was twenty-four; social workers said she was twenty-seven. See Ransdall, "Report on the Scottsboro Case," 16.
3. Ibid., 12–13, 17.

4. *LD* 9 (June 1933): 70–71; *LD* 9 (July 1933): 12–13; *LD* 9 (Aug. 1933): 36–37, 46; *LD* 9 (Oct. 1933): 65, 67; *LD* 9 (Dec. 1933): 89; *LD* 10 (March 1934): 19, 23; Ransdall, "Report on the Scottsboro Case," 16–17; Hays, *Trial by Prejudice,* 25–26. See also, Woodward, *Origins of the New South;* Tindall, *Emergence of the New South;* Fite, *Cotton Fields No More;* Kirby, *Southern Worlds Lost;* Daniel, *Breaking the Land;* Wright, *Old South, New South;* Hall, *Like a Family.*
5. *LD* 9 (June 1933): 70–71; *LD* 9 (July 1933): 12–13; *LD* 9 (Aug. 1933): 36–37, 46; *LD* 9 (Oct. 1933): 65, 67; *LD* 9 (Dec. 1933): 89.
6. Ransdall, "Report on the Scottsboro Case," 14–17; *Jackson* (Miss.) *Daily News,* Feb. 1931, quoted in Hall, "The Mind That Burns in Each Body," 340.
7. Carter, *Scottsboro,* 6; Crenshaw and Miller, *Scottsboro,* 14–15; *HT,* 26 March 1931: A traveling salesman "heard [Ruby Bates] speak to some of those in the crowd in answer to the questions"; Ransdall, "Report on the Scottsboro Case," 3; Report of Douglas McKenzie, 14 April 1931, ILD Papers; JB to WWA, 14 April 1931, CIC Papers. See also Record at 41, *Weems* v. *Alabama,* U.S. Supreme Court (No. 100; Oct. Term, 1932); SDC, *Opinion of Judge Horton,* 18–19.
8. Record at 22–25, *Powell* v. *Alabama,* U.S. Supreme Court (No. 98; Oct. Term, 1932).
9. Record, *Powell* v. *Alabama,* U.S. Supreme Court (No. 98; Oct. Term, 1932); Record, *Patterson* v. *Alabama,* U.S. Supreme Court (No. 99; Oct. Term, 1932); Record, *Weems* v. *Alabama,* U.S. Supreme Court (No. 100; Oct. Term, 1932).
10. Record at 39, *Powell* v. *Alabama,* U.S. Supreme Court (No. 98; Oct. Term, 1932); Record at 22–23, *Weems* v. *Alabama,* U.S. Supreme Court (No. 100; Oct. Term, 1932).

CHAPTER 4

1. Allen, "Communism in the Deep South," 26–87.
2. Ibid.
3. Allen, "Communism in the Deep South," 108–33; Lowell Wakefield to ILD, 7–10 April 1931, ILD Papers; *SW,* 4 April 1931; *DW,* 10 April 1931; Ransdall, "Report on the Scottsboro Case," 9; Wilson, "Freight-Car Case," 40.
4. *DW,* 10 April 1931; Report of Douglas McKenzie, 14 April 1931, ILD Papers.
5. Report of Douglas McKenzie, 14 April 1931; Report of George Chamlee ("The People of the State of Alabama Versus the Scottsboro Defendants"), 21 April 1931; Report of George Chamlee ("Statement of Facts in the Scottsboro Case"), n.d., ILD Papers; *DW,* 10–11 April 1931.
6. Report of Douglas McKenzie, 14 April 1931, ILD Papers.
7. *DW,* 10 April 1931; Minor, "The Negro and His Judases," 632–33.
8. *DW,* 11 April 1931.
9. Draper, *American Communism,* 302–6; Howe and Coser, *American Communist Party,* 177–82.
10. Draper, *American Communism,* 315–56; Klehr, *Heyday of American Communism,* 324–48; Howe and Coser, *American Communist Party,* 204–9; Naison, *Communists in Harlem,* 3–25; Allen, "Communism in the Deep South," 67. See also Kelley, *Hammer and Hoe.*
11. Howe and Coser, *American Communist Party,* 182–88.
12. Minor, "The Negro and His Judases," 637–39; *Liberator,* 30 May 1931, quoted in Naison, *Communists in Harlem,* 62. See also *DW,* 17 Oct. 1931.
13. ILD Papers, Scottsboro Case, Publicity and Organization, Publicity Tours, 1931–32.
14. Naison, *Communists in Harlem,* 68–69.
15. Naison, *Communists in Harlem,* 57–89; Howe and Coser, *American Communist Party,* 209–16; Record, *The Negro and the Communist Party;* Record, *Race and Radicalism;* Nolan,

Communism Versus the Negro; Carter, *Scottsboro,* 88–90, 137–54; Klehr, *Heyday of American Communism,* 324–48; Martin, "International Labor Defense and Black America." For membership estimates, see Beecher, "Share Croppers' Union in Alabama," 131–32; Stone, "Agrarian Conflict in Alabama"; Rosen, "Alabama Share Croppers Union"; Rosengarten, *All God's Dangers,* 559–61; Painter, *Hosea Hudson,* 17–18, 114; Klehr, *Heyday of American Communism,* 4–7, 25–27, 91–92, 136–38, 153–54, 324–48; Kelley, *Hammer and Hoe.* Allen, "Communism in the Deep South," 122.
16. Cowley, *Dream of the Golden Mountains,* 51–82; Adamic, *My America,* 109–10; Theodore Dreiser to "Dear Friend," May 1931; Lincoln Steffens to "Dear Friend," July 1931, Oct. 1931; John Dos Passos to "Dear Friend," 19 June 1931, ACLU Papers; Dreiser, "Lynching," *AN,* 27 May 1931. Copies of these letters may also be found in the ILD, CIC, and NAACP Papers.

CHAPTER 5

1. White, "The Negro and the Communists," 66.
2. Myrdal, *An American Dilemma,* II:822–26; Autrey, "NAACP in Alabama," 110–18. See also Zangrando, *The NAACP Crusade Against Lynching.*
3. WFW to Bob (Bagnall) and Herbert (Seligman), 3 May 1931, ACLU Papers.
4. White, *A Man Called White,* 28–43; Meier and Rudwick, "Walter Francis White"; Meier and Rudwick, "The Rise of the Black Secretariat," 114–19. See also Cannon, *A Gentle Knight;* Tillman, "Walter Francis White."
5. White, *A Man Called White,* 3–27; Meier and Rudwick, "Walter Francis White."
6. White, *A Man Called White,* 28–119; Meier and Rudwick, "Walter Francis White."
7. White, "The Negro and the Communists," 66.
8. Ibid., 69–70.
9. Ibid., 67.
10. Du Bois, "The Negro and Communism," 314–15.
11. White, "The Negro and the Communists," 72.
12. *TNR* 66 (29 April 1931): 285–86; *TNR* 66 (13 May 1931): 243; *TNR* 67 (8 July 1931): 189–90; Wilson, "Freight-Car Case," 38–43; *CC* 48 (1 July 1931): 859; *CC* 48 (22 July 1931): 941; *CC* 49 (13 Jan. 1932): 49; *CC* 49 (6 April 1932): 435; *TN* 132 (29 April 1931): 465; *TN* 132 (3 June 1931): 608–10; *TN* 134 (20 Jan. 1932): 61–62; *Crisis* 39 (March 1932): 81–83; Arthur Garfield Hays to RNB, 29 Dec. 1931, ACLU Papers; *NYT,* 15 Sept., 28, 30 Dec. 1931, 3, 5 Jan. 1932; Carter, *Scottsboro,* 94–100.

CHAPTER 6

1. Forrest Bailey to HR, 29 April 1931, ACLU Papers; HR, interview by Mary Frederickson, 6 Nov. 1974, Southern Oral History Program interview #4007 (G-50), transcript, 1–8, Southern Historical Collection, University of North Carolina, Chapel Hill; HR to Bailey, 27 April 1931, ACLU Papers.
2. Excerpt from a Confidential Report on the Scottsboro Case by HR, 7 May 1931; HR to Forrest Bailey, 6, 9, 13 May 1931, ACLU Papers.
3. Ransdall, "Report on the Scottsboro Case," 1–3, 4–5.
4. Ibid., 5–6.
5. Ransdall, "Report on the Scottsboro Case," 6–7, 9; *Powell* v. *Alabama,* 287 U.S. 45 (1932); *New York Times,* 8 Nov. 1932.
6. Ransdall, "Report on the Scottsboro Case," 7–8.
7. Ibid., 11.
8. Ibid., 12–14.

9. Ibid., 14, 16.
10. Ibid., 15–17.
11. HR to Forrest Bailey, 6 May 1931, ACLU Papers; Ransdall, "Report on the Scottsboro Case," 17, 21.
12. Ransdall, "Report on the Scottsboro Case," 3, 15.
13. Ibid., 18.
14. Ibid., 19.
15. HR, interview by Mary Frederickson, 20; Forrest Bailey to HR, 25 June 1931, ACLU Papers; *DW,* 14 July 1931; White, "The Negro and the Communists," 62–72; NAACP News Release, 24 April 1931, NAACP Papers; NAACP, *The Scottsboro Case* (New York, 1931), ACLU Papers.
16. HR, interview by Mary Frederickson, 8–16.
17. WFW to Bob (Bagnall) and Herbert (Seligman), 3 May 1931, NAACP Papers; HR to Forrest Bailey, 6 May 1931; Excerpt from a Confidential Report on the Scottsboro Case by HR, 7 May 1931; HR to Forrest Bailey, 9 May 1931, ACLU Papers.
18. Excerpt from a Confidential Report on the Scottsboro Case by HR, 7 May 1931, ACLU Papers.
19. Ransdall, "Report on the Scottsboro Case," 18; HR, interview by Mary Frederickson, 14–16.
20. Ransdall, "Report on the Scottsboro Case," 20–22.

CHAPTER 7

1. *SPA,* 2, 9 April 1931; *CNS,* 8 April 1931; *JCS,* 9 April 1931; *CDT,* 12 April 1931; *Fairhope Courier,* 9 April 1931; *MA,* 14, 27 April 1931; JB, "The Scottsboro Case," May 1931, CIC Papers. The protest mail referred to here and hereafter is in ASF.
2. *JCS,* 7, 21, 28 May 1931; *Rockford* (Tenn.) *Times,* July 1931, reprinted in *NR* 19 (Sept. 1931); *CDT,* 18 July 1931; *SPA,* 23 April, 7, 21 May 1931; *MA,* 19 July 1931; Jordan, *Unpublished Inside Story.*
3. *BN,* 7–15 June 1931; *MA,* 13 June 1931.
4. "Militia in the Courtroom," *STJ,* 9 April 1931; "The Mob in the Courtroom," *STJ,* n.d., clipping in the CIC Papers. See also "The Scottsboro Case," *STJ,* reprinted in *BP,* 30 March 1932.
5. *NYT,* 22–24 Jan., 25–26 March 1932; *BAH,* 23 Jan., 25 March 1932; *Powell* v. *State,* 224 Ala. 540 (1932); Carter, *Scottsboro,* 156–60. Chief Justice John Anderson dissented.
6. *BN,* 12 June 1931; Crenshaw and Miller, *Scottsboro,* 59.
7. *JCS,* 7 May 1931. See also *SPA,* 23, 30 April, 7 May 1931; *BAH,* 15 June 1931; *Monroe* (La.) *News Star,* 9 Oct. 1931; *DD,* 3 Oct. 1931.
8. For white Alabamans' views of the Sharecroppers' Union, see any Alabama newspaper in the days and weeks following 17 July 1931 or the TINCF, 1931, "Agriculture—Labor Conditions." For the shooting of the Birmingham "society girls," see *BN, BP,* and *BAH,* beginning 4 Aug. 1931 and TINCF, 1931, "Crime." For the Birmingham meetings, see Report of Lt. Ralph E. Hurst, 19 Oct. 1932, in Alabama Executive Files, drawer 32, ADAH; *NYT,* 14 May 1932; *DW,* 16 May, 4, 10 Oct. 1932; Painter, *Hosea Hudson,* 94–145; Kelley, *Hammer and Hoe; Memphis Commercial Appeal,* 17 July 1931; *MA,* 18 July 1931.
9. Mrs. L. Miller to Benjamin M. Miller, 13 April 1931; F. W. Fischer to Miller, 17 July 1931; A. L. Beverell to Miller, 3 July 1931; Belle Alkali Company to Miller, 4 Aug. 1931, ASF.
10. *JCS,* quoted in *BN,* 15 June 1931; *SPA,* 1 Oct. 1931.

CHAPTER 8

1. Sosna, *In Search of the Silent South,* 20–41; Tindall, *Emergence of the New South,* 177–83. See also Dykeman and Stokely, *Seeds of Southern Change.*
2. Hall, *Revolt Against Chivalry,* esp. 159–91; Sosna, *In Search of the Silent South,* 26–27; Tindall, *Emergence of the New South,* 175–84; Kneebone, *Southern Liberal Journalists,* 3–21. See also Eagles, *Jonathan Daniels;* Salmond, *Southern Rebel;* Williamson, *Crucible of Race;* Loveland, *Lillian Smith.*
3. Hall, *Revolt Against Chivalry,* 59–129.
4. JB, "The Scottsboro Case," May 1931; WWA to WFW, 21 May 1931, CIC Papers.
5. JB to WWA, 14 April 1931; JB, "Partial Report Scottsboro Alabama Case," 23 April 1931; "The Scottsboro Case," 1 May 1931; "The Scottsboro Case," May 1931; "The Scottsboro Case, Report No. 3," 7 May 1931, CIC Papers; "The Scottsboro Case, Report No. 4," 8 June 1931, CIC Papers; Leo Thiel to JB, 19 May 1931, CIC Papers.
6. JB, "The Scottsboro Case, Report No. 4," 8 June 1931, CIC Papers.
7. JB, "The Scottsboro Case," 1 May 1931; "The Scottsboro Case," May 1931; "The Scottsboro Case, Report No. 3," 7 May 1931, CIC Papers.
8. CIC officials sometimes took credit for thwarting the mob at Scottsboro, but their own correspondence indicates that their phone calls to local and state law enforcement officials came after the sheriff of Jackson County had called the governor to secure the National Guard. See John Abercrombie to WWA, 30 March 1931, CIC Papers. Mrs. J. F. Hooper to JDA, 28 April 1931; Mary M. McCoy to JDA, 21 April 1931; Daisy Morris to JDA, 27 April 1931; JDA to Mrs. L. P. Donovan, 2 July 1931, ASWPL Papers. See also Hall, *Revolt Against Chivalry,* 197–201, 202–3.
9. Jeannette Adams to JDA, 30 April 1931, CIC Papers; JDA to L. P. Donovan, 7 July 1931, ASWPL Papers; Nellie G. Hooper to JDA, 28 April 1931; Jeannette Adams to JDA, 30 April 1931, CIC Papers. See also Daisy Morris to JDA, 27 April 1931, CIC Papers; Hall, *Revolt Against Chivalry,* 201–7.
10. WWA, "Dedicated for Mr. Eaton—United Press," July 1931; WWA to Carter Taylor, 5 Aug. 1931; GFM to WFW, 22 Jan. 1932, CIC Papers.
11. GFM to Bruce Bliven, 25 Aug. 1931, CIC Papers.
12. WWA to Eleanor Copenhaver, 6 May 1931; WWA to Louise Young, 20 May 1931; WWA to WFW, 21 May 1931, CIC Papers.
13. R. B. Eleazer to William M. Scott, 12 June 1931; WWA to WFW, 23 June 1931, CIC Papers; John P. West to Benjamin M. Miller, 18 June 1931; Thomas E. Anderson to Miller, 13 July 1931; Alfred Truitt to Miller, 12 April 1932, ASF; *BP,* 18 Jan. 1932; *BN,* 25 March 1932; *BAH,* 9 April 1932; *NYT,* 10 Jan., 1 May 1932; *Talladega Daily Home,* 1 June 1932; Carter, *Scottsboro,* 159.
14. *BR,* 16 May 1931; Mrs. Eliot Smith to Benjamin M. Miller, 28 March 1932; Earl Sims to Miller, 14 April 1932, ASF.

CHAPTER 9

1. Woodward, *Origins of the New South,* 205–35, 350–68; Tindall, *Emergence of the New South,* 143–83, 540–74. See also Du Bois, *Souls of Black Folk;* Redding, *No Day of Triumph;* McMillen, *Dark Journey.*
2. Washington, *Up From Slavery;* Washington, *My Larger Education;* Du Bois, "Of Booker T. Washington and Others," in *Souls of Black Folk;* Woodward, *Origins of the New South,* 350–68; Harlan, *Booker T. Washington.*
3. Robert R. Moton to Benjamin M. Miller, 14 April 1931, ASF.
4. The *Reporter* went bankrupt in 1934. Allen Jones, "Alabama," in Suggs, *The Black*

Press in the South, 61; Moorman and Barrell, *Leaders of the Colored Race in Alabama,* 87.
5. *BR,* 13 June 1931.
6. *BR,* 2, 9 May, 8 Aug. 1931.
7. *BR,* 30 May 1931, 6 Feb. 1932.
8. *BR,* 14 Nov. 1931, 23 Jan., 2 April 1932.
9. *ST,* 16 April 1931. For more on Johnson, see Matthews, "Black Newspapermen and the Black Community in Georgia."
10. *ST,* 4 Feb., 2, 16, 23 June, 7, 21 July, 11 Aug., 1, 22 Sept. 1932; *Negro Worker,* 15 June 1932, reprinted in Cunard, *Negro,* 144.
11. *ST,* 5, 12 Jan. 1933.

CHAPTER 10

1. Naison, *Communists in Harlem,* 57–94.
2. *BR,* 23 May 1931.
3. *CD,* 9 May 1931; *DW,* 11 May 1931; *NM* 7 (July 1931): 14–15; *NM* 7 (Nov. 1931): 18–21; *NM* 7 (Feb. 1932): 10; *NM* 7 (June 1932): 10; *Opportunity* 9 (Dec. 1931): 379; Hughes, *I Wonder as I Wander,* 39–69; Hughes, "Christ in Alabama"; Hughes, "Southern Gentlemen." See also Rampersad, *Langston Hughes* I:211–41.
4. *DW,* 24 April 1931.
5. *CD,* 9, 16, 30 May 1931; RW to WFW, 15 May 1931, NAACP Papers; *Atlanta World,* 15 May 1931; *BAA,* 16 May 1931; *NJG,* 16 May 1931; Minor, "The Negro and His Judases," 633–34; *PC,* 14, 19 April, 16, 23, 30 May 1931; ANP News Release, n.d. (1931), CIC Papers.
6. *OCBD,* 14 May 1931; *BAA,* 9 May 1931; *CD,* 9 May 1931; *New York News and Harlem Home Journal,* 23 May 1931, cited in Naison, *Communists in Harlem,* 61. See also *WW,* 20 July 1931; *St. Louis Argus,* 23–24 July 1931; *BAA,* 13 June, 11 July 1931.
7. *WW,* 24 July 1931; the *World* printed White's response on 31 July 1931.
8. *BAA,* 25 July, 1 Aug. 1931; *WW,* 24 July 1931. Cf. "War in Alabama," *NJG,* 25 July 1931; *AN,* 22 July 1931; and the ANP story of John Henry Calhoun, 23 July 1931, which appeared that week in a host of black newspapers, among them the *PC* and *St. Louis Argus.*
9. This and what follows is based on Du Bois, "Negro Editors on Communism," 117–19, 154–56, 170.

CHAPTER 11

1. Painter, *Hosea Hudson,* 84.
2. Ibid., 1–44, 52–74.
3. Ibid., 80, 77–80, 82.
4. Ibid., 83–84.
5. Ibid., 85–86.
6. Ibid., 87–94.
7. Allen, "Communism in the Deep South," 56; Painter, *Hosea Hudson,* 94–126.
8. Rosengarten, *All God's Dangers,* 296–303.
9. Ibid., 298–304.
10. Ibid., 559–61.
11. Painter, *Hosea Hudson,* epigraph, 101, 130–35, 141.
12. Rosengarten, *All God's Dangers,* 299–305.
13. Ibid., 305–12. This and what follows is Cobb's version of the story; it appears to be the most accurate of the accounts sympathetic to the Union and it is corroborated

in significant ways by some unsympathetic accounts: for example, *MA,* 24 Dec. 1932. For the perspectives of white southerners, see *BN, BAH, BP,* and *MA* between 20 Dec. 1932 and 10 Jan. 1933. Cf. *DW;* Beecher, "Share Croppers' Union in Alabama," 131–32; Painter, *Hosea Hudson,* 146–56; Solomon, "Red and Black"; Stone, "Agrarian Conflict in Alabama"; Rosen, "Alabama Share Croppers Union"; Jamieson, *Labor Unionism in American Agriculture,* 290–302; Kelley, *Hammer and Hoe,* 34–57. See also TINCF, 1932, "Agriculture—Labor Conditions."
14. *BP,* 22 Dec. 1932.
15. Painter, *Hosea Hudson,* 150–56; *DW,* 9 Jan. 1933.
16. Rosengarten, *All God's Dangers,* 331–43; Stone, "Agrarian Conflict in Alabama," 525; *DW,* 27, 28 April 1933. See also *CD,* 7 Jan., 8 April 1933.
17. Rosengarten, *All God's Dangers,* 340–41.
18. Autrey, "NAACP in Alabama," 110–18; Painter, *Hosea Hudson,* 86, 15–16, 271; Rosengarten, *All God's Dangers,* 299; Mamie Williams to the United Front Scottsboro Committee, printed in *DW,* 29 May 1931; Janie Patterson to *DW,* 9 May 1931; Beecher, "Share Croppers' Union in Alabama," 127.
19. Painter, *Hosea Hudson,* 80, 95; Hudson, *Black Worker,* 4.
20. Rosengarten, *All God's Dangers,* 7; Nate Cobb, interview with Theodore Rosengarten, quoted in Naison, "Black Agrarian Radicalism in the Great Depression," 55.

CHAPTER 12

1. *DW,* 11 April, 9 May 1931, 10 Feb. 1932; *Liberator,* 5 May 1931; *LD* 8 (Aug. 1932): 144; Branche, "Report of Neuropsychiatric Examination" of HP, CN, OM, and OP.
2. The Pattersons, Ada Wright, Mamie Williams, and Viola Montgomery were behind the ILD from May 1931 on; Josephine Powell switched for the last time in August; Ida Norris in September or October. Weems's and Roberson's parents were dead. See Carter, *Scottsboro,* 90–99.
3. Ada Wright, n.d., to the ILD, ILD Papers; *DW,* 25 April 1931; Janie Patterson to the ILD, reprinted in *DW,* 9 May 1931.
4. ILD Papers, "Publicity Tours"; *DW,* 27 April 1932. Cf. Carter, *Scottsboro,* 171–73.
5. WFW to Bob (Bagnall) and Herbert (Seligman), 3 May 1931, ACLU Papers; William Pickens to WFW, 6 June 1931, NAACP Papers; White, "The Negro and the Communists," 67; *PC,* 16 May 1931. White's public comments, which must have circulated in an NAACP news release, appeared in dozens of newspapers. See also WFW to Herbert Turner, 11 May 1931; WFW to Dean (Pickens), 12 May 1931, NAACP Papers.
6. *DW,* 17 July 1931; Richard Moore to Frank, 25 March 1933; Ada Wright to the ILD, n.d., ILD Papers.
7. *DW,* 27 May 1931; Richard Moore to Frank, 25 March 1933, ILD Papers.

CHAPTER 13

1. *Powell* v. *Alabama,* 287 U.S. 45 (1932); the *NYT* reprinted the entire decision on 8 Nov. 1932.
2. *NYT,* 8 Nov. 1932; Haywood, "Scottsboro Decision," 1065–75; letter of Louis Colman, *TN* 135 (7 Dec. 1932): 560.
3. Haywood, "Scottsboro Decision," 1065–75; letter of Louis Colman, *TN* 135 (7 Dec. 1932): 560.
4. *NYT,* 8, 13 Nov. 1932; Haywood, "Scottsboro Decision," 1065–67.
5. WFW, quoted in *BAA,* 19 Nov. 1932; *Mt. Clemens Leader,* 12 Nov. 1932; *NYT,* 8 Nov. 1932; *NYDN,* 12 Nov. 1932.

6. Ernst, "Dissenting Opinion"; *TN* 135 (7 Dec. 1932): 545. See also *BAA,* 12 Nov. 1932; *NJG,* 12 Nov. 1932; *Washington Tribune,* 23 Dec. 1932.
7. *NYT,* 13 Nov. 1932, reprinted in Kurland, *Felix Frankfurter.*
8. Oliver Wendell Holmes wrote the majority opinion in *Moore.* The decision affirmed his lone dissent in *Frank* v. *Magnum* 237 U.S. 309 (1915), the Leo Frank Case, in which he declared that it is the court's duty "to declare lynch law as little valid when practiced by a regularly drawn jury as when administered by one elected by a mob intent on death"; see Miller, *Petitioners,* 235; Cortner, *A Mob Intent on Death. NYT,* 13 Nov. 1932.

CHAPTER 14

1. HP to Janie Patterson, 8 April 1931, printed in *DW,* 16 April 1931; CW to George Maurer, n.d., ILD Papers; CN to WFW, 16 Aug. 1931, CIC Papers.
2. RWR to Ada Wright, 19 June 1931; OP to Josephine Powell, 7 Dec. 1932, ILD Papers.
3. OM to William Patterson, 9 Nov. 1932; HP to William Patterson, 19 Dec. 1932, ILD Papers.
4. RWR to George Maurer, 6 Sept. 1931, printed in *DW,* 14 Sept. 1931.
5. Branche, "Report of Neuropsychiatric Examination" of RWR and AW. See also *DW,* 11, 16 April 1931.
6. *SB,* 26–28; Branche, "Report of Neuropsychiatric Examination" of HP.
7. Branche, "Report of Neuropsychiatric Examination" of HP; *SB,* 28.
8. *SB,* 30–31; HP to J. Louis Engdahl, 10 Dec. 1931, ILD Papers.
9. *SB,* 31–32. For more on Kilby Prison, see also *LSB,* esp. 47–57, 177–91; Moos, *Penal Administration.* For three perspectives from the other side of the bars, see March, *Alabama Bound.*
10. *LSB,* 17–47. See also Branche, "Report of Neuropsychiatric Examination" of CN.
11. *LSB,* 28.
12. Ibid., 36–46.
13. Ibid., 17–18, 45–46.
14. Ibid., 18.
15. Ibid., 46.
16. *LSB,* 50–56; *SB,* 25, 50–57. See also Moos, *Penal Administration,* 137–38; March, *Alabama Bound,* 53–61; *MA,* 1, 5, 8, 10–12 March 1932.
17. *LSB,* 54, 257–61.
18. *NYT,* 22 March 1933; *SB,* 35.
19. *NYT,* 10 March 1933.
20. Ibid.
21. Ibid.

CHAPTER 15

1. Johnson, "Let Freedom Ring."
2. See Leibowitz, *The Defender;* Pasley, *Not Guilty!;* Reynolds, *Courtroom.*
3. Johnson, "Let Freedom Ring," 21.
4. This account is based on Leibowitz, *The Defender,* 170–81; Reynolds, *Courtroom,* 179–89. Cf. Johnson, "Let Freedom Ring," 21–24.
5. William L. Patterson to SSL, 28 Jan. 1933, ILD Papers. Part of this letter, and part of Leibowitz's reply, is reprinted in Reynolds, *Courtroom,* 249–51.
6. Leibowitz, *The Defender,* 189–90; SSL to William L. Patterson, 31 Jan. 1933, ILD Papers.

7. SSL to William L. Patterson, 31 Jan. 1933, ILD Papers.
8. Allen, "Scottsboro Struggle." See also "The Scottsboro Struggle and the Next Steps," *Communist* 12 (June 1933): 570–82. William L. Patterson to George Chamlee, 24 Dec. 1932, ILD Papers.
9. William L. Patterson to SSL, 6 Feb. 1933, ILD Papers; Leibowitz, *The Defender,* 189–90.
10. Phillips, *American Negro Slavery;* Phillips, *Life and Labor.* See also Novick, *That Noble Dream,* 72–80.
11. Stampp, *Causes of the Civil War;* Stampp, *Era of Reconstruction,* 3–23.
12. Joseph Le Conte, quoted in Foner, *Reconstruction,* 609. See also Du Bois, *Black Reconstruction,* 711–29; Stampp, *Era of Reconstruction,* 3–23; Foner, *Reconstruction,* xix–xxvii, 602–12.
13. Novick, *That Noble Dream,* 47–50, 72–80, 224–39; Kirby, *Media-Made America,* 1–8; Du Bois, *Black Reconstruction,* 718–29; Dunning, *Reconstruction;* Fleming, *Civil War and Reconstruction in Alabama;* Fleming, *The Sequel of Appomattox;* Burgess, *Reconstruction and the Constitution;* Rhodes, *History of the United States;* Wilson, *History of the American People.*
14. Dixon, *The Clansman;* Kirby, *Media-Made America,* 1–38; Rogin, " 'The Sword Became a Flashing Vision,' " 151–52.
15. Bowers, *The Tragic Era;* Kirby, *Media-Made America,* 23–34; Novick, *That Noble Dream,* 230–31.
16. Schlesinger, review of *The Tragic Era.* See also Kirby, *Media-Made America,* 34–35.
17. See, for example, Buck, *Road to Reunion.*
18. Stampp, *Era of Reconstruction,* 3–23; Novick, *That Noble Dream,* 72–80, 84.

CHAPTER 16

1. ADAH, *Alabama Official and Statistical Register,* 1935, 32.
2. Spivak, *A Man in His Time,* 207–10; Owen, *History of Alabama,* III: 990.
3. ADAH, *Alabama Official and Statistical Register,* 1935, 98; *Powell* v. *State,* 224 Ala. 540 (1932).
4. *NYT,* 22–24 Jan., 25 March 1932; *BAH,* 23 Jan. 1932; *Powell* v. *Alabama,* 287 U.S. 45 (1932); *NYT,* 11 Oct. 1932; *Powell* v. *State,* 224 Ala. 540 (1932); *NYT,* 11 March 1933.
5. Owsley, "Scottsboro"; O'Brien, *Idea of the American South,* 172. See also *BAH,* 20 July 1933.
6. Owsley, "Scottsboro," 259, 264, 270.
7. *MA,* 20 July 1931.
8. Owsley, "Scottsboro," 266, 270–76.
9. Owsley, "Scottsboro," 279–81; O'Brien, *Idea of the American South,* 170–71.
10. *JCS,* 6 April 1933.
11. Bowers, *The Tragic Era,* 52.
12. Letter of F. B. Cullen to *BN,* reprinted in *JCS,* 27 April 1933; Bowers, *The Tragic Era,* 48; Owsley, "Scottsboro," 267.

CHAPTER 17

1. *NYT,* 13 March 1933.
2. *NYT,* 14 March 1933.
3. *NYT, NYWT,* and *NYHT,* 14 March 1933.
4. *NYT,* 15 March 1933; Spivak, *A Man in His Time,* 220–22.

5. Leibowitz, *The Defender,* 194–97; Pasley, *Not Guilty,* 238; *NYHT,* 30 April 1933.
6. *NYT,* 28 March 1933; Motion to quash indictment at 28–99, *Alabama* v. *Patterson,* Morgan County (27 March 1933); Carter, *Scottsboro,* 194–97.
7. Motion to quash indictment at 36–39, *Alabama* v. *Patterson,* Morgan County (27 March 1933).
8. *JCS,* 16, 23 April 1931; *DD,* 28 March 1933; *NYT,* 28 March 1933; Motion to quash indictment at 32–34, *Alabama* v. *Patterson,* Morgan County (27 March 1933).
9. *NYT,* 28 March 1933; Motion to quash indictment at 30, 83, 85, *Alabama* v. *Patterson,* Morgan County (27 March 1933).
10. Motion to quash indictment at 99–217, *Alabama* v. *Patterson,* Morgan County (27 March 1933).
11. Hammond, "The South Speaks," 465–66; Spivak, *A Man in His Time,* 207–10; *NYWT,* 5 April 1933; Leibowitz, *The Defender,* 197.
12. Motion to quash indictment at 118–19, *Alabama* v. *Patterson,* Morgan County (27 March 1933).
13. Motion to quash indictment at 99–217, *Alabama* v. *Patterson,* Morgan County (27 March 1933); Hammond, "The South Speaks," 466; *DD,* 31 March 1933; Leibowitz, *The Defender,* 202; *DD,* 4 April 1933; Carter, *Scottsboro,* 196–97.
14. *DD,* 28–31 March 1933; *NYT,* 29–31 March 1933; Vorse, "Scottsboro Trial," 276–77.
15. Vorse, "Scottsboro Trial," 276; *DD,* 31 March 1933; *NYT,* 31 March 1933.
16. Reynolds, *Courtroom,* 266; *DD,* 31 March, 1 April 1933; *NYT,* 31 March, 1 April 1933.

CHAPTER 18

1. *DD,* 3 April 1933.
2. Record at 16–132, *Alabama* v. *Patterson,* Morgan County (31 March 1933); *DD,* 3–4 April 1933; *NYT,* 5 April 1933.
3. Record at 72–78, 327–331, *Alabama* v. *Patterson,* Morgan County (31 March 1933); *DD,* 3 April 1933; *NYT,* 6 April 1933.
4. Record at 60–128, *Alabama* v. *Patterson,* Morgan County (31 March 1933).
5. *DD,* 3–4 April 1933; Vorse, "Scottsboro Trial," 277; *BAA,* 8, 15 April 1931.
6. Record at 17–26, 159, *Alabama* v. *Patterson,* Morgan County (31 March 1933); *DD,* 3–4, April 1933. See also *BAA,* 8 April 1933.
7. Record at 89, 101, 104, *Alabama* v. *Patterson,* Morgan County (31 March 1933).
8. Record at 132–56, 161–98, *Alabama* v. *Patterson,* Morgan County (31 March 1933); Hays, *Trial by Prejudice,* 119.
9. Record at 255–88, *Alabama* v. *Patterson,* Morgan County (31 March 1933).
10. Record at 255–88, *Alabama* v. *Patterson.*
11. Record at 298–325, *Alabama* v. *Patterson.*
12. Record at 346–482, 801–2, *Alabama* v. *Patterson,* Morgan County (31 March 1933); *DD,* 5 April 1933; *NYT,* 6 April 1933.
13. Record at 354–482, *Alabama* v. *Patterson,* Morgan County (31 March 1933).
14. Record at 453, *Alabama* v. *Patterson.*
15. Record at 453–54, *Alabama* v. *Patterson.*
16. *DD,* 5–6 April 1933; Record at 398–401, *Alabama* v. *Patterson,* Morgan County (31 March 1933); Hays, *Trial by Prejudice,* 121–22; *NYT,* 6 April 1933; *NYHT,* 5 April 1933; *NYDN,* 6 April 1933.
17. Record at 482–530, *Alabama* v. *Patterson,* Morgan County (31 March 1933).
18. Record at 530–633, *Alabama* v. *Patterson.*
19. *JCS,* 9 March 1933; *DD,* 27–30 March, 3, 6 April 1933; *BAA,* 8 April 1933; *NYT,*

11, 25–26, 30 March, 7 April 1933; Record at 662–750, 803–7, *Alabama* v. *Patterson*, Morgan County (31 March 1933).

20. Hammond, "The South Speaks," 465; *DW*, 6 April 1933; *DD*, 8 April 1933; *HT*, 9 April 1933.

21. *NYWT*, 5 April 1933; *DD*, 6 April 1933; *NYT*, 7–8 April 1933; Robert B. Eleazer to George E. Haynes, 11 April 1933, CIC Papers; Vorse, "Scottsboro Trial," 276–78; Hammond, "The South Speaks," 465–66; Hays, *Trial by Prejudice*, 126–27; Spivak, "When Mobs Marched on Decatur," *Louisiana Weekly*, clipping, n.d. (May 1933), CIC Papers.

22. *NYT*, 8 April 1933; *NYHT*, 8 April 1933; Reynolds, *Courtroom*, 274.

23. *NYT*, 9–10 April 1933; *HT*, 9 April 1933; *AC*, 9 April 1933; Spivak, *A Man in His Time*, 230. See also Hammond, "The South Speaks," 466.

24. Leibowitz, *The Defender*, 243–44.

25. Palsey, *Not Guilty!*, 265–66; *NYT*, 8–9 April 1933; *DD*, 8 April 1933; *BP*, 8 April 1933.

26. *NYT*, 9 April 1933; *HT*, 9 April 1933.

27. *NYT*, 9 April 1933.

CHAPTER 19

1. Carter, *Scottsboro*, 200; Reynolds, *Courtroom*, 266.

2. Record at 6–161, *Alabama* v. *Patterson*, Morgan County (31 March 1933); *DD*, 3–4 April 1933; *SPA*, 6 April 1933; *HT*, 3 April 1933; *Athens Courier*, 6 April 1933, quoted in Goodrich, "James Edwin Horton," 57; *MA*, 4 April 1933. See also *BAH*, 4 April 1933, quoted in Carter, *Scottsboro*, 214.

3. *JCS*, 28 May 1931.

4. *NYT*, 18 March 1933; Goodrich, "James Edwin Horton," 15–17.

5. Goodrich, "James Edwin Horton," 15–17; *NYT*, 2 April 1933.

6. Vorse, "Scottsboro Trial," 277–78; *NYWT*, 5 April 1933; *NYHT*, 3 April 1933; *Sylacauga* (Ala.) *News*, 7 April 1933.

7. Record at 132–60, *Alabama* v. *Patterson*, Morgan County (31 March 1933).

8. Record at 161–98, *Alabama* v. *Patterson*, Morgan County (31 March 1933); *DD*, 4 April 1933; *BAH*, 4 April 1933; *CDT*, 4 April 1933, quoted in Carter, *Scottsboro*, 214.

9. *DD*, 4 April 1933. See also Record at 198–203, 236–39, 244–48, 255–58, 288–90, *Alabama* v. *Patterson*, Morgan County (31 March 1933).

10. Record at 203–98, *Alabama* v. *Patterson*, Morgan County (31 March 1933); *DD*, 4 April 1933.

11. Record at 298–482, *Alabama* v. *Patterson*, Morgan County (31 March 1933); *DD*, 5 April 1933.

12. Record at 573–672, *Alabama* v. *Patterson*, Morgan County (31 March 1933).

13. Record at 573–633, 676–746, *Alabama* v. *Patterson*.

14. Ibid.

15. Record at 676–746, *Alabama* v. *Patterson*.

16. Record at 685–91, 703, 720–22, 726–27, *Alabama* v. *Patterson*.

17. Crenshaw and Miller, *Scottsboro*, 87; Record at 695–97, 708–9, *Alabama* v. *Patterson*, Morgan County (31 March 1933).

18. Record at 741–43, *Alabama* v. *Patterson*, Morgan County (31 March 1933).

19. *DD*, 8 April 1933; *AC*, 8 April 1933.

20. *NYT*, 8–9 April 1933; *DD*, 8 April 1933; *BP*, 8 April 1933; Pasley, *Not Guilty!*, 265–66.

21. *DD*, 8 April 1933; *NYT*, 9 April 1933.

22. *HT*, 9 May 1933; Thomas E. Knight, Jr., to Charles J. Cargile, 13 May 1933, TEK

Papers; *DD*, 6 April 1933; *RTD* 7 April 1933; *NYT*, 8 April 1933; *HT*, 7 April 1933; WGM to WWA, 17 April 1933, CIC Papers; *AC*, 8–10 April 1933; Vorse, "Scottsboro Trial," 356.
23. *NYT*, 10 April 1933; *NYDN*, 10 April 1933.
24. *SPA*, 6 April 1933.

CHAPTER 20

1. *NYDN*, 10 April 1933; *NYT*, 11 April 1933.
2. *NYDN*, 10 April 1933; *NYT*, 10–11 April 1933; *NYHT*, 11 April 1933; Hays, *Trial by Prejudice*, 32–33.
3. *NYHT*, 8, 11 April 1933; *NYWT*, 11 April 1933.
4. *NYT*, *NYHT*, and *NYWT*, 4–10 April 1933. Cf. *DD*, *HT*, and *MA*. For a striking example of the difference between stories based on the AP and UP dispatches, see the change in the stories in the *RNO*, 1–10 April 1933, after the editor switched from the former to the latter in mid-trial.
5. *NYHT*, 11 April 1933; *NYT*, 10 April 1933.
6. *NYT*, 11–12, 16–17 April 1933; *NYEJ*, 11 April 1933; *NYDN*, 11 April 1933; *NYDM*, 13 April 1933; *NYEP*, 10 April 1933.
7. For reports on Hitler, Germany, and German Jews, see almost any major metropolitan daily newspaper on any day in the last week of March and the first week of April. My summary is based on the *NYEP*, *NYHT*, and *NYT*. For a different perspective on perceptions of Germany in the American press, see Lipstadt, *Beyond Belief*, esp. 13–40. See also, American Jewish Committee, *The Jews in Nazi Germany*.
8. *NYEP*, 3–7, 13 April 1933.
9. *NYEP*, 17 April 1933; *NYEJ*, 7, 13 April 1933; *NYDM*, 15 April 1933. See also *New York New Leader*, 15 April 1933; *CC* 50 (19 April 1933): 521; letter of Maurice Le Frak, *NYWT*, 13 April 1933; *BP*, 10 April 1933; Kneebone, *Southern Liberal Journalists*, 176–80.
10. *Portland* (Oreg.) *Advocate*, 10 June 1933; *KCC*, 5 May 1933; *CD*, 8 April 1933; *NYT*, 10–11 April 1931.
11. Leibowitz, *The Defender*, 197; *NYT*, 10–11 April 1931.
12. *NYWT*, 10–11 April 1933; unlabeled clipping, 11 May 1933, CIC Papers.
13. *NYT*, 11–17 April 1933; *NYDN*, 14–17 April 1933.
14. *NYWT*, 17 April 1933; *NYHT*, 18 April 1933; *NYT*, 18 April 1933; Goodrich, "James Edwin Horton," 93.
15. *NYHT*, 18, 30 April 1933.
16. *NYWT*, 17 April 1933; *NYHT*, 18 April 1933; SSL to Judge James Edwin Horton, Jr., 18 April 1933, printed in *KCC*, 28 April 1933; Goodrich, "James Edwin Horton," 93.
17. *NYHT*, 18 April 1933; *NYWT*, 11 April 1933; *NYDN*, 17 April 1933. See also *NYT*, 6, 24 May 1933; *AN*, 30 Aug. 1933.

CHAPTER 21

1. *LSB*, 149–61; *SB*, 44–48. See also *NYHT*, 28 April 1933; *NYT*, *BN*, and *BAH*, 28–29 April 1933; *DW*, 1 May 1933.
2. *DD*, 31 March 1933; *NYT*, 12 May 1933; Report by Benjamin J. Davis, Jr., on interview with Scottsboro Boys in Birmingham, 13 May 1933, ILD Papers; *DW*, 11–12, 20 May 1933; *Seattle Northwest Enterprise*, 18 May 1933, clipping, CIC Papers; *LSB*, 156–57.

3. See Moos, *Penal Administration,* 134–35; March, *Alabama Bound,* esp. 30–50; *SB,* 101–2; *LSB,* 185; *HT,* 10 Jan. 1932.
4. *SB,* 46–48; *LSB,* 149–53.
5. *LSB,* 149–53.
6. *SB,* 44–48.
7. *LSB,* 151.

CHAPTER 22

1. Lynch, *Facts of Reconstruction;* Lynch, "Some Historical Errors of James Ford Rhodes"; Lynch, "More About the Historical Errors of James Ford Rhodes."
2. George Myers to James Ford Rhodes, 21 Nov. 1917; Myers to Rhodes, 8 Jan. 1918, in Garraty, *The Barber and the Historian,* 75, 77–78.
3. Ibid.
4. Lynch, "Communications: *The Tragic Era*"; Woodson, review of *The Tragic Era.*
5. Du Bois, "Of the Dawn of Freedom," in *Souls of Black Folk;* Du Bois, "Reconstruction and Its Benefits," Du Bois, *Black Reconstruction in America,* 725–26. A few white historians deserted to the black historians' side in the 1930s, but the impact of their work on the academic historiography of Reconstruction, let alone popular historiography, would not be felt for another thirty years. See, for example, Simkins and Woody, *South Carolina During Reconstruction;* Simkins, "New Viewpoints of Southern Reconstruction."
6. Naison, "Black Agrarian Radicalism," 55; Painter, *Hosea Hudson,* 80; Hudson, *Black Worker,* 4; former slave quoted in Foner, *Reconstruction,* 611.
7. *NYWT,* 10 April 1933; *NYT,* 10 April 1933; Theodore Bassett quoted in Naison, *Communists in Harlem,* 82–83; *AN,* 12 April 1933.
8. *Philadelphia Ledger,* quoted in *NJG,* 15 April 1933; *OCBD,* 13 April 1933. See also *ST,* 20 April 1933; *BR,* 18 Feb., 15 April 1933.
9. *NYEP,* 10 April 1933; *NYEJ, NYDN,* and *NYT,* 11 April 1933; I. F. Coles to WFW, 14 April 1933; WFW to the Branches, 12 April 1933, NAACP Papers; *BR,* 13 May 1933; Naison, *Communists in Harlem,* 82.
10. Naison, *Communists in Harlem,* 83–89.
11. *BAA,* 15 April 1933; *AN,* 19 April 1933; *New York Age,* 15 April 1933; Naison, *Communists in Harlem,* 82–83; "Brown" to "Dear Sir," 15 April 1933, NAACP Papers. See also *Cleveland Call and Post,* 15 April 1933; *Palmetto Leader,* 1 July 1933.

CHAPTER 23

1. *HT,* 12 April 1933; *RTD,* 12 April 1933; *RNO,* quoted in *Literary Digest* 115 (22 April 1933): 4; *Richmond News Leader,* quoted in *NJG,* 15 April 1933. See also *BP,* 15 April 1933.
2. *RTD,* 12 April 1933; *CC* 50 (10 May 1933): 630; Virginius Dabney to JB, 1 June 1932, CIC Papers; Dabney, *Liberalism in the South,* 256–68; Graves, "Fiat Justitia," 218.
3. Cothran, "South of Scottsboro," 323; Cason, "Black Straws," 84–85.
4. Cason, "Black Straws," 84–85; Cothran, "South of Scottsboro," 324.
5. Cason, "Black Straws," 86; Cothran, "South of Scottsboro," 325, 328; Cason, "Middle Class and Bourbon," in Couch, *Culture in the South,* 497.
6. SCSL, "Lynchings and What They Mean,"; Raper, *Tragedy of Lynching;* Kneebone, *Southern Liberal Journalists,* 74–75, 81–84; Sosna, *In Search of the Silent South,* 31–36; *NYHT,* 8 April 1933; *The World Tomorrow* 16 (June 1933): 428; Cason, "The Forgotten Negro," 75; Dabney, *Liberalism in the South,* 250.

7. WWA, "Dedicated for Mr. Eaton—United Press," July 1931, CIC Papers; Cothran, "South of Scottsboro," 328.
8. James E. Clarke to Francis J. Grimké, 9 May 1933, in Grimké, *Works of Francis James Grimké* 3: 479–80; Cothran, "South of Scottsboro," 326.
9. Dollard, *Caste and Class,* 134–72, esp. 170; Cash, *Mind of the South,* 118; Deutsch, *Psychology of Women,* esp. I:126, 261–62.
10. *Raleigh* (N.C.) *Times,* reprinted in *CD,* 27 May 1933.
11. J. F. Hayden to Benjamin M. Miller, 20 July 1931, ASF.
12. See Smith, *Strange Fruit;* Smith, *Killers of the Dream.*
13. Raper, *Tragedy of Lynching,* 1–54.
14. Cason, *Ninety Degrees in the Shade,* 113–20. Cf. Cason, "The Forgotten Negro," 75, 79.
15. Cason, *Ninety Degrees in the Shade,* 120; Raper, *Tragedy of Lynching;* Hall, *Revolt Against Chivalry,* 129–57.
16. WWA to George E. Haynes, 25 Feb. 1933, CIC Papers; *RNO,* 16, 21 April 1933.
17. WGM to WWA, 17 April 1933, CIC Papers.
18. Milton, *Age of Hate;* Dabney, *Liberalism in the South,* 154–55; *BAH,* 6, 10 May 1933.
19. WGM to WWA, 17 April 1933, CIC Papers.
20. Deutsch, *Psychology of Women* I: 262.
21. *Greensboro Daily News,* quoted in *NJG,* 15 April 1933; *Charlotte Observer,* n.d., clipping, CIC Papers; *RNO,* 8–9 April 1933.
22. *RNO,* 8–9 April 1933.

CHAPTER 24

1. *NYWT,* 17 April 1933; *DD,* 22 June 1933; *HT,* 22 June 1933. Except where otherwise noted, this chapter is based on the complete text of Horton's decision: Decision on motion for a new trial, *Alabama* v. *Patterson,* Morgan County (22 June 1933). The version of Horton's decision that circulated most widely in the 1930s was SDC, *The Scottsboro Case: Opinion of Judge James Edwin Horton, Jr.;* there are copies in the ACLU, CIC, SDC, NAACP, and ILD Papers. That pamphlet was reprinted in *SB,* 260–68, and except for Horton's discussion and citation of precedents, it is complete.
2. Goodrich, "James Edwin Horton," 21–24; Graves, "Fiat Justitia," 218.
3. Goodrich, "James Edwin Horton," 25–38.
4. *Limestone Democrat,* 23 March 1933, quoted in Goodrich, "James Edwin Horton," 21–22; Thomas E. Knight, Jr., to Marcus W. Crenshaw, 20 Sept. 1933, TEK Papers.
5. Goodrich, "James Edwin Horton," 25–38; Graves, "Fiat Justitia," 218.
6. *BAA,* 8 April 1933; Record at 2–5, 398–401, *Alabama* v. *Patterson,* Morgan County (31 March 1933).
7. Graves, "Fiat Justitia," 218; Goodrich, "James Edwin Horton," 57. My account of Horton's encounter with Dr. Lynch is based on Carter, *Scottsboro,* 214–16. Carter corresponded with and interviewed Horton in 1966 and 1967. Horton died in 1973.
8. Carter, *Scottsboro,* 214–16.
9. *DD,* 21 June 1933.
10. *NYT,* 9 April 1933; *AC,* 9 April 1933.

CHAPTER 25

1. *DW,* 10–12 April 1931; Report of Douglas McKenzie, 14 April 1931; Report of George Chamlee ("The People of the State of Alabama Versus the Scottsboro Defen-

dants"), 21 April 1931; Report of George Chamlee ("Statement of Facts in the Scottsboro Case"), n.d.; "Names of Witnesses, Families, Etc.," n.d., ILD Papers; Chamlee, "Is Lynching Ever Defensible?"; Wilson, "The Freight-Car Case."
2. JB, "The Scottsboro Case," 1 May 1931; JB, "The Scottsboro Case, Report No. 4," 8 June 1931; Leo Thiel to JB, 19 May 1931, CIC Papers; WFW to Bob (Bagnall) and Herbert (Seligman), 3 May 1931, NAACP Papers; HR to Forrest Bailey, 6 May 1931, ACLU Papers.
3. Record at 63–65, *Patterson* v. *Alabama,* U.S. Supreme Court (No. 99; Oct. Term, 1932).
4. Record at 65–66, *Patterson* v. *Alabama.*
5. Record at 66–68, *Patterson* v. *Alabama.*
6. Record at 68–70, *Patterson* v. *Alabama.*
7. Record at 70–75, *Patterson* v. *Alabama.*
8. *JCS,* 28 May 1931; *CDT,* 6 June 1931, cited in Carter, *Scottsboro,* 79.
9. Record at 156–60, *Patterson* v. *Alabama,* U.S. Supreme Court (No. 99; Oct. Term 1932).
10. Record at 156–60, *Patterson* v. *Alabama.*
11. *NYWT,* 14 July 1931.
12. Ransdall, "Report on the Scottsboro Case."
13. Ibid., 13–14.
14. Vorse, "How Scottsboro Happened," 356–57.
15. For an early, indispensable, and controversial discussion of racism, antiracism, and rape, see Brownmiller, *Against Our Will,* 210–55. Cf. Davis,, "Rape, Racism and the Myth of the Black Rapist," in Davis, *Women, Race, and Class;* Stafford, "Brownmiller on Rape"; Whitfield, *A Death in the Delta,* 111–16.
16. See Hall, *Revolt Against Chivalry,* 201–6.
17. JDA, "The Lynchers' View of Lynching," typescript, 11, ASWPL Papers; Theodore Dreiser, "Lynching," *AN,* 27 May 1931; Dreiser to ASWPL, 13 July 1931, in Elias, *Letters of Theodore Dreiser* II: 535; *BAA,* 15 April 1933; Hughes, "Southern Gentlemen." More generally, see Hall, *Revolt Against Chivalry,* 201–6.
18. *NYT,* 9 April 1933.

CHAPTER 26

1. Record at 200–2, 482–505, 732, 794–801, *Alabama* v. *Patterson,* Morgan County (31 March 1933); *DD,* 30 Nov. 1933; SDC, *Opinion of Judge Horton,* 18–19. See also chapter 3.
2. See, for example, Raper, *Tragedy of Lynching,* 94–95, 319–20, 462–64; NAACP, *Thirty Years of Lynching.*
3. Vorse, "Scottsboro Trial," 277; *BAA,* 8 April 1933.
4. Record at 530–633, 662–750, *Alabama* v. *Patterson,* Morgan County (31 March 1933); Vorse, "How Scottsboro Happened," 357.
5. Ransdall, "Report on the Scottsboro Case," 14–16; Record at 55, *Alabama* v. *Patterson,* Morgan County (31 March 1933); *LD* 9 (June 1933): 70–71; *LD* 9 (July 1933): 12–13; *LD* 9 (Aug. 1933): 36–37, 46; *LD* 9 (Oct. 1933): 65, 67; *LD* 9 (Dec. 1933): 89; *LD* 10 (March 1934): 19, 23; *NYHT,* 4 March 1934; *NYWT,* 3 May 1933; *DW,* 18 April, 4 May 1933, 11 July 1937. As early as June 1931, Will Alexander had heard that "one of the white girls" might be willing to withdraw her accusation; see WWA to WFW, 3 July 1931, CIC Papers.
6. *LD* 10 (March 1934): 19, 23.
7. *LD* 10 (March 1934): 19, 23; Ruby Bates to Earl Streetman, 5 Jan. 1932, ILD Papers (nearly identical versions of Bates's letter are printed in Hays, *Trial by Prejudice,* 115–

16, and *SB,* 258–59); *HT,* 6–7 Jan. 1932; *CDT,* 7–8, 15 Jan. 1932. See also Carter, *Scottsboro,* 186–88.
8. *LD* 10 (March 1934): 19, 23; Crenshaw and Miller, *Scottsboro,* 91; Record at 726–27, *Alabama* v. *Patterson,* Morgan County (31 March 1933).
9. *CT,* 7–13, 15 Jan. 1932; *HT,* 6–7, 11 Jan. 1932.
10. *CT,* 7–13, 15 Jan. 1932; *HT,* 6–7, 11 Jan. 1932.
11. *LD* 10 (March 1934): 19, 23; WFW to Alfred Baker Lewis, 11 March 1933, NAACP Papers. See also Report of interview of secretary and assistant secretary with SSL, 1 Oct. 1934; Remarks of SSL to the American Scottsboro Committee, 17 Oct. 1934, NAACP Papers.
12. *LD* 10 (March 1934): 19, 23; Harry Emerson Fosdick to Benjamin M. Miller, 17 Nov. 1933, ASF.
13. Record at 676–746, *Alabama* v. *Patterson,* Morgan County (31 March 1933).
14. *NYWT,* 3 May 1933.
15. *Northwest Enterprise* (Wash.), 18 May 1933, clipping in CIC Papers.
16. *NYT,* 7–10 May 1933; *NYHT,* 8–9 May 1933; *NYWT,* 8–9 May 1933; *HT,* 7–9 May 1933.
17. *NYHT,* 9 May 1933; *NYWT,* 9 May 1933.
18. *NYWT,* 3 May 1933.
19. Ibid.

CHAPTER 27

1. *BP,* 10 April, 23 June 1933; *BN,* 23 June 1933; *BAH,* 23–24 June 1933.
2. *Lafayette Sun* and *Huntsville Builder* quoted in Work, *Negro Year Book: 1937–1938,* 115–16; letter of William Moseley, *BAH,* 27 Oct. 1933. See also *MA,* 23 June 1933.
3. Crenshaw and Miller, *Scottsboro,* 120.
4. *JCS,* 6 April 1933; *Pickens County Herald, Wiregrass Journal,* and *Alabama Courier* are quoted in *JCS,* 29 June 1933.
5. *NYT,* 23 Nov. 1933; *HT,* 7–9 May 1933.
6. *HT,* 7, 9 May 1933; editorial, *Charlotte Observer,* n.d., reprinted in *BAH,* 16 April 1933. For more on the sharecroppers, see chapter 11; Stone, "Agrarian Conflict in Alabama," 523–25; Rosen, "Alabama Share Croppers Union"; Beecher, "Share Croppers' Union in Alabama," 131–32; Painter, *Hosea Hudson,* 154; Kelley, *Hammer and Hoe,* 48–53; Owsley, "Scottsboro," 281; Crenshaw and Miller, *Scottsboro,* 57–59, 70–71.
7. Stone, "Agrarian Conflict in Alabama," 523–25; Owsley, "Scottsboro," 281.
8. SCSL, *Plight of Tuscaloosa,* 9–16.
9. Ibid., 19–20.
10. SCSL, *Plight of Tuscaloosa,* 22–24; *Literary Digest* 1 (2 Sept. 1933): 8.
11. SCSL, *Plight of Tuscaloosa,* 17–20, 34–36.
12. Ibid.
13. *JCS,* 17 Nov. 1932; *SPA,* 13 April 1933.
14. *BP,* 23 June 1933; letter of George W. Read, *BN,* 12 Oct. 1933, quoted in Carter, *Scottsboro,* 271.
15. *NYT,* 23–24 June 1933; *MA,* 23–24 June 1933; *JCS,* 22 June 1933; J. Thomas Heflin to Thomas Knight, 23 June 1933, TEK Papers.
16. Goodrich, "James Edwin Horton," 109–17.

CHAPTER 28

1. *NYT,* 10, 18–19 April 1933; *KCC,* 28 April 1933; *NYDN,* 11 April 1933; *NYHT,* 11, 18 April 1933; *NYWT,* 17 April 1933; *TN* 136 (19 April 1933): 434; Hammond, "The South Speaks," 466.
2. *DW,* 13 April 1933; *OCBD,* n.d. (week of 20 April 1933), clipping, CIC Papers. See also *TNR* 75 (5 July 1933): 191.
3. *CD,* 1 July 1933; *BAA,* 1 July 1933. See also *CD,* 11 July 1933.
4. *CT,* 23 June 1933; *JCS,* 23 June 1933; *NYT,* 23–24 June 1933; *BAH,* 23 June 1933; *MA,* 24 June 1933; WGM to WWA, 27 July 1933; WGM to RNB, 21 Oct. 1933; WWA to WGM, 23 Oct. 1933, CIC Papers; Carter, *Scottsboro,* 272–73.
5. *NYT,* 29 Oct., 21–23 Nov. 1933; *BAH,* 21 Nov. 1933; Basso, "Five Days in Decatur," 162; Hammond, "Due Process of Law," 701–2; *NYHT,* 27 Nov. 1933; *BAA,* 2 Dec. 1933; *DD,* 20 Nov. 1933.
6. *NYT,* 13 Oct., 19–21 Nov., 7 Dec. 1933; SCSL, *The Plight of Tuscaloosa; TNR* 76 (23 Aug. 1933): 34–35; WWA to William Callahan, 27 Nov. 1933, CIC Papers; *BP,* 18 Nov. 1933; *BAA,* 28 Oct. 1933; *DD,* 17 Nov. 1933; *NYHT,* 23, 28 Nov. 1933.
7. *NYHT,* 27–30 Nov. 1933; *DD,* 27–30 Nov. 1933; *TN* 137 (13 Dec. 1933): 666; *BAA,* 2, 9 Dec. 1933; *NYT,* 10, 19–21, 30 Nov., 1, 8 Dec. 1933; *TNR* 77 (13 Dec. 1933): 116–17.
8. *Huntsville Community Builder,* quoted in *NYHT,* 22 Nov. 1933; *NYT,* 7 Dec. 1933.
9. NCDPP to FDR, 20 Nov. 1933, ACLU Papers; *DW,* 16 Nov. 1933. See also, *NYT,* 10, 21 Nov. 1933; *DD,* 20–23 1933; *BAA,* 2 Dec. 1933; *TNR* 77 (6 Dec. 1933): 85–86. All of the affidavits are in Record, *Norris* v. *Alabama,* U.S. Supreme Court (No. 534; Oct. Term, 1934).
10. *DD,* 24–25 Nov., 2 Dec. 1933; *NYT,* 26 Nov. 1933; *NYHT,* 26 Nov. 1933; Hammond, "Due Process of Law," 701–2. See also Record, *Norris* v. *Alabama,* U.S. Supreme Court (No. 534; Oct. Term, 1934).
11. Record at 1–125, *Alabama* v. *Patterson,* Morgan County (No. 1977; 27 Nov. 1933); *DD, NYT,* and *NYHT,* 28 Nov. 1933; *NYDN,* 1 Dec. 1933.
12. *Alabama* v. *Patterson,* Morgan County (No. 1977; 27 Nov. 1933); *Alabama* v. *Norris,* Morgan County (No. 1977; 1 Dec. 1933); *NYT,* 28–30 Nov., 3–5 Dec. 1933; *DD,* 28–30 Nov., 2–5 Dec. 1933; *NYHT,* 28–30 Nov., 3–5 Dec. 1933; *NYDN,* 28 Nov., 1 Dec. 1933.
13. *DD,* 16, 25, 27–30 Nov. 1933; *BAA,* 2, 9 Dec. 1933; *NYT,* 21, 29–30 Nov. 1933; *NYHT,* 29–30 Nov. 1933; *NYDN,* 1 Dec. 1933; *TNR* 77 (29 Nov. 1933): 59; Hammond, "Due Process of Law," 701–2; Basso, "Five Days in Decatur," 161–65; *DW,* 16 Nov., 6 Dec. 1933.
14. *NYT,* 1 Dec. 1933; *NYHT,* 1 Dec. 1933; *DD,* 30 Nov. 1933; *CC* 50 (13 Dec. 1933): 1563–64; *TNR:* 77 (13 Dec. 1933): 114.
15. *NYHT,* 2 Dec. 1933; *NYT,* 2 Dec. 1933. Cf. *DD,* 2 Dec. 1933.
16. *NYT,* 1–7 Dec. 1933; *NYHT,* 1–7 Dec. 1933; *DD,* 30 Nov., 1–7 Dec. 1933.
17. *NYT,* 1–7 Dec. 1933; *NYHT,* 1–7 Dec. 1933; *DD,* 30 Nov., 1–7 Dec. 1933.
18. *NYT,* 2, 7 Dec. 1933; *NYHT,* 7 Dec. 1933.

CHAPTER 29

1. ADAH, *Alabama Official and Statistical Register,* 1935, 109–10.
2. *NYT,* 29 Oct. 1933; *NYHT,* 27 Nov. 1933; ADAH, *Alabama Official and Statistical Register,* 1931–1935; Carter, *Scottsboro,* 274–76.
3. *NYT,* 23 Nov. 1933.

4. *NYT,* 20–23 Nov. 1933; *NYHT,* 22 Nov. 1933; *DD,* 20–23 Nov. 1933. See also Record, *Norris* v. *Alabama,* U.S. Supreme Court (No. 534; Oct. Term, 1934).
5. *DD,* 24–25 Nov., 2 Dec. 1933; *NYT,* 24–26 Nov. 1933; *NYHT,* 26 Nov. 1933. See also *TN* 137 (6 Dec. 1933): 635.
6. *NYT,* 21, 23, 28 Nov., 1–2 Dec. 1933; *NYHT,* 23 Nov., 2 Dec. 1933; *NYDN,* 28 Nov. 1933.
7. *DD,* 25–29 Nov., 4 Dec. 1933; *BAA,* 2, 9 Dec. 1933; *NYT,* 29–30 Nov. 1933; *NYDN,* 1 Dec. 1933; *NYHT,* 29–30 Nov., 5 Dec. 1933.
8. *NYT,* 21, 23 Nov., 1–2 Dec. 1933; *NYHT,* 23 Nov., 2 Dec. 1933.
9. *NYHT,* 30 Nov. 1933. See also Record at 329, *Alabama* v. *Patterson,* Morgan County, (31 March 1933).
10. *NYT,* 30 Nov., 1 Dec. 1933; *Weems* v. *State,* 224 Ala. 524 (1932); *Patterson* v. *State,* 224 Ala. 531 (1932); *Memphis Commercial Appeal,* reprinted in *OCBD,* 20 April 1933; *DD,* 8 April, 30 Nov. 1933; *NYHT,* 30 Nov. 1933; Basso, "Five Days in Decatur," 163.
11. Thomas E. Knight to Marcus W. Crenshaw, 20 Sept. 1933, TEK Papers.
12. Record at 72–73, 329, *Alabama* v. *Patterson,* Morgan County (31 March 1933).
13. *NYT,* 1 Dec. 1933. See for example Walling Keith, "Alabama Is Afraid of Ghosts," *MA,* 13 April 1933. Hall, *Revolt Against Chivalry,* 155–56; Hall, "The Mind That Burns in Each Body," 331–33.
14. *Powell* v. *State,* 224 Ala. 540 (1932) at 26; letter of John Gould Fletcher, *TN* 137 (27 Dec. 1933): 734–35; letter of William T. Seibels, *NYHT,* 21 April 1933. See also William J. Mahoney, Jr., "Alabama's Scottsboro Case," *MA,* 14 Aug. 1931.
15. J. Thomas Heflin to Thomas Knight, 23 June 1933, TEK Papers; *NYHT,* 1 Dec. 1933; *DD,* 30 Nov. 1933.
16. Letter of F. B. Cullen to *BN,* reprinted in *JCS,* 27 April 1933; Sylvia F. Metcalf to GFM, 21 Sept. 1930, ASWPL Papers; *Powell* v. *State,* 224 Ala. 540 (1932) at 4.
17. *JCS,* 6 April 1933; Hammond, "Due Process of Law," 701–2; *DD,* 28 Nov. 1933; Reynolds, *Courtroom,* 282; Record at 155–80, *Alabama* v. *Patterson,* Morgan County (No. 1977; 27 Nov. 1933); Record at 248–53, *Alabama* v. *Norris,* Morgan County (No. 1977; 1 Dec. 1933); Basso, "Five Days in Decatur," 162.
18. Basso, "Five Days in Decatur," 163; Hammond, "Due Process of Law," 701–2.
19. *BP,* 10, 15 April 1933.
20. Basso, "Five Days in Decatur," 163; *NYHT,* 30 Nov. 1933. See also Reynolds, *Courtroom,* 305.

CHAPTER 30

1. *DD,* 28 Nov., 2 Dec. 1933; Record at 1–125, *Alabama* v. *Patterson,* Morgan County (No. 1977; 27 Nov. 1933); Record at 2–71, *Alabama* v. *Norris,* Morgan County (No. 1977; 1 Dec. 1933). See also *NYT,* 28 Nov. 1933; *NYHT,* 27 Nov. 1933; Hammond, "Due Process of Law," 701–2; *NYDN,* 28 Nov. 1933.
2. *NYT,* 29 Nov. 1933; *NYHT,* 27, 29 Nov. 1933; *DD,* 29 Nov. 1933; Basso, "Five Days in Decatur," 161–64; Hammond, "Due Process of Law," 701–2; *BAA,* 2 Dec. 1933.
3. *NYT,* 29 Nov. 1933; *BAA,* 2 Dec. 1933.
4. *NYT,* 29–30 Nov., 5 Dec. 1933.
5. Record at 277–332, *Alabama* v. *Patterson,* Morgan County (No. 1977; 27 Nov. 1933); *NYT, NYHT,* and *DD,* 29 Nov. 1933.
6. Basso, "Five Days in Decatur," 163; *NYHT,* 30 Nov. 1933; *NYT,* 30 Nov. 1933; *NYT,* 5 Dec. 1933.
7. *DD,* 30 Nov. 1933; *NYHT,* 30 Nov. 1933; Basso, "Five Days in Decatur," 163–64.

8. *DD,* 30 Nov. 1933; *NYHT,* 30 Nov. 1933.
9. For Callahan's charge, see *NYT,* 1 Dec. 1933; Record at 515–36, *Alabama* v. *Patterson,* Morgan County (No. 1977; 27 Nov. 1933).
10. Callahan omitted this paragraph in his charge to Clarence Norris's jury. See *NYT,* 5 Dec. 1933, or Record at 266–83, *Alabama* v. *Norris,* Morgan County (No. 1977; 1 Dec. 1933); Basso, "Five Days in Decatur," 162–63.
11. *NYT,* 1 Dec. 1933.
12. *Huntsville Builder* cited in Work, *Negro Year Book: 1937–1938,* 115–16. See also *Newport News Daily Press,* quoted in *NJG,* 15 April 1933; *Alabama Courier,* 29 June 1933, quoted in Goodrich, "James Edwin Horton," 103; *TNR* 74 (5 April 1933): 217.
13. *Strasburg* (Va.) *Daily,* 2 Dec. 1933.

CHAPTER 31

1. *NYT,* 6–7 Dec. 1933.
2. HP to Benjamin J. Davis, 14 Jan. 1934; HP to William Patterson, 15 Jan. 1934, ILD Papers.
3. HP to Janie Patterson, Feb. 1934, ILD Papers.
4. HP to Janie Patterson, 4 May 1934; HP to Joseph Brodsky, 20 Aug. 1934, ILD Papers.
5. CW to ILD, 7 Jan. 1934; CW to Mina, 5 Oct. 1934, ILD Papers.
6. Branche, "Report of Neuropsychiatric Examination" of CW.
7. CW to ILD, 7 Jan. 1934; CW to Mina, 14, 22, 28 Sept. 1934, ILD Papers; Report on Georgia–Alabama Delegation of NCDPP, July 1934, ACLU Papers. For more on the doghouse, see March, *Alabama Bound,* 6–50.
8. RWR and EW to "Freddie" (Frieda) Brown, 4 Jan. 1934, ILD Papers.
9. Report on Georgia–Alabama Delegation of NCDPP, July 1934, ACLU Papers; Moos, *Penal Administration,* 132–34. See also *DW,* 13 March, 8, 28 April 1934; *NYT,* 24–26 March 1934.
10. Letter of VM, *LD* 8 (Aug. 1932): 144; Branche, "Report of Neuropsychiatric Examination" of OM.
11. Branche, "Report of Neuropsychiatric Examination" of OM; Memorandum of Benjamin J. Davis on interview with Scottsboro boys in Birmingham, 13 May 1933, ILD Papers.
12. VM to [William] Patterson, 7 Nov. 1932; VM to "Friend and Fellow Worker," 24 Feb. 1934, ILD Papers.
13. VM to "Friend and Fellow Worker," 24 Feb. 1934; OM to VM, 3 May 1934; OM to VM, 4 May 1934, ILD Papers.
14. Report on Georgia–Alabama Delegation of NCDPP, July 1934, ACLU Papers.
15. *NYT,* 6 Jan., 25 Feb., 10 March, 22, 26 May, 29 June 1934; *NYP,* 28 Dec. 1934; Carter, *Scottsboro,* 303–8.
16. The sixty-day stay made the date 8 Feb. 1935, but that date was suspended on 8 Jan. 1935, when the U.S. Supreme Court agreed to review the case.
17. *LSB,* 144–45; Carter, *Scottsboro,* 311–19.
18. *LSB,* 144–45; *MA,* 13 Oct. 1934; *TN* 139 (21 Nov. 1934): 577; *TN* 139 (28 Nov. 1934): 607–8; *TN* 139 (5 Dec. 1934): 635–36; *TN* 139 (12 Dec. 1934): 661, 674; *TN* 139 (19 Dec. 1934): 712; *TNR* 80 (17 Oct. 1934): 254–55; *TNR* 81 (5 Dec. 1934): 89–91; *CC* 51 (7 Nov. 1934): 1401–2; *CC* 51 (28 Nov. 1934): 1507–8.
19. *DW,* 31 Oct., 1 Nov. 1934.
20. CN to Joseph Brodsky, 29 Oct. 1934, ILD Papers.
21. HP to Osmond Fraenkel, 8 Oct. 1934, ILD Papers.

22. HP to John Wexley, 5 March 1934, ILD Papers.
23. HP to Joseph Brodsky, 27 Oct. 1934, ILD Papers.

CHAPTER 32

1. Report of interview of secretary and assistant secretary with SSL, 1 Oct. 1934; WFW to SSL, 2 Oct. 1934; Memorandum, Charles Houston to WFW, 12 Oct. 1934; Minutes of a meeting of the Temporary American Scottsboro Committee, 17 Oct. 1934; Remarks of SSL to the American Scottsboro Committee, 17 Oct. 1934; Statement of SSL on the Scottsboro Case, 26 Oct. 1934, NAACP Papers; *NYT,* 2, 4–5, 7, 11–13, 21, 31 Oct., 3–4, 7, 16 Nov. 1934; *DW,* Oct. and Nov. 1934; *NYHT,* 11 Oct. 1934; *CD,* 13 Oct. 1934; Carter, *Scottsboro,* 308–19.
2. *NYT,* 8–9 Jan. 1935; Memorandum of conversation with SSL on Scottsboro Case, 23 Jan. 1935, ACLU Papers; *CD,* 9 Feb. 1935; *DW,* 11–12 Feb. 1935.
3. Reynolds, *Courtroom,* 282–85; *NYT,* 16 Feb. 1935; *DW,* 19 Feb. 1935; ILD News Release, 19 Feb. 1935, ACLU Papers.
4. Reynolds, *Courtroom,* 282–85; ILD News Release, 19 Feb. 1935, ACLU Papers.
5. *NYP,* 2 April 1935; *NYHT,* 2 April 1935; *NYT,* 2–3 April 1935; SSL to BG, 30 April 1935, AKC Papers; *DD,* 29–30 April, 2–3 May 1935.
6. *NYP,* 2 April 1935; *DW,* 2 April 1935.
7. Memorandum on Conference Re Joint Action in Scottsboro Cases, 10 Oct. 1935; Memorandum for the files from the Secretary, 14 Oct. 1935; Memorandum Re Meeting of Committee on Joint Action in the Scottsboro Cases, 21 Nov. 1935, NAACP Papers; Carter, *Scottsboro,* 330–35.
8. RNB to William H. Tayloe, 11 Nov. 1935; RNB to Tayloe, 18 Nov. 1935; RNB to Tayloe, 9 Dec. 1935; RNB to James H. Dillard, 18 Nov. 1935; RNB to Morris Ernst, 22 Nov. 1935; RNB to Ernst, 3 Dec. 1935; RNB to WGM, 17 Dec. 1935; RNB to SSL, 12 Dec. 1935; RNB to SSL, 18 Dec. 1935; SSL to RNB, 20 Dec. 1935, ACLU Papers; Norman Thomas to Mrs. James Boyd, 17 Jan. 1936, NAACP Papers.
9. Carter, *Scottsboro,* 330–35; SDC News Release, 28 Dec. 1935, AKC Papers; *DW,* 30 Dec. 1935.
10. *NYEP,* 17 Nov. 1935.

CHAPTER 33

1. *NYT,* 2 April 1935; *MA,* 2 April 1935.
2. CN to SSL, 1 April 1935, reprinted in *MA,* 2 April 1935, and *BW,* 5 April 1935.
3. See, for example, Birdie Robinson to Benjamin M. Miller, n.d.; "A black woman from Cleveland" to Miller, 16 April 1934; "An Alabama Mother" to Mrs. Bibb Graves, 1 May 1935, ASF.
4. *Norris* v. *Alabama,* 294 U.S. 587 (1935). The *NYT* printed the complete text of the decision on 2 April 1935.
5. *SW,* May 1935. Cf. *BW,* 5 April 1935; *ST,* 29 Aug. 1935.
6. *NYT,* 6–7 April 1935; *BAA,* 13 April 1935; *Richmond Planet,* 13 April 1935; *CD,* 25 May 1935; *Literary Digest,* 13 April 1935; *BAH,* 3 April 1935; Federal Council of Churches, "Southern Editors on the Scottsboro Case," *Information Service* 14 (20 April 1935); *MA,* 2 April 1935.
7. *BAH,* 3 April 1935; *Raleigh Times,* quoted in Federal Council of Churches, "Southern Editors on the Scottsboro Case," *Information Service* 14 (20 April 1935); *Jackson Daily News,* quoted in *BAA,* 13 April 1935. See also *Richmond Planet,* 13 April 1935.
8. *DD,* 6 April 1935; *CD,* 29 June 1935.

9. *Scott* v. *Sandford* 19 How. (60 U.S.) 393 (1857). See Blaustein and Zangrando, *Civil Rights*.
10. *Slaughterhouse Cases,* 16 Wall. (83 U.S.) 36 (1873); *U.S.* v. *Cruikshank,* 92 U.S. 542 (1876); *Civil Rights Cases,* 109 U.S. 3 (1883); *Plessy* v. *Ferguson,* 163 U.S. 537 (1896).
11. *Strauder* v. *West Virginia* 100 U.S. 303 (1880); *Guinn* v. *U.S.,* 238 U.S. 347 (1915); *Moore* v. *Dempsey,* 261 U.S. 86 (1923). See Blaustein and Zangrando, *Civil Rights;* Hall, *Oxford Companion,* 599–600, 844; Witt, *Congressional Quarterly Guide,* 527.
12. *Grovey* v. *Townsend,* 295 U.S. 45 (1935); *NYHT,* 2 April 1935.
13. *NJG,* 13 April 1935.
14. *NYT,* 2 April, 14 Nov. 1935.

CHAPTER 34

1. *TSBF,* 43–49; Klehr, *Heyday of American Communism,* 167–223; Naison, *Communists in Harlem,* 169–227; *NYT,* 14, 17 Nov. 1935, 28 Dec. 1935, 5, 7, 9, 12, 14, 20 Jan. 1936.
2. *NYT,* 21 Jan. 1936; *SB,* 62. For Patterson's fourth trial, see *NYT,* 5–30 Jan. 1936, 2 Feb. 1936; *NYHT,* 21–25 Jan. 1936; *DW,* 20–25 Jan. 1936; *NYP,* 21–29, Jan., 3 Feb. 1936; *New York American,* 21–24 Jan. 1936; *NYWT,* 21–24 Jan. 1936; *New York Journal,* 23–25 Jan. 1936; Beals, "Scottsboro Puppet Show"; Beals, "Scottsboro Interview"; Hammond, "Trial of Haywood Patterson"; Record, *Patterson* v. *Alabama,* Morgan County (No. 2366; 6 Jan. 1936); Record, *Patterson* v. *Alabama,* U.S. Supreme Court (Oct. Term, 1937), cert. denied 302 U.S. 733 (1937).
3. *NYT,* 21–22 Jan. 1936; Record at 12–13, *Patterson* v. *Alabama,* U.S. Supreme Court (Oct. Term, 1937).
4. *NYT,* 21 Jan. 1936; Record at 37–59, *Patterson* v. *Alabama,* U.S. Supreme Court (Oct. Term, 1937).
5. Record at 44, 47, 69, 70, passim, *Patterson* v. *Alabama,* U.S. Supreme Court (Oct. Term, 1937); *NYT,* 22 Jan. 1936.
6. *NYT,* 22 Jan. 1936; Record at 101–9, 74–76, *Patterson* v. *Alabama,* U.S. Supreme Court (Oct. Term, 1937); *SB,* 62.
7. *BAA,* 15 Feb. 1936; Record at 110–37, *Patterson* v. *Alabama,* U.S. Supreme Court (Oct. Term, 1937); Beals, "Scottsboro Interview," 179.
8. *NYP,* 23 Jan. 1936; *NYT,* 23 Jan. 1936; *Time* 27 (3 Feb. 1936): 13; Beals, "Scottsboro Puppet Show," 150; Hammond, "Trial of Haywood Patterson," 14.
9. *NYT,* 23–24 Jan. 1936.
10. *NYP,* 29 Jan. 1936; Reynolds, *Courtroom,* 299–300; Carter, *Scottsboro,* 348.
11. *NYP,* 29 Jan. 1936.
12. Hammond, "Trial of Haywood Patterson," 14; *NYT,* 24 Jan. 1936; *DW,* 24 Jan. 1936.
13. *NYT,* 25 Jan. 1936.
14. *HT,* 24–28 Jan. 1936; *DD,* 25–28 Jan. 1936; *MA,* 25–29 Jan. 1936; *NYT,* 25–28 Jan. 1936; *NYHT, NYP, DW, New York Journal,* and *New York American,* 25–27 Jan. 1936; Beals, "Scottsboro Interview," 178–79; *LSB,* 162–64.
15. *NYT,* 26 Jan. 1936.
16. *NYT,* 26 Jan. 1936; *New York American,* 26 Jan. 1936; OM to AD, 26 Jan. 1936, NAACP Papers; *DW,* 27 Jan. 1936.
17. Branche, "Report of Neuropsychiatric Examination" of OP.
18. *NYHT, NYP,* and *NYT,* 25 Jan. 1936.
19. Memorandum of Joseph Gelders on Mrs. Josephine Powell's account of her visit with OP, 3 Feb. 1936; Josephine Powell to AD, 30 Jan. 1936, NAACP Papers.

20. Joseph Gelders to MS, 3 Feb. 1936; Memorandum of Joseph Gelders on Mrs. Josephine Powell's account of her visit with OP, 3 Feb. 1936, NAACP Papers.
21. Branche, "Report of Neuropsychiatric Examination" of OP; *LSB*, 165–66.

CHAPTER 35

1. *MA,* 25–29 Jan. 1936. See also chapter 34.
2. *MA,* 26 Jan. 1936.
3. *MA,* 26–28 Jan. 1936.
4. Van Doren, "Eight Who Must Not Die," 608–10.
5. JB to Arthur Raper, 1 Aug. 1931, CIC Papers; *MA,* 26 Jan. 1936.
6. *BAH,* 4 Dec. 1935.
7. Owen, *Story of Alabama* 3:75–76; WGM to RNB, 24 Jan. 1936, ACLU Papers.
8. WGM to AKC, 31 Jan. 1936, ACLU Papers.
9. WGM to RNB, 30 Jan. 1936, ACLU Papers.
10. *BAH,* 25–26 Jan. 1936; *BN,* 25–26 Jan. 1936.
11. *SPA,* 9 April 1931; William Mahoney, Jr., "Alabama's Scottsboro Case," *Baltimore Evening Sun,* 14 Aug. 1931. See also *MA,* 17 Aug. 1937.
12. *Dothan Eagle,* reprinted in *MA,* 16 Aug. 1931; *MA,* 12, 24 July 1931; *TNR* 74 (5 April 1933): 217; *MA,* 4 April 1935; *DD,* 19 April 1935, quoted in Carter, *Scottsboro,* 327.

CHAPTER 36

1. Branche, "Report of Neuropsychiatric Examination" of CN; CN to Lucille Milner, 2 April 1936, ACLU Papers.
2. AW to AD, 2 Oct. 1936, ILD Papers.
3. WR to Mina, 15 Sept. 1934; WR to Mina, 22 Sept. 1934; WR to Mina, 29 Sept. 1934; WR to Mina, 8 Oct. 1934; WR to AD, 8 Nov. 1934, ILD Papers.
4. OM to AD, 18 July 1936, ILD Papers.
5. OM to AD, 2 Oct. 1936, ILD Papers.
6. OM to AD, 20 Sept. 1936, ILD Papers.
7. OM to AD, 2 Oct. 1936, ILD Papers.
8. OM to AD, 1 Nov. 1936, ILD Papers.
9. AD to OM, 10 Nov. 1936, ILD Papers.
10. OM to AD, 12 Nov. 1936, ILD Papers.
11. Report by Benjamin J. Davis, Jr., on Interview with Scottsboro Boys in Birmingham, 13 May 1933, ILD Papers.
12. HP to AD, 22 Aug. 1936; HP to AD, 21 Sept. 1936, ILD Papers.
13. HP to AD, 21 Sept. 1936, ILD Papers.
14. HP to AD, 19 Oct. 1936, ILD Papers.
15. HP to AD, 28 Oct. 1936; AD to HP, 28 Oct. 1936; HP to AD, 30 Oct. 1936, ILD Papers.
16. HP to AD, 6 Nov. 1936, ILD Papers.
17. HP to AD, 11 Dec. 1936.
18. Ibid.
19. Ibid.
20. EW to AD, 12 Dec. 1936, ILD Papers; *TSBF,* 25–26.
21. Branche, "Report of Neuropsychiatric Examination" of HP.
22. Branche, "Report of Neuropsychiatric Examination" of OM, AW, and RWR.

23. Branche, "Report of Neuropsychiatric Examination" of RWR.
24. Branche, "Report of Neuropsychiatric Examination" of EW and CW.
25. Branche, "Report of Neuropsychiatric Examination" of OP and WR.
26. Branche, "Report of Neuropsychiatric Examination" of WR.
27. OM to AD, 22 March 1937, ILD Papers.

CHAPTER 37

1. AKC, "Out in All Weathers," typescript, 1–15; AKC, "Allan Knight Chalmers," typescript, AKC Papers; *Jersey City Journal,* 31 Dec. 1935; *NYT,* 24 Jan. 1972.
2. AKC, "Out in All Weathers," 5, 11–15; AKC, "Allan Knight Chalmers," AKC Papers.
3. AKC, "Out in All Weathers," 12–14; AKC, "Allan Knight Chalmers," AKC Papers.
4. AKC, "Out in All Weathers," 1–25; AKC, "Allan Knight Chalmers," AKC Papers; *Jersey City Journal,* 31 Dec. 1935.
5. *TSBF,* 43–46.
6. Ibid., 49–52.
7. Ibid., 53–56.
8. AKC to RNB, 1 Feb. 1936, ACLU Papers; WGM to AKC, 31 Jan. 1937; GFM to Norman Thomas, 14 Feb. 1936, ACLU Papers; Joseph Gelders to MS, 5 Feb. 1936, NAACP Papers.
9. *TSBF,* 56–58.
10. Ibid., 57–63.
11. Ibid., 63–64.
12. Owen, *Story of Alabama* 5:1072; Report by Lawrence Gellert of the Meeting of the Citizens Scottsboro Aid Committee of Birmingham, 31 March 1933, ILD Papers; *TSBF,* 65–68.
13. AKC to Mrs. Frederick M. Paist, 25 Feb. 1936, AKC Papers.
14. Minutes of the SDC Meeting, 17 Feb. 1936, AKC Papers; *TSBF,* 68.
15. WGM to AKC, 14 Feb. 1936, ACLU Papers; WGM to AKC, 20 Feb. 1936, AKC Papers.
16. WGM to AKC, 20 Feb. 1936; HME to AKC, 24 March 1936; AKC to HME, 27 March 1936, AKC Papers.
17. HME to AKC, 25 April 1936; HME to AKC, 29 April 1936; HME to AKC, 4 May 1936; Waights Taylor to AKC, 5 June 1936, AKC Papers.
18. MS to HME, 10 June 1936; HME to MS, 11 June 1936; SDC Press Release, 11 June 1936; AKC to HME, 11 June 1936; HME to AKC, 12 June 1936; AKC to HME, 13 June 1936; HME to AKC, 16 June 1936, AKC Papers; *TSBF,* 115.
19. AKC to HME, 11 June 1936, AKC Papers.
20. RNB to Rev. Stewart Meacham, 4 June 1936; Meacham to RNB, 6 June 1936; HME to AKC, 30 June 1936; AKC to MS and RS, n.d., ACLU Papers; HME to AKC, 14 Jan. 1937, AKC Papers.
21. HME to AKC, 14 Jan. 1937; AKC to Joseph Gelders, 19 Feb. 1937; Gelders to AKC, 23 Feb. 1937, AKC Papers; *TSBF,* 75–76.
22. *TSBF,* 76–78.
23. Ibid., 82–85.
24. HME to AKC, 30 June 1936; AKC to MS and RS, n.d., ACLU Papers; MS to AKC, 10 Sept. 1936; AKC to HME, 2 Dec. 1936, AKC Papers; Carter, *Scottsboro,* 358–60.
25. AKC to James E. Mills, 18 Dec. 1936; AKC to BG, 8 Dec. 1936, AKC Papers; *TSBF,* 25–26.

CHAPTER 38

1. Reynolds, *Courtroom,* 205–12, 307–23; Kennedy, *The Airman and the Carpenter,* 385–87.
2. Reynolds, *Courtroom,* 291–93.
3. *NYT,* 12 June 1936; AKC to HME, 11 June 1936, AKC Papers; Reynolds, *Courtroom,* 291–93.
4. Reynolds, *Courtroom,* 291–93; AKC to HME, 11 June 1936, AKC Papers.
5. Reynolds, *Courtroom,* 292–93; MS to AKC, 10 Sept. 1936, AKC Papers.
6. Reynolds, *Courtroom,* 294–95; *TSBF,* 91–94.
7. *TSBF,* 94–96, 98–99; typescript of official agreement, 16 Jan. 1937, AKC Papers.
8. *TSBF,* 93–96.
9. Marion Norris to AKC, 5 Jan. 1937; Norris to AKC, 9 Jan. 1937; Minutes of the SDC Meeting, 12 Jan. 1937; MS to SSL, 13 Jan. 1937; MS to "Boys and Relatives," 14 Jan. 1937, AKC Papers.
10. *TSBF,* 96–99; AKC to FJ, 24 Feb. 1937; AKC to FJ, 1 May 1937; AKC to FJ, 12 May 1937; FJ to AKC, 14 May 1937; AKC to HME, 26 May 1937; FJ to Hon. Jos. H. Nathan, 28 May 1937; HME to AKC, 28 May 1937, AKC Papers; Shapiro, "Behind the Scenes," 171.
11. *BAH,* 18–19 May 1937; *NYT,* 23 May 1937.
12. *DD,* 25 May 1937; *NYT,* 26 May 1937.
13. *MA,* 12 June 1937; AKC to FJ, 12 June 1937; FJ to AKC, 12 June 1937; AKC to WNS, 14 June 1937; WNS to FJ, 26 June 1937, AKC Papers.
14. WNS to FJ, 26 June 1937, AKC Papers.

CHAPTER 39

1. Hollis, *Grover C. Hall,* 1–7.
2. Ibid., 8–14, 24–26.
3. Ibid., 8–14, 24–69.
4. Hollis, *Grover C. Hall,* 33–39; *MA,* 3–5, 14, 19–20 July, 5, 20 Aug. 1927.
5. Hollis, *Grover C. Hall,* 33–39.
6. Hollis, *Grover C. Hall,* 40–43; Owen, *Story of Alabama* 1:306–7; Carter, *Scottsboro,* 9.
7. *MA,* March–Sept. 1931, esp. 27 March, 14 April, 19–20 May, 13, 15, 19 June, 1, 4, 8, 12, 19–20, 24 July, 26–27 Aug., 28 Sept. 1931.
8. *JCS,* 23 March 1933; *MA,* 13 Aug. 1937.
9. *JCS,* 23 March 1933; *MA,* 13 June, 19 July 1931, 16 April 1932.
10. *MA,* 12 June 1937.
11. *MA,* 13 Oct. 1934, 2–7 April 1935.
12. *MA,* 2–7 April 1935.
13. See *MA,* 26–28 Jan. 1936; chapter 35; GCH to FJ, 11 June 1937, AKC Papers.
14. *MA,* 13 Aug. 1937; GCH to FJ, 11 June 1937, AKC Papers; *MA,* 12 June 1937.
15. *MA,* 12 June 1937.
16. GCH to FJ, 11 June 1937; FJ to AKC, 12 June 1937, AKC Papers; *HT,* 13 June 1937; Carter, *Scottsboro,* 366.
17. Marion Norris to AKC, 18 June 1937; FJ to WNS, 19 June 1937; MS to AKC, 22 June 1937; FJ to AKC, 22 June 1937; WNS to FJ, 26 June 1937, AKC Papers.
18. *TSBF,* 99–102; AKC to FJ, 2 July 1937, AKC Papers.
19. *TSBF,* 99–102; AKC to FJ, 2 July 1937, AKC Papers.
20. *TSBF,* 99–102; Marion Norris to AKC, 29 June 1937; Norris to FJ, 2 July 1937; FJ to Norris, 3 July 1937, AKC Papers.

CHAPTER 40

1. *NYT,* 29 June, 7, 13 July 1937; *DD,* 3, 6–8 July 1937; *BAH,* 1, 7, 9 July 1937; WNS to FJ, 26 June 1937, AKC Papers; Shapiro, "Behind the Scenes," 170–71.
2. Marion Norris to AKC, 20 July 1937; Norris to "Frances," 20 July 1937, AKC Papers.
3. *DD,* 12 July 1937; *NYT,* 13 July 1937; *BAH,* 13 July 1937.
4. *DD,* 13 July 1937; *NYT,* 14 July 1937; *BAH,* 14 July 1937.
5. *DD,* 14 July 1937; *NYT,* 14–15 July 1937; *BAH,* 14–15 July 1937.
6. *DD,* 14 July 1937; *NYT,* 15 July 1937; *BAH,* 15 July 1937.
7. *NYT,* 15 July 1937.
8. *NYT, DD,* and *BAH,* 16 July 1937; Crusader News Agency News Release, 19 July 1937, ACLU Papers; Marion Norris to AKC, 20 July 1937, AKC Papers.
9. Marion Norris to AKC, 20 July 1937, AKC Papers; *NYT,* 18–19 July 1937.
10. *NYT,* 20 July 1937; *NYP,* 22 July 1937; Shapiro, "Behind the Scenes," 170–71.
11. *NYT,* 21 July 1937.
12. Ibid.
13. Ibid., 22 July 1937.
14. Ibid.
15. Ibid., 23 July 1937.
16. Ibid., 23–24 July 1937.
17. Ibid.
18. *DD,* 23 July 1937; *NYT,* 24 July 1937.
19. *DD,* 24 July 1937; *NYT,* 25 July 1937.
20. *DD,* 24 July 1937; *NYP,* 24 July 1937; *NYT,* 25 July 1937; *NYHT,* 25 July 1937.
21. *DD,* 24 July 1937; *NYT, NYHT,* and *DW,* 25 July 1937; ANP News Release, n.d., Claude Barnett Papers.
22. *NYT,* 25–26 July 1937; *NYHT,* 26 July 1937.
23. *NYT,* 27 July 1937.
24. *NYP,* 29 July 1937; *NYT,* 30 July 1937.

CHAPTER 41

1. *TSBF,* 103–5; AKC to HME, 21 Sept. 1937; AKC, "Out in All Weathers," typescript, 5, 13–16, AKC Papers.
2. *NYT,* 25 July 1937; *TSBF,* 100–4.
3. AKC to RS, 30 Aug. 1937; SDC, *Four Free, Five in Prison,* AKC Papers.
4. AKC to BG, 20 Sept. 1937; BG to AKC, 20 Sept. 1937; AKC to FJ, 20 Sept. 1937; AKC to FJ, 28 Oct. 1937, AKC Papers.
5. *TSBF,* 113.
6. AKC to RNB, 28 Dec. 1937, ACLU Papers; Apollo Theatre playbill, Aug. 1937, NAACP Papers.
7. AKC to FJ, 11 Feb. 1938; Minutes of the SDC Meeting, 28 March 1938; AKC to HME, 29 March 1938; GCH to AKC, 2 April 1938; GCH to AKC, 6 May 1938; AKC to BG, 1 April 1938; AKC to BG, 4 May 1938, AKC Papers.
8. BG to AKC, 23 May 1938; AKC to HME, 30 May 1938; HME to AKC, 7 July 1938; MS to AKC, 12 July 1938, AKC Papers. See also *NYT,* 6 July 1938.
9. Carter, *Scottsboro,* 386–87; *NYT,* 17 Aug. 1938.
10. *NYT,* 17–18 Aug., 12 Oct. 1938; AKC to HME, 7 Oct. 1938; GCH to AKC, 12 Oct. 1938; AKC to HME, 13 Oct. 1938, AKC Papers.
11. AKC to HME, 6 June 1938; AKC to EM, 14 Oct. 1938; EM to AKC, 15 Oct.

1938; EM to AKC, 17 Oct. 1938; AKC to GCH, 19 Oct. 1938; AKC to EM, 24 Oct. 1938; EM to AKC, 27 Oct. 1938, AKC Papers; *TSBF,* 129, 141–42.
12. BG to AKC, 17 Oct. 1938; BG to AKC, 29 Oct. 1938; GCH to AKC, 1 Nov. 1938; Joseph Gelders to MS, 1 Nov. 1938, AKC Papers; *TSBF,* 125–26.
13. GCH to AKC, 2 Nov. 1938; AKC to GCH, 2 Nov. 1938; AKC to HME, FJ, and GCH, 5 Nov. 1938, AKC Papers; *TSBF,* 126–33.
14. *TSBF,* 126–33; AKC to HME, FJ, and GCH, 5 Nov. 1938, AKC Papers.
15. *TSBF,* 133–35. WFW to ER, 11 Nov. 1938, AKC Papers.
16. *TSBF,* 133–42, 166–67; WFW to ER, 11 Nov. 1938; AKC to FJ, 11 Nov. 1938, AKC Papers.
17. FJ to AKC, 14 Nov. 1938; JC to AKC, 14 Nov. 1938; AKC to GCH, 18 Nov. 1938; Carroll Kilpatrick to AKC, 19 Nov. 1938; AKC to GCH, 21 Nov. 1938, AKC Papers.
18. AKC to GCH, 18 Nov. 1938, AKC Papers; *TSBF,* 142–44; FDR to BG, 7 Dec. 1938, FDR Library, Hyde Park, New York.
19. *TSBF,* 149–50.
20. AKC to BG, 19 Dec. 1938; SDC, *A Record of Broken Promises,* AKC Papers.
21. *TSBF,* 150–54; AKC to GCH, 22 Dec. 1938; AKC to HME, FJ, GCH, JC, and Donald Comer, 22 Dec. 1938; SDC, *A Record of Broken Promises,* AKC Papers; *BW,* 6 Jan. 1939.
22. GCH to AKC, 23 Dec. 1938; Donald Comer to AKC, 23 Dec. 1938; JC to AKC, 23 Dec. 1938; FJ to AKC, 28 Dec. 1938, AKC Papers; *TSBF,* 151–52, 154–62.

CHAPTER 42

1. *MA,* 25 July 1937; *Baltimore Evening Sun,* 13 Aug. 1937.
2. Hollis, *Grover C. Hall*, 33–43, 53–55; Gilbert, "Bibb Graves as a Progressive," 30.
3. HME, JC, FJ, and James Mills to BG, 10 Dec. 1937, AKC Papers.
4. GCH to AKC, 2 April 1937, AKC Papers.
5. GCH to AKC, 6 May 1938; GCH to BG, 6 May 1938; GCH to BG, 7 July 1938, AKC Papers.
6. *MA,* 18 Aug. 1938; Carter, *Scottsboro,* 388.
7. GCH to AKC, 18 Aug. 1938; GCH to MS, 9 Sept. 1938; MS to AKC, 19 Sept. 1938; GCH to AKC, 12 Oct. 1938, AKC Papers.
8. For Hall's account of his meeting with Graves and of Graves's meeting with the defendants, see GCH to AKC, 1 Nov. 1938, GCH Papers, AKC Papers.
9. GCH to AKC, 1 Nov. 1938, GCH Papers, AKC Papers; GCH to AKC, 2 Nov. 1938, AKC Papers.
10. FJ to GCH, 17 Nov. 1938, GCH Papers.
11. Ibid.
12. JC to GCH, 16 Nov. 1938; JC to GCH, 18 Nov. 1938, GCH Papers.
13. GCH to JC, 15 Nov. 1938, GCH Papers; *TSBF,* 133–35.
14. FJ to AKC, 14 Nov. 1938; JC to AKC, 14 Nov. 1938, AKC Papers.
15. GCH to BG, 14 Nov. 1938, GCH Papers.

CHAPTER 43

1. GCH to AKC, 15 Nov. 1938; AKC to GCH, 18 Nov. 1938, AKC Papers; *TSBF,* 142–43.
2. Krueger, *Promises to Keep;* Reed, "Southern Conference for Human Welfare," 1–43; Foreman, "Decade of Hope," 137–50; R. F. Hall, "Southern Conference for Human

Welfare," 57–65; R. F. Hall, "Those Southern Liberals," 490–92; Martin, "Rise and Fall of Popular Front Liberalism in the South," 119–44; Mason, "Southerners Look at the South," 17–18, 40; Carroll Kilpatrick to AKC, 19 Nov. 1938, AKC Papers; FDR to Judge Louise O. Charlton, 19 Nov. 1938, reprinted in Southern Conference for Human Welfare, *Report of the Proceedings*.

3. Krueger, *Promises to Keep;* Reed, "Southern Conference for Human Welfare," 30–33, 44–63; Kelley, *Hammer and Hoe,* 176–92; Southern Conference for Human Welfare, *Report of the Proceedings;* R. F. Hall, "Those Southern Liberals," 490–92.

4. Kelley, *Hammer and Hoe,* 188; JC to AKC, 23 Dec. 1938; FJ to AKC, 28 Dec. 1938, AKC Papers, GCH Papers.

5. *TSBF,* 149–50; GCH to AKC, 23 Dec. 1938; GCH to BG, 23 Dec. 1938, AKC Papers.

6. GCH to AKC, 23 Dec. 1938; GCH to AKC, 29 Dec. 1938, AKC Papers.

7. GCH to AKC, 24 Aug. 1939, AKC Papers; Hollis, *Grover C. Hall,* 88.

8. *TSBF,* 172–74.

9. Ibid., 174–77.

10. *MA,* 13 Feb. 1940.

11. General Statement of Alex Smith, Chairman of the State Board of Pardons and Paroles; Opinion of Alex Smith; Opinion of Robert Hill; Opinion of Edwina Mitchell, 8 March 1940, AKC Papers; *NYT,* 13 March 1940.

12. *MA,* 9 March 1940.

13. *TSBF,* 179–90.

14. Ibid.

15. RNB to GCH, 12 June 1940; GCH to RNB, n.d., ACLU Papers.

16. *TSBF,* 179–90, 74.

17. Hollis, *Grover C. Hall,* 90–91; *TSBF,* 74.

CHAPTER 44

1. *NYT,* 25–26 July 1937; *DW,* 25 July 1937; *NYHT,* 26 July 1937; *CD,* 31 July 1937.

2. *NYT,* 26–27 July 1937; *CD,* 31 July 1937.

3. *NYT,* 26–31 July 1937; *Statesville* (N.C.) *Landmark,* 29 July 1937; *CD,* 7 Aug. 1937.

4. Notes of Marion Norris, 6–10 Aug. 1937, AKC Papers.

5. Ibid.

6. Carter, *Scottsboro,* 384; Notes of Marion Norris, 6–10 Aug. 1937, AKC Papers; *NYT,* 16 Aug. 1937; MS to RWR, EW, OM, and WR, 18 Aug. 1937, NAACP Papers; *DW,* 27 Aug. 1937; *NYP,* clipping, n.d. (Aug. 1937), ACLU Papers.

7. RS to AKC, 25 Aug. 1937; MS to OM, RWR, EW, and WR, 25 Aug. 1937, NAACP Papers; *TSBF,* 117; "ALW" to RNB, 3 Sept. 1937; Minutes of the SDC Meeting, 20 Oct. 1937; Schedule for National Scottsboro Tour, ACLU Papers; *EJ* 12 (Jan. 1938): 3.

CHAPTER 45

1. CN to RB, 24 July 1937, ILD Papers.

2. RB to CN, 27 July 1937; CN to RB, 3 Aug. 1937, ILD Papers.

3. CN to RS, 23 Sept. 1937; CN to MS, 24 Sept. 1937; CN to Joseph Brodsky, 25 Oct. 1937, NAACP Papers.

4. CN to MS, 27 Oct. 1937; CN to MS, 25 Nov. 1937; CN to MS, 6 Dec. 1937, NAACP Papers.

5. MS to CN, 17 Jan. 1938, NAACP Papers; CN to MS, 18 Jan. 1938, AKC Papers.

6. CN to MS, 18 Jan. 1938, AKC Papers.
7. *TSBF,* 82–85, 93; HP to MS, 23 May 1937, NAACP Papers.
8. *NYT,* 29 Aug. 1937.
9. *NYT,* 29 Aug. 1937; SDC News Release, 31 Aug. 1937, NAACP Papers.
10. CN to MS, 11 Feb. 1938; CN to MS, 27 Feb. 1938, NAACP Papers; CN to AKC, 15 March 1938; AKC to CN, 13 April 1938, AKC Papers; *NYT,* 17, 28 June, 6, 10 July, 17–18 Aug. 1938.

CHAPTER 46

1. *NYT,* 20 July 1937; AW to "Readers," 24 July 1937, ILD Papers.
2. *NYT,* 27 July 1937; AW to "My dearest sister," 25 Aug. 1937; AW to Ada Wright, n.d. (Aug. 1937), NAACP Papers; AW to AKC, 28 April 1943, AKC Papers; *LSB,* 179.
3. AW to MS, 22 Sept. 1937; AW to MS, 20 Oct. 1937, NAACP Papers.
4. Anonymous to MS, Oct. 1937, NAACP Papers; *DW,* 9 Sept. 1937.
5. AW to MS, 11 Dec. 1937; AW to MS, 24 Jan. 1938; AW to MS, 3 Feb. 1938; AW to MS, 12 Feb. 1938; AW to MS, 14 Feb. 1938; AW to MS, 20 Feb. 1938; AW to MS, 25 Feb. 1938; AW to MS, 14 March 1938; MS to AW, 16 March 1938; AW to MS, 20 March 1938, NAACP Papers.
6. Anonymous to SDC, 24 March 1938; Ada Wright to RS, 29 March 1938, NAACP Papers.
7. Anonymous to SDC, 24 March 1938, NAACP Papers.

CHAPTER 47

1. *SB,* 65–69; *NYT,* 27 July 1937; HP to AD, 9 Sept. 1937; HP to RS, 26 Sept. 1937, ILD Papers.
2. *SB,* 73–76; HP to AD, 9 Sept. 1937, ILD Papers; HP to AD, 24 Sept. 1937, NAACP Papers.
3. HP to AD, 24 Sept. 1937, NAACP Papers. See also HP to AD, 9 Sept. 1937; HP to AD, n.d., ILD Papers; HP to MS, 11 Oct. 1937, NAACP Papers.
4. *NYT,* 12 Sept., 9, 23, 26 Oct. 1937; HP to MS, 30 Nov. 1937; HP to MS, 15 Dec. 1937, NAACP Papers.
5. HP to MS, 10 Dec. 1937; HP to MS, 15 Dec. 1937; HP to MS, 19 Dec. 1937; HP to MS, 23 March 1938, NAACP Papers.
6. HP to MS, 15 Dec. 1937; HP to "Honorable President," n.d. (21 Dec. 1937); Daniel M. Lyons to HP, 31 Dec. 1937, NAACP Papers.
7. HP to MS, 19 Dec. 1937; MS to HP, 27 Dec. 1937, NAACP Papers; AKC to HP, 28 Dec. 1937, AKC Papers; HP to MS, 29 Dec. 1937; HP to MS, 2 Jan. 193[8], NAACP Papers.
8. *SB,* 67–68; HP to AKC, 25 Dec. 1937, AKC Papers; HP to MS, 2 Jan. 1938, NAACP Papers.
9. HP to MS, 3 June 1938; HP to MS, 8 June 1938; HP to MS, 18 June 1938, NAACP Papers; HP to AD, 2 July 1938; HP to AD, 5 July 1938, ILD Papers; HP to MS and AKC, 12 July 1938, AKC Papers; HP to MS, 14 July 1938, NAACP Papers; HP to AKC, 27 July 1938; RS to AKC, 30 Aug. 1938, AKC Papers; HP to MS, n.d. (Aug. 1938); HP to AKC, 7 Sept. 1938, NAACP Papers.

CHAPTER 48

1. *TSBF,* 147; *LSB,* 174; CN to AKC, Dec. 1938, AKC Papers.
2. AW to AKC, 5 Dec. 1938, AKC Papers; *TSBF,* 147–49.
3. AW to MS, 16 Nov. 1938, NAACP Papers; AKC to AW, CN, OP, HP, and CW, 1 Dec. 1938, AKC Papers.
4. AW to MS, 3 Dec. 1938, NAACP Papers; AW to AKC, 5 Dec. 1938, AKC Papers; AW to MS, 27 Nov. 1938, NAACP Papers; *TSBF,* 147.
5. CN to AKC, Dec. 1938, AKC Papers; *TSBF,* 147.
6. AKC to AW, 13 Dec. 1938; AW to AKC, 15 Dec. 1938, AKC Papers; *TSBF,* 148–49.
7. HP to AKC, n.d. (Dec. 1938), NAACP Papers; *SB,* 100–2.

CHAPTER 49

1. OM to *KCC,* 12 Jan. 1938, NAACP Papers; Minutes of the SDC Meeting, 17 Feb. 1938, ACLU Papers.
2. AD to AKC, 28 Feb. 1938, ACLU Papers.
3. RW to RS, 28 Feb. 1939, ACLU Papers.
4. Ibid.
5. RW to RS, 28 Feb. 1939, ACLU Papers; RW to RS, 4 March 1939; AKC to EM, 21 March 1939, AKC Papers; Minutes of the SDC Meeting, 9 June 1939; RW to EM, 17 Aug. 1939; EM to RW, 21 Aug. 1939, ACLU Papers.
6. VM to "My Dear Friend," 27 Aug. 1939, ILD Papers; EM to RW, 21 Aug. 1939, ACLU Papers.
7. AKC to OM, 20 Oct. 1939; RW to AKC, 9 Nov. 1939; OM to AKC, 2 Dec. 1939; AKC to OM, 5 Dec. 1939; OM to AKC, 7 Dec. 1939; OM to AKC, 14 Dec. 1939, AKC Papers.
8. AKC to HH, 8 Jan. 1940; OM to AKC, 22 Jan. 1940, AKC Papers.
9. AKC to OM, 25 Jan. 1940; OM to AKC, 20 Feb. 1940; OM to AKC, 1 March 1940, AKC Papers; OM to RS, 6 March 1940, NAACP Papers; James McClendon to RW, 27 July 1940; McClendon to TM, 29 July 1940; AKC to JC, 31 Oct. 1940, AKC Papers; Carter, *Scottsboro,* 401.
10. EM to AKC, 4 Oct. 1940; AKC to EM, 7 Oct. 1940; MS to AKC, 7 Oct. 1940; RW to OM, 21 Oct. 1940; OM to RW, 23 Oct. 1940; RW to AKC, 23 Dec. 1940, AKC Papers.
11. RW to AKC, 25 Sept. 1941; Allen F. Jackson to RW, 27 Dec. 1941; RW to Jackson, 12 Jan. 1942, AKC Papers.
12. OM to RW, 23 Oct. 1940, AKC Papers.
13. Allen F. Jackson to RW, 27 Dec. 1941, AKC Papers; Memorandum for the file on the Scottsboro Case from RW, 10 June 1942, NAACP Papers.
14. EM to RW, 19 Oct. 1942, AKC Papers; AKC to EM, n.d. (Oct. 1942), AKC Papers; WR to HH, 14 July 1942, ILD Papers.
15. Frances Levkoff to AKC, n.d. (April 1939); Levkoff to AKC, n.d. (April 1939); AKC to Levkoff, 1 May 1939, AKC Papers; Memorandum for the file on the Scottsboro Case from RW, 10 June 1942, NAACP Papers; Levkoff to AKC, n.d. (Jan. 1943); AKC to Levkoff, 14 Jan. 1943; Levkoff to AKC, n.d. (Feb. 1943); AKC to Levkoff, 9 Feb. 1943; Memorandum for the Files—on OM from RW, 7 April 1943, AKC Papers.
16. Memorandum to the Files from RW, 2 April 1952; Jawn A. Sandifer to RW, 7 April 1952, NAACP Papers.

CHAPTER 50

1. HP to MS, 14 March 1938, NAACP Papers.
2. *SB,* 95–98.
3. Ibid., 116–19.
4. Ibid., 112.
5. Ibid., 79–85.
6. Ibid.
7. Ibid.
8. Ibid., 127–32.
9. *SB,* 142–47; JC to AKC, 20 Oct. 1941, AKC Papers.
10. *SB,* 148–49; HP to AKC, n.d., AKC Papers.
11. *SB,* 149–56.
12. *SB,* 156–66; HP to AKC, n.d. (1943); HP to AKC, n.d. (1943); HP to AKC, n.d. (1943), AKC Papers.
13. *SB,* 166–68.

CHAPTER 51

1. CW to HH, 3 Nov. 1941; AW to RB, 28 April 1939, ILD Papers.
2. AW to MS, 14 June 1939, NAACP Papers; AW to AKC, 23 Oct. 1939, AKC Papers; AW to HH, 15 March 1942, ILD Papers.
3. AW to HH, 14 Feb. 1943; AW to RS, 2 Aug. 1939, ILD Papers; AW to AKC, 17 Dec. 1939; AW to AKC, 16 Sept. 1943, AKC Papers.
4. CN to HH, 2 Aug. 1942, ILD Papers; AKC to AW, 17 Dec. 1942; AW to AKC, 25 Dec. 1942, AKC Papers.
5. *LSB,* 184–91.
6. Edwina Mitchell to AKC, 14 Aug. 1943; RW to James J. McClendon, 27 Dec. 1943; Report from Ohio Parole Board, 28 Dec. 1943; AW to AKC, 16 Sept. 1943; AW to AKC, 22 Sept. 1943; AW to AKC, 8 Nov. 1943, AKC Papers.
7. "Charlie Weems Set Free," clipping, n.d. (Nov. 1943); ILD Press Release, Nov. 1943, ACLU Papers; CW to HH, 12 Oct. 1943; CW to HH, 17 Dec. 1943; CW to HH, n.d. (April 1944), ILD Papers.
8. W. P. Shirley to AKC, 5 Jan. 1944; AW and CN to AKC, 8 Jan. 1944, AKC Papers; CN to HH, n.d. (Jan. 1944); AW to HH, n.d. (Jan.–Feb. 1944), ILD Papers; *LSB,* 192–96.
9. AW to AKC, 28 Jan. 1944; J. E. Lindsay to Alabama Board of Parole, 29 Jan. 1944; AW to AKC, Feb. 1944; RW to AKC, 2 Feb. 1944; AW to AKC, 12 Feb. 1944; AW to AKC, n.d. (March 1944), AKC Papers; AW to HH, n.d. (Jan.–Feb. 1944), ILD Papers.
10. *LSB,* 196–98; AKC to CN, 3 March 1944, AKC Papers; CN to HH, 1 May 1944, ILD Papers; AKC to CN, 9 May 1944; AKC to AW, 9 May 1944, AKC Papers.
11. AW to AKC, 11 June 1944, AKC Papers; *LSB,* 197; AW to AKC, n.d. (June 1944), AKC Papers; CN to HH, 15 June 1944, ILD Papers.
12. E. D. Nixon to AKC, 31 May 1946, AKC Papers; *LSB,* 198–200.
13. *LSB,* 200–201.
14. *LSB,* 201–5; EM to AKC, 14 Jan. 1944, AKC Papers.
15. RW to Henry W. McGee, 25 Oct. 1946; Memorandum to Mrs. Waring from RW, 4 Nov. 1946; RW to AW, 24 Dec. 1946, NAACP Papers; AW to AKC, 7 Feb. 1947; AW to AKC, n.d. (1947); AW to AKC, n.d. (1947); AW to AKC, n.d., AKC Papers; AW to AKC, n.d. (Sept. 1947); AW to AKC, n.d. (Oct. 1947); George Chamlee to RW, 17 March 1948, NAACP Papers; *TSBF,* 232.
16. Joseph B. Robinson to TM, 31 Jan. 1950; AKC to TM, n.d. (July–Aug. 1950);

AW to RW, 15 July 1950; AW to RW, 24 July 1950; Madison S. Jones to AKC, 27 July 1950; Jones to Robinson, 27 July 1950; Memorandum to RW from Mr. Jones, 28 July 1950, NAACP Papers.
17. AW to RW, 24 July 1950, NAACP Papers; AW to AKC, n.d. (June–July 1950), AKC Papers.
18. Memorandum to RW from Mr. Jones, 28 July 1950; Memorandum to RW from Madison Jones, 31 July 1950; NAACP Press Release, 19 July 1951; Calendar of Events, 23 June to 12 July, n.d., NAACP Papers.
19. Statement of James Andrew Wright, 22 Oct. 1951, NAACP Papers.
20. Jawn A. Sandifer to TM, 23 July 1951; NAACP Press Release, 21 Feb. 1952, NAACP Papers; AW to AKC, n.d. (1952), AKC Papers.
21. RW to AKC, 15 May 1952; RW to AW, 31 Oct. 1952; AKC to RW, 4 Feb. 1955, NAACP Papers.
22. RW to AW, 1 March 1955; AW to RW, n.d. (Nov. 1955), NAACP Papers.

CHAPTER 52

1. *SB,* 171–79.
2. Ibid., 173–74.
3. Ibid., 179–82.
4. Ibid., 183–90.
5. *SB,* 190–229; HP to AKC, 13 Jan. 1945; HP to AKC, 5 Feb. 1945; Edwina Mitchell to AKC, 2 March 1945; HP to AKC, 3 March 1945; HP to AKC, 5 Oct. 1945; AKC to W. H. Swearingen, 11 Oct. 1945; HP to AKC, 5 Nov. 1945; HP to AKC, 19 Jan. 1946, AKC Papers; Mitchell to AKC, 31 Dec. 1946, AKC Papers.
6. *SB,* 228–29.
7. Ibid., 222–30.
8. Ibid., 229–32.
9. Ibid., 232–35.
10. Ibid.
11. Ibid., 235–41.
12. Ibid., 241–44.
13. *SB,* 245–46; I. F. Stone, "Fugitive's Book Tells of Nazi-Like Horror Camps in Southland, U.S.A.," *York* (Pa.) *Gazette and Daily,* 2 June 1950.
14. *TSBF,* 231–38; Horne, *Communist Front?,* 292; *NYT,* 28 June, 11, 13 July 1950.
15. *NYT,* 19, 22 Dec. 1950, 26 Aug. 1952; *Detroit Free Press,* 19 Dec. 1950, 25 Sept. 1951.

CHAPTER 53

1. *LSB,* 205–8.
2. Ibid., 208–11.
3. Ibid., 214.
4. Ibid., 215–18.
5. Ibid.
6. Ibid., 216–18.
7. *LSB,* 221–25; AKC to AW, 6 Nov. 1944, AKC Papers; Kunstler, "From Scottsboro to Goetz," 20; *NYT,* 18 Aug. 1959.
8. *LSB,* 219–21, 225–26.
9. *LSB,* 227–30; *NYT,* 9 Oct. 1976.
10. *LSB,* 226.

11. Ibid., 230–31.
12. Ibid.
13. Ibid., 231–33.
14. *LSB,* 233–34; Bass, *Taming the Storm,* 323–46.
15. *NYT,* 9 Oct. 1976; *LSB,* 235–36.
16. *LSB,* 236–37.
17. *NYT,* 19 Oct. 1976; *LSB,* 237–38.
18. William R. Robinson to CN, 22 Oct. 1976, reprinted in *LSB,* 277; Bill Baxley and Milton C. Davis to the Board of Pardons and Paroles, 25 Oct. 1976, reprinted in *LSB,* 278–81; *NYT,* 26 Oct. 1976.
19. *LSB,* 240; *NYT,* 26 Oct. 1976.
20. *NYT,* 26 Oct. 1976; *LSB,* 241–42.
21. Carter, *Scottsboro,* rev. ed., 417–18; *NYT,* 29 Oct. 1976.
22. *LSB,* 242–44; *NYT,* 30 Nov. 1976.
23. *LSB,* 245–46; *NYT,* 2 Dec. 1976.
24. *NYT,* 2 Dec. 1976.
25. *LSB,* 242; Carter, *Scottsboro,* rev. ed., 456–62; *NYT,* 9, 12–13 July 1977, 12 Jan. 1978, 6 Oct., 9 Dec. 1981, 26 Jan. 1989.

CHAPTER 54

1. This account is based on the program for, my notes from, and a tape recording of the Memorial Service for Clarence Norris, 31 Jan. 1989.
2. *NYT,* 7 April 1977; Kunstler, "From Scottsboro to Goetz," 20.

Bibliography

Aaron, Daniel. *Writers on the Left: Episodes in American Literary Communism.* New York, 1961.

Adamic, Louis. *My America.* New York, 1938.

Allen, James. "Communism in the Deep South. The Opening: 1930–31—A Political Memoir." Typescript. 1984.

———. "The Scottsboro Struggle." *Communist* 12 (May 1933): 437–48.

American Jewish Committee. *The Jews in Nazi Germany: The Factual Record of Their Persecution by the National Socialists.* New York, 1933.

Autrey, Dorothy. "The National Association for the Advancement of Colored People in Alabama, 1913–1952." Ph.D. diss., University of Notre Dame, 1985.

Baldwin, Hanson W., and Shepard Stone, eds. *We Saw It Happen: The News Behind the News That's Fit to Print.* New York, 1939.

Bass, Jack. *Taming the Storm: The Life and Times of Judge Frank M. Johnson, Jr.* New York, 1993.

Basso, Hamilton. "Five Days in Decatur." *The New Republic* 77 (20 December 1933): 161–64.

Beals, Carleton. "Scottsboro Interview." *The Nation* 142 (12 February 1936): 178–79.

———. "The Scottsboro Puppet Show." *The Nation* 142 (5 February 1936): 149–50.

Beecher, John. "The Share Croppers' Union in Alabama," *Social Forces* 13 (October 1934): 125–32.

Blaustein, Albert P., and Robert L. Zangrando. *Civil Rights and the American Negro: A Documentary History.* New York, 1968.

Bowers, Claude G. *The Tragic Era.* Cambridge, Mass., 1929.

Branche, G. C. "Report of Neuropsychiatric Examination" of Olen Montgomery, Haywood Patterson, Clarence Norris, Ozie Powell, Willie Roberson, Charlie Weems, Eugene Williams, Andy Wright, and Roy Wright. 10 January 1937. Mimeo. There are copies of these reports in the ACLU, AKC, and NAACP Papers.

Brownmiller, Susan. *Against Our Will.* New York, 1975.

Buck, Paul H. *The Road to Reunion.* Boston, 1937.

Burgess, John W. *Reconstruction and the Constitution, 1866–1876.* New York, 1902.

Cannon, Poppy. *A Gentle Knight: My Husband Walter White.* New York, 1956.

Carmer, Carl. *Stars Fell on Alabama.* New York, 1934.

Carter, Dan T. *Scottsboro: A Tragedy of the American South.* Baton Rouge, 1969.

———. *Scottsboro: A Tragedy of the American South.* Rev. ed. Baton Rouge, 1979.

Cash, W. J. *The Mind of the South.* New York, 1941.

Cason, Clarence. "Black Straws in the Wind." *North American Review* 236 (July 1933): 81–86.

———. "The Forgotten Negro." *North American Review* 234 (July 1932): 75–81.

———. "Middle Class and Bourbon." In W. T. Couch, ed., *Culture in the South.* Chapel Hill, 1934.

———. *Ninety Degrees in the Shade.* Chapel Hill, 1935.

Chalmers, Allan Knight. *They Shall Be Free.* New York, 1951.

Chamlee, George W., and John P. Fort, "Is Lynching Ever Defensible?" *Forum* 76 (1926): 811–17.

Collingwood, R. G. *The Idea of History.* Oxford, 1946.

Collins, Winfield H. *The Truth About Lynching and the Negro in the South.* New York, 1918.

Commission on Interracial Cooperation. *The Commission on Interracial Cooperation Papers, 1919–1944 and the Association of Southern Women for the Prevention of Lynching Papers, 1930–1942: A Guide to the Microfilm Editions.* Edited by Mitchell F. Ducey. Ann Arbor, 1984.

———. *The Crime of Mob Murder.* Atlanta, n.d.

———. *The Mob Still Rides: A Review of the Lynching Record, 1931–1935.* Atlanta, n.d.

Cortner, Richard C. *A Mob Intent on Death: The NAACP and the Arkansas Riot Cases.* Middletown, Conn., 1988.

———. *A "Scottsboro" Case in Mississippi: The Supreme Court and Brown v. Mississippi.* Jackson, Miss., 1986.

Cothran, Ben. "South of Scottsboro." *Form and Century* 93 (9 June 1935): 323–29.

Cowley, Malcolm. *The Dream of the Golden Mountains: Remembering the 1930s.* New York, 1980.

Crenshaw, Files, Jr., and Kenneth A. Miller. *Scottsboro: The Firebrand of American Communism.* Montgomery, Ala., 1936.

Cruden, Robert. *James Ford Rhodes: The Man, the Historian, and His Work.* Cleveland, 1961.

Cunard, Nancy, ed. *Negro: An Anthology.* 1934. Reprint. New York, 1970.

Dabney, Virginius. *Liberalism in the South.* Chapel Hill, 1932.
Daniel, Pete. *Breaking the Land: The Transformation of Cotton, Tobacco, and Rice Cultures Since 1880.* Urbana, Ill., 1985.
———. *Standing at the Crossroads: Southern Life in the Twentieth Century.* New York, 1986.
Davis, Angela Y. *Women, Race, and Class.* New York, 1981.
Deutsch, Helene. *The Psychology of Women.* 2 vols. 1944. Reprint. New York, 1973.
Dixon, Thomas. *The Clansman.* New York, 1905.
Dollard, John. *Caste and Class in a Southern Town.* New Haven, 1937.
Draper, Theodore. *American Communism and Soviet Russia: The Formative Period.* 1960. Reprint. New York, 1986.
Du Bois, W.E.B. *Black Reconstruction in America.* 1935. Reprint. New York, 1963.
———. *Dusk of Dawn.* 1940. Reprint. New York, 1986.
———. "The Negro and Communism." *Crisis* 38 (September 1931): 314–15.
———. "Reconstruction and Its Benefits." *American Historical Review* 15 (1910): 781–99.
———. *The Souls of Black Folk.* Chicago, 1903.
———, ed. "Negro Editors on Communism." *Crisis* 39 (April 1932): 117–19, and *Crisis* 39 (May 1932): 154–56, 170.
Dunning, William A. *Reconstruction: Political and Economic.* New York, 1907.
Durr, Virginia Foster. *Outside the Magic Circle: The Autobiography of Virginia Foster Durr.* Edited by Hollinger F. Barnard. Tuscaloosa, 1985.
Dykeman, Wilma, and James Stokely. *Seeds of Southern Change: The Life of Will Alexander.* Chicago, 1962.
Eagles, Charles W. *Jonathan Daniels and Race Relations: The Evolution of a Southern Liberal.* Knoxville, Tenn., 1982.
Elias, Robert H., ed. *Letters of Theodore Dreiser.* 2 vols. Philadelphia, 1959.
Ernst, Morris. "Dissenting Opinion." *The Nation* 135 (7 December 1932): 559.
Fite, Gilbert C. *Cotton Fields No More: Southern Agriculture, 1865–1980.* Lexington, Ky., 1984.
Fleming, Walter L. *Civil War and Reconstruction in Alabama.* New York, 1905.
———. *The Sequel of Appomattox.* New Haven, 1919.
Foner, Eric. *Reconstruction: America's Unfinished Revolution, 1863–1877.* New York, 1988.
Foreman, Clark. "The Decade of Hope." *Phylon* 12 (1951): 137–50.
Franklin, John Hope. *Race and History: Selected Essays, 1938–1988.* Baton Rouge, 1989.
Fredrickson, George. *The Black Image in the White Mind: The Debate on Afro-American Character and Destiny, 1817–1914.* New York, 1971.
Garraty, John A., ed. *The Barber and the Historian: The Correspondence of George A. Meyers and James Ford Rhodes, 1910–1923.* Columbus, Ohio, 1956.
Gilbert, William E. "Bibb Graves as a Progressive, 1927–1930." *Alabama Review* 10 (January 1957): 15–30.
Goodrich, Gillian White. "James Edwin Horton, Jr.: Scottsboro Judge." Master's thesis, University of Alabama at Birmingham, 1974.

Graves, John Temple II. "Fiat Justitia, Ruat Coelum." *The New Republic* 94 (30 March 1938): 218.

———. *The Fighting South*. New York, 1943.

Grimké, Francis James. *The Works of Francis James Grimké*. 4 vols. Edited by Carter G. Woodson. Washington, D.C., 1942.

Hall, Jacquelyn Dowd. "The Mind That Burns in Each Body." In Ann Snitow, Christine Stansell, and Sharon Thompson, eds., *Powers of Desire: The Politics of Sexuality*. New York, 1983.

———. *Revolt Against Chivalry: Jessie Daniel Ames and the Women's Campaign Against Lynching*. New York, 1979.

Hall, Jacquelyn Dowd, et al. *Like a Family: The Making of a Southern Cotton Mill World*. Chapel Hill, 1987.

Hall, Kermit L., et al., eds., *Oxford Companion to the Supreme Court*. New York, 1992.

Hall, Robert F. "The Southern Conference for Human Welfare." *Communist* 18 (January 1939): 57–65.

———. "Those Southern Liberals." *Dissent* 26 (Fall 1979): 490–92.

Hammond, John Henry. "Due Process of Law in Alabama." *The Nation* 137 (20 December 1933): 701–2.

———. "The South Speaks." *The Nation* 136 (26 April 1933): 465–66.

———. "The Trial of Haywood Patterson." *The New Republic* 86 (12 February 1936): 13–14.

Hammond, John, and Irving Townsend. *John Hammond on Record: An Autobiography*. New York, 1977.

Harlan, Louis R. *Booker T. Washington: The Making of a Black Leader, 1856–1901*. New York, 1972.

———. *Booker T. Washington: The Wizard of Tuskegee, 1901–1915*. New York, 1983.

Hays, Arthur Garfield. *Trial by Prejudice*. 1933. Rev. ed. New York, 1935.

Haywood, Harry. "The Scottsboro Decision." *Communist* 11 (December 1932): 1065–1075.

Herndon, Angelo. *Let Me Live*. 1937. Reprint. New York, 1969.

Hollis, Daniel Webster. *An Alabama Newspaper Tradition: Grover C. Hall and the Hall Family*. Tuscaloosa, 1983.

Horne, Gerald. *Communist Front? The Civil Rights Congress, 1946–1956*. Rutherford, N.J., 1988.

Howe, Irving, and Lewis Coser. *The American Communist Party: A Critical History, 1919–1957*. Boston, 1957.

Hudson, Hosea. *Black Worker in the Deep South*. New York, 1972.

Hughes, Langston. *I Wonder As I Wander: An Autobiographical Journey*. New York, 1956.

———. *Scottsboro Limited: Four Poems and a Play in Verse*. Illustrated by Prentis Taylor. New York, 1932.

———. "Southern Gentlemen, White Prostitutes, Mill-Owners, and Negroes." *Contempo* 1 (December 1931): 1.

Ingalls, Robert P. "Antiradical Violence in Birmingham During the 1930s." *Labor History* 47 (November 1981): 521–44.

Isserman, Maurice. "Three Generations: Historians View American Communism." *Labor History* 26 (Fall 1985): 517–45.

Jamieson, Stuart Marshall. *Labor Unionism in American Agriculture.* 1946. Reprint. New York, 1976.

Johnson, Alva. "Let Freedom Ring." *New Yorker* 8 (4 June 1932): 21–24.

———. "Let Freedom Ring." *New Yorker* 8 (11 June 1932): 18–22.

Jordan, J. Glenn. *The Unpublished Inside Story of the Infamous Scottsboro Case.* Huntsville, Ala., 1932.

Kelley, Robin D. G. *Hammer and Hoe: Alabama Communists During the Great Depression.* Chapel Hill, 1990.

Kennedy, Ludovic. *The Airman and the Carpenter: The Lindbergh Kidnapping and the Framing of Richard Hauptmann.* New York, 1985.

Kirby, Jack Temple. *Darkness at the Dawning: Race and Reform in the Progressive South.* Philadelphia, 1972.

———. *Media-Made America: The South in the American Imagination.* 1978. Reprint. Athens, Ga., 1986.

———. *Rural Worlds Lost: Agriculture, Rural Life, Folks, 1920–1960.* Baton Rouge, 1986.

Kirby, John B. *Black Americans in the Roosevelt Era: Liberalism and Race.* Knoxville, Tenn., 1980.

Kitchens, John W., ed. *Guide to the Microfilm Edition of the Tuskegee Institute News Clippings File.* Tuskegee Institute, Ala., 1978.

Klehr, Harvey. *The Heyday of American Communism: The Depression Decade.* New York, 1984.

Kneebone, John. *Southern Liberal Journalists and the Issue of Race, 1920–1944.* Chapel Hill, 1985.

Krueger, Thomas A. *And Promises to Keep: The Southern Conference for Human Welfare, 1938–1948.* Nashville, 1967.

Kunstler, William. "From Scottsboro to Goetz." *Village Voice* 30 (26 March 1985): 1, 13–20.

Kurland, Philip B., ed. *Felix Frankfurter on the Supreme Court: Extrajudicial Essays on the Court and Constitution.* Cambridge, Mass., 1970.

Leibowitz, Robert. *The Defender: The Life and Career of Samuel S. Leibowitz, 1893–1933.* Englewood Cliffs, N.J., 1981.

Leuchtenburg, William E. *Franklin D. Roosevelt and the New Deal.* New York, 1963.

Lewis, David Levering. *When Harlem Was in Vogue.* 1979. Reprint. New York, 1982.

Lipstadt, Deborah E. *Beyond Belief: The American Press and the Coming of the Holocaust, 1933–1945.* New York, 1986.

Loveland, Anne C. *Lillian Smith: A Southerner Confronting the South.* Baton Rouge, 1986.

Lyn, Conrad. *There Is a Fountain: The Autobiography of a Civil Rights Lawyer.* Westport, Conn., 1979.

Lynch, John R. "Communications: *The Tragic Era.*" Review of *The Tragic Era,* by Claude Bowers. *Journal of Negro History* 16 (January 1931): 103–20.

———. *The Facts of Reconstruction.* New York, 1913.

———. "More About the Historical Errors of James Ford Rhodes." *Journal of Negro History* 3 (April 1918): 139–57.

———. "Some Historical Errors of James Ford Rhodes." *Journal of Negro History* 2 (October 1917): 345–68.

McMillen, Neil R. *Dark Journey: Black Mississippians in the Age of Jim Crow*. Urbana, Ill., 1989.

McNeil, Genna Rae. *Groundwork: Charles Hamilton Houston and the Struggle for Civil Rights*. Philadelphia, 1983.

McPherson, James M. *Ordeal by Fire: The Civil War and Reconstruction*. New York, 1982.

March, Ray A. *Alabama Bound: Forty Years Inside a Prison System*. Tuscaloosa, 1978.

Martin, Charles H. *The Angelo Herndon Case and Southern Justice*. Baton Rouge, 1976.

———. "The International Labor Defense and Black America." *Labor History* 26 (Spring 1985): 165–94.

———. "The Rise and Fall of Popular Front Liberalism in the South: The Southern Conference for Human Welfare, 1938–1948." In *Perspectives on the American South* 3 (1985): 119–44.

Mason, Lucy Randolph. "Southerners Look at the South." *North Georgia Review* 3 (Spring 1939): 17–18, 40.

Matthews, John M. "Black Newspapermen and the Black Community in Georgia, 1890–1930." *Georgia Historical Quarterly* 68 (Fall 1984): 356–81.

Meier, August, and Elliot Rudwick. *From Plantation to Ghetto*. 3rd ed. New York, 1976.

———. "The Rise of the Black Secretariat in the NAACP, 1909–1935." In Meier and Rudwick, eds., *Along the Color Line: Explorations in the Black Experience*. Urbana, Ill., 1976.

———. "Walter Francis White." In Rayford Logan and Michael R. Winston, eds., *Dictionary of American Negro Biography*. New York, 1982.

Miller, Loren. *The Petitioners: The Story of the Supreme Court of the United States and the Negro*. New York, 1966.

Minor, Robert. "The Negro and His Judases." *Communist* 10 (July 1931): 632–39.

Moorman, J. H., and E. L. Barrell, eds. *Leaders of the Colored Race in Alabama*. Mobile, Ala., 1928.

Moos, Malcolm C. *State Penal Administration in Alabama*. Tuscaloosa, 1942.

Murray, Hugh T., Jr. "Aspects of the Scottsboro Campaign." *Science and Society* 35 (Summer 1971): 177–92.

———. "Changing America and the Changing Image of Scottsboro." *Phylon* 38 (1977): 82–92.

———. "The NAACP Versus the Communist Party: The Scottsboro Rape Cases, 1931–1932." In Bernard Sternsher, ed., *The Negro in Depression and War: Prelude to Revolution, 1930–1945*. Chicago, 1969.

Myrdal, Gunnar. *An American Dilemma: The Negro Problem and Modern Democracy*. 2 vols. New York, 1944.

Naison, Mark. "Black Agrarian Radicalism in the Great Depression: The

Threads of a Lost Tradition." *Journal of Ethnic Studies* 1 (Fall 1983): 47–65.

———. *Communists in Harlem During the Depression*. 1983. Reprint. New York, 1984.

National Association for the Advancement of Colored People. *Guide to the Papers of the NAACP, Part 6: The Scottsboro Case, 1931–1950*. Edited by Dan T. Carter, Randolph Boehm, and Martin Schipper. Frederick, Md., 1986.

———. *Thirty Years of Lynching in the United States, 1889–1918*. New York, 1919.

Nolan, William A. *Communism Versus the Negro*. Chicago, 1951.

Norris, Clarence, and Sybil D. Washington. *The Last of the Scottsboro Boys: An Autobiography*. New York, 1979.

Novick, Peter. *That Noble Dream: The "Objectivity Question" and the American Historical Profession*. Cambridge, Mass., 1988.

O'Brien, Michael. *The Idea of the American South, 1920–1941*. Baltimore, 1979.

Owen, Marie Bankhead. *The Story of Alabama: A History of the State*. 5 vols. New York, 1949.

Owen, Thomas M. *History of Alabama and Dictionary of Alabama Biography*. 4 vols. Chicago, 1921.

Owsley, Frank L. "Scottsboro, the Third Crusade: The Sequel to Abolition and Reconstruction." *American Review* 1 (June 1933): 257–85.

Painter, Nell Irvin. *The Narrative of Hosea Hudson: His Life as a Negro Communist in the South*. Cambridge, Mass., 1979.

Pasley, Fred D. *Not Guilty! The Story of Samuel S. Leibowitz*. New York, 1933.

Patterson, Haywood, and Earl Conrad. *Scottsboro Boy*. New York, 1950.

Pells, Richard H. *Radical Visions and American Dreams: Culture and Social Thought in the Depression Years*. New York, 1973.

Phillips, Ulrich B. *American Negro Slavery*. New York, 1918.

———. *Life and Labor in the Old South*. Boston, 1929.

Raboteau, Albert J. *Slave Religion: The "Invisible Institution" in the Antebellum South*. New York, 1980.

Rampersad, Arnold. *The Life of Langston Hughes*. 2 vols. New York, 1986–89.

Ransdall, Hollace. "Report on the Scottsboro, Alabama, Case." New York: American Civil Liberties Union, 1931. Mimeo. There are copies of this report in the ACLU, NAACP, CIC, and ILD Papers.

Raper, Arthur. *The Tragedy of Lynching*. Chapel Hill, 1933.

Record, Wilson. *The Negro and the Communist Party*. Chapel Hill, 1951.

———. *Race and Radicalism: The NAACP and the Communist Party in Conflict*. Ithaca, 1964.

Redding, J. Saunders. *No Day of Triumph*. New York, 1945.

Reed, Linda. "The Southern Conference for Human Welfare and the Southern Conference Educational Fund, 1938–1963." Ph.D. diss., Indiana University, 1986.

Reynolds, Quentin. *Courtroom: The Story of Samuel S. Leibowitz*. New York, 1950.

Rhodes, James Ford. *History of the United States from the Compromise of 1850 to the Final Restoration of Home Rule at the South*. 7 vols. New York, 1892–1907.

Rodgers, Daniel T. "Regionalism and the Burdens of Progress." In J. Morgan Kousser and James M. McPherson, eds., *Region, Race, and Reconstruction: Essays in Honor of C. Vann Woodward*. New York, 1982.

Rogin, Michael. " 'The Sword Became a Flashing Vision': D. W. Griffith's *The Birth of a Nation*." *Representations* 9 (Winter 1985): 150–95.

Rosen, Dale. "The Alabama Share Croppers Union." B.A. honors essay, Radcliffe College, 1969.

Rosengarten, Theodore. *All God's Dangers: The Life of Nate Shaw*. New York, 1975.

Ross, Barbara Joyce. *J. E. Springarn and the Rise of the NAACP, 1911–1939*. New York, 1972.

Rukeyser, Muriel. *Theory of Flight*. New Haven, 1935.

Salmond, John. *A Southern Rebel: The Life and Times of Aubrey Willis Williams, 1890–1965*. Chapel Hill, 1983.

Schlesinger, Arthur M. Review of *The Tragic Era*, by Claude Bowers. *The New Republic* 60 (9 October 1929): 210–11.

Schlesinger, Arthur M., Jr. *The Age of Roosevelt: The Crisis of the Old Order, 1919–1933*. Boston, 1957.

Scottsboro Defense Committee. *Four Free, Five in Prison—on the Same Evidence: What the Nation's Press Says about the Scottsboro Case*. New York, 1937.

———. *A Record of Broken Promises*. New York, 1938.

———. *The Scottsboro Case: Opinion of Judge James Edwin Horton, Jr.* New York, 1936.

Shapiro, Morris. "Behind the Scenes at Scottsboro." *The Nation* 145 (14 August 1937): 170–71.

Simkins, Francis B. "New Viewpoints of Southern Reconstruction." *Journal of Southern History* 5 (February 1939): 49–61.

Simkins, Francis B., and Robert H. Woody. *South Carolina During Reconstruction*. Chapel Hill, 1932.

Sitkoff, Harvard. *A New Deal for Blacks: The Emergence of Civil Rights as a National Issue*. New York, 1978.

Smith, Lillian. *Killers of the Dream*. New York, 1949.

———. *Strange Fruit*. New York, 1944.

Solomon, Mark. "Red and Black: Negroes and Communism." Ph.D. diss., Harvard University, 1972.

Sosna, Morton. *In Search of the Silent South: Southern Liberals and the Race Issue*. New York, 1977.

Southern Commission on the Study of Lynching. *Lynchings and What They Mean*. Atlanta, 1931.

———. *The Plight of Tuscaloosa: A Case Study of Conditions in Tuscaloosa County, Alabama, 1933*. Atlanta, 1933.

Southern Conference for Human Welfare. *Report of the Proceedings of the Southern Conference for Human Welfare, Birmingham, Alabama, November 20–23, 1938*. Birmingham, 1938.

Spivak, John. *A Man in His Time*. New York, 1967.

Stafford, Jean. "Brownmiller on Rape: A Scare Worse Than Death." *Esquire* 84 (November 1975): 50–52.

Stampp, Kenneth M. *The Era of Reconstruction, 1865–1877.* New York, 1965.

———, ed. *The Causes of the Civil War.* Englewood Cliffs, N.J., 1974.

Stone, Olive Matthews. "Agrarian Conflict in Alabama: Sections, Races, and Classes in a Rural State from 1800 to 1938." Ph.D. diss., University of North Carolina, 1939.

Stott, William. *Documentary Expression and Thirties America.* 1973. Reprint. Chicago, 1986.

Suggs, Henry Lewis, ed. *The Black Press in the South, 1865–1979.* Westport, Conn., 1983.

Terkel, Studs. *Hard Times.* New York, 1970.

Tillman, Nathaniel P. "Walter Francis White, A Study in Intergroup Leadership." Ph.D. diss., University of Wisconsin, 1961.

Tindall, George B. *The Emergence of the New South, 1913–1945.* Baton Rouge, 1967.

Vorse, Mary Heaton. "How Scottsboro Happened." *The New Republic* 74 (10 May 1933): 356–58.

———. "The Scottsboro Trial," *The New Republic* 74 (19 April 1933): 276–78.

Walker, Alyce Billings, ed. *Alabama: A Guide to the Deep South.* 1941. Reprint. New York, 1975.

Washington, Booker T. *My Larger Education: Being Chapters from My Experience.* New York, 1911.

———. *Up From Slavery.* New York, 1901.

Weiss, Nancy J. *Farrell to the Party of Lincoln: Black Politics in the Age of FDR.* Princeton, 1983.

West, Caroll Van. "Perpetuating the Myth of America: Scottsboro and Its Interpreters." *South Atlantic Quarterly* 80 (Winter 1981): 37–48.

Wexley, John. *They Shall Not Die.* New York, 1934.

White, Walter Francis. *A Man Called White: The Autobiography of Walter White.* New York, 1948.

———. "The Negro and the Communists." *Harper's Monthly* 164 (December 1931): 62–72.

———. *Rope and Faggot: A Biography of Judge Lynch.* New York, 1929.

Whitfield, Stephen J. *A Death in the Delta: The Story of Emmett Till.* New York, 1988.

Wilkins, Roy, and Tom Mathews. *Standing Fast: The Autobiography of Roy Wilkins.* New York, 1982.

Williamson, Joel. *The Crucible of Race: Black/White Relations in the American South Since Emancipation.* New York, 1984.

Wilson, Edmund. "The Freight-Car Case." *The New Republic* 68 (26 August 1931): 38–43.

———. *Letters on Literature and Politics, 1912–1972.* Edited by Elena Wilson. New York, 1977.

———. *The Thirties.* Edited by Leon Edel. New York, 1980.

Wilson, Woodrow. *A History of the American People.* 5 vols. New York, 1902.

Witt, Elder. *Congressional Quarterly Guide to the U.S. Supreme Court*. Washington, D.C., 1990.

Woodson, Carter G. Review of *The Tragic Era,* by Claude Bowers. *Journal of Negro History* 15 (January 1930): 117–19.

Woodward, C. Vann. *Origins of the New South, 1877–1913*. Baton Rouge, 1951.

———. *Thinking Back: The Perils of Writing History*. Baton Rouge, 1986.

Work, Monroe N., ed. *Negro Year Book: An Annual Encyclopedia of the Negro, 1912–1956*. Tuskegee Institute, Ala., 1912–1956.

Wright, Gavin. *Old South, New South: Revolutions in the Southern Economy Since the Civil War*. New York, 1986.

Zangrando, Robert L. *The NAACP Crusade Against Lynching, 1909–1950*. Philadelphia, 1980.

Zinn, Howard. *The Twentieth Century: A People's History*. 1980. Reprint. New York, 1984.

Acknowledgments

I have had many wonderful teachers, and I would like to thank some of them here: Maria DeBella, Alice Alldian, Michael Marcus, David Naylor, Marvin Bram, the late John Lydenberg, James Crenner, Thomas Bender, Patricia Bonomi, Albert Raboteau, James McPherson, and Daniel Rodgers.

For the extraordinary support I have received at Pantheon, I would like to thank Alan Turkus, Edward Cohen, Susan Norton, Claudine O'Hearn, and my editor, Daniel Frank. Dan is an editor—a reader, a fan, a critic, a wizard with a pencil, a fresh set of eyes—and I am happy to have one.

For generous financial assistance at crucial moments over the past seven years, I would like to thank Princeton University, the American Historical Association, the Charlotte W. Newcombe Foundation, the American Council of Learned Societies, and Harvard University's Joseph H. Clark Fund and William F. Milton Fund.

For special help with my research, I would like to thank Gillian Goodrich of Birmingham, Alabama; Virginia Hamilton of the University of Alabama in Birmingham; Dianne Jackson and Miriam Jones of the Alabama Department of Archives and History; Randolph Boehm of University Publications of America; Raymond Teichman of the Franklin D. Roosevelt Library; Jane Hammond of the Cornell University Law Library; Robin Kelley of the University of Michigan; Sule Greg Wilson and Diana Lachatanere of the Schomburg Center for Research in Black Culture; Charles Niles of Boston University's Mugar Memorial Library; John Henneman of Princeton University's Firestone Library; Jean Holliday of Princeton's Seeley Mudd Library; and three research assistants at Harvard, Nishani Naidoo, Hyung-Joon Bak, and Jon Rosenberg.

And finally, for all kinds of encouragement, advice, criticism, suggestions, conversations, arguments, help, and friendship along the way, I would like to thank Dan Carter, Nell Painter, Douglas

Greenberg, Stanley Katz, David Landes, Judy Vishniac, Susan Borges, Harvey Rishikof, Daniel Goldhagen, Stephen Aiken, Susan Hannah, Stephen Russell, Elaine McIlroy, Daniel Gross, Martha Hodes, Reid Mitchell, Henri Cole, Daniel Ernst, Drake McFeely, Louis Masur, William McFeely, Mary McFeely, Burton Goodman, Wendy Goodman, Sandra Goodman, Robert Goodman, Jill Mohrer, Rachel Lehr, Jackson Goodman, Samuel Goodman, and Jennifer McFeely.

Index